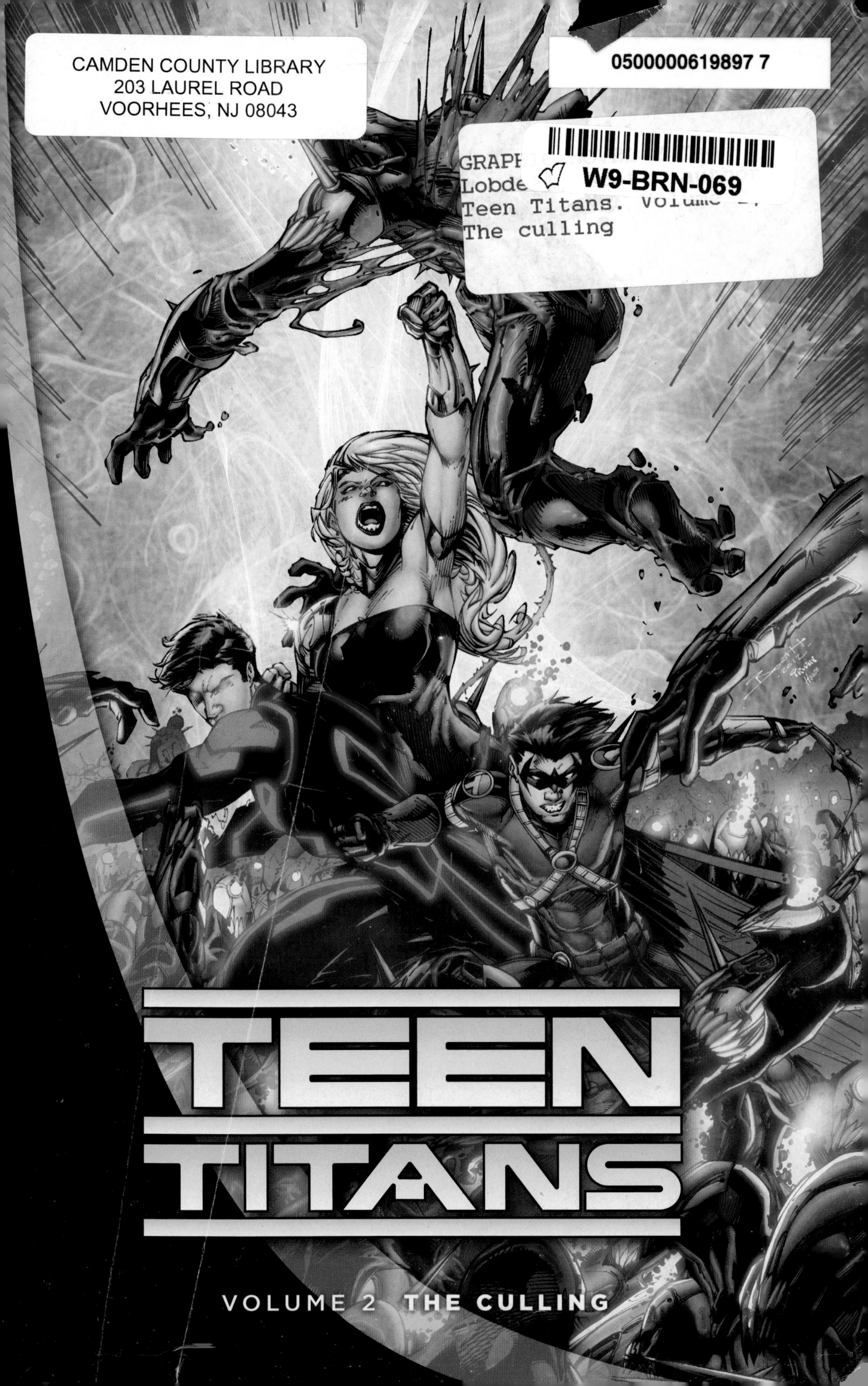

TEEN TITANS

VOLUME 2 **THE CULLING**

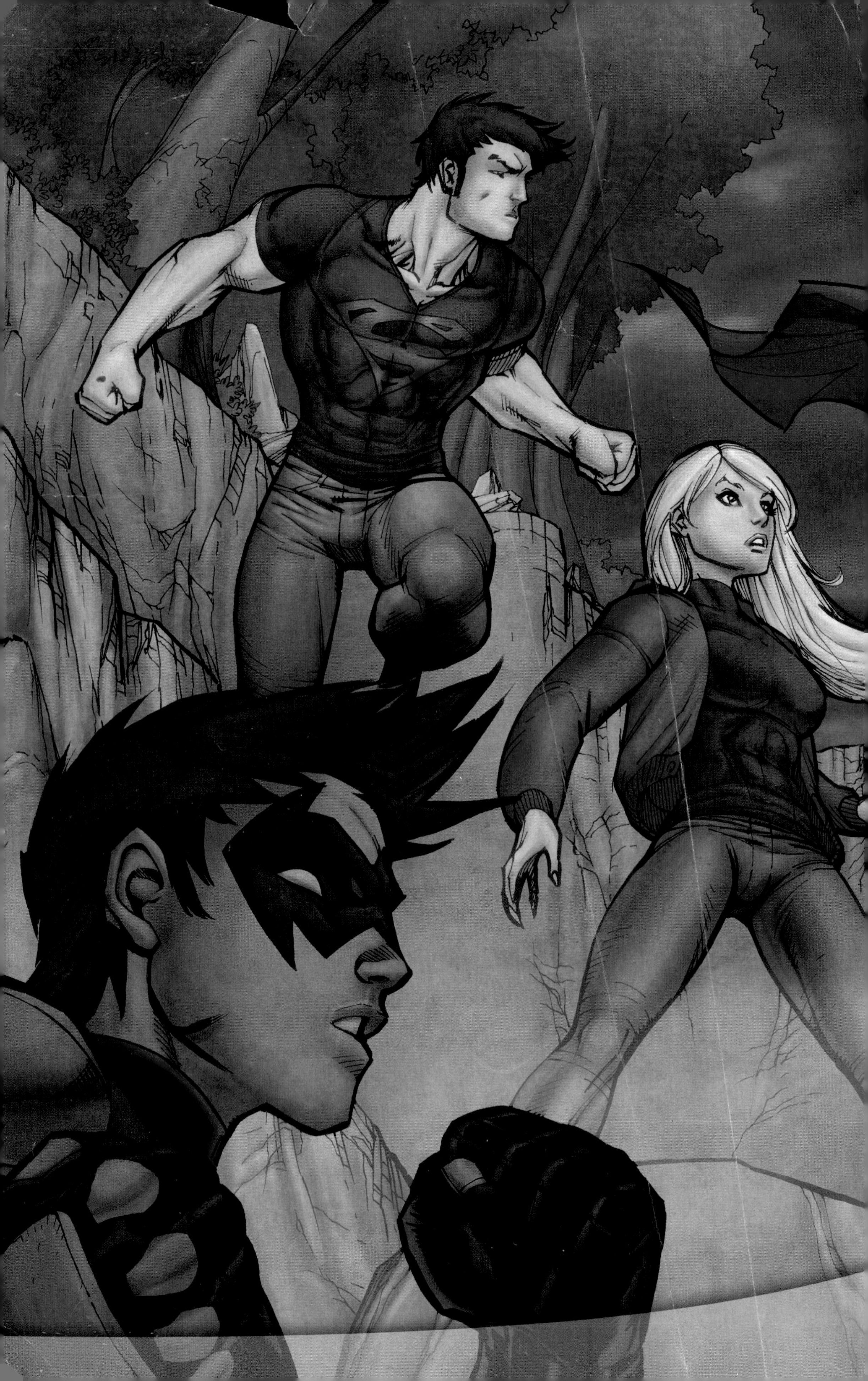

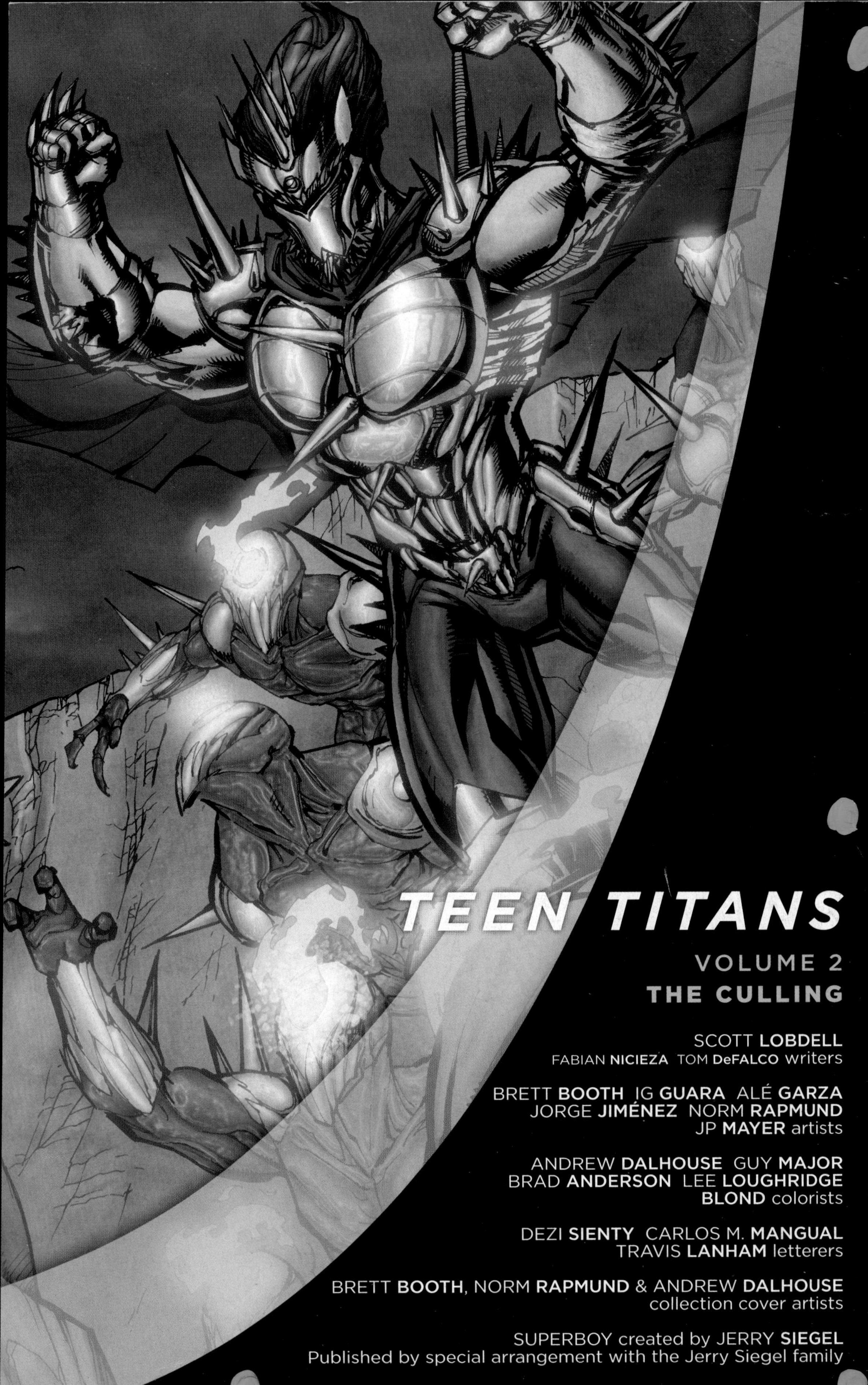

TEEN TITANS

VOLUME 2
THE CULLING

SCOTT **LOBDELL**
FABIAN **NICIEZA** TOM **DeFALCO** writers

BRETT **BOOTH** IG **GUARA** ALÉ **GARZA**
JORGE **JIMÉNEZ** NORM **RAPMUND**
JP **MAYER** artists

ANDREW **DALHOUSE** GUY **MAJOR**
BRAD **ANDERSON** LEE **LOUGHRIDGE**
BLOND colorists

DEZI **SIENTY** CARLOS M. **MANGUAL**
TRAVIS **LANHAM** letterers

BRETT **BOOTH**, NORM **RAPMUND** & ANDREW **DALHOUSE**
collection cover artists

SUPERBOY created by JERRY **SIEGEL**
Published by special arrangement with the Jerry Siegel family

EDDIE BERGANZA BOBBIE CHASE Editors – Original Series WIL MOSS Associate Editor – Original Series
DARREN SHAN KATIE KUBERT Assistant Editors – Original Series ROBIN WILDMAN Editor
ROBBIN BROSTERMAN Design Director – Books ROBBIE BIEDERMAN Publication Design

BOB HARRAS Senior VP – Editor-in-Chief, DC Comics

DIANE NELSON President DAN DIDIO and JIM LEE Co-Publishers GEOFF JOHNS Chief Creative Officer
JOHN ROOD Executive VP – Sales, Marketing & Business Development AMY GENKINS Senior VP – Business & Legal Affairs
NAIRI GARDINER Senior VP – Finance JEFF BOISON VP – Publishing Planning MARK CHIARELLO VP – Art Direction & Design
JOHN CUNNINGHAM VP – Marketing TERRI CUNNINGHAM VP – Editorial Administration
ALISON GILL Senior VP – Manufacturing & Operations HANK KANALZ Senior VP – Vertigo & Integrated Publishing
JAY KOGAN VP – Business & Legal Affairs, Publishing JACK MAHAN VP – Business Affairs, Talent
NICK NAPOLITANO VP – Manufacturing Administration SUE POHJA VP – Book Sales
COURTNEY SIMMONS Senior VP – Publicity BOB WAYNE Senior VP – Sales

TEEN TITANS VOLUME 2: THE CULLING

DC Comics, 1700 Broadway, New York, NY 10019
A Warner Bros. Entertainment Company.
Printed by RR Donnelley, Salem, VA, USA. 5/17/13. First Printing.

ISBN: 978-1-4012-4103-2

Library of Congress Cataloging-in-Publication Data

Lobdell, Scott.
Teen Titans. Volume 2, The culling / Scott Lobdell, Brett Booth.
pages cm
"Originally published in single magazine form in Teen Titans 8-14, DC Universe Presents 12."
ISBN 978-1-4012-4103-2
1. Graphic novels. I. Booth, Brett, illustrator. II. Title. III. Title: Culling.
PN6728.T34L64 2013
741.5'973—dc23
2013003526

SUSTAINABLE
FORESTRY
INITIATIVE

Certified Chain of Custody
At Least 20% Certified Forest Content
www.sfiprogram.org
SFI-01042
APPLIES TO TEXT STOCK ONLY

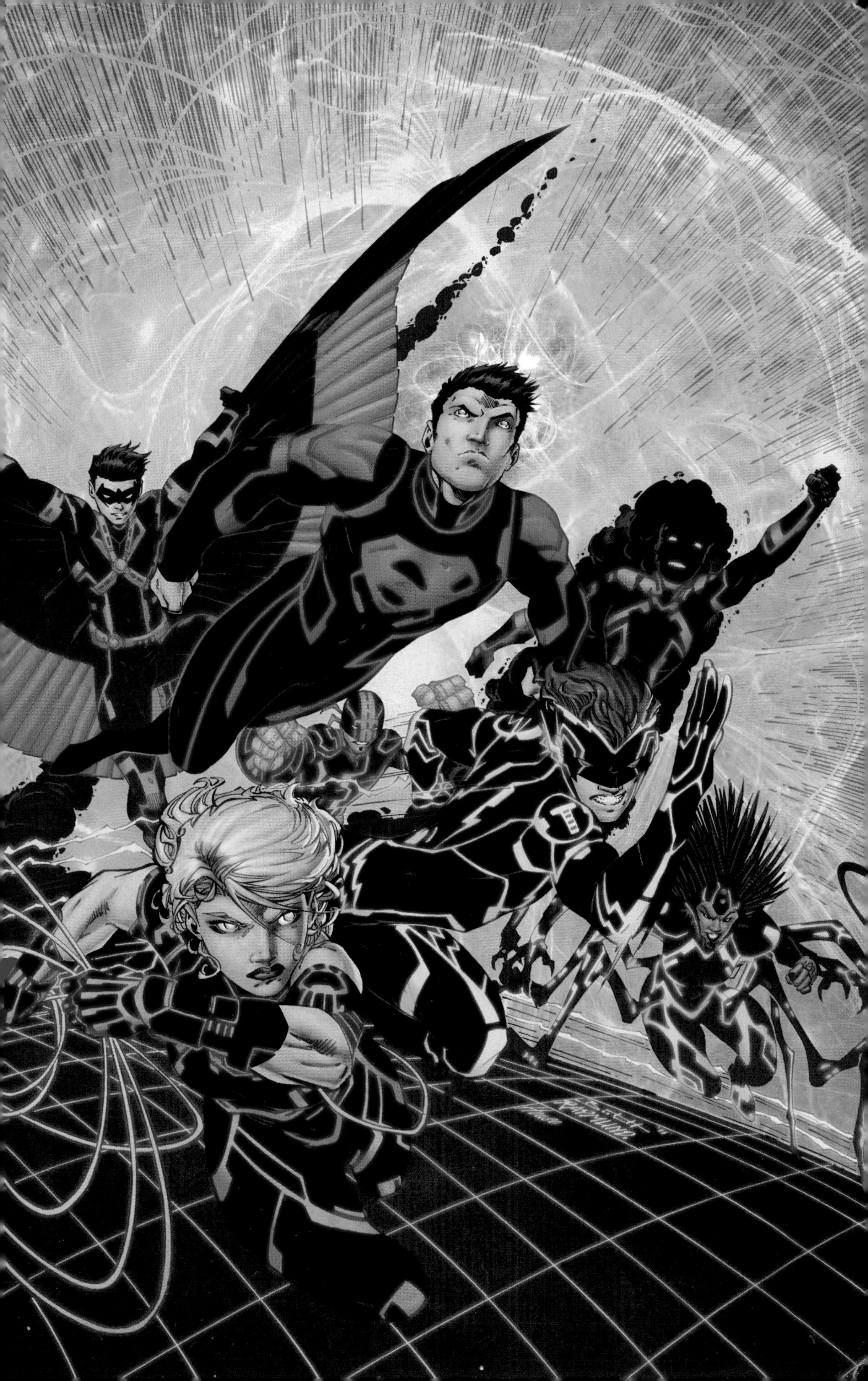

PREVIOUSLY...

For months, the mysterious organization known as N.O.W.H.E.R.E. has been kidnapping super-powered teenagers and holding them in a hidden testing facility. For almost as long, Red Robin, Batman's former kid partner, has been fighting back. Once the threat became too large for him to go it alone, he recruited Cassie (sometimes called "Wonder Girl"), brick-wielding Bunker, insectoid Skitter and N.O.W.H.E.R.E. escapees Kid Flash and Solstice to join his cause. These young Teen Titans broke into N.O.W.H.E.R.E. in an attempt to rescue their one-time enemy Superboy, but were captured while trying to escape. Now they are in the clutches of N.O.W.H.E.R.E.'s cruel leader Harvest...

A DARK OMEN

SCOTT LOBDELL
writer

IG GUARA
penciller

JP MAYER
inker

cover art by
BRETT BOOTH, NORM RAPMUND & ANDREW DALHOUSE

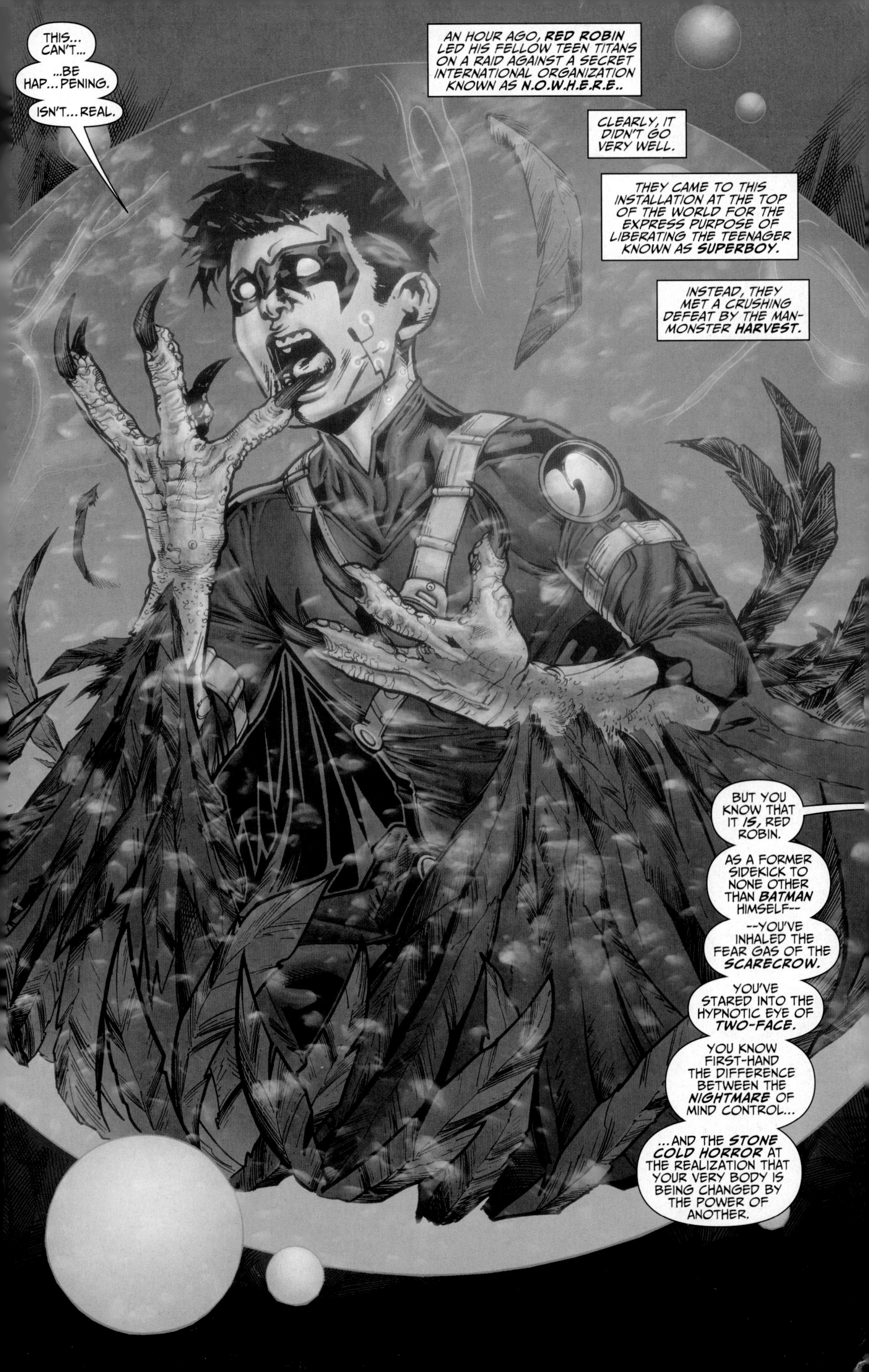
THIS... CAN'T...
...BE HAP...PENING.
ISN'T...REAL.
AN HOUR AGO, RED ROBIN LED HIS FELLOW TEEN TITANS ON A RAID AGAINST A SECRET INTERNATIONAL ORGANIZATION KNOWN AS N.O.W.H.E.R.E..
CLEARLY, IT DIDN'T GO VERY WELL.
THEY CAME TO THIS INSTALLATION AT THE TOP OF THE WORLD FOR THE EXPRESS PURPOSE OF LIBERATING THE TEENAGER KNOWN AS SUPERBOY.
INSTEAD, THEY MET A CRUSHING DEFEAT BY THE MAN-MONSTER HARVEST.
BUT YOU KNOW THAT IT IS, RED ROBIN.
AS A FORMER SIDEKICK TO NONE OTHER THAN BATMAN HIMSELF--
--YOU'VE INHALED THE FEAR GAS OF THE SCARECROW.
YOU'VE STARED INTO THE HYPNOTIC EYE OF TWO-FACE.
YOU KNOW FIRST-HAND THE DIFFERENCE BETWEEN THE NIGHTMARE OF MIND CONTROL...
...AND THE STONE COLD HORROR AT THE REALIZATION THAT YOUR VERY BODY IS BEING CHANGED BY THE POWER OF ANOTHER.

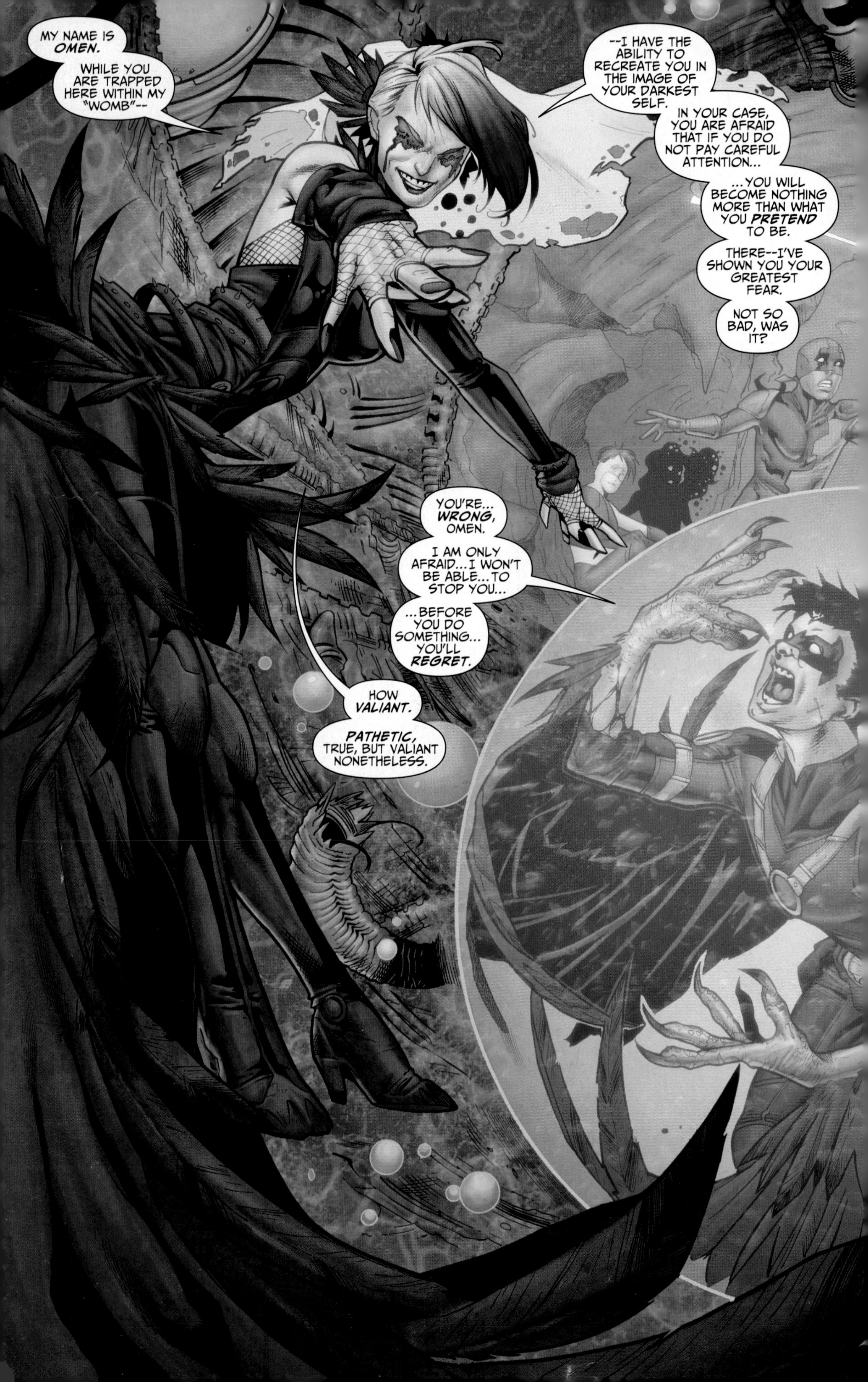
MY NAME IS OMEN.
WHILE YOU ARE TRAPPED HERE WITHIN MY "WOMB"--
--I HAVE THE ABILITY TO RECREATE YOU IN THE IMAGE OF YOUR DARKEST SELF.
IN YOUR CASE, YOU ARE AFRAID THAT IF YOU DO NOT PAY CAREFUL ATTENTION...
...YOU WILL BECOME NOTHING MORE THAN WHAT YOU PRETEND TO BE.
THERE--I'VE SHOWN YOU YOUR GREATEST FEAR.
NOT SO BAD, WAS IT?
YOU'RE... WRONG, OMEN.
I AM ONLY AFRAID...I WON'T BE ABLE...TO STOP YOU...
...BEFORE YOU DO SOMETHING... YOU'LL REGRET.
HOW VALIANT.
PATHETIC, TRUE, BUT VALIANT NONETHELESS.

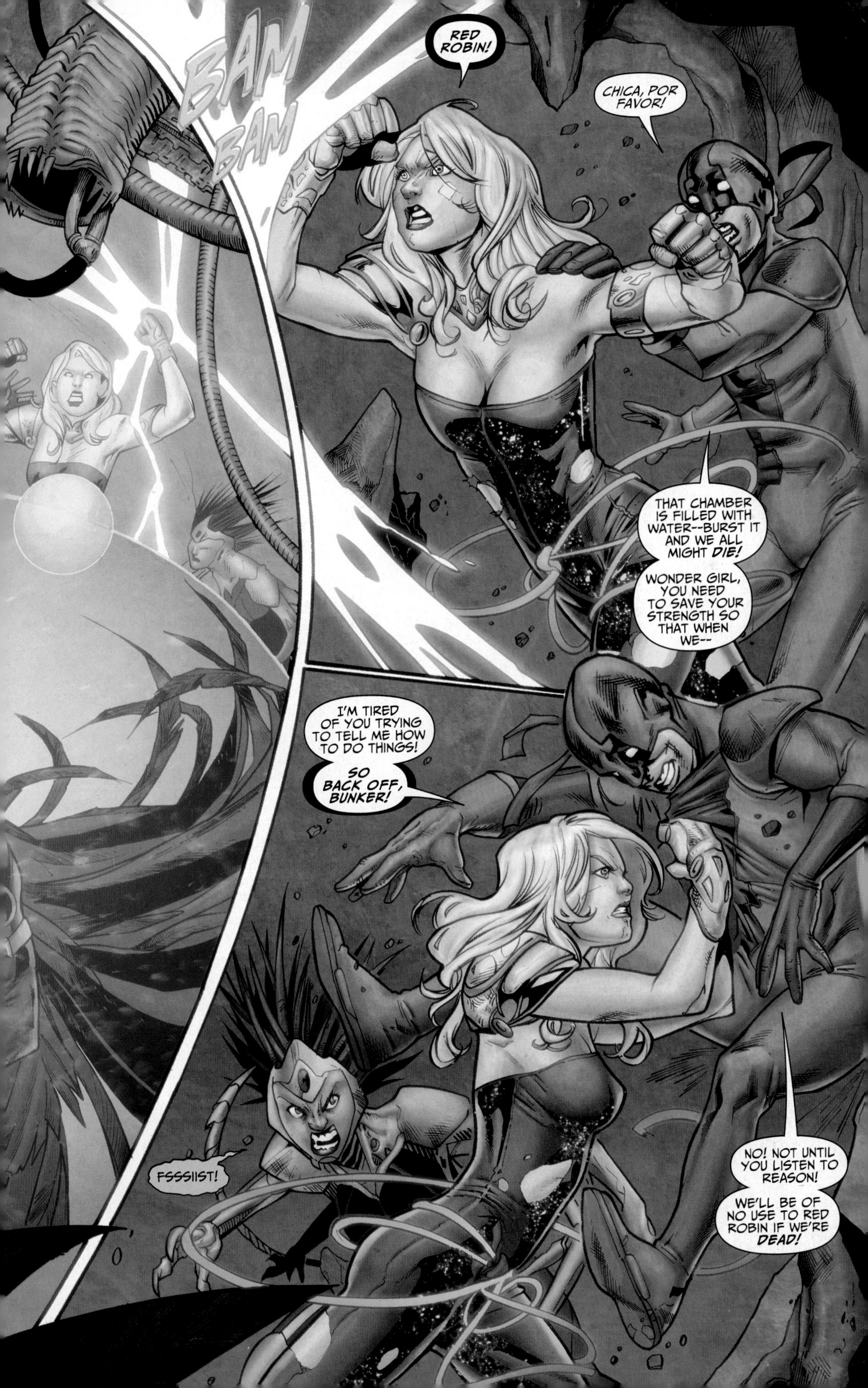
BAM
BAM
RED ROBIN!
CHICA, POR FAVOR!
THAT CHAMBER IS FILLED WITH WATER--BURST IT AND WE ALL MIGHT DIE!
WONDER GIRL, YOU NEED TO SAVE YOUR STRENGTH SO THAT WHEN WE--
I'M TIRED OF YOU TRYING TO TELL ME HOW TO DO THINGS!
SO BACK OFF, BUNKER!
FSSSIIST!
NO! NOT UNTIL YOU LISTEN TO REASON!
WE'LL BE OF NO USE TO RED ROBIN IF WE'RE DEAD!

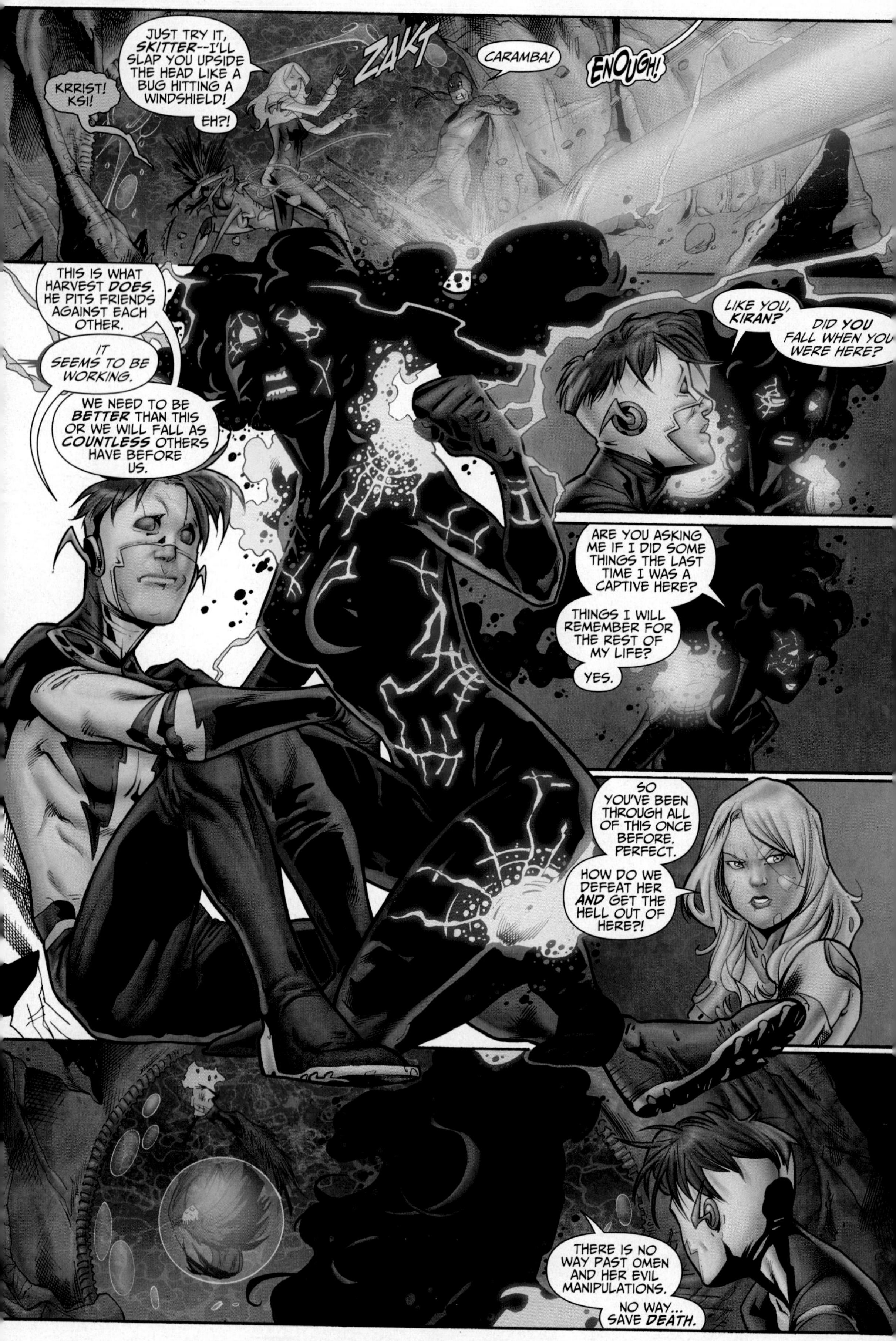

JUST TRY IT, SKITTER--I'LL SLAP YOU UPSIDE THE HEAD LIKE A BUG HITTING A WINDSHIELD!
KRRIST! KSI!
EH?!
ZAKT
CARAMBA!
ENOUGH!
THIS IS WHAT HARVEST DOES. HE PITS FRIENDS AGAINST EACH OTHER.
IT SEEMS TO BE WORKING.
WE NEED TO BE BETTER THAN THIS OR WE WILL FALL AS COUNTLESS OTHERS HAVE BEFORE US.
LIKE YOU, KIRAN?
DID YOU FALL WHEN YOU WERE HERE?
ARE YOU ASKING ME IF I DID SOME THINGS THE LAST TIME I WAS A CAPTIVE HERE?
THINGS I WILL REMEMBER FOR THE REST OF MY LIFE?
YES.
SO YOU'VE BEEN THROUGH ALL OF THIS ONCE BEFORE. PERFECT.
HOW DO WE DEFEAT HER AND GET THE HELL OUT OF HERE?!
THERE IS NO WAY PAST OMEN AND HER EVIL MANIPULATIONS.
NO WAY... SAVE DEATH.

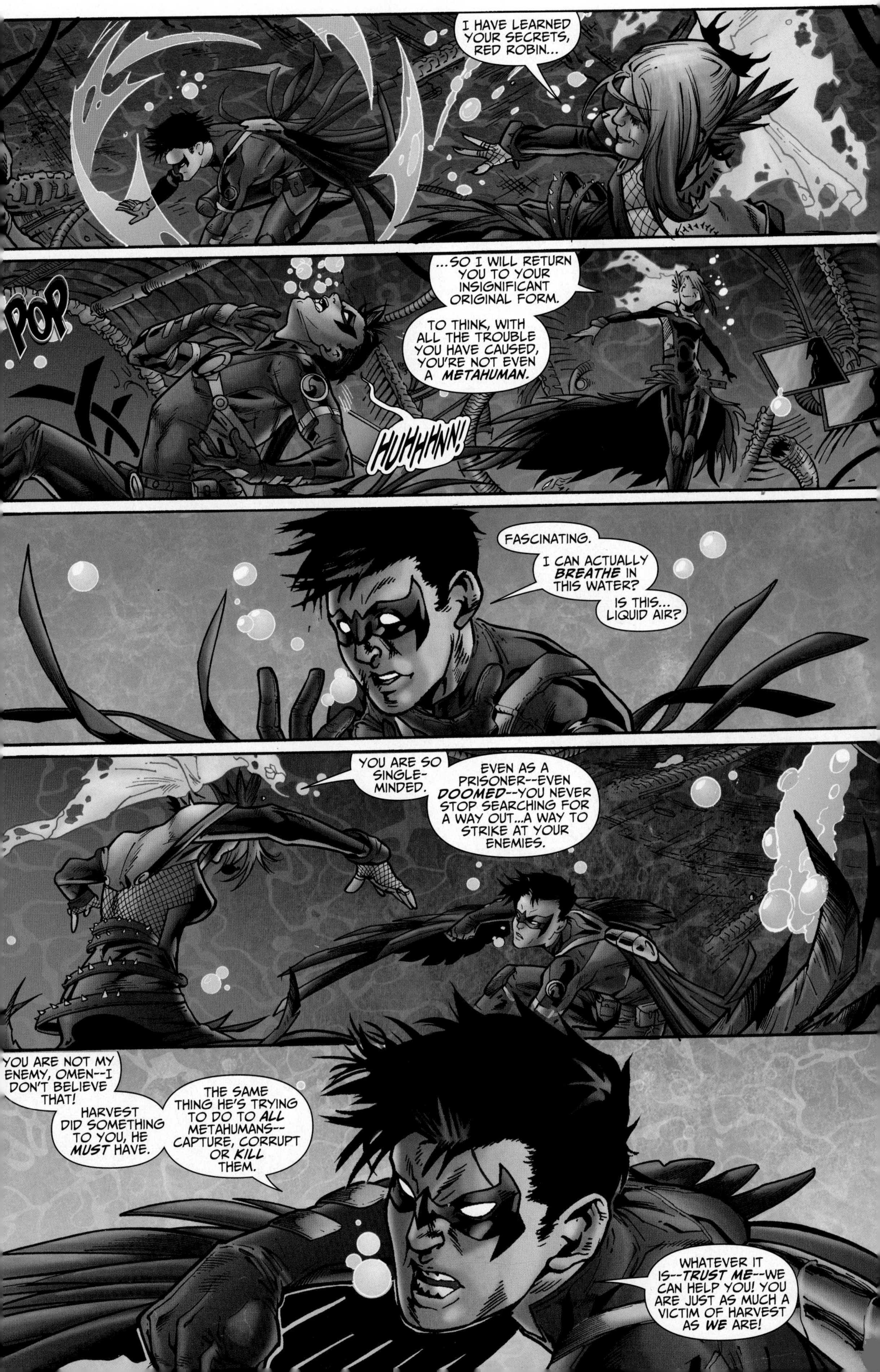
I HAVE LEARNED YOUR SECRETS, RED ROBIN...
...SO I WILL RETURN YOU TO YOUR INSIGNIFICANT ORIGINAL FORM.
TO THINK, WITH ALL THE TROUBLE YOU HAVE CAUSED, YOU'RE NOT EVEN A METAHUMAN.
POP
HUHHHNN!
FASCINATING.
I CAN ACTUALLY BREATHE IN THIS WATER?
IS THIS... LIQUID AIR?
YOU ARE SO SINGLE-MINDED.
EVEN AS A PRISONER--EVEN DOOMED--YOU NEVER STOP SEARCHING FOR A WAY OUT...A WAY TO STRIKE AT YOUR ENEMIES.
YOU ARE NOT MY ENEMY, OMEN--I DON'T BELIEVE THAT!
HARVEST DID SOMETHING TO YOU, HE MUST HAVE.
THE SAME THING HE'S TRYING TO DO TO ALL METAHUMANS--CAPTURE, CORRUPT OR KILL THEM.
WHATEVER IT IS--TRUST ME--WE CAN HELP YOU! YOU ARE JUST AS MUCH A VICTIM OF HARVEST AS WE ARE!

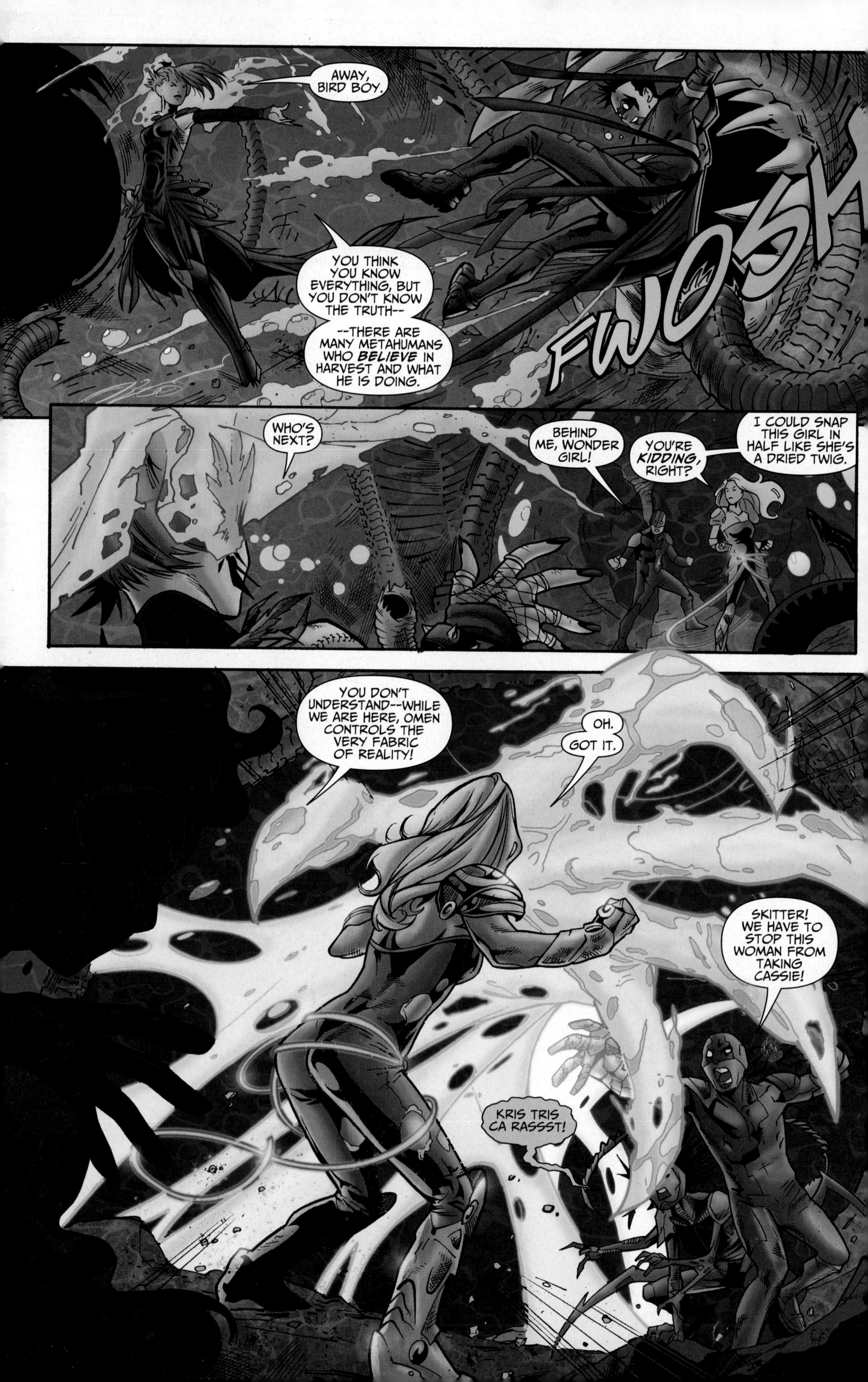

AWAY, BIRD BOY.
YOU THINK YOU KNOW EVERYTHING, BUT YOU DON'T KNOW THE TRUTH--
--THERE ARE MANY METAHUMANS WHO *BELIEVE* IN HARVEST AND WHAT HE IS DOING.
FWOSK
WHO'S NEXT?
BEHIND ME, WONDER GIRL!
YOU'RE *KIDDING*, RIGHT?
I COULD SNAP THIS GIRL IN HALF LIKE SHE'S A DRIED TWIG.
YOU DON'T UNDERSTAND--WHILE WE ARE HERE, OMEN CONTROLS THE VERY FABRIC OF REALITY!
OH. GOT IT.
SKITTER! WE HAVE TO STOP THIS WOMAN FROM TAKING CASSIE!
KRIS TRIS CA RASSST!

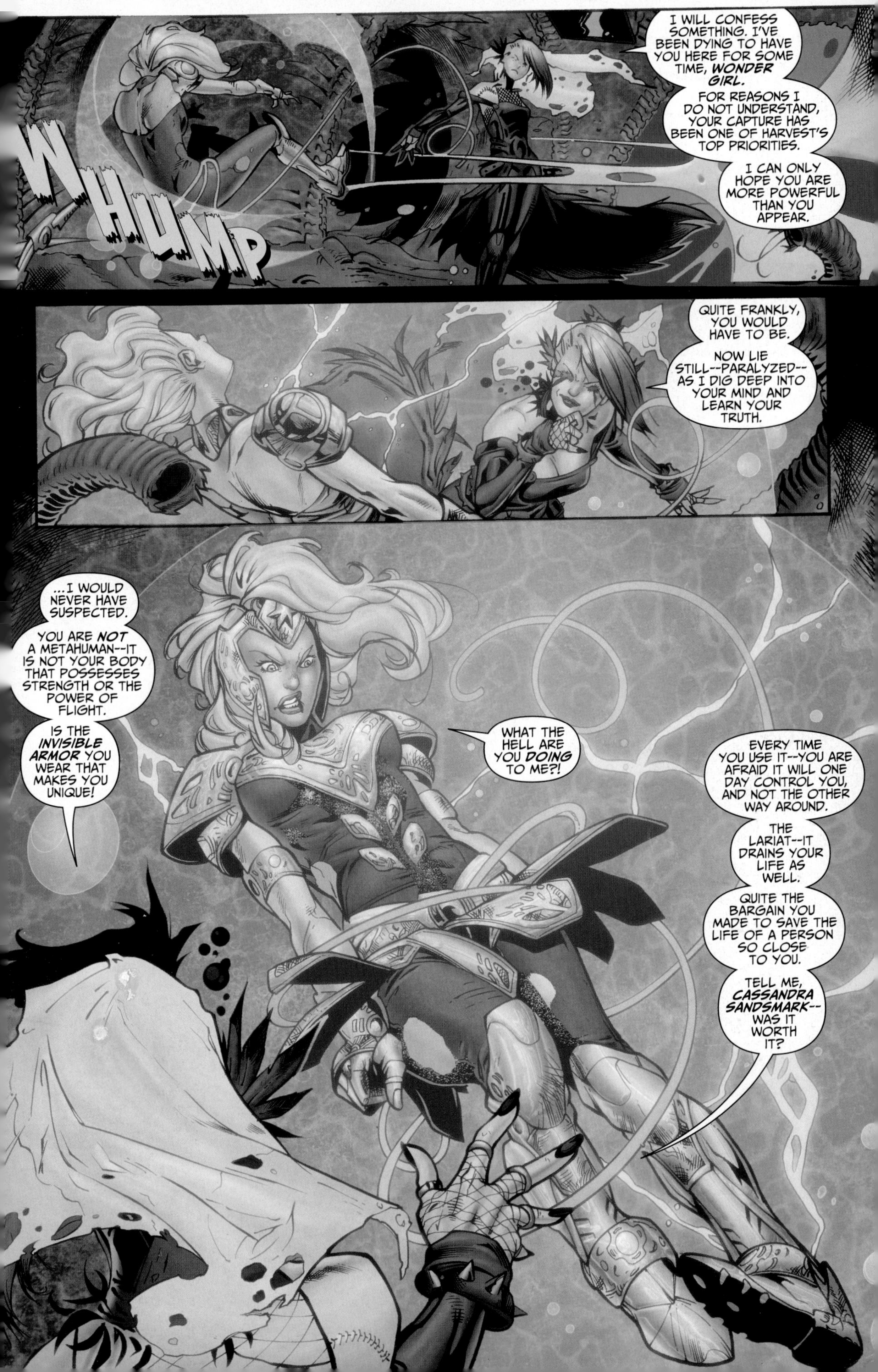

WHUMP
I WILL CONFESS SOMETHING. I'VE BEEN DYING TO HAVE YOU HERE FOR SOME TIME, WONDER GIRL.
FOR REASONS I DO NOT UNDERSTAND, YOUR CAPTURE HAS BEEN ONE OF HARVEST'S TOP PRIORITIES.
I CAN ONLY HOPE YOU ARE MORE POWERFUL THAN YOU APPEAR.
QUITE FRANKLY, YOU WOULD HAVE TO BE.
NOW LIE STILL--PARALYZED--AS I DIG DEEP INTO YOUR MIND AND LEARN YOUR TRUTH.
...I WOULD NEVER HAVE SUSPECTED.
YOU ARE NOT A METAHUMAN--IT IS NOT YOUR BODY THAT POSSESSES STRENGTH OR THE POWER OF FLIGHT.
IS THE INVISIBLE ARMOR YOU WEAR THAT MAKES YOU UNIQUE!
WHAT THE HELL ARE YOU DOING TO ME?!
EVERY TIME YOU USE IT--YOU ARE AFRAID IT WILL ONE DAY CONTROL YOU, AND NOT THE OTHER WAY AROUND.
THE LARIAT--IT DRAINS YOUR LIFE AS WELL.
QUITE THE BARGAIN YOU MADE TO SAVE THE LIFE OF A PERSON SO CLOSE TO YOU.
TELL ME, CASSANDRA SANDSMARK--WAS IT WORTH IT?

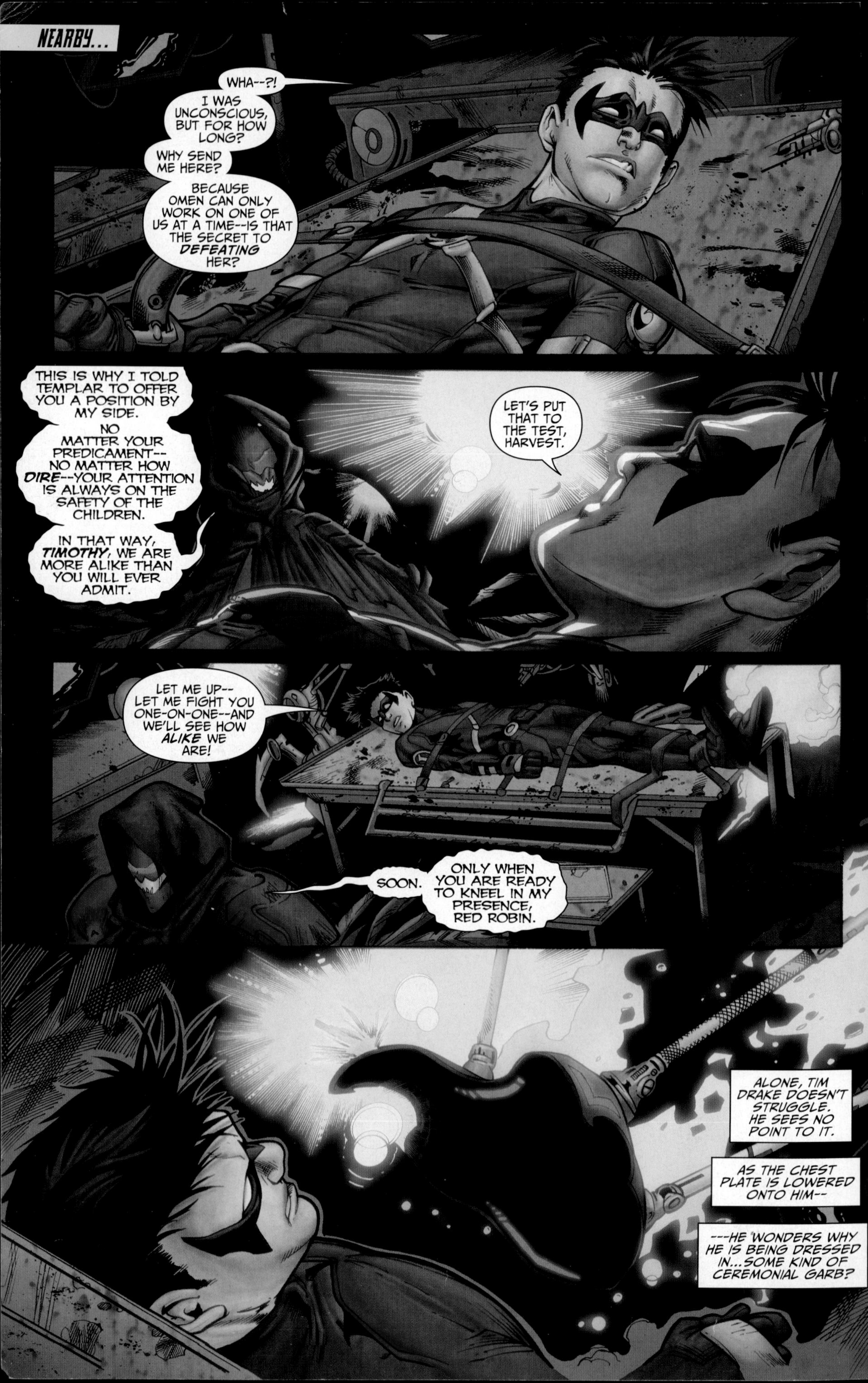
NEARBY...
WHA--?!
I WAS UNCONSCIOUS, BUT FOR HOW LONG?
WHY SEND ME HERE?
BECAUSE OMEN CAN ONLY WORK ON ONE OF US AT A TIME--IS THAT THE SECRET TO DEFEATING HER?
THIS IS WHY I TOLD TEMPLAR TO OFFER YOU A POSITION BY MY SIDE.
NO MATTER YOUR PREDICAMENT-- NO MATTER HOW DIRE--YOUR ATTENTION IS ALWAYS ON THE SAFETY OF THE CHILDREN.
IN THAT WAY, TIMOTHY, WE ARE MORE ALIKE THAN YOU WILL EVER ADMIT.
LET'S PUT THAT TO THE TEST, HARVEST.
LET ME UP-- LET ME FIGHT YOU ONE-ON-ONE--AND WE'LL SEE HOW ALIKE WE ARE!
SOON.
ONLY WHEN YOU ARE READY TO KNEEL IN MY PRESENCE, RED ROBIN.
ALONE, TIM DRAKE DOESN'T STRUGGLE. HE SEES NO POINT TO IT.
AS THE CHEST PLATE IS LOWERED ONTO HIM--
---HE WONDERS WHY HE IS BEING DRESSED IN...SOME KIND OF CEREMONIAL GARB?

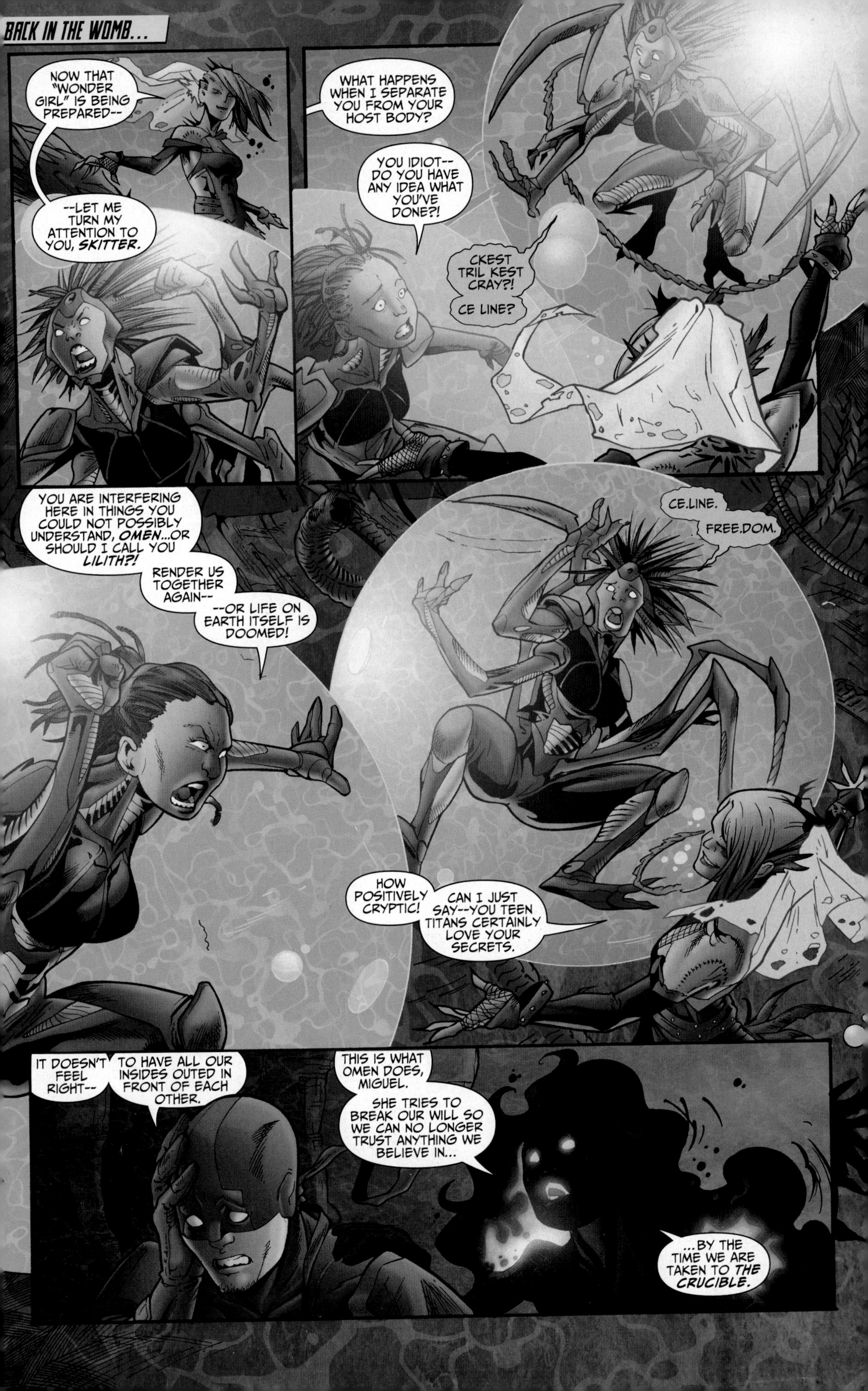
BACK IN THE WOMB...
NOW THAT "WONDER GIRL" IS BEING PREPARED--
--LET ME TURN MY ATTENTION TO YOU, SKITTER.
WHAT HAPPENS WHEN I SEPARATE YOU FROM YOUR HOST BODY?
YOU IDIOT--DO YOU HAVE ANY IDEA WHAT YOU'VE DONE?!
CKEST TRIL KEST CRAY?!
CE LINE?
YOU ARE INTERFERING HERE IN THINGS YOU COULD NOT POSSIBLY UNDERSTAND, OMEN...OR SHOULD I CALL YOU LILITH?!
RENDER US TOGETHER AGAIN--
--OR LIFE ON EARTH ITSELF IS DOOMED!
CE.LINE.
FREE.DOM.
HOW POSITIVELY CRYPTIC!
CAN I JUST SAY--YOU TEEN TITANS CERTAINLY LOVE YOUR SECRETS.
IT DOESN'T FEEL RIGHT--
TO HAVE ALL OUR INSIDES OUTED IN FRONT OF EACH OTHER.
THIS IS WHAT OMEN DOES, MIGUEL.
SHE TRIES TO BREAK OUR WILL SO WE CAN NO LONGER TRUST ANYTHING WE BELIEVE IN...
...BY THE TIME WE ARE TAKEN TO THE CRUCIBLE.

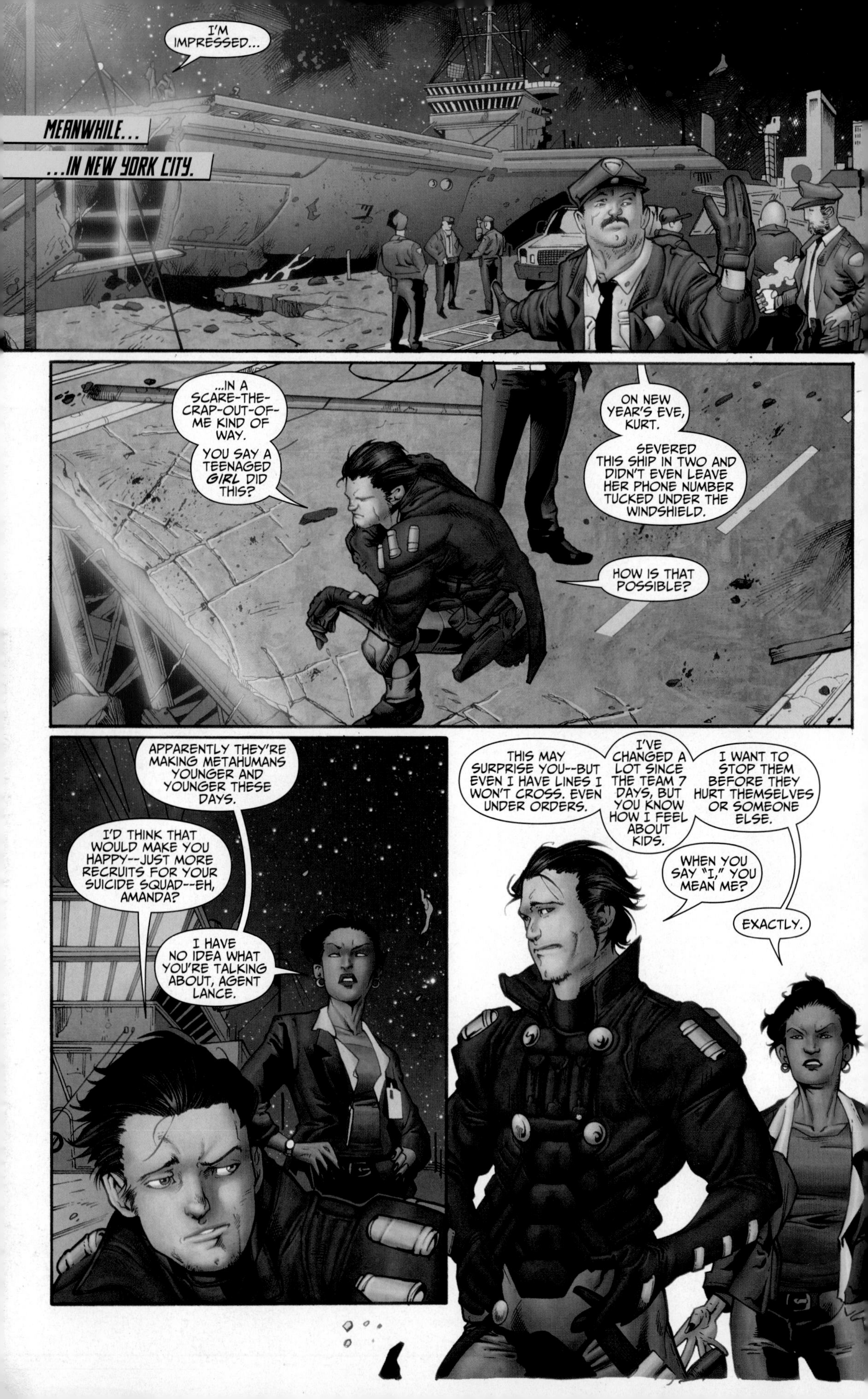
I'M IMPRESSED...
MEANWHILE...
...IN NEW YORK CITY.
...IN A SCARE-THE-CRAP-OUT-OF-ME KIND OF WAY.
YOU SAY A TEENAGED GIRL DID THIS?
ON NEW YEAR'S EVE, KURT.
SEVERED THIS SHIP IN TWO AND DIDN'T EVEN LEAVE HER PHONE NUMBER TUCKED UNDER THE WINDSHIELD.
HOW IS THAT POSSIBLE?
APPARENTLY THEY'RE MAKING METAHUMANS YOUNGER AND YOUNGER THESE DAYS.
I'D THINK THAT WOULD MAKE YOU HAPPY--JUST MORE RECRUITS FOR YOUR SUICIDE SQUAD--EH, AMANDA?
I HAVE NO IDEA WHAT YOU'RE TALKING ABOUT, AGENT LANCE.
THIS MAY SURPRISE YOU--BUT EVEN I HAVE LINES I WON'T CROSS. EVEN UNDER ORDERS.
I'VE CHANGED A LOT SINCE THE TEAM 7 DAYS, BUT YOU KNOW HOW I FEEL ABOUT KIDS.
I WANT TO STOP THEM BEFORE THEY HURT THEMSELVES OR SOMEONE ELSE.
WHEN YOU SAY "I," YOU MEAN ME?
EXACTLY.

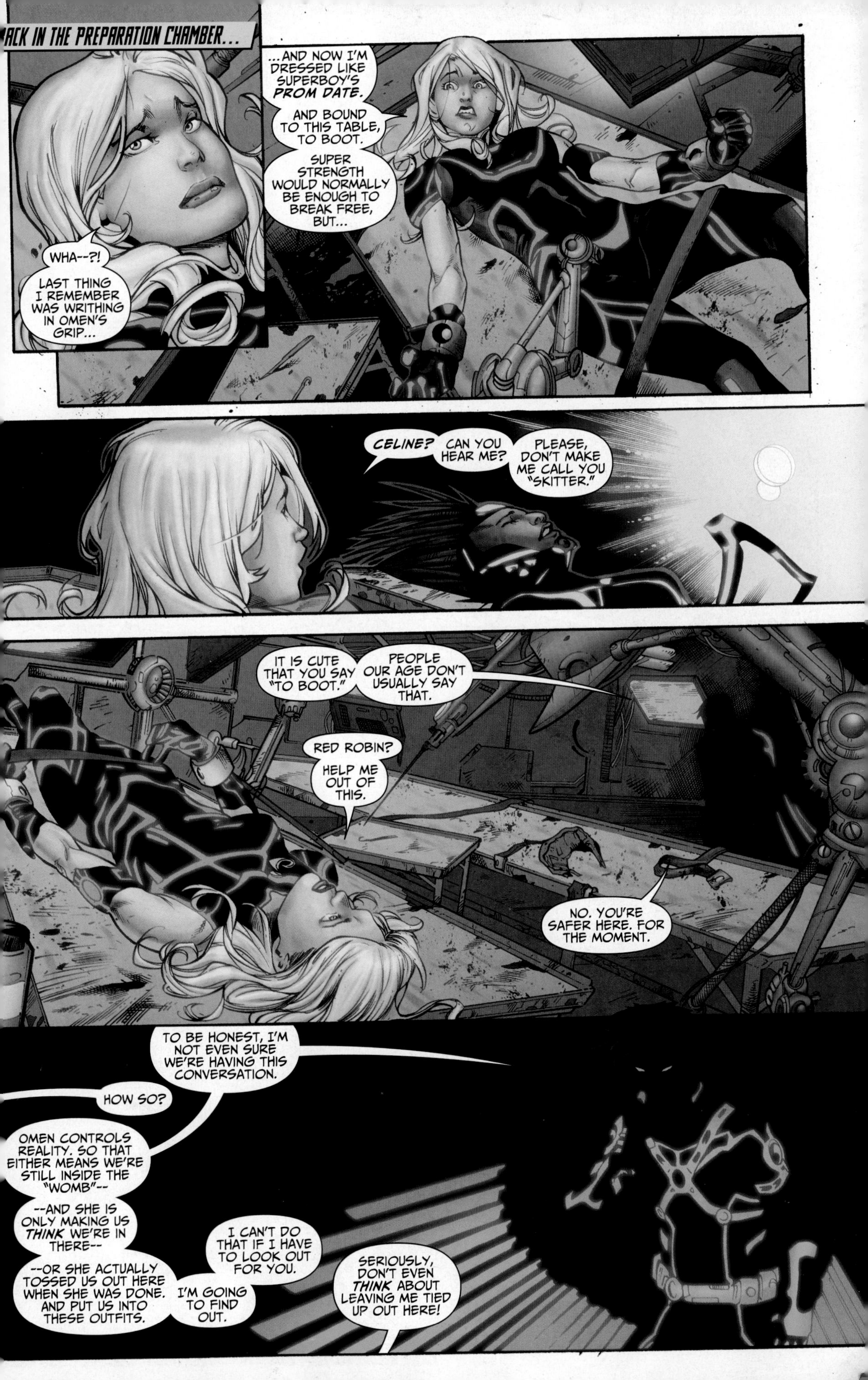

ACK IN THE PREPARATION CHAMBER...
WHA--?!
LAST THING I REMEMBER WAS WRITHING IN OMEN'S GRIP...
...AND NOW I'M DRESSED LIKE SUPERBOY'S PROM DATE.
AND BOUND TO THIS TABLE, TO BOOT.
SUPER STRENGTH WOULD NORMALLY BE ENOUGH TO BREAK FREE, BUT...
CELINE?
CAN YOU HEAR ME?
PLEASE, DON'T MAKE ME CALL YOU "SKITTER."
IT IS CUTE THAT YOU SAY "TO BOOT."
PEOPLE OUR AGE DON'T USUALLY SAY THAT.
RED ROBIN?
HELP ME OUT OF THIS.
NO. YOU'RE SAFER HERE. FOR THE MOMENT.
TO BE HONEST, I'M NOT EVEN SURE WE'RE HAVING THIS CONVERSATION.
HOW SO?
OMEN CONTROLS REALITY. SO THAT EITHER MEANS WE'RE STILL INSIDE THE "WOMB"--
--AND SHE IS ONLY MAKING US THINK WE'RE IN THERE--
--OR SHE ACTUALLY TOSSED US OUT HERE WHEN SHE WAS DONE. AND PUT US INTO THESE OUTFITS.
I'M GOING TO FIND OUT.
I CAN'T DO THAT IF I HAVE TO LOOK OUT FOR YOU.
SERIOUSLY, DON'T EVEN THINK ABOUT LEAVING ME TIED UP OUT HERE!

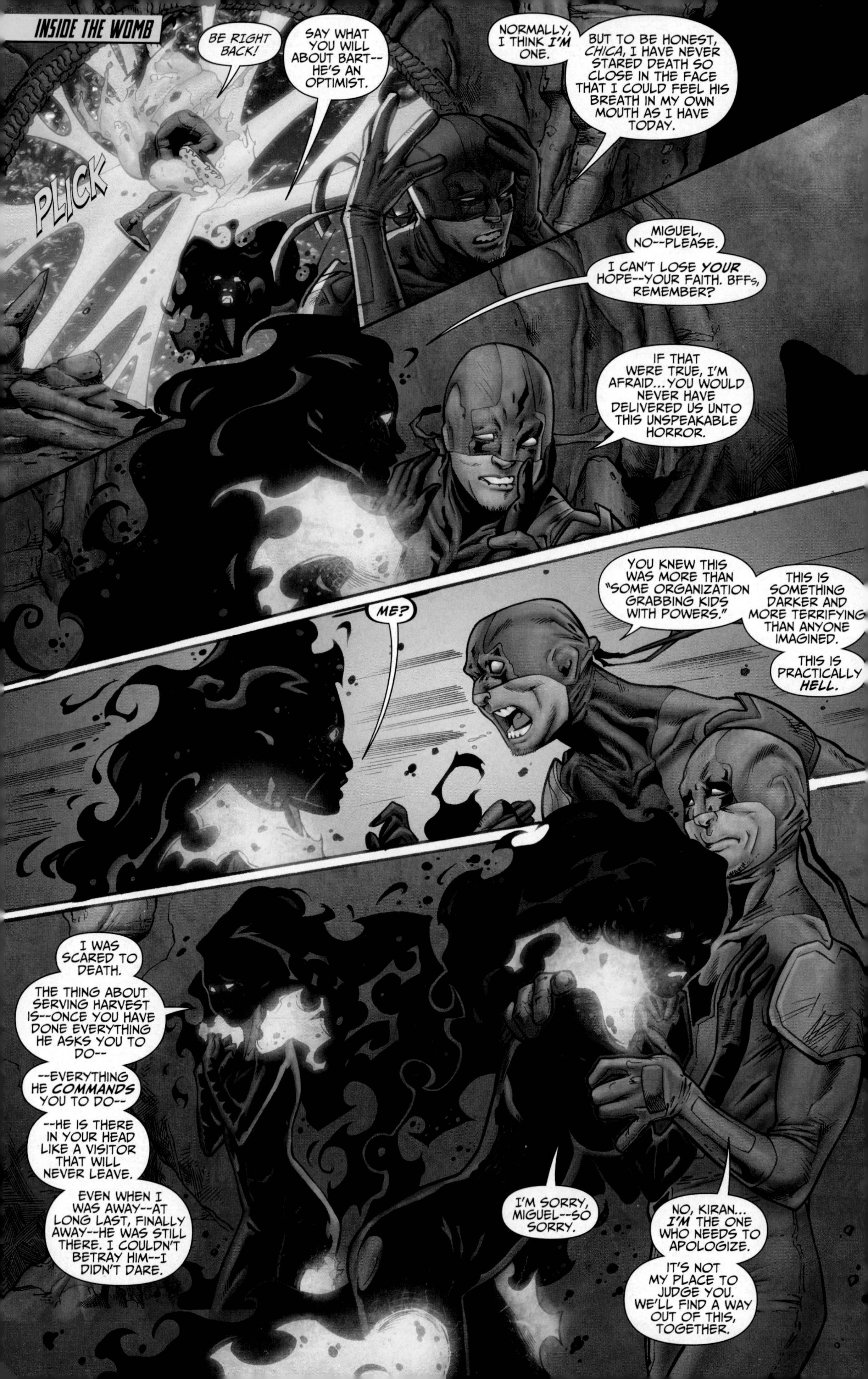
INSIDE THE WOMB
BE RIGHT BACK!
SAY WHAT YOU WILL ABOUT BART--HE'S AN OPTIMIST.
NORMALLY, I THINK I'M ONE.
BUT TO BE HONEST, CHICA, I HAVE NEVER STARED DEATH SO CLOSE IN THE FACE THAT I COULD FEEL HIS BREATH IN MY OWN MOUTH AS I HAVE TODAY.
PLICK
MIGUEL, NO--PLEASE.
I CAN'T LOSE YOUR HOPE--YOUR FAITH. BFFs, REMEMBER?
?
IF THAT WERE TRUE, I'M AFRAID...YOU WOULD NEVER HAVE DELIVERED US UNTO THIS UNSPEAKABLE HORROR.
ME?
YOU KNEW THIS WAS MORE THAN "SOME ORGANIZATION GRABBING KIDS WITH POWERS."
THIS IS SOMETHING DARKER AND MORE TERRIFYING THAN ANYONE IMAGINED.
THIS IS PRACTICALLY HELL.
I WAS SCARED TO DEATH.
THE THING ABOUT SERVING HARVEST IS--ONCE YOU HAVE DONE EVERYTHING HE ASKS YOU TO DO--
--EVERYTHING HE COMMANDS YOU TO DO--
--HE IS THERE IN YOUR HEAD LIKE A VISITOR THAT WILL NEVER LEAVE.
EVEN WHEN I WAS AWAY--AT LONG LAST, FINALLY AWAY--HE WAS STILL THERE. I COULDN'T BETRAY HIM--I DIDN'T DARE.
I'M SORRY, MIGUEL--SO SORRY.
NO, KIRAN... I'M THE ONE WHO NEEDS TO APOLOGIZE.
IT'S NOT MY PLACE TO JUDGE YOU. WE'LL FIND A WAY OUT OF THIS, TOGETHER.

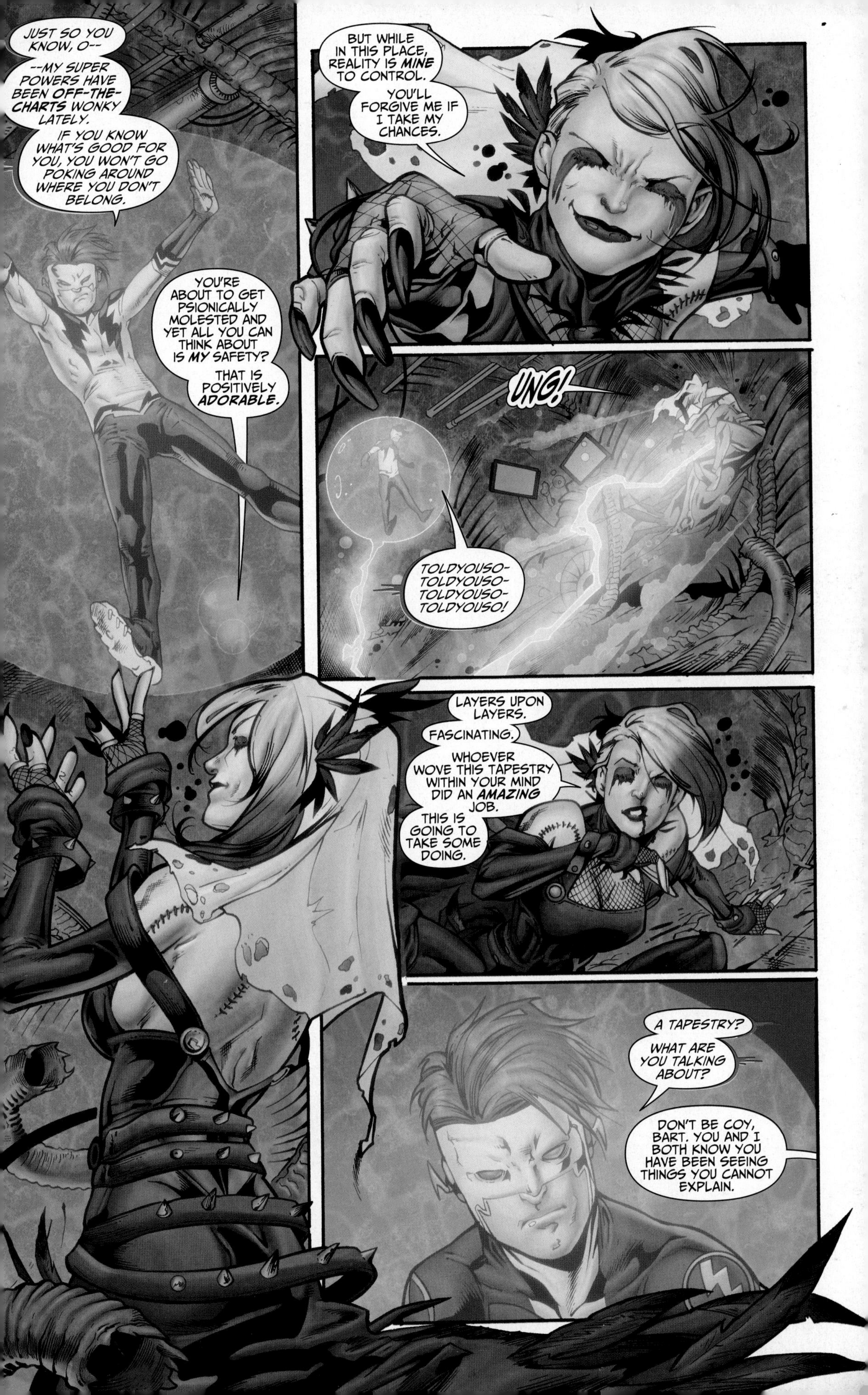

JUST SO YOU KNOW, O--
--MY SUPER POWERS HAVE BEEN **OFF-THE-CHARTS** WONKY LATELY.
IF YOU KNOW WHAT'S GOOD FOR YOU, YOU WON'T GO POKING AROUND WHERE YOU DON'T BELONG.
YOU'RE ABOUT TO GET PSIONICALLY MOLESTED AND YET ALL YOU CAN THINK ABOUT IS **MY** SAFETY?
THAT IS POSITIVELY **ADORABLE.**
BUT WHILE IN THIS PLACE, REALITY IS **MINE** TO CONTROL.
YOU'LL FORGIVE ME IF I TAKE MY CHANCES.
UNG!
TOLDYOUSO-TOLDYOUSO-TOLDYOUSO-TOLDYOUSO!
LAYERS UPON LAYERS.
FASCINATING.
WHOEVER WOVE THIS TAPESTRY WITHIN YOUR MIND DID AN **AMAZING** JOB.
THIS IS GOING TO TAKE SOME DOING.
A TAPESTRY?
WHAT ARE YOU TALKING ABOUT?
DON'T BE COY, BART. YOU AND I BOTH KNOW YOU HAVE BEEN SEEING THINGS YOU CANNOT EXPLAIN.

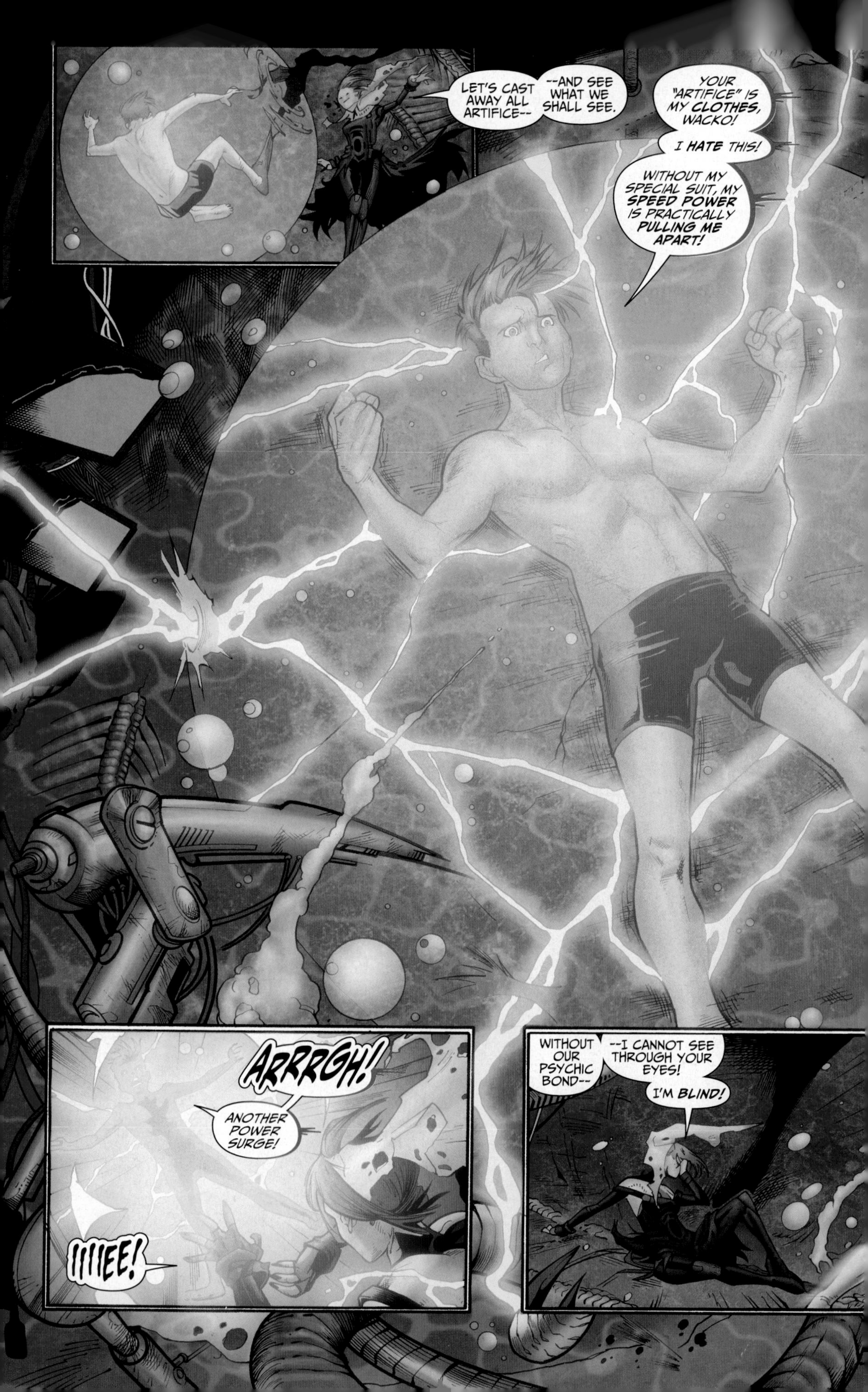
LET'S CAST AWAY ALL ARTIFICE--
--AND SEE WHAT WE SHALL SEE.
YOUR "ARTIFICE" IS MY CLOTHES, WACKO!
I HATE THIS!
WITHOUT MY SPECIAL SUIT, MY SPEED POWER IS PRACTICALLY PULLING ME APART!
ARRRGH!
ANOTHER POWER SURGE!
IIIIIEE!
WITHOUT OUR PSYCHIC BOND--
--I CANNOT SEE THROUGH YOUR EYES!
I'M BLIND!

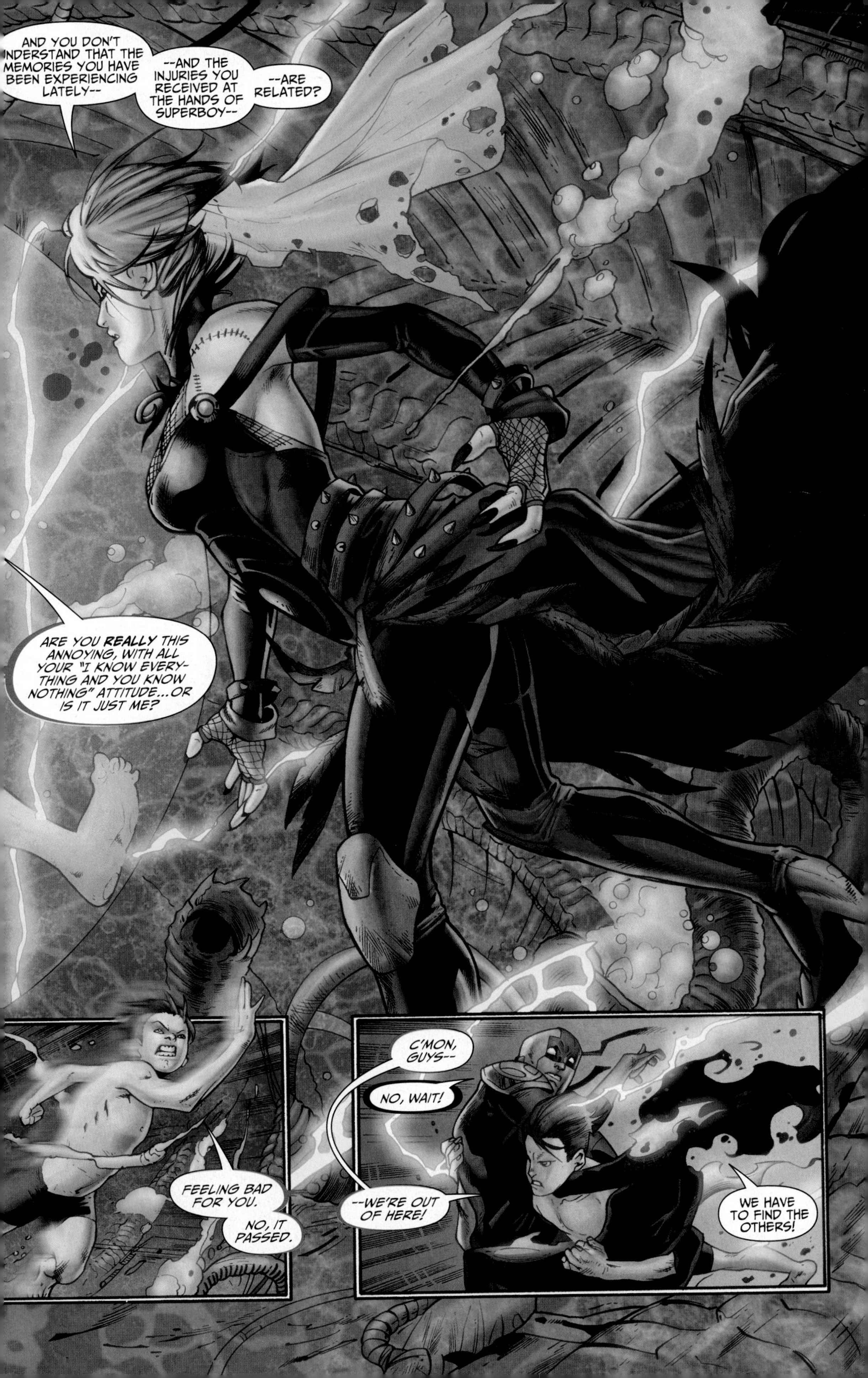

AND YOU DON'T UNDERSTAND THAT THE MEMORIES YOU HAVE BEEN EXPERIENCING LATELY--
--AND THE INJURIES YOU RECEIVED AT THE HANDS OF SUPERBOY--
--ARE RELATED?
ARE YOU **REALLY** THIS ANNOYING, WITH ALL YOUR "I KNOW EVERYTHING AND YOU KNOW NOTHING" ATTITUDE...OR IS IT JUST ME?
FEELING BAD FOR YOU.
NO, IT PASSED.
C'MON, GUYS--
NO, WAIT!
--WE'RE OUT OF HERE!
WE HAVE TO FIND THE OTHERS!

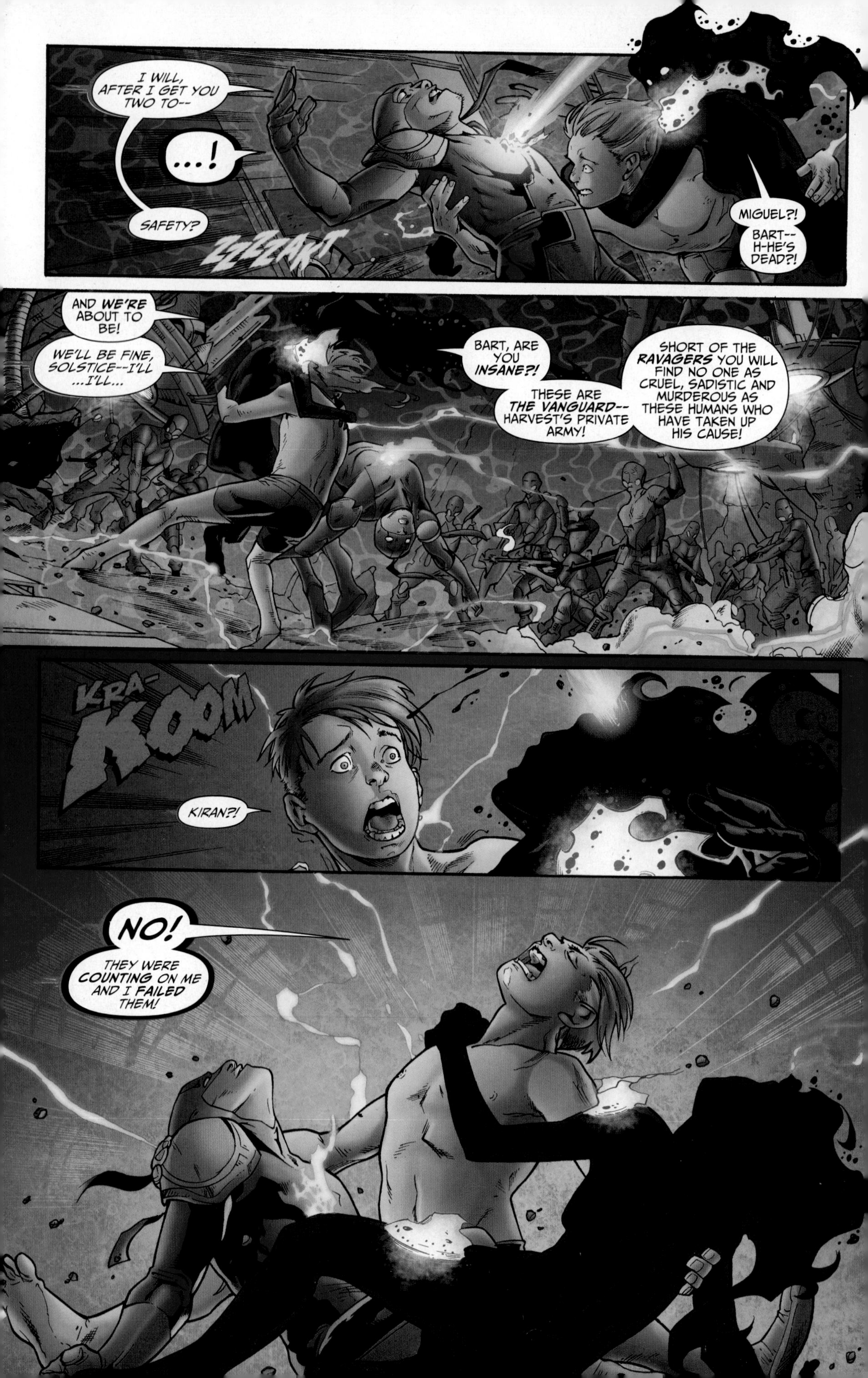
I WILL, AFTER I GET YOU TWO TO--
...!
SAFETY?
ZZZZZAKT
MIGUEL?! BART-- H-HE'S DEAD?!
AND WE'RE ABOUT TO BE!
WE'LL BE FINE, SOLSTICE--I'LL ...I'LL...
BART, ARE YOU INSANE?!
THESE ARE THE VANGUARD-- HARVEST'S PRIVATE ARMY!
SHORT OF THE RAVAGERS YOU WILL FIND NO ONE AS CRUEL, SADISTIC AND MURDEROUS AS THESE HUMANS WHO HAVE TAKEN UP HIS CAUSE!
KRA-KOOM
KIRAN?!
NO!
THEY WERE COUNTING ON ME AND I FAILED THEM!

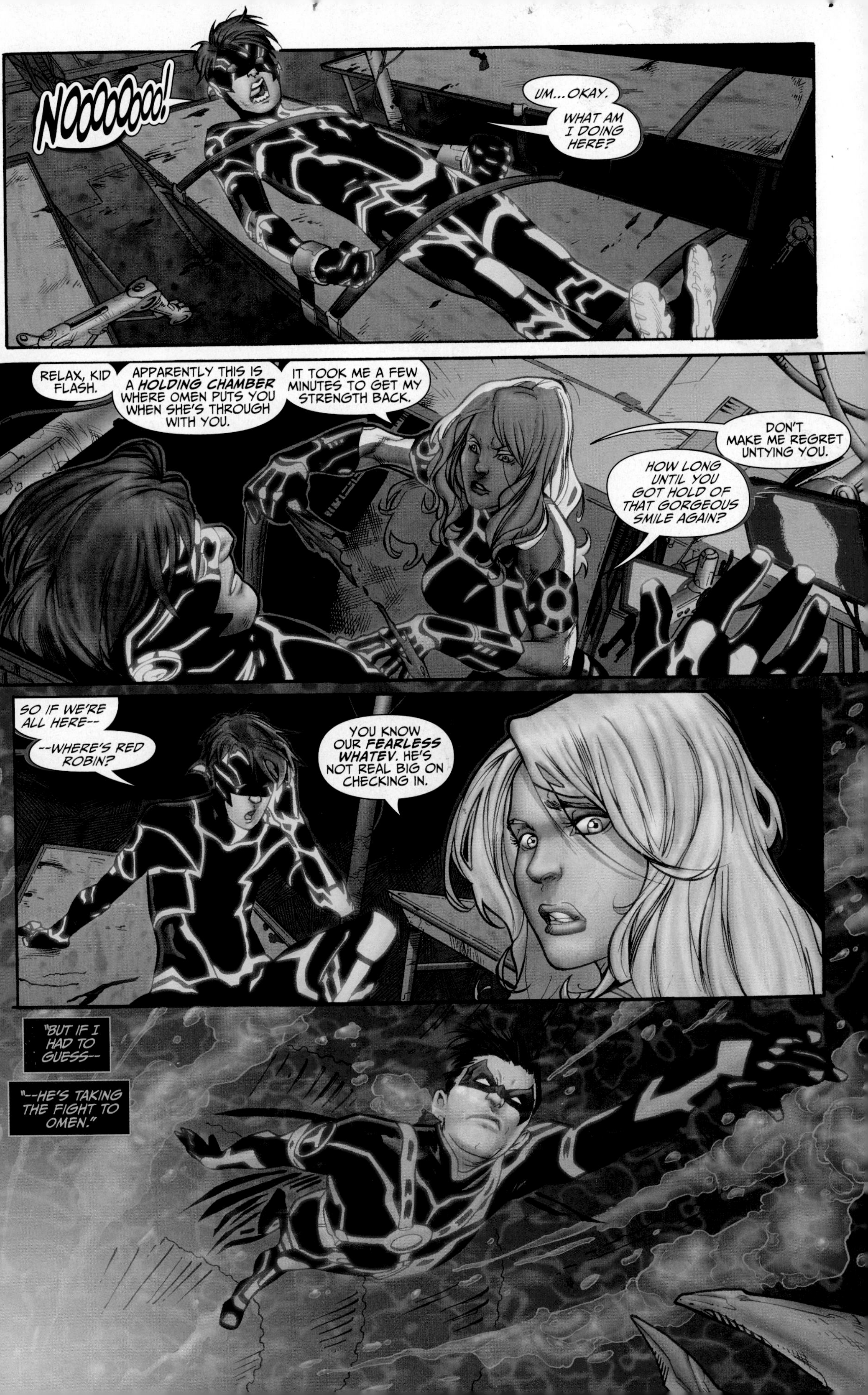
NOOOOOOOO!
UM...OKAY.
WHAT AM I DOING HERE?
RELAX, KID FLASH.
APPARENTLY THIS IS A HOLDING CHAMBER WHERE OMEN PUTS YOU WHEN SHE'S THROUGH WITH YOU.
IT TOOK ME A FEW MINUTES TO GET MY STRENGTH BACK.
DON'T MAKE ME REGRET UNTYING YOU.
HOW LONG UNTIL YOU GOT HOLD OF THAT GORGEOUS SMILE AGAIN?
SO IF WE'RE ALL HERE--
--WHERE'S RED ROBIN?
YOU KNOW OUR FEARLESS WHATEV. HE'S NOT REAL BIG ON CHECKING IN.
"BUT IF I HAD TO GUESS--
"--HE'S TAKING THE FIGHT TO OMEN."

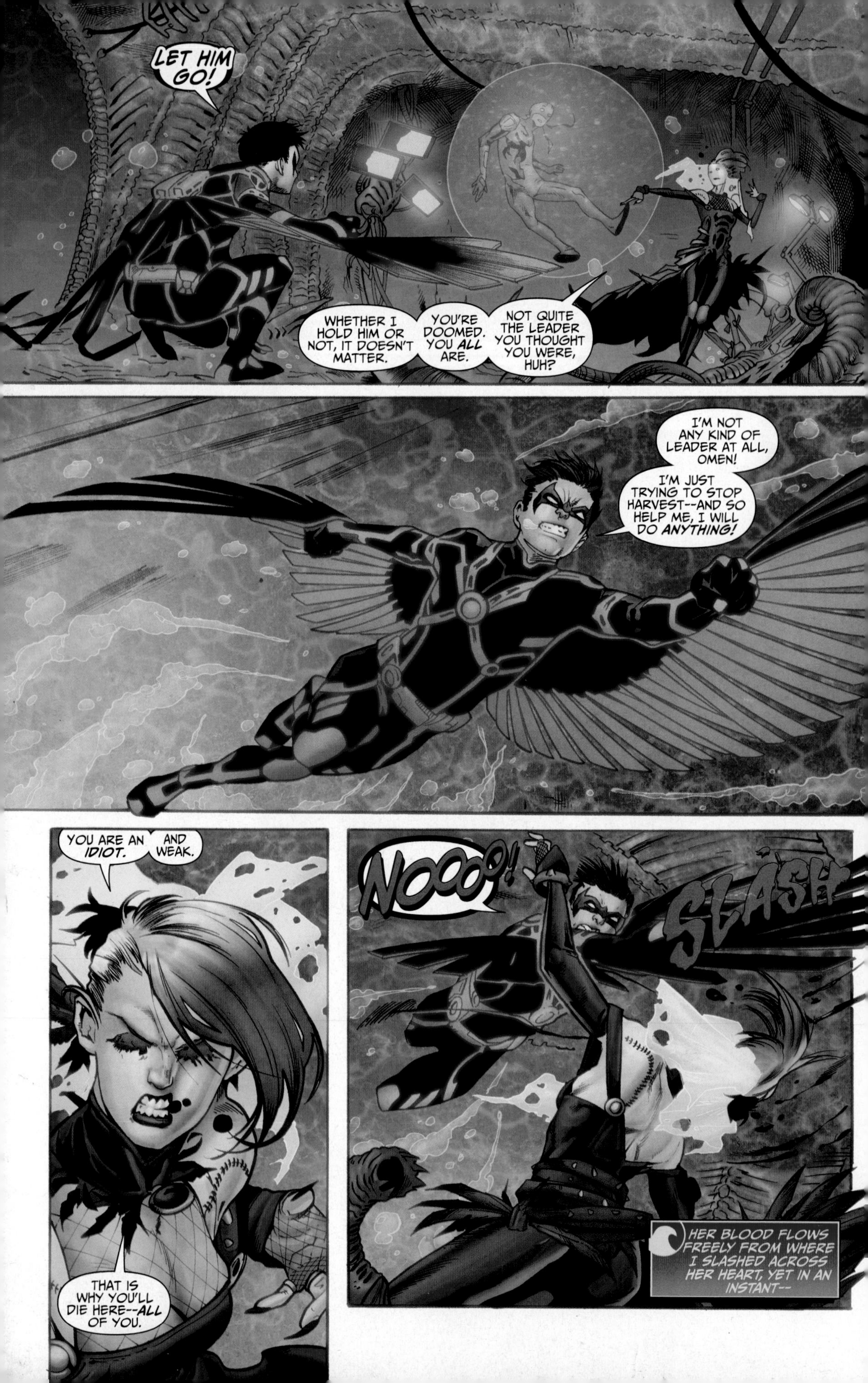

LET HIM GO!
WHETHER I HOLD HIM OR NOT, IT DOESN'T MATTER.
YOU'RE DOOMED. YOU ALL ARE.
NOT QUITE THE LEADER YOU THOUGHT YOU WERE, HUH?
I'M NOT ANY KIND OF LEADER AT ALL, OMEN!
I'M JUST TRYING TO STOP HARVEST--AND SO HELP ME, I WILL DO ANYTHING!
YOU ARE AN IDIOT.
AND WEAK.
THAT IS WHY YOU'LL DIE HERE--ALL OF YOU.
NOOOO!
SLASH
HER BLOOD FLOWS FREELY FROM WHERE I SLASHED ACROSS HER HEART, YET IN AN INSTANT--

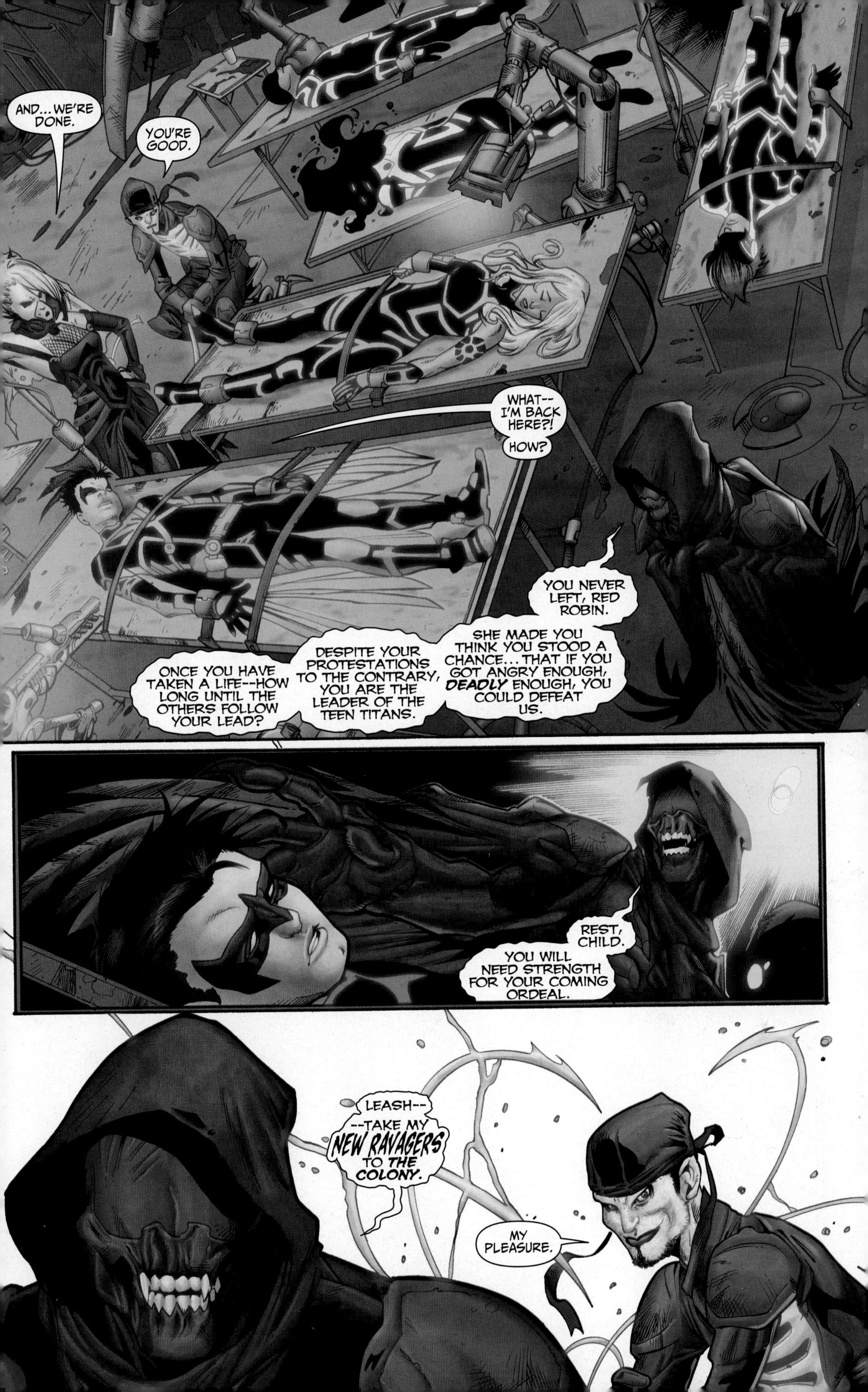
AND...WE'RE DONE.
YOU'RE GOOD.
WHAT-- I'M BACK HERE?!
HOW?
YOU NEVER LEFT, RED ROBIN.
SHE MADE YOU THINK YOU STOOD A CHANCE...THAT IF YOU GOT ANGRY ENOUGH, DEADLY ENOUGH, YOU COULD DEFEAT US.
DESPITE YOUR PROTESTATIONS TO THE CONTRARY, YOU ARE THE LEADER OF THE TEEN TITANS.
ONCE YOU HAVE TAKEN A LIFE--HOW LONG UNTIL THE OTHERS FOLLOW YOUR LEAD?
REST, CHILD.
YOU WILL NEED STRENGTH FOR YOUR COMING ORDEAL.
LEASH--
--TAKE MY NEW RAVAGERS TO THE COLONY.
MY PLEASURE.

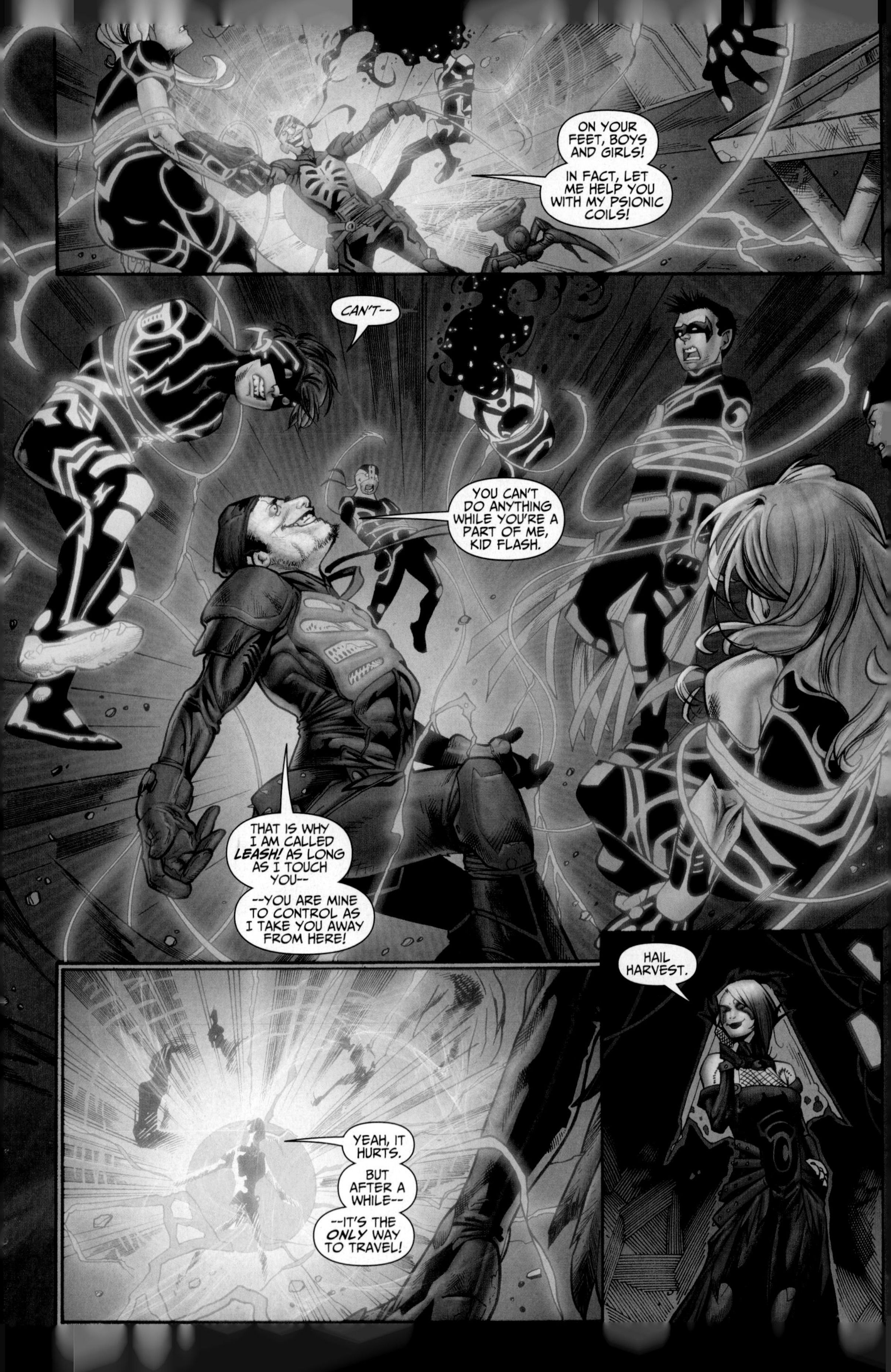
ON YOUR FEET, BOYS AND GIRLS!
IN FACT, LET ME HELP YOU WITH MY PSIONIC COILS!
CAN'T--
YOU CAN'T DO ANYTHING WHILE YOU'RE A PART OF ME, KID FLASH.
THAT IS WHY I AM CALLED *LEASH!* AS LONG AS I TOUCH YOU--
--YOU ARE MINE TO CONTROL AS I TAKE YOU AWAY FROM HERE!
YEAH, IT HURTS.
BUT AFTER A WHILE--
--IT'S THE *ONLY* WAY TO TRAVEL!
HAIL HARVEST.

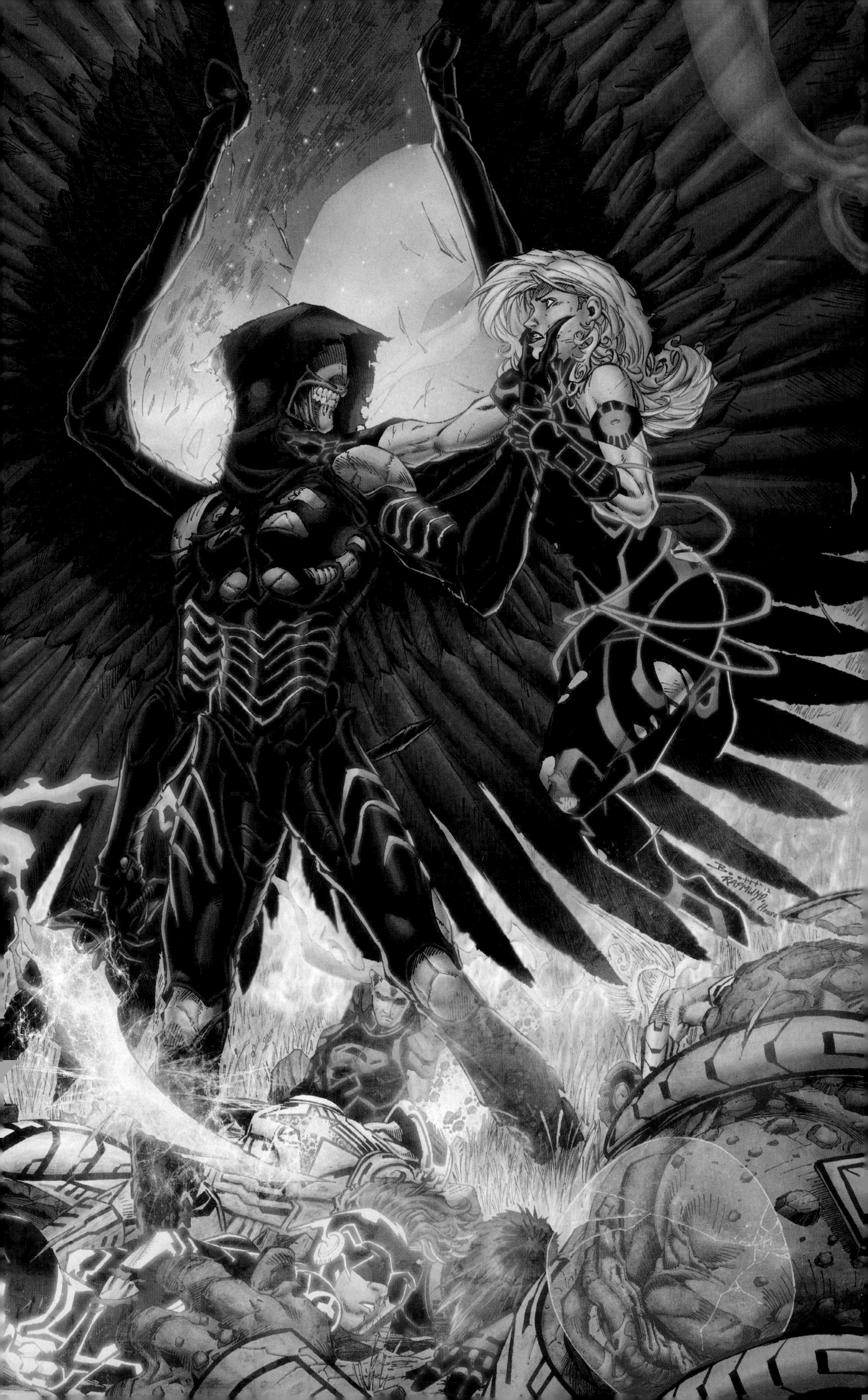

After being transported to the underground facility known as the Colony, the Teen Titans learned they would be competing in "The Culling," N.O.W.H.E.R.E.'s meta-teen battle royal. Losers die while winners join Harvest's forces as "Ravagers." In the melee, the Teen Titans joined forces with a time-displaced team from the 31st century — the Legion Lost. Together, they rescued survivors and took down the Ravagers, but the teens' powers fail when Harvest himself joins the fight...

THE CULLING: IF THIS BE VICTORY—!

SCOTT LOBDELL
writer

TOM DEFALCO
scripter

IG GUARA
penciller

JP MAYER
inker

cover art by
BRETT BOOTH, NORM RAPMUND & ANDREW DALHOUSE

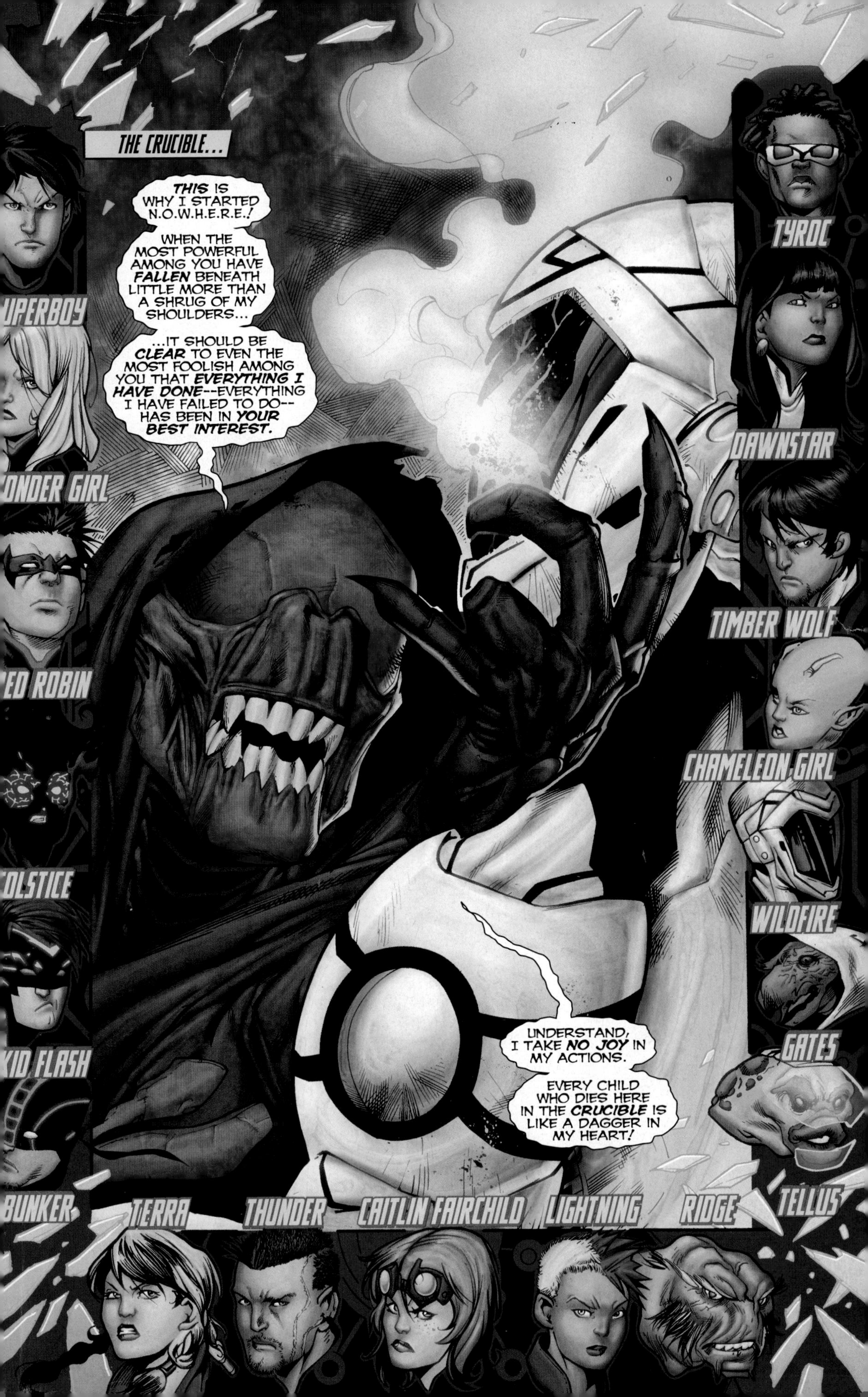
THE CRUCIBLE...
THIS IS WHY I STARTED N.O.W.H.E.R.E.! WHEN THE MOST POWERFUL AMONG YOU HAVE FALLEN BENEATH LITTLE MORE THAN A SHRUG OF MY SHOULDERS...
...IT SHOULD BE CLEAR TO EVEN THE MOST FOOLISH AMONG YOU THAT EVERYTHING I HAVE DONE--EVERYTHING I HAVE FAILED TO DO--HAS BEEN IN YOUR BEST INTEREST.
UNDERSTAND, I TAKE NO JOY IN MY ACTIONS.
EVERY CHILD WHO DIES HERE IN THE CRUCIBLE IS LIKE A DAGGER IN MY HEART!
UPERBOY
ONDER GIRL
ED ROBIN
OLSTICE
KID FLASH
BUNKER
TERRA
THUNDER
CAITLIN FAIRCHILD
LIGHTNING
RIDGE
TELLUS
TYROC
DAWNSTAR
TIMBER WOLF
CHAMELEON GIRL
WILDFIRE
GATES

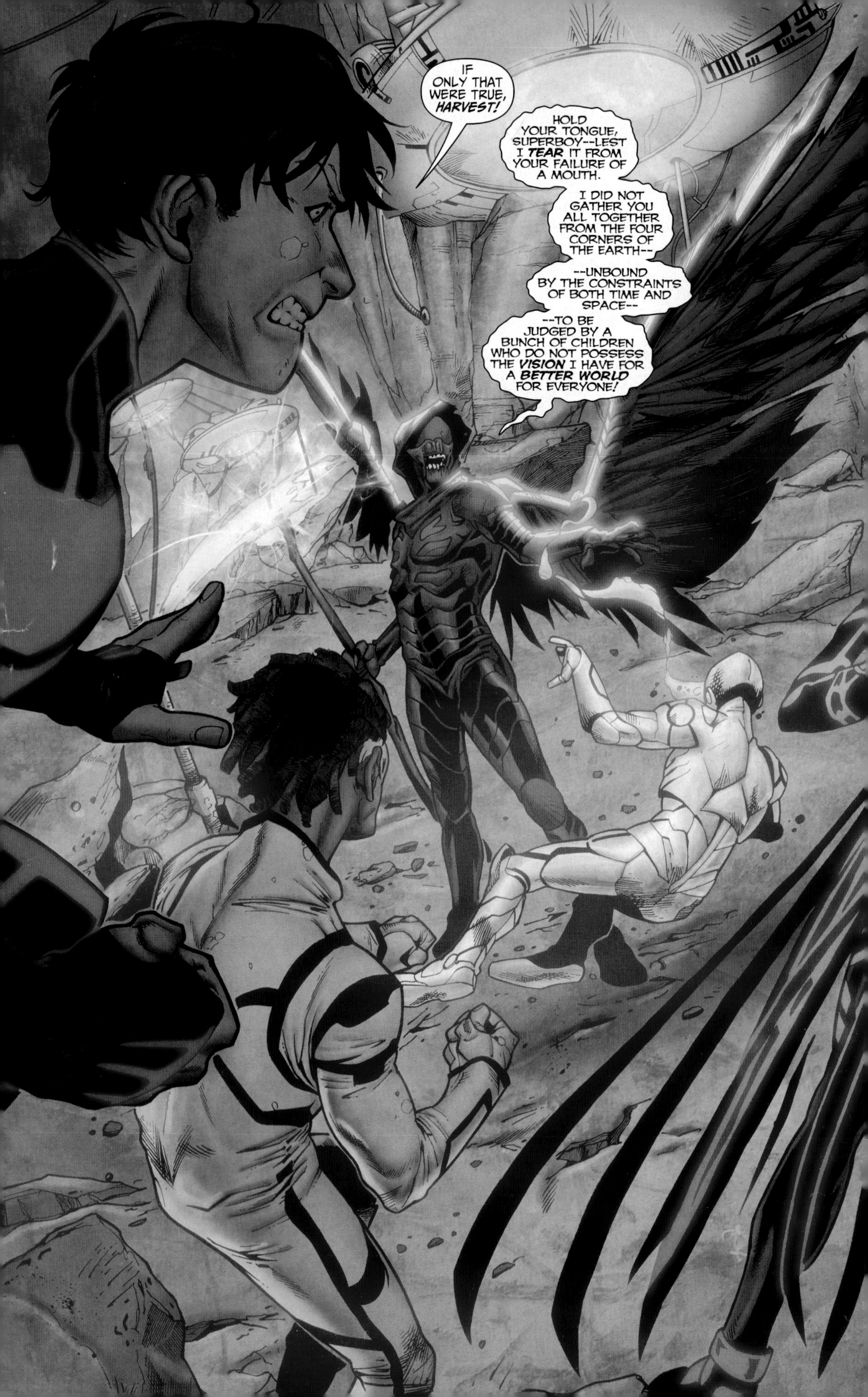

IF ONLY THAT WERE TRUE, HARVEST!
HOLD YOUR TONGUE, SUPERBOY--LEST I TEAR IT FROM YOUR FAILURE OF A MOUTH.
I DID NOT GATHER YOU ALL TOGETHER FROM THE FOUR CORNERS OF THE EARTH--
--UNBOUND BY THE CONSTRAINTS OF BOTH TIME AND SPACE--
--TO BE JUDGED BY A BUNCH OF CHILDREN WHO DO NOT POSSESS THE VISION I HAVE FOR A BETTER WORLD FOR EVERYONE!

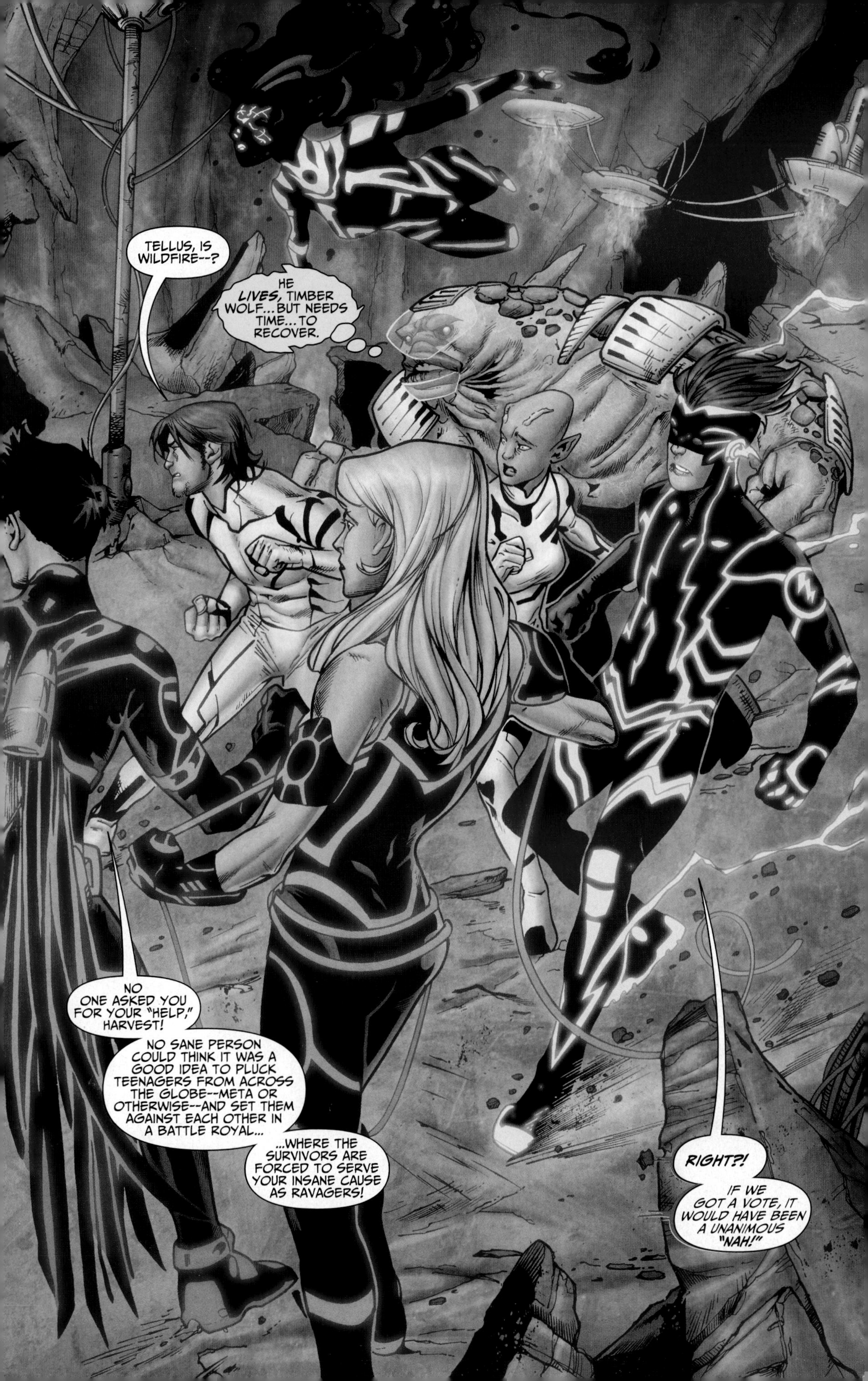
TELLUS, IS WILDFIRE--?
HE *LIVES,* TIMBER WOLF...BUT NEEDS TIME...TO RECOVER.
NO ONE ASKED YOU FOR YOUR "HELP," HARVEST!
NO SANE PERSON COULD THINK IT WAS A GOOD IDEA TO PLUCK TEENAGERS FROM ACROSS THE GLOBE--META OR OTHERWISE--AND SET THEM AGAINST EACH OTHER IN A BATTLE ROYAL...
...WHERE THE SURVIVORS ARE FORCED TO SERVE YOUR INSANE CAUSE AS RAVAGERS!
RIGHT?!
IF WE GOT A VOTE, IT WOULD HAVE BEEN A UNANIMOUS *"NAH!"*

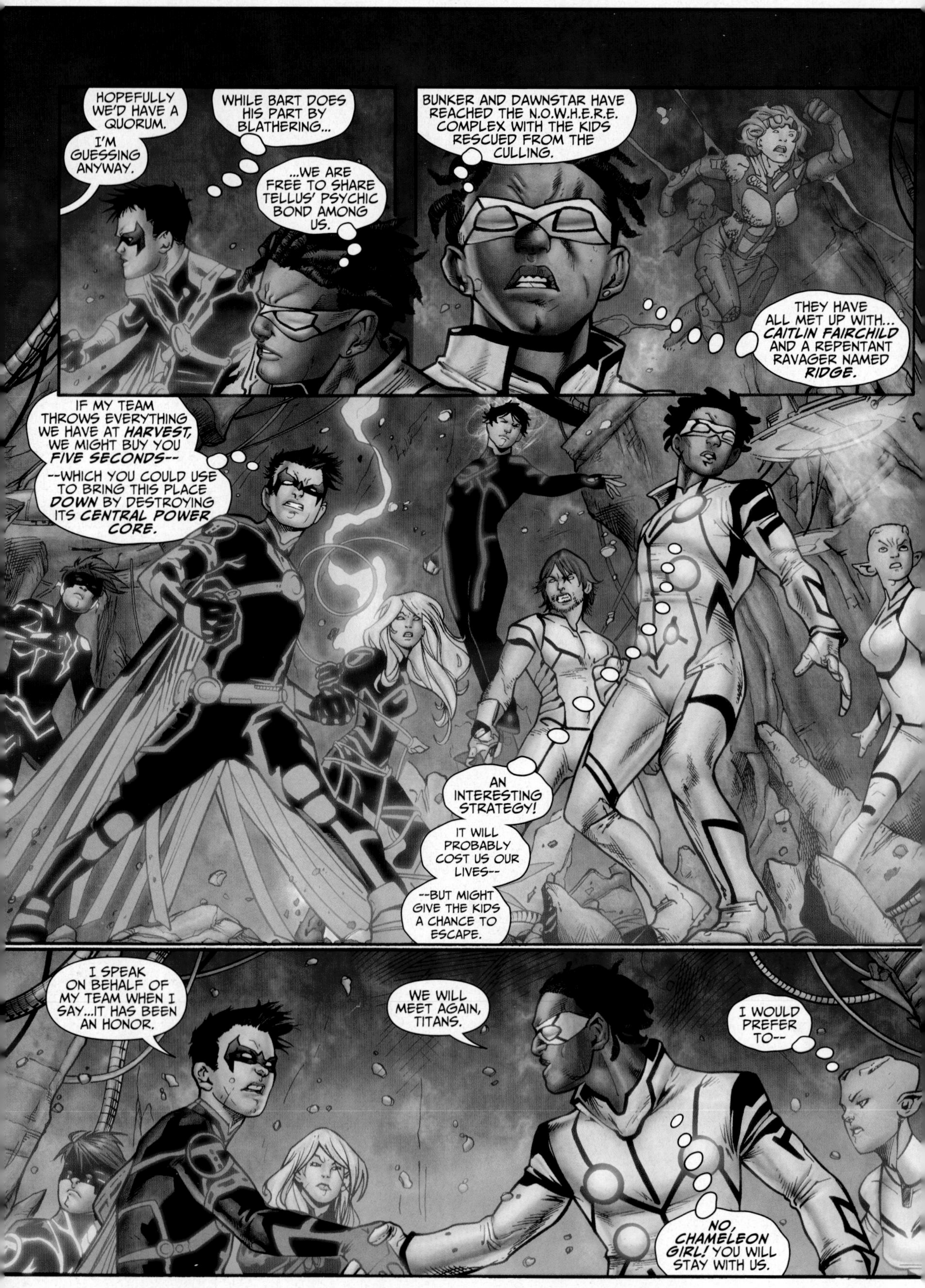
HOPEFULLY WE'D HAVE A QUORUM.
I'M GUESSING ANYWAY.
WHILE BART DOES HIS PART BY BLATHERING...
...WE ARE FREE TO SHARE TELLUS' PSYCHIC BOND AMONG US.
BUNKER AND DAWNSTAR HAVE REACHED THE N.O.W.H.E.R.E. COMPLEX WITH THE KIDS RESCUED FROM THE CULLING.
THEY HAVE ALL MET UP WITH... CAITLIN FAIRCHILD AND A REPENTANT RAVAGER NAMED RIDGE.
IF MY TEAM THROWS EVERYTHING WE HAVE AT HARVEST, WE MIGHT BUY YOU FIVE SECONDS--
--WHICH YOU COULD USE TO BRING THIS PLACE DOWN BY DESTROYING ITS CENTRAL POWER CORE.
AN INTERESTING STRATEGY!
IT WILL PROBABLY COST US OUR LIVES--
--BUT MIGHT GIVE THE KIDS A CHANCE TO ESCAPE.
I SPEAK ON BEHALF OF MY TEAM WHEN I SAY...IT HAS BEEN AN HONOR.
WE WILL MEET AGAIN, TITANS.
I WOULD PREFER TO--
NO, CHAMELEON GIRL! YOU WILL STAY WITH US.

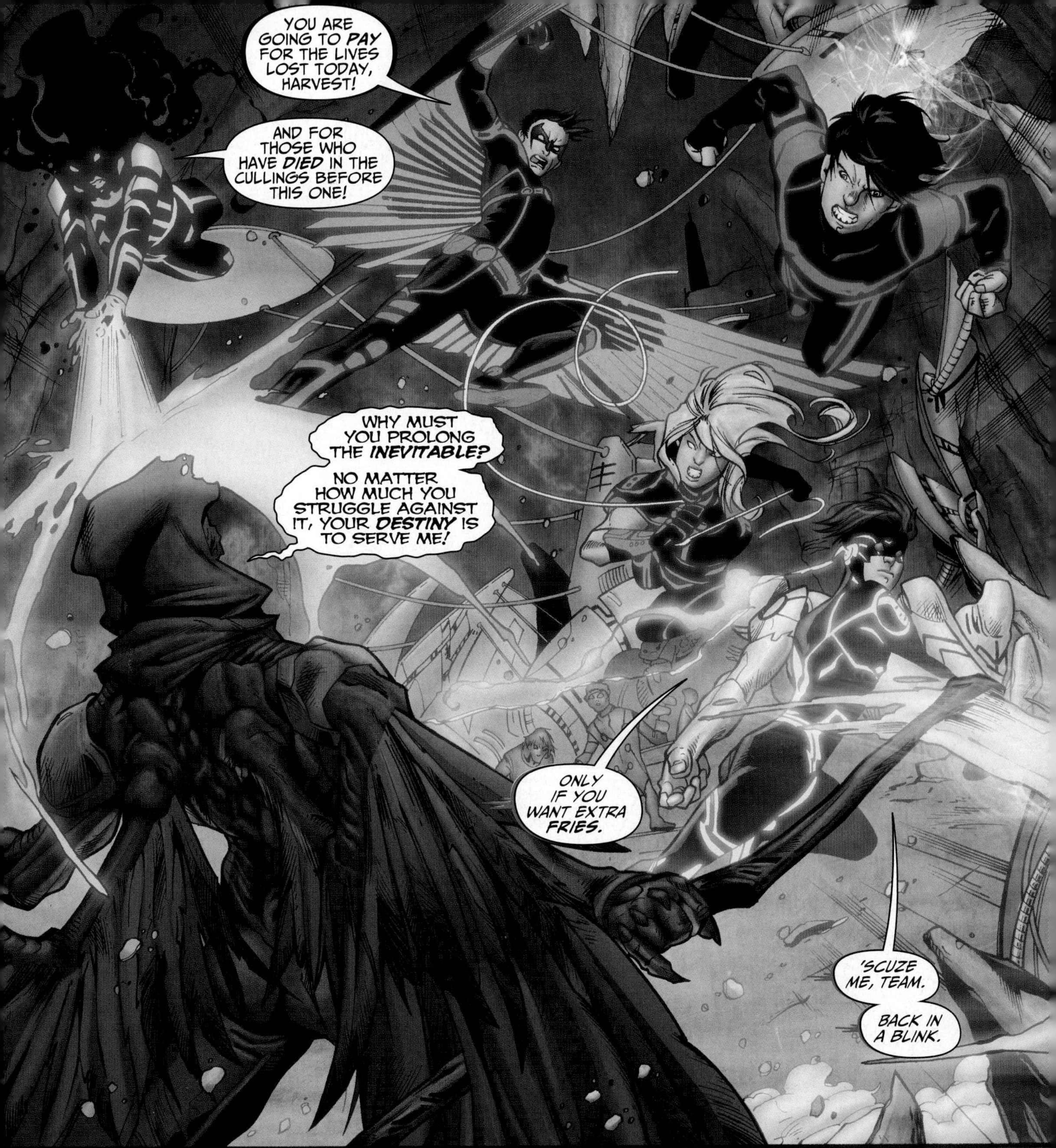
YOU ARE GOING TO PAY FOR THE LIVES LOST TODAY, HARVEST!
AND FOR THOSE WHO HAVE DIED IN THE CULLINGS BEFORE THIS ONE!
WHY MUST YOU PROLONG THE INEVITABLE?
NO MATTER HOW MUCH YOU STRUGGLE AGAINST IT, YOUR DESTINY IS TO SERVE ME!
ONLY IF YOU WANT EXTRA FRIES.
'SCUZE ME, TEAM.
BACK IN A BLINK.
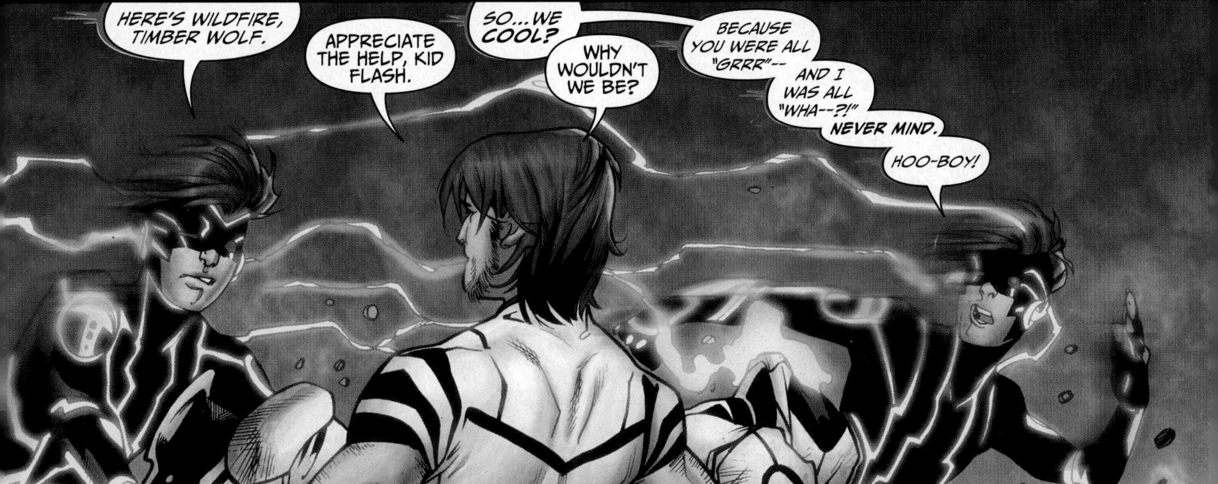
HERE'S WILDFIRE, TIMBER WOLF.
APPRECIATE THE HELP, KID FLASH.
SO...WE COOL?
WHY WOULDN'T WE BE?
BECAUSE YOU WERE ALL "GRRR"-- AND I WAS ALL "WHA--?!"
NEVER MIND.
HOO-BOY!

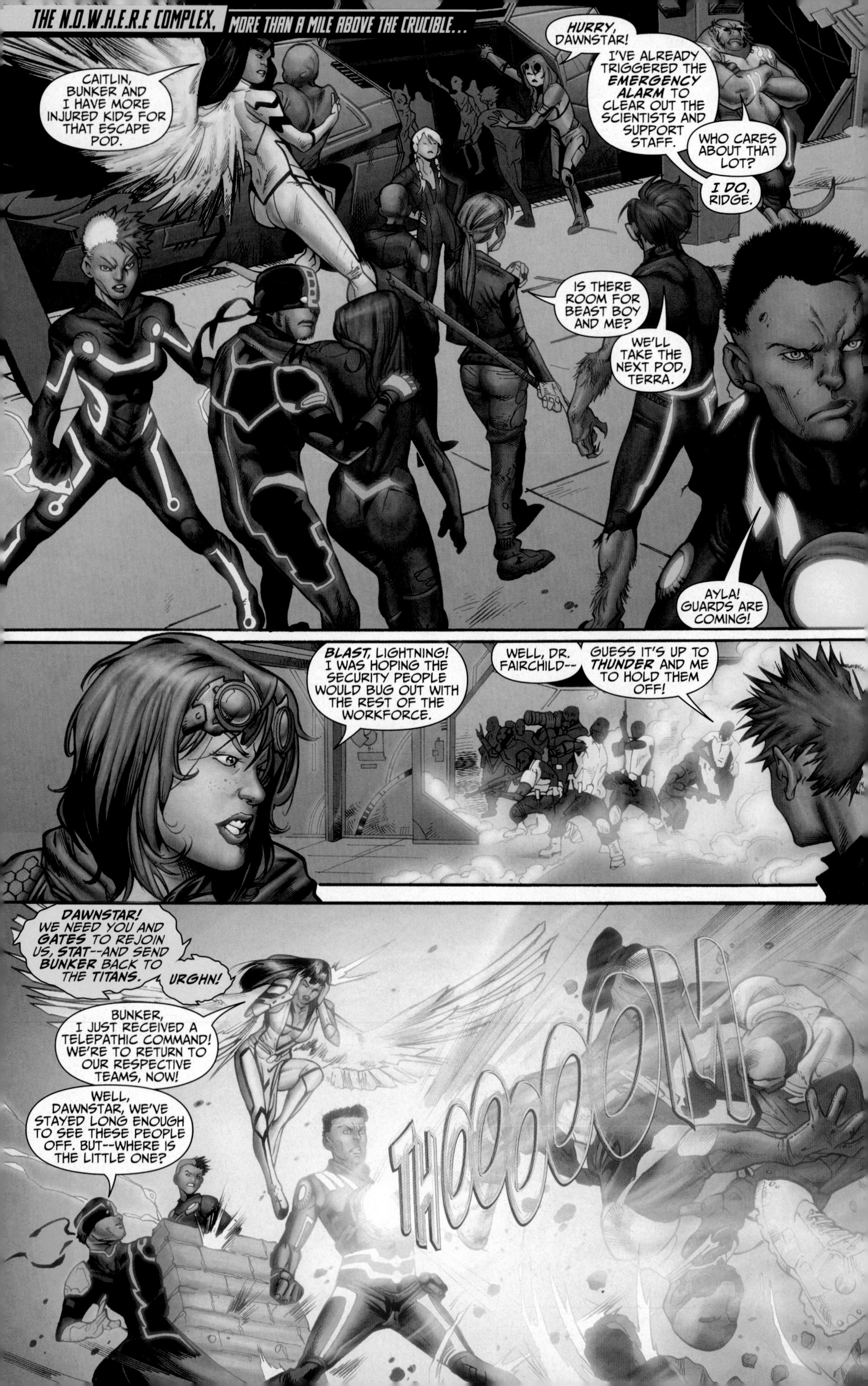
THE N.O.W.H.E.R.E COMPLEX, MORE THAN A MILE ABOVE THE CRUCIBLE...
CAITLIN, BUNKER AND I HAVE MORE INJURED KIDS FOR THAT ESCAPE POD.
HURRY, DAWNSTAR! I'VE ALREADY TRIGGERED THE EMERGENCY ALARM TO CLEAR OUT THE SCIENTISTS AND SUPPORT STAFF.
WHO CARES ABOUT THAT LOT?
I DO, RIDGE.
IS THERE ROOM FOR BEAST BOY AND ME?
WE'LL TAKE THE NEXT POD, TERRA.
AYLA! GUARDS ARE COMING!
BLAST, LIGHTNING! I WAS HOPING THE SECURITY PEOPLE WOULD BUG OUT WITH THE REST OF THE WORKFORCE.
WELL, DR. FAIRCHILD--
GUESS IT'S UP TO THUNDER AND ME TO HOLD THEM OFF!
DAWNSTAR! WE NEED YOU AND GATES TO REJOIN US, STAT--AND SEND BUNKER BACK TO THE TITANS.
URGHN!
BUNKER, I JUST RECEIVED A TELEPATHIC COMMAND! WE'RE TO RETURN TO OUR RESPECTIVE TEAMS, NOW!
WELL, DAWNSTAR, WE'VE STAYED LONG ENOUGH TO SEE THESE PEOPLE OFF. BUT--WHERE IS THE LITTLE ONE?
THOOOOOOM

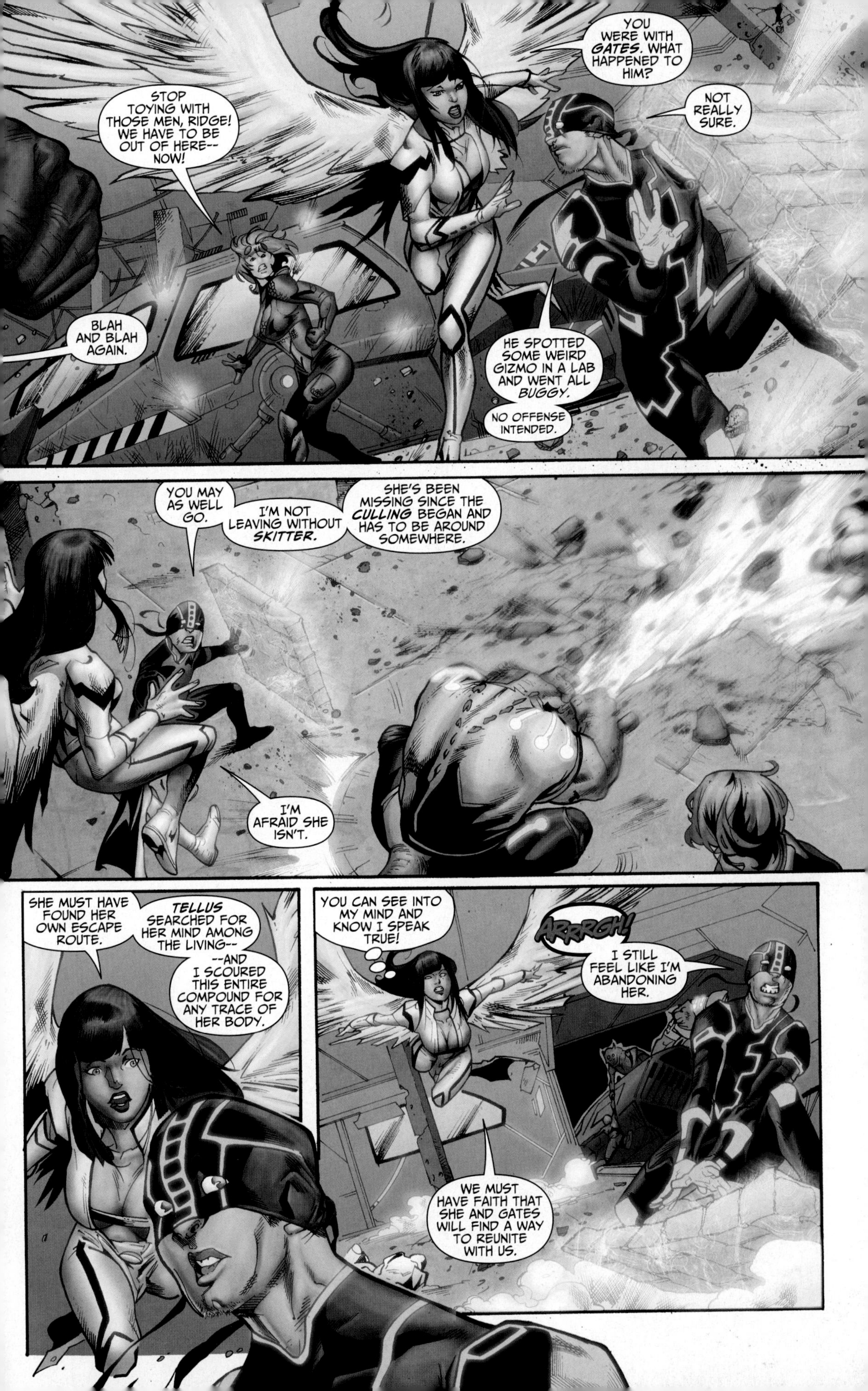

STOP TOYING WITH THOSE MEN, RIDGE! WE HAVE TO BE OUT OF HERE--NOW!
YOU WERE WITH GATES. WHAT HAPPENED TO HIM?
NOT REALLY SURE.
BLAH AND BLAH AGAIN.
HE SPOTTED SOME WEIRD GIZMO IN A LAB AND WENT ALL BUGGY.
NO OFFENSE INTENDED.
YOU MAY AS WELL GO.
I'M NOT LEAVING WITHOUT SKITTER.
SHE'S BEEN MISSING SINCE THE CULLING BEGAN AND HAS TO BE AROUND SOMEWHERE.
I'M AFRAID SHE ISN'T.
SHE MUST HAVE FOUND HER OWN ESCAPE ROUTE.
TELLUS SEARCHED FOR HER MIND AMONG THE LIVING--
--AND I SCOURED THIS ENTIRE COMPOUND FOR ANY TRACE OF HER BODY.
YOU CAN SEE INTO MY MIND AND KNOW I SPEAK TRUE!
ARRRGH!
I STILL FEEL LIKE I'M ABANDONING HER.
WE MUST HAVE FAITH THAT SHE AND GATES WILL FIND A WAY TO REUNITE WITH US.

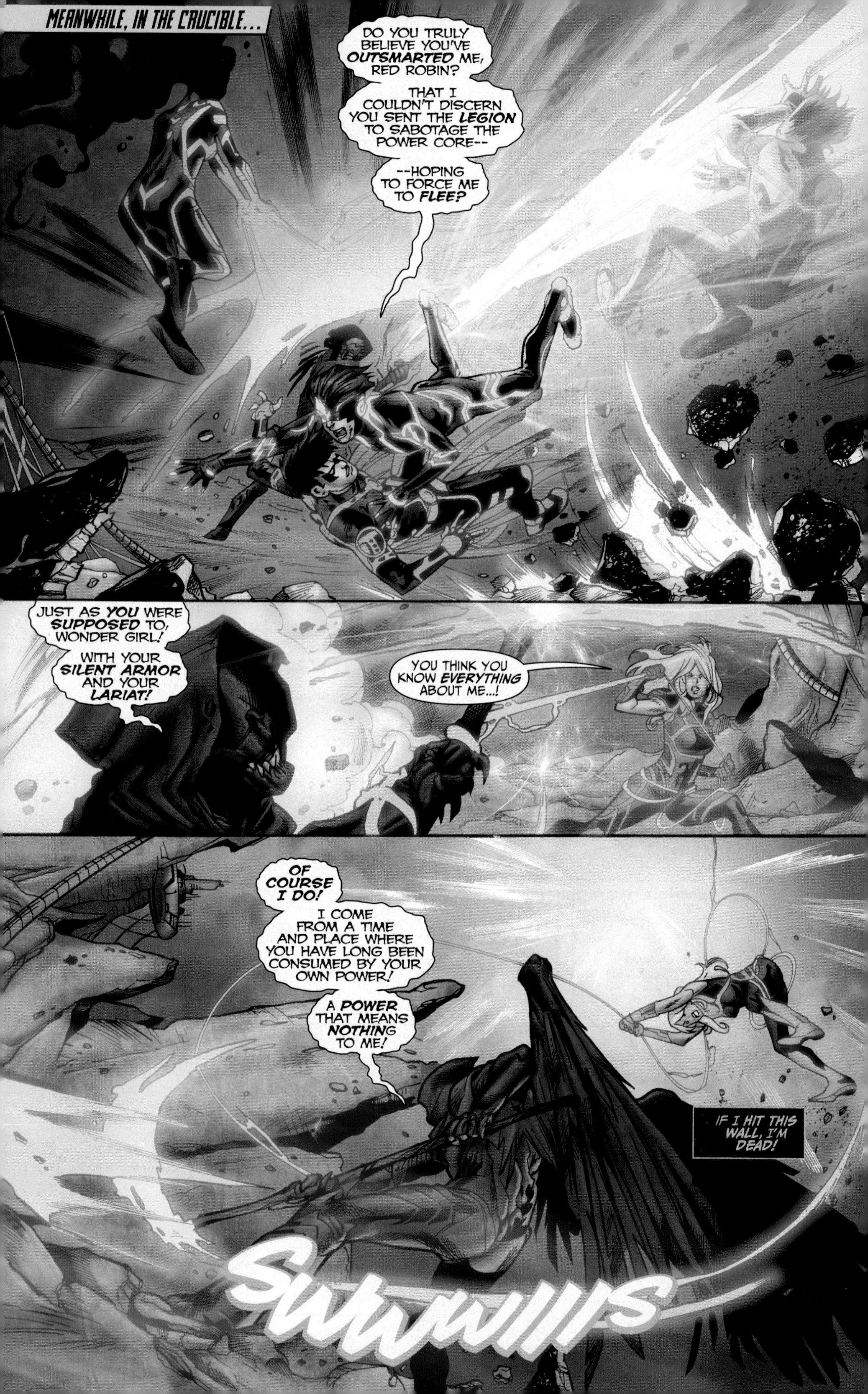
MEANWHILE, IN THE CRUCIBLE...
DO YOU TRULY BELIEVE YOU'VE OUTSMARTED ME, RED ROBIN?
THAT I COULDN'T DISCERN YOU SENT THE LEGION TO SABOTAGE THE POWER CORE--
--HOPING TO FORCE ME TO FLEE?
JUST AS YOU WERE SUPPOSED TO, WONDER GIRL!
WITH YOUR SILENT ARMOR AND YOUR LARIAT!
YOU THINK YOU KNOW EVERYTHING ABOUT ME...!
OF COURSE I DO!
I COME FROM A TIME AND PLACE WHERE YOU HAVE LONG BEEN CONSUMED BY YOUR OWN POWER!
A POWER THAT MEANS NOTHING TO ME!
IF I HIT THIS WALL, I'M DEAD!
SWWWIIIIS

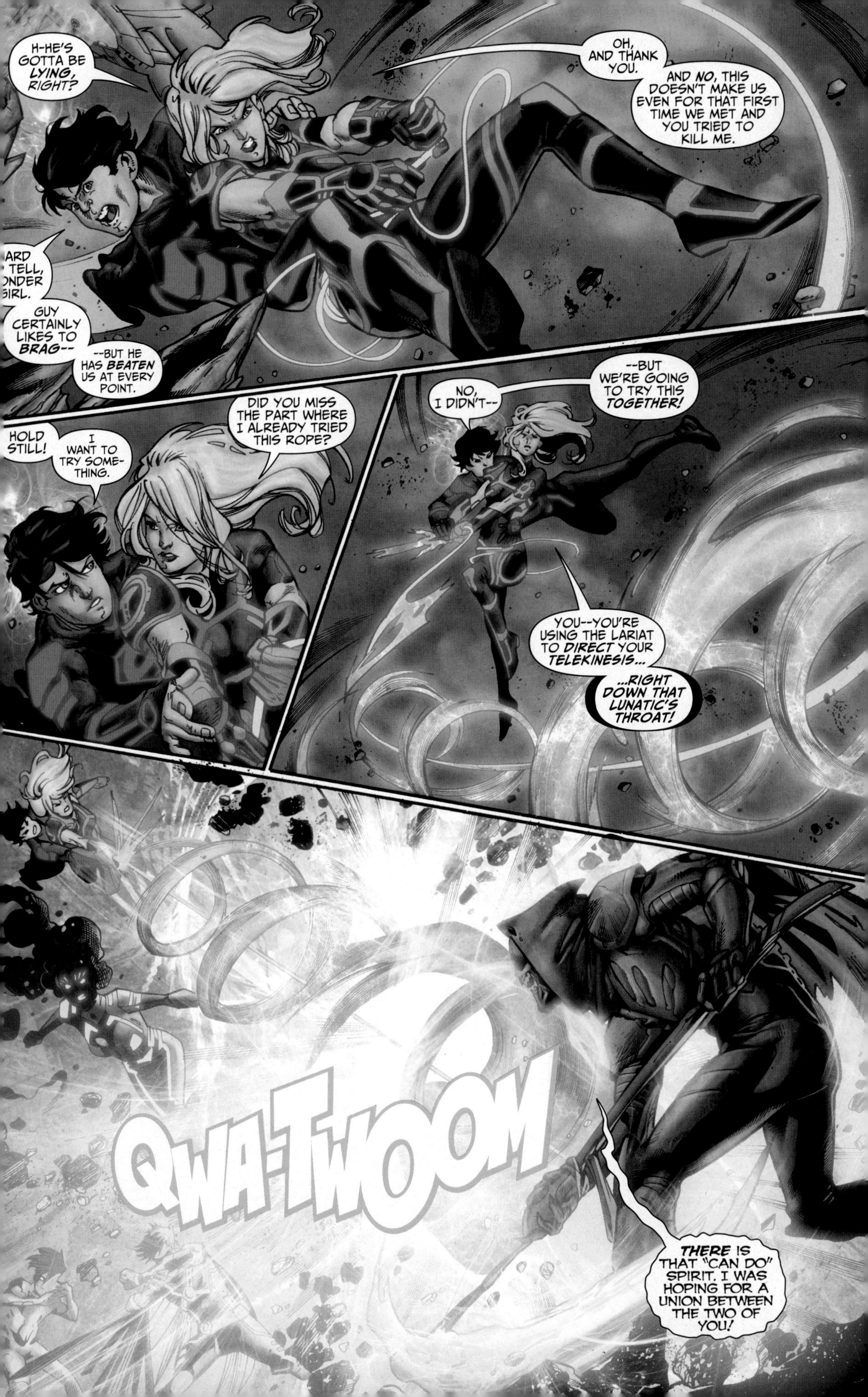
H-HE'S GOTTA BE LYING, RIGHT?
OH, AND THANK YOU.
AND NO, THIS DOESN'T MAKE US EVEN FOR THAT FIRST TIME WE MET AND YOU TRIED TO KILL ME.
GUY CERTAINLY LIKES TO BRAG--
--BUT HE HAS BEATEN US AT EVERY POINT.
HOLD STILL!
I WANT TO TRY SOMETHING.
DID YOU MISS THE PART WHERE I ALREADY TRIED THIS ROPE?
NO, I DIDN'T--
--BUT WE'RE GOING TO TRY THIS TOGETHER!
YOU--YOU'RE USING THE LARIAT TO DIRECT YOUR TELEKINESIS...
...RIGHT DOWN THAT LUNATIC'S THROAT!
QWA-TWOOM
THERE IS THAT "CAN DO" SPIRIT. I WAS HOPING FOR A UNION BETWEEN THE TWO OF YOU!

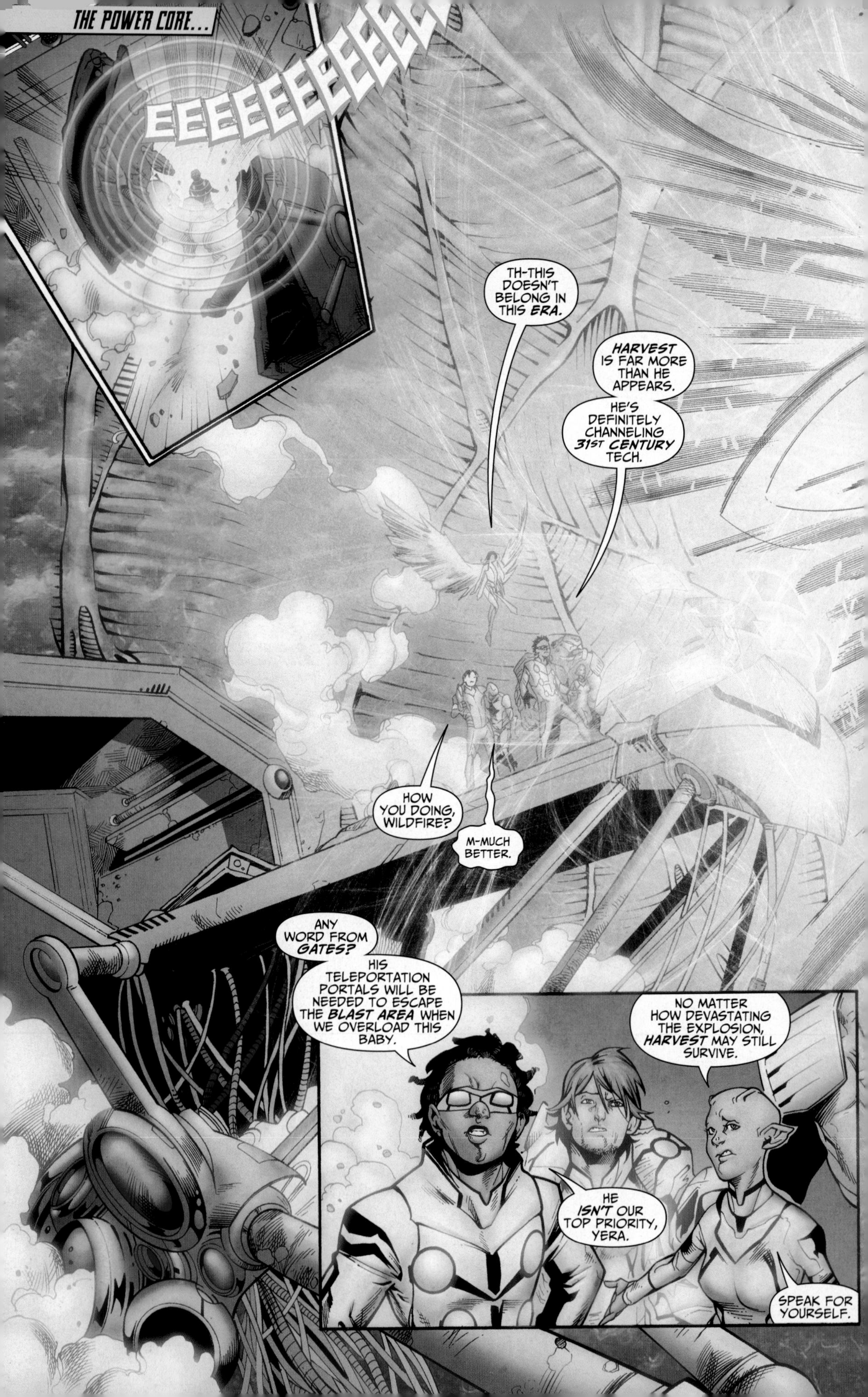
THE POWER CORE...
EEEEEEEEEEEL
TH-THIS DOESN'T BELONG IN THIS ERA.
HARVEST IS FAR MORE THAN HE APPEARS.
HE'S DEFINITELY CHANNELING 31ST CENTURY TECH.
HOW YOU DOING, WILDFIRE?
M-MUCH BETTER.
ANY WORD FROM GATES?
HIS TELEPORTATION PORTALS WILL BE NEEDED TO ESCAPE THE BLAST AREA WHEN WE OVERLOAD THIS BABY.
NO MATTER HOW DEVASTATING THE EXPLOSION, HARVEST MAY STILL SURVIVE.
HE ISN'T OUR TOP PRIORITY, YERA.
SPEAK FOR YOURSELF.

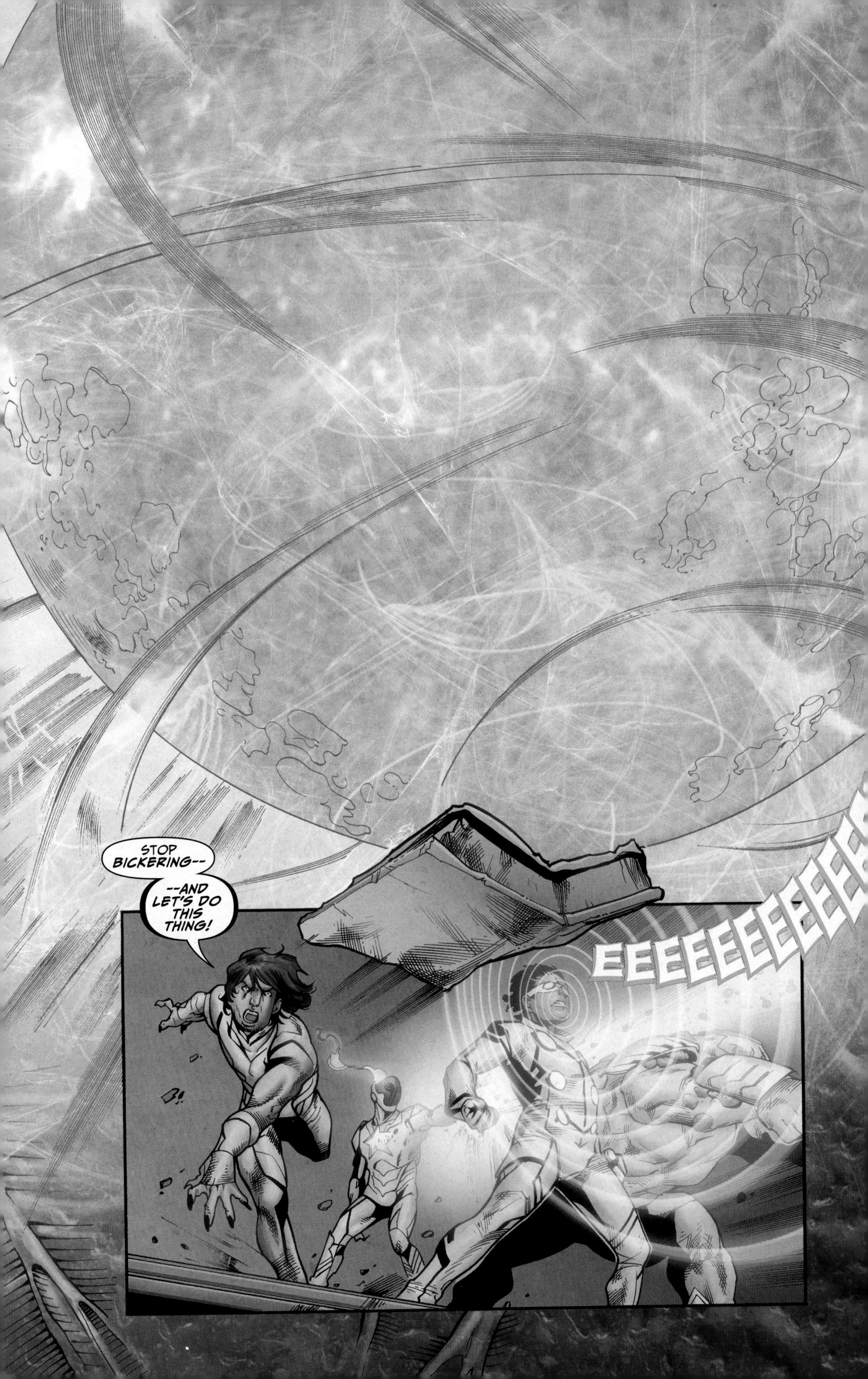
STOP BICKERING--
--AND LET'S DO THIS THING!
EEEEEEEEEEEEEEEEEE

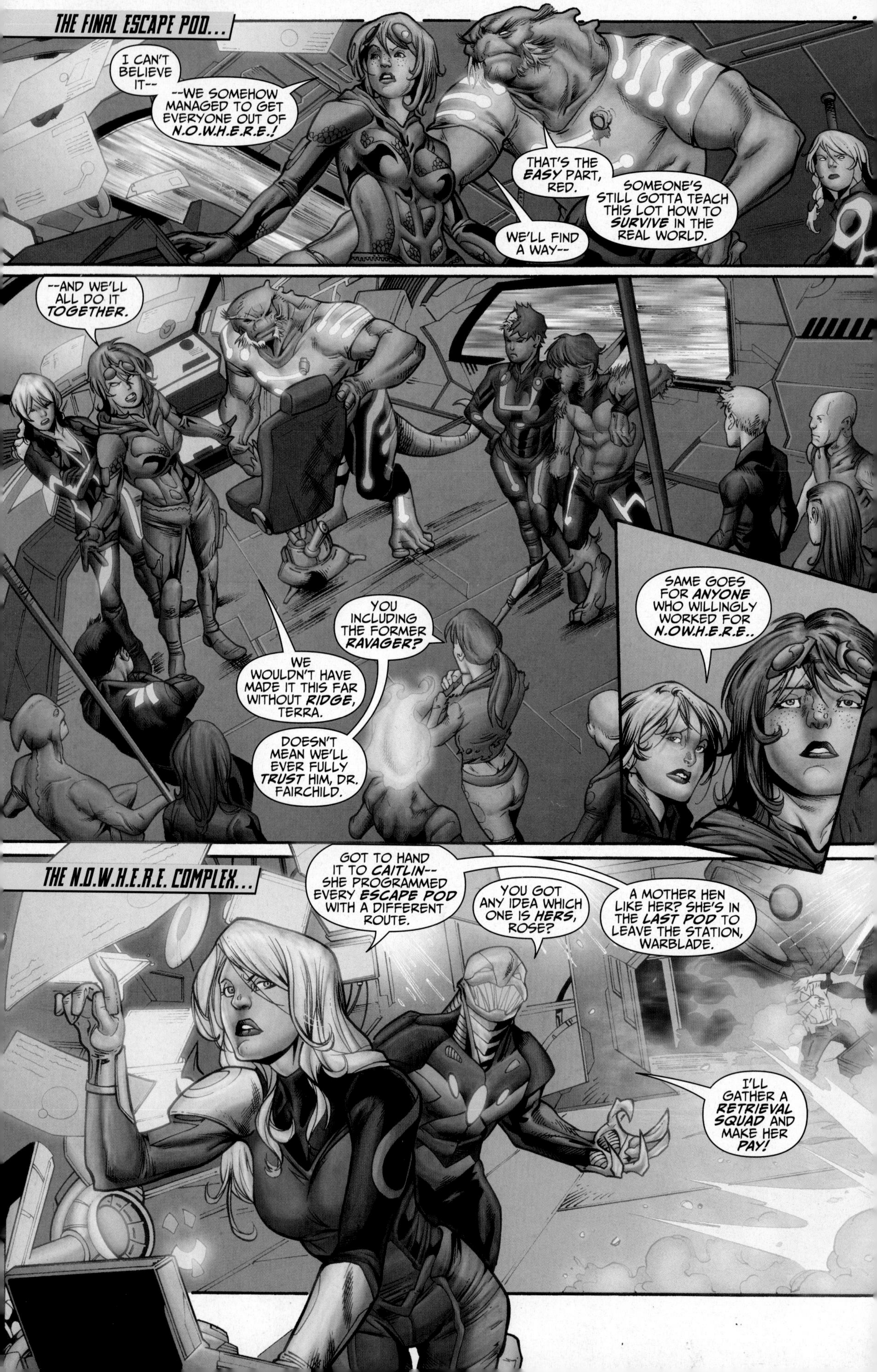
THE FINAL ESCAPE POD...
I CAN'T BELIEVE IT--
--WE SOMEHOW MANAGED TO GET EVERYONE OUT OF N.O.W.H.E.R.E.!
THAT'S THE EASY PART, RED.
SOMEONE'S STILL GOTTA TEACH THIS LOT HOW TO SURVIVE IN THE REAL WORLD.
WE'LL FIND A WAY--
--AND WE'LL ALL DO IT TOGETHER.
WE WOULDN'T HAVE MADE IT THIS FAR WITHOUT RIDGE, TERRA.
YOU INCLUDING THE FORMER RAVAGER?
DOESN'T MEAN WE'LL EVER FULLY TRUST HIM, DR. FAIRCHILD.
SAME GOES FOR ANYONE WHO WILLINGLY WORKED FOR N.O.W.H.E.R.E..
THE N.O.W.H.E.R.E. COMPLEX...
GOT TO HAND IT TO CAITLIN-- SHE PROGRAMMED EVERY ESCAPE POD WITH A DIFFERENT ROUTE.
YOU GOT ANY IDEA WHICH ONE IS HERS, ROSE?
A MOTHER HEN LIKE HER? SHE'S IN THE LAST POD TO LEAVE THE STATION, WARBLADE.
I'LL GATHER A RETRIEVAL SQUAD AND MAKE HER PAY!

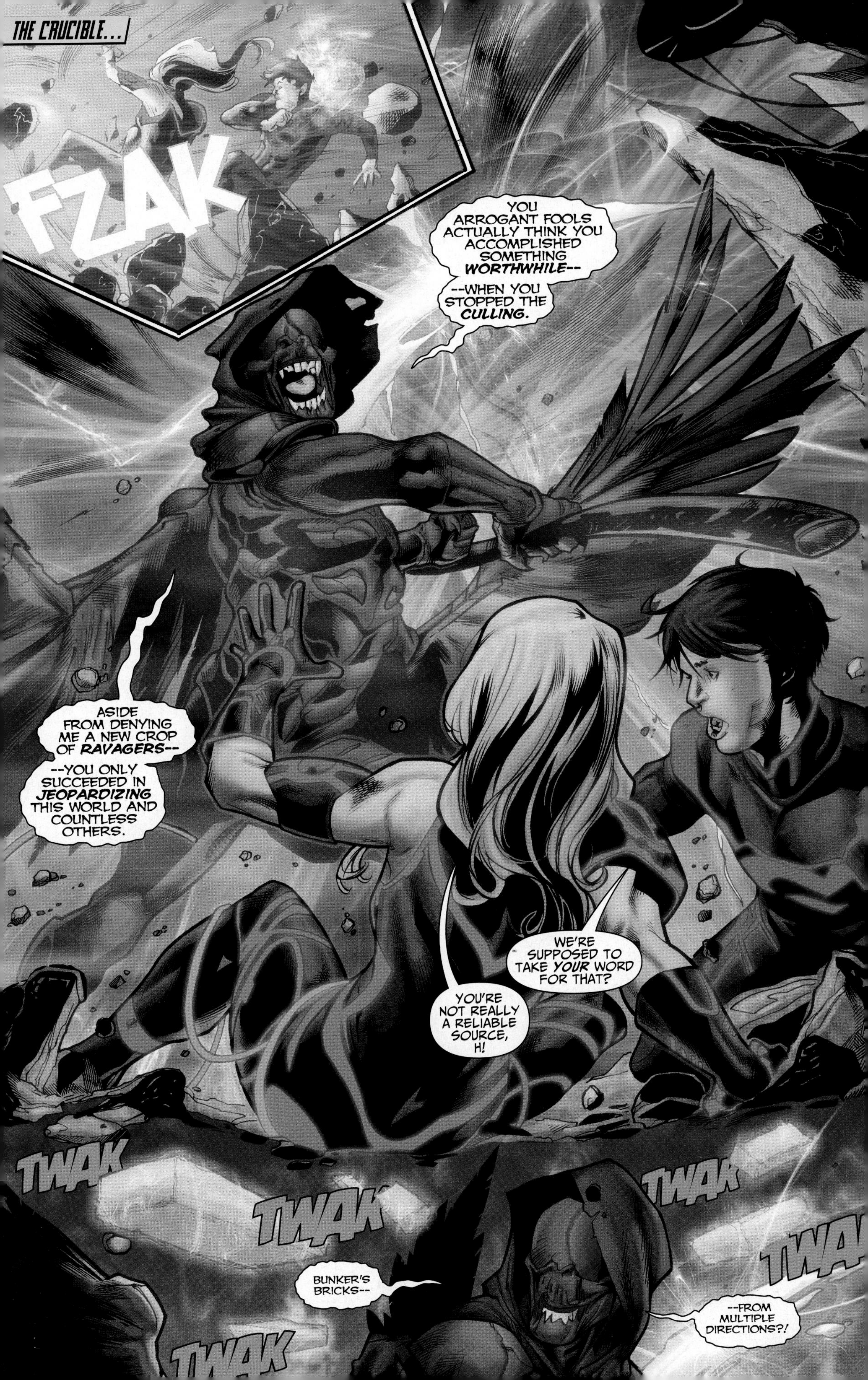
THE CRUCIBLE...
FZAK
YOU ARROGANT FOOLS ACTUALLY THINK YOU ACCOMPLISHED SOMETHING WORTHWHILE--
--WHEN YOU STOPPED THE CULLING.
ASIDE FROM DENYING ME A NEW CROP OF RAVAGERS--
--YOU ONLY SUCCEEDED IN JEOPARDIZING THIS WORLD AND COUNTLESS OTHERS.
WE'RE SUPPOSED TO TAKE YOUR WORD FOR THAT?
YOU'RE NOT REALLY A RELIABLE SOURCE, H!
TWAK
TWAK
TWAK
TWAK
BUNKER'S BRICKS--
--FROM MULTIPLE DIRECTIONS?!
TWAK

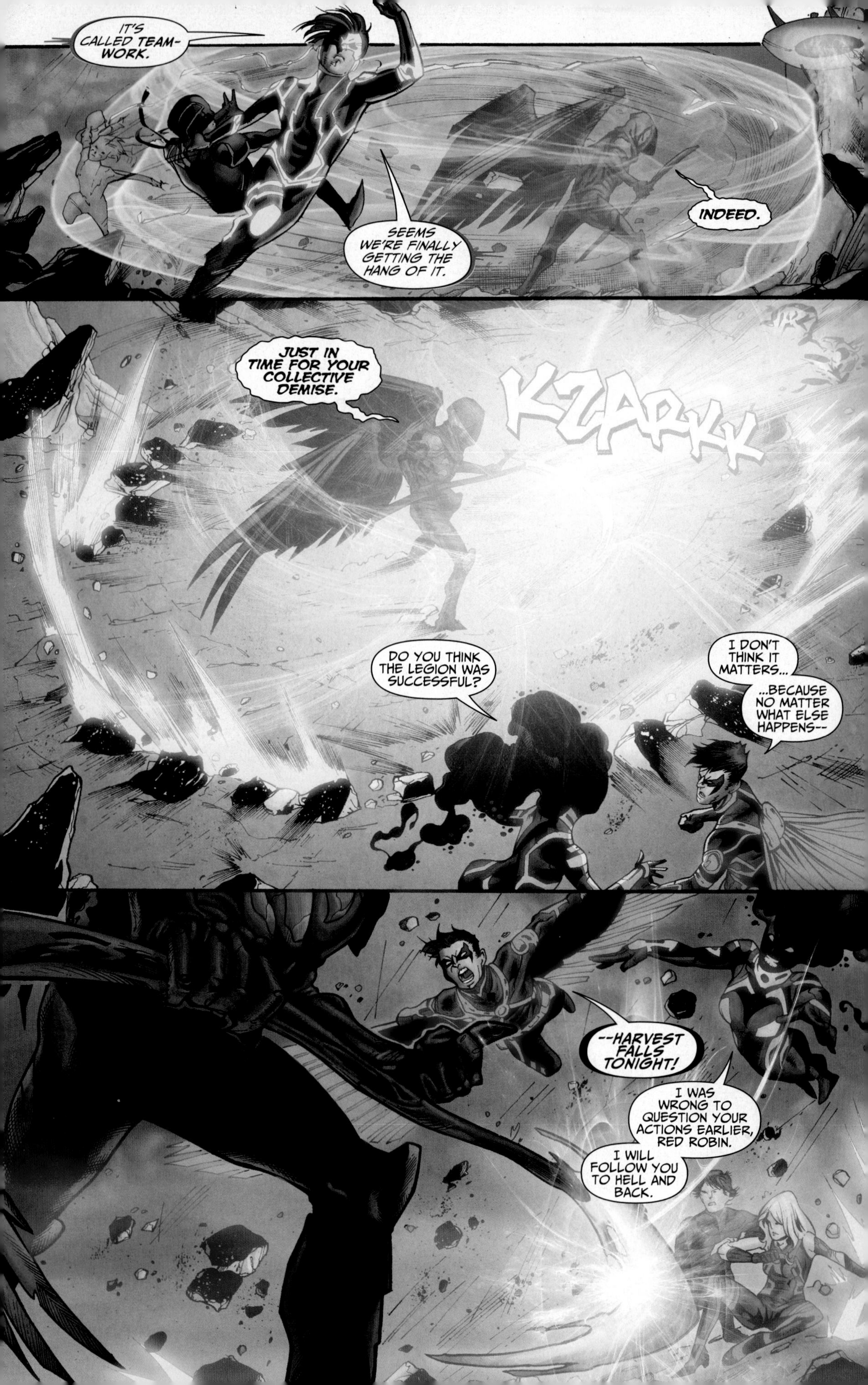
IT'S CALLED TEAM-WORK.
SEEMS WE'RE FINALLY GETTING THE HANG OF IT.
INDEED.
JUST IN TIME FOR YOUR COLLECTIVE DEMISE.
KZARKK
DO YOU THINK THE LEGION WAS SUCCESSFUL?
I DON'T THINK IT MATTERS...
...BECAUSE NO MATTER WHAT ELSE HAPPENS--
--HARVEST FALLS TONIGHT!
I WAS WRONG TO QUESTION YOUR ACTIONS EARLIER, RED ROBIN.
I WILL FOLLOW YOU TO HELL AND BACK.

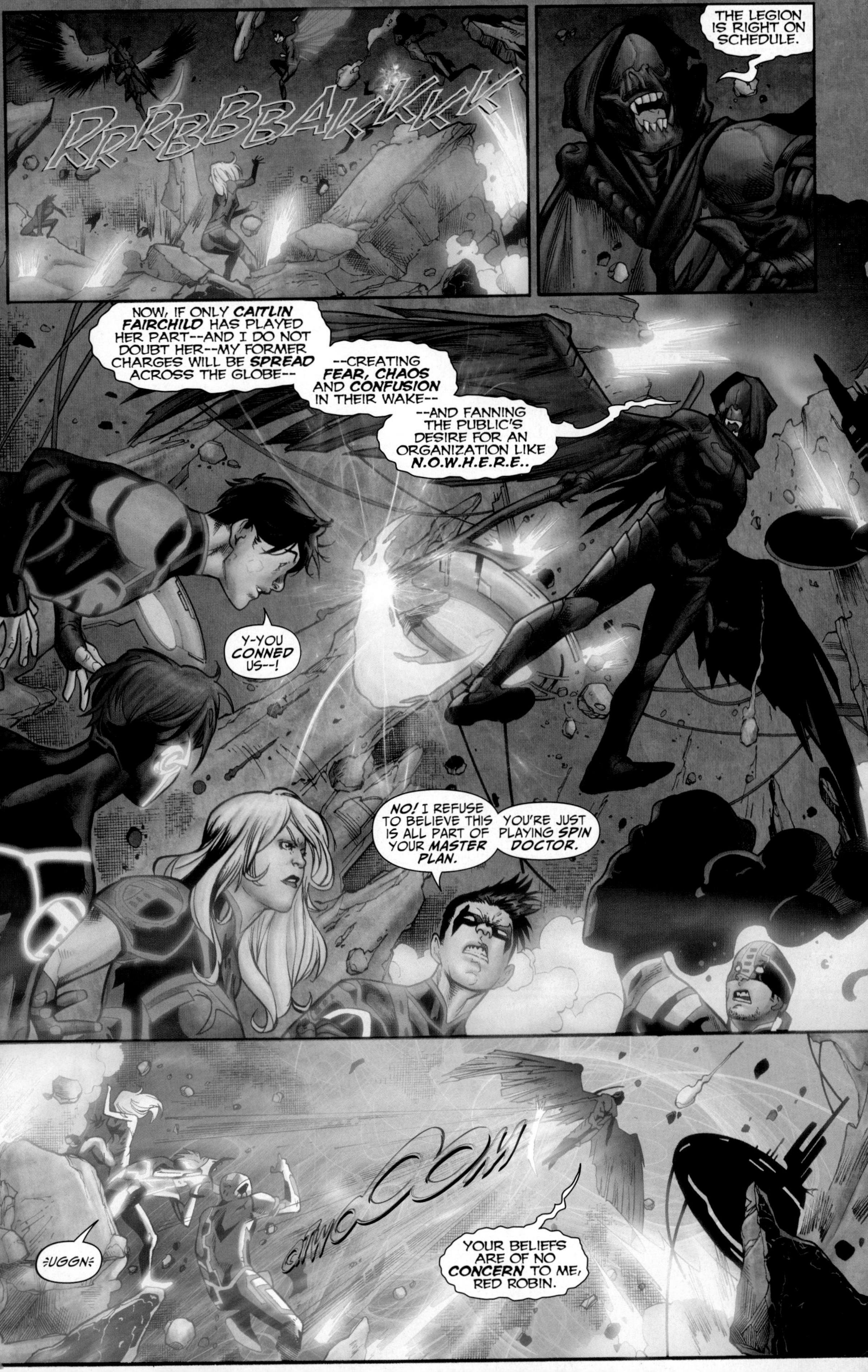
RRRBBBAKKKK
THE LEGION IS RIGHT ON SCHEDULE.
NOW, IF ONLY CAITLIN FAIRCHILD HAS PLAYED HER PART--AND I DO NOT DOUBT HER--MY FORMER CHARGES WILL BE SPREAD ACROSS THE GLOBE--
--CREATING FEAR, CHAOS AND CONFUSION IN THEIR WAKE--
--AND FANNING THE PUBLIC'S DESIRE FOR AN ORGANIZATION LIKE N.O.W.H.E.R.E..
Y-YOU CONNED US--!
NO! I REFUSE TO BELIEVE THIS IS ALL PART OF YOUR MASTER PLAN.
YOU'RE JUST PLAYING SPIN DOCTOR.
UGGN
YOUR BELIEFS ARE OF NO CONCERN TO ME, RED ROBIN.

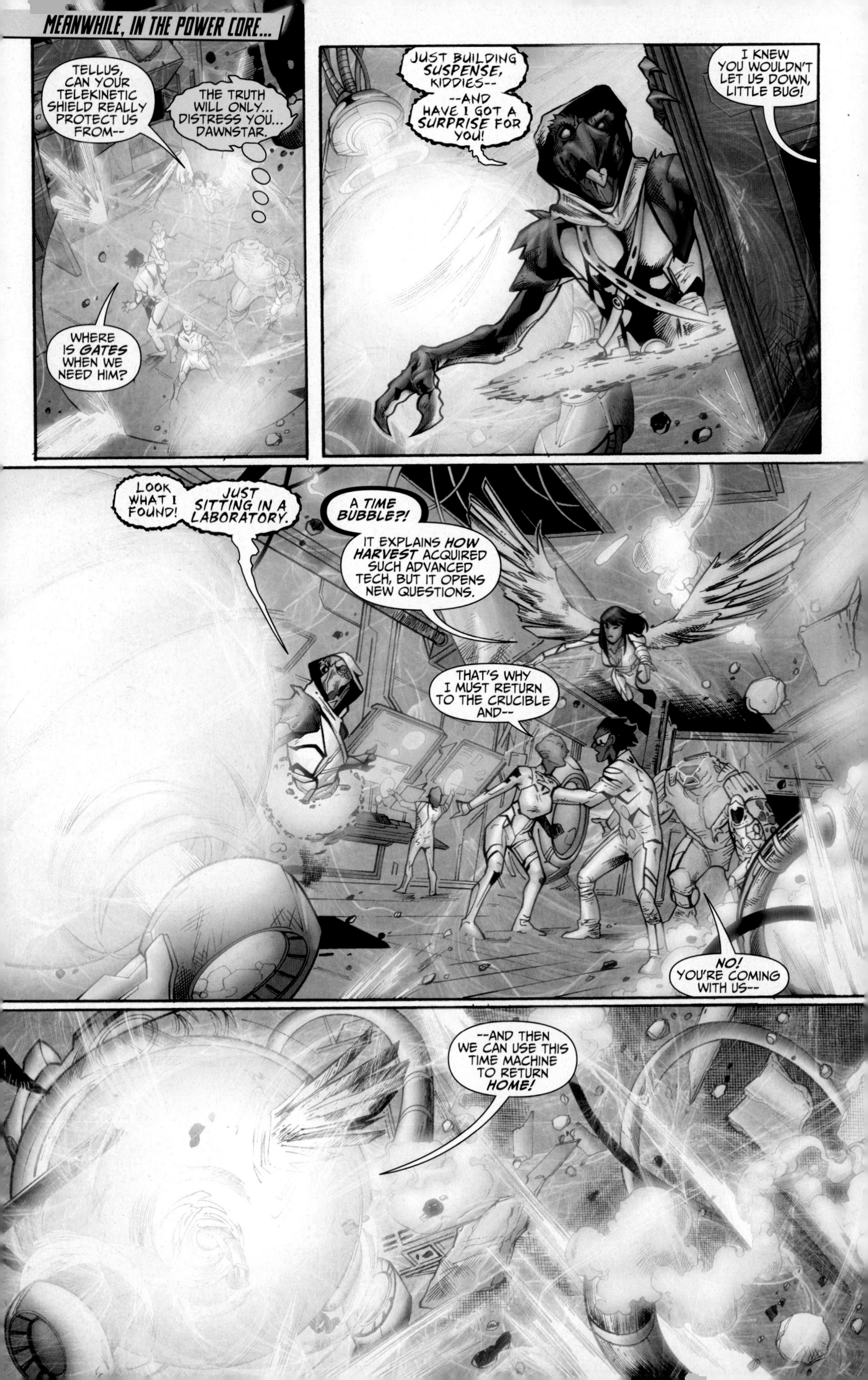
MEANWHILE, IN THE POWER CORE...
TELLUS, CAN YOUR TELEKINETIC SHIELD REALLY PROTECT US FROM--
THE TRUTH WILL ONLY... DISTRESS YOU... DAWNSTAR.
WHERE IS GATES WHEN WE NEED HIM?
JUST BUILDING SUSPENSE, KIDDIES--
--AND HAVE I GOT A SURPRISE FOR YOU!
I KNEW YOU WOULDN'T LET US DOWN, LITTLE BUG!
LOOK WHAT I FOUND!
JUST SITTING IN A LABORATORY.
A TIME BUBBLE?!
IT EXPLAINS HOW HARVEST ACQUIRED SUCH ADVANCED TECH, BUT IT OPENS NEW QUESTIONS.
THAT'S WHY I MUST RETURN TO THE CRUCIBLE AND--
NO! YOU'RE COMING WITH US--
--AND THEN WE CAN USE THIS TIME MACHINE TO RETURN HOME!

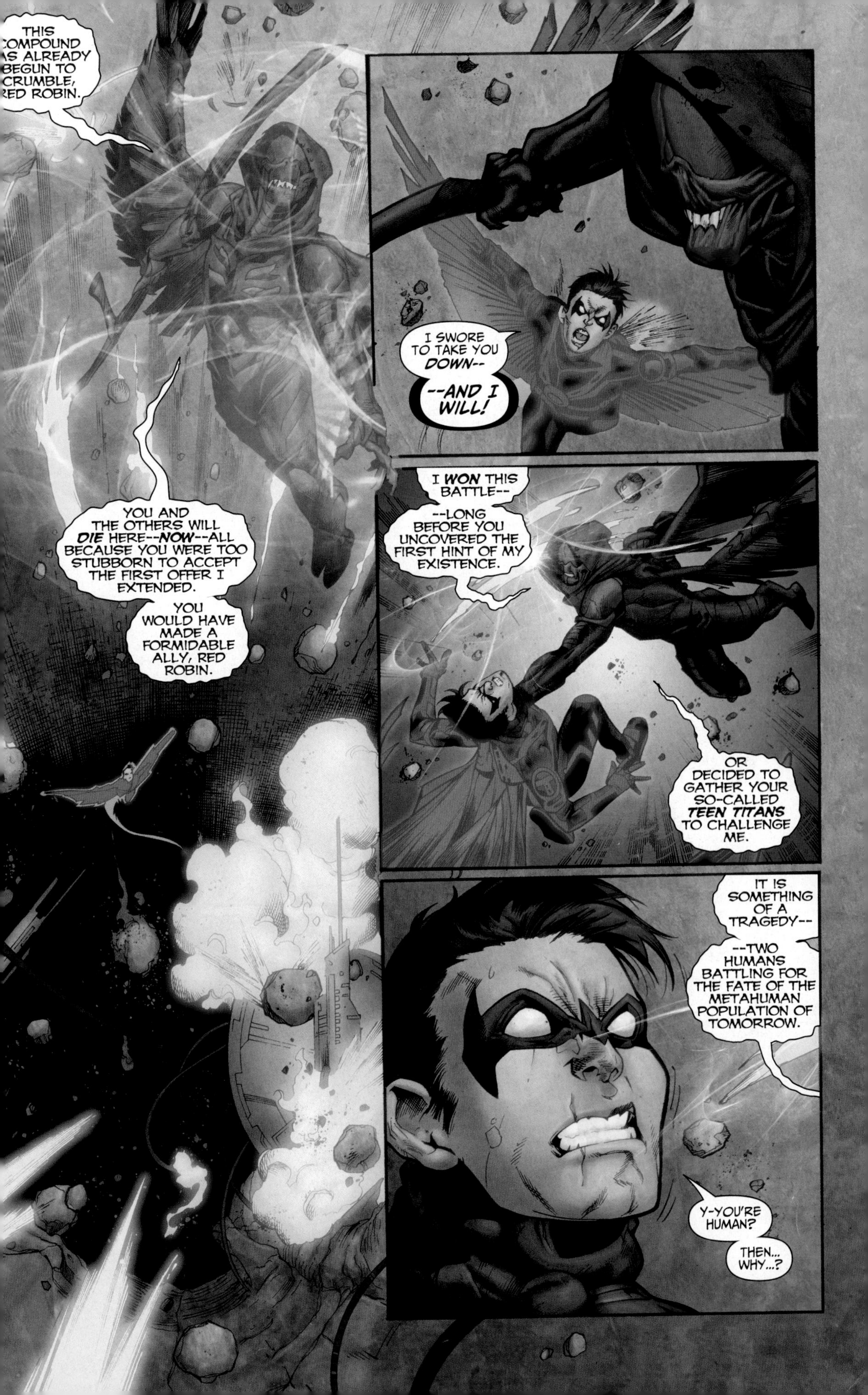
THIS COMPOUND AS ALREADY BEGUN TO CRUMBLE, RED ROBIN.
I SWORE TO TAKE YOU DOWN--
--AND I WILL!
YOU AND THE OTHERS WILL DIE HERE--NOW--ALL BECAUSE YOU WERE TOO STUBBORN TO ACCEPT THE FIRST OFFER I EXTENDED.
YOU WOULD HAVE MADE A FORMIDABLE ALLY, RED ROBIN.
I WON THIS BATTLE--
--LONG BEFORE YOU UNCOVERED THE FIRST HINT OF MY EXISTENCE.
OR DECIDED TO GATHER YOUR SO-CALLED TEEN TITANS TO CHALLENGE ME.
IT IS SOMETHING OF A TRAGEDY--
--TWO HUMANS BATTLING FOR THE FATE OF THE METAHUMAN POPULATION OF TOMORROW.
Y-YOU'RE HUMAN?
THEN... WHY...?

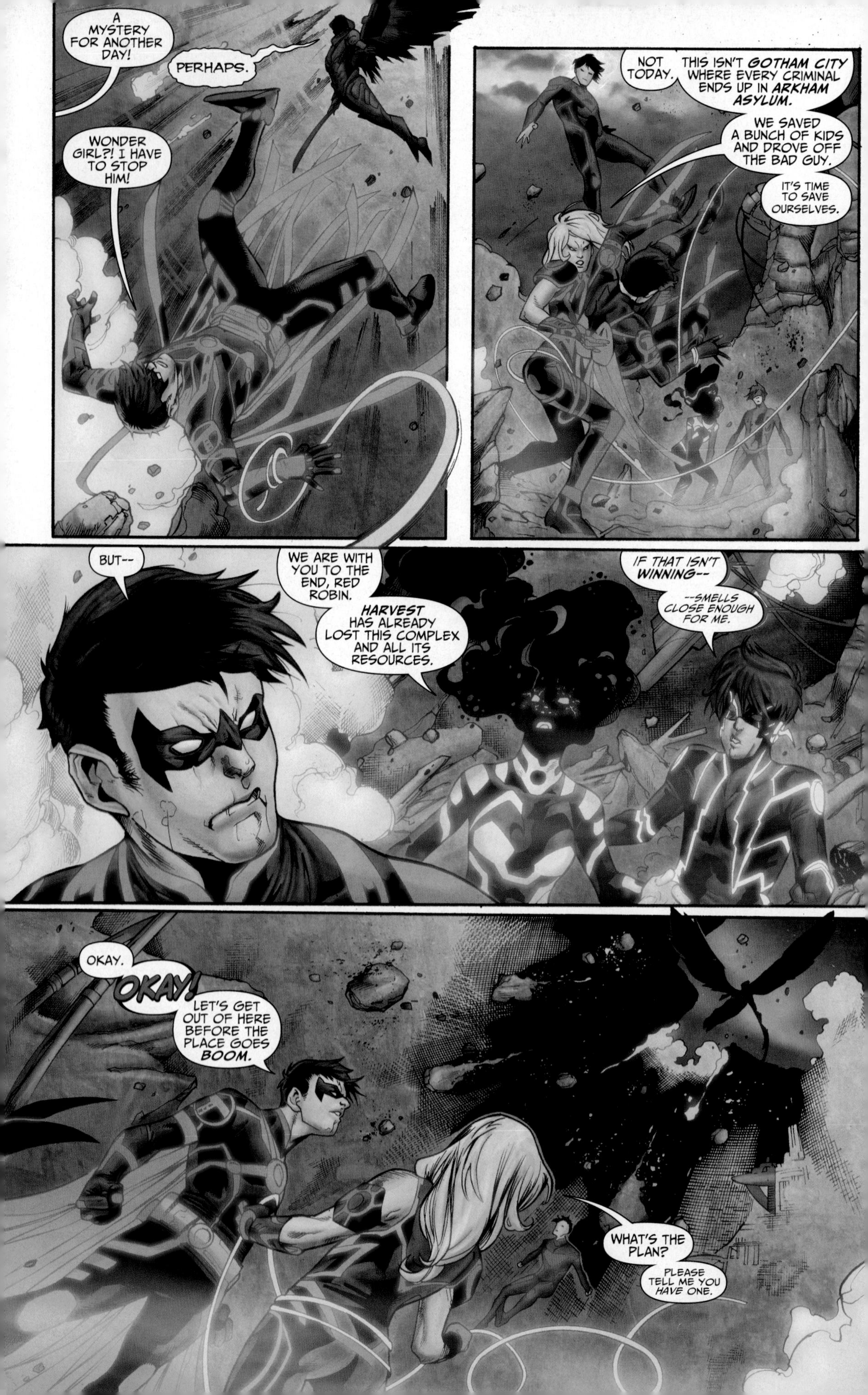
A MYSTERY FOR ANOTHER DAY!
PERHAPS.
WONDER GIRL?! I HAVE TO STOP HIM!
NOT TODAY.
THIS ISN'T GOTHAM CITY WHERE EVERY CRIMINAL ENDS UP IN ARKHAM ASYLUM.
WE SAVED A BUNCH OF KIDS AND DROVE OFF THE BAD GUY.
IT'S TIME TO SAVE OURSELVES.
BUT--
WE ARE WITH YOU TO THE END, RED ROBIN.
HARVEST HAS ALREADY LOST THIS COMPLEX AND ALL ITS RESOURCES.
IF THAT ISN'T WINNING--
--SMELLS CLOSE ENOUGH FOR ME.
OKAY.
OKAY!
LET'S GET OUT OF HERE BEFORE THE PLACE GOES BOOM.
WHAT'S THE PLAN?
PLEASE TELL ME YOU HAVE ONE.

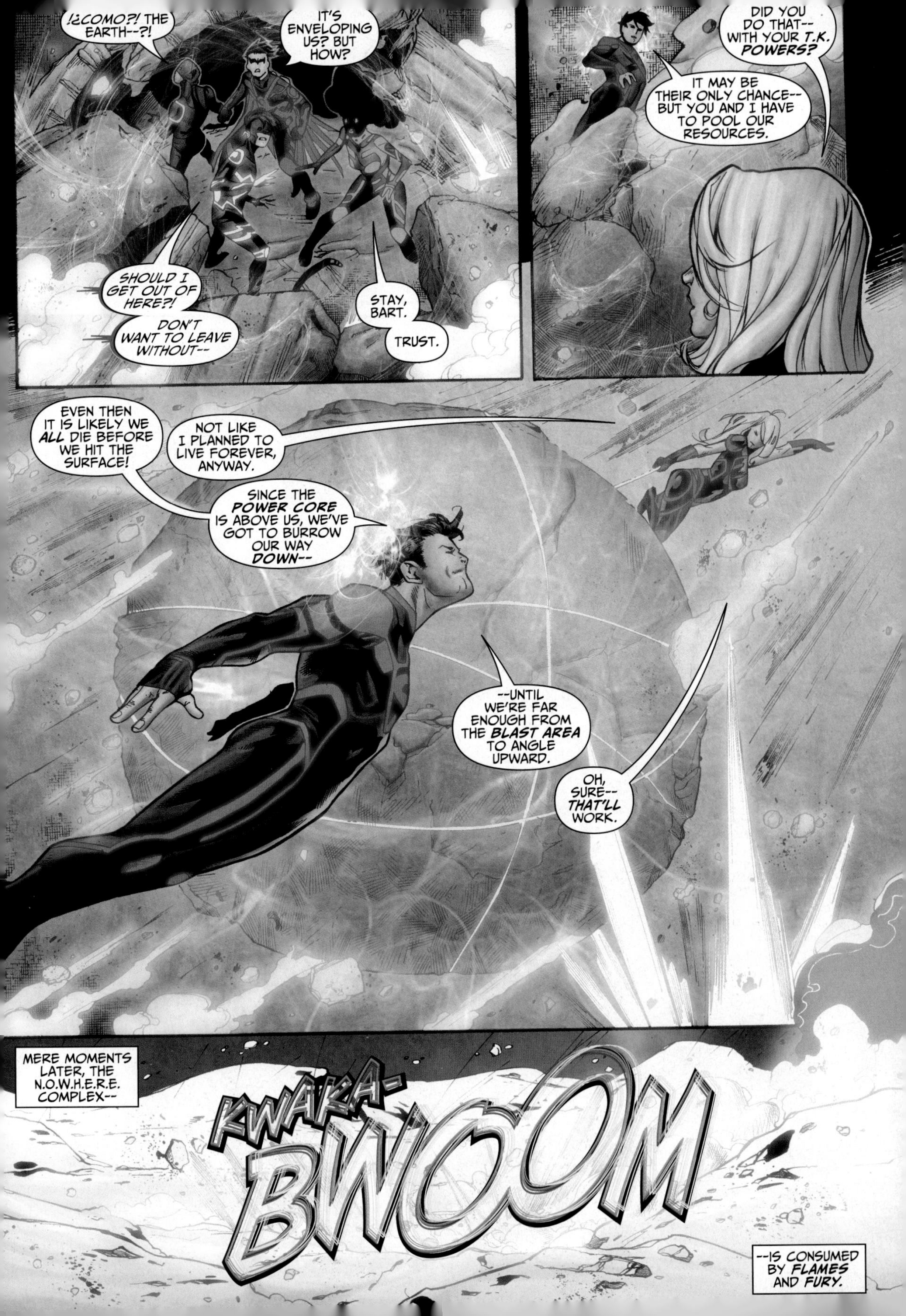

¡¿COMO?! THE EARTH--?!
IT'S ENVELOPING US? BUT HOW?
SHOULD I GET OUT OF HERE?!
DON'T WANT TO LEAVE WITHOUT--
STAY, BART.
TRUST.
DID YOU DO THAT--WITH YOUR T.K. POWERS?
IT MAY BE THEIR ONLY CHANCE--BUT YOU AND I HAVE TO POOL OUR RESOURCES.
EVEN THEN IT IS LIKELY WE ALL DIE BEFORE WE HIT THE SURFACE!
NOT LIKE I PLANNED TO LIVE FOREVER, ANYWAY.
SINCE THE POWER CORE IS ABOVE US, WE'VE GOT TO BURROW OUR WAY DOWN--
--UNTIL WE'RE FAR ENOUGH FROM THE BLAST AREA TO ANGLE UPWARD.
OH, SURE--THAT'LL WORK.
MERE MOMENTS LATER, THE N.O.W.H.E.R.E. COMPLEX--
KWAKA-BWOOM
--IS CONSUMED BY FLAMES AND FURY.

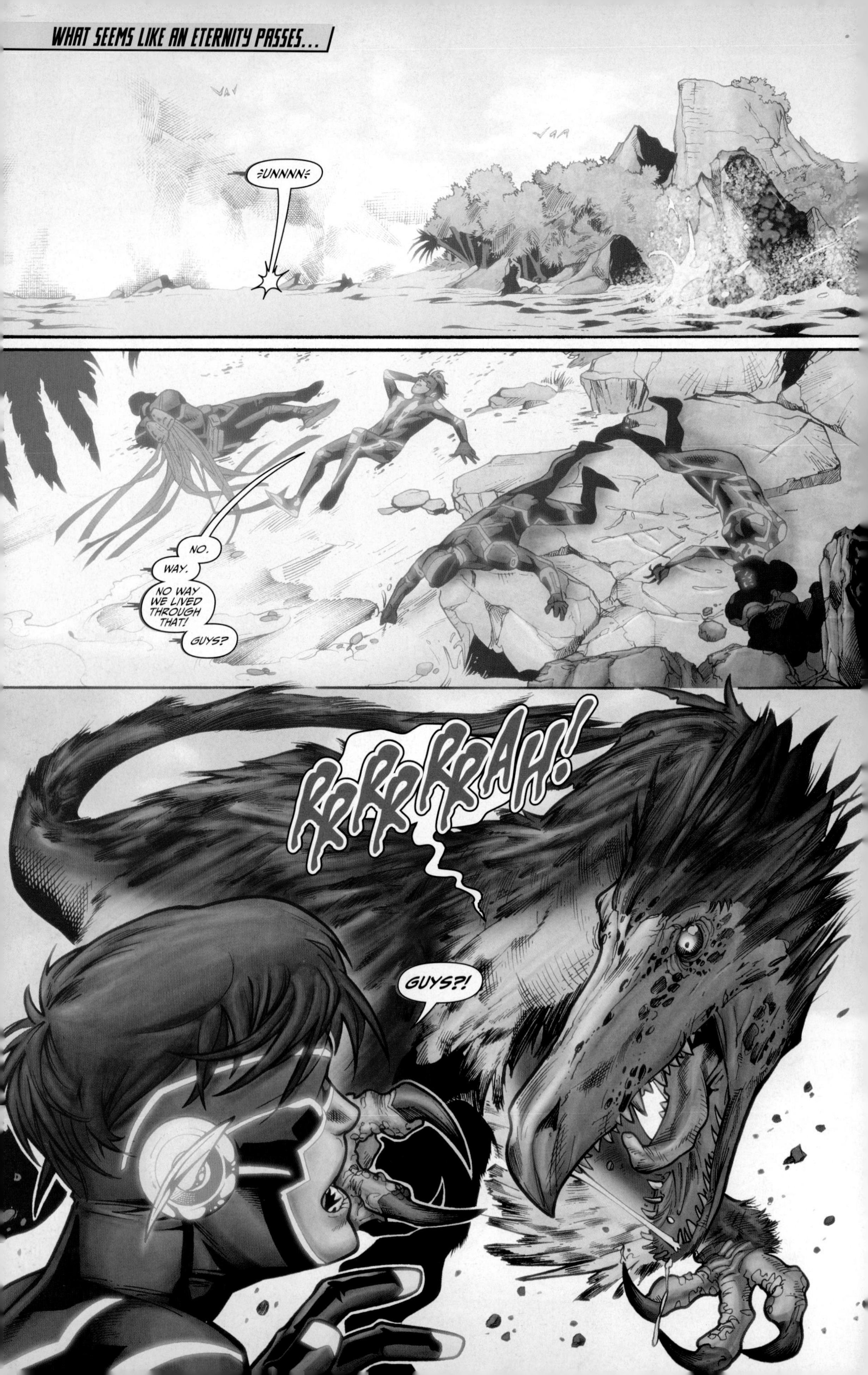
WHAT SEEMS LIKE AN ETERNITY PASSES...
UNNNN
NO.
WAY.
NO WAY WE LIVED THROUGH THAT!
GUYS?
RRRRRRAH!
GUYS?!

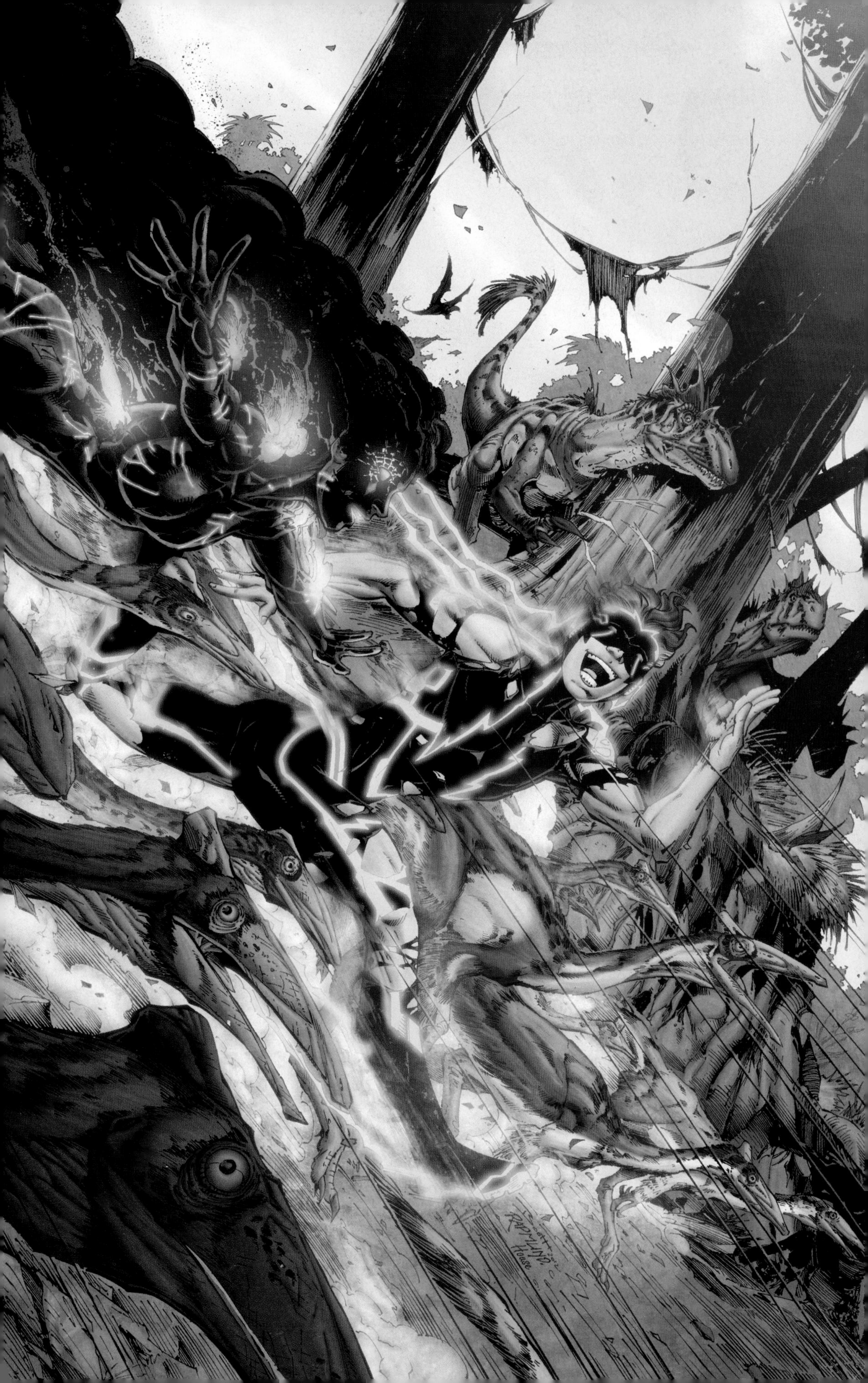

SAUR FEELINGS

SCOTT LOBDELL
writer

BRETT BOOTH
penciller

NORM RAPMUND
inker

cover art by
BRETT BOOTH, NORM RAPMUND & ANDREW DALHOUSE

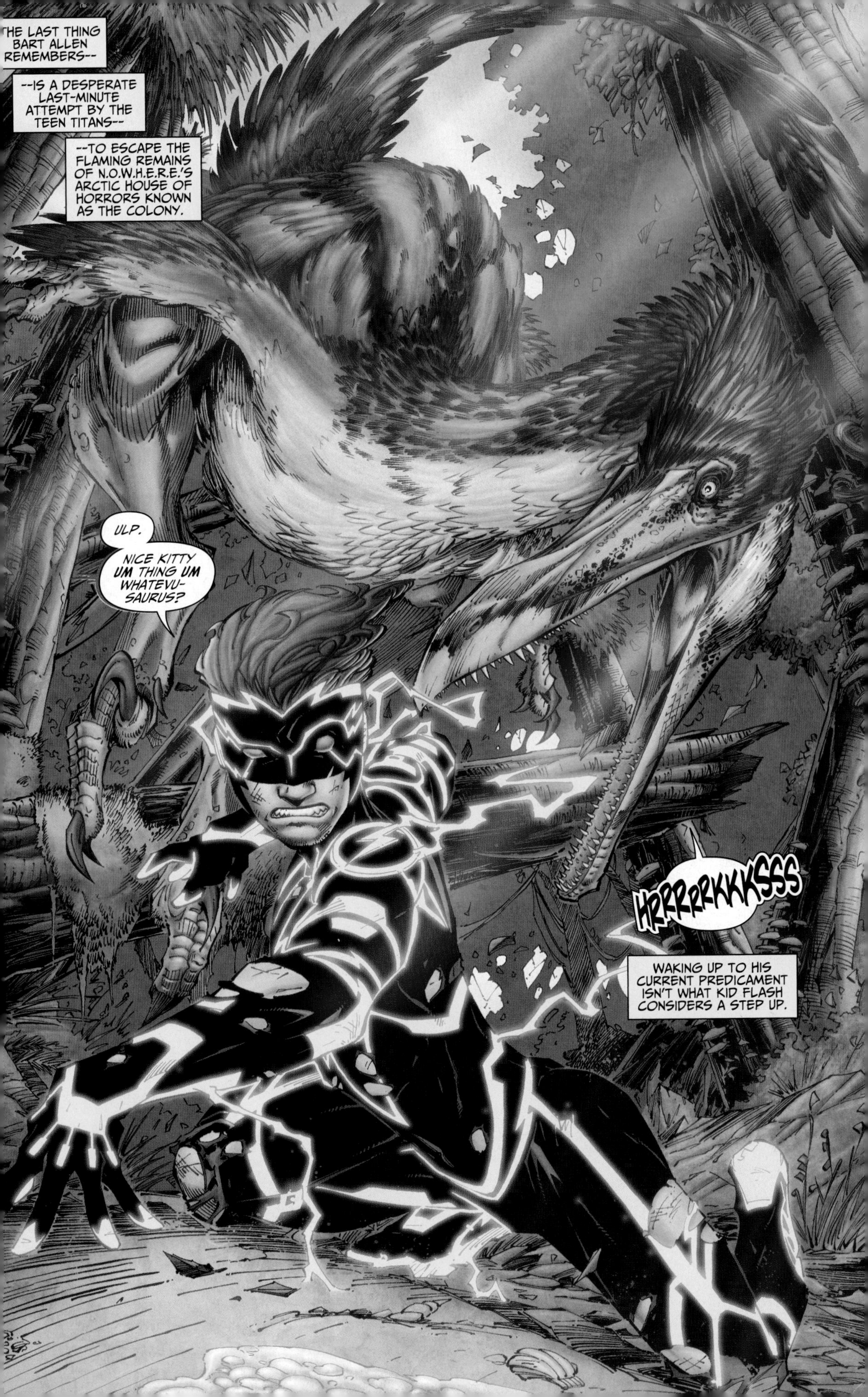
THE LAST THING BART ALLEN REMEMBERS--
--IS A DESPERATE LAST-MINUTE ATTEMPT BY THE TEEN TITANS--
--TO ESCAPE THE FLAMING REMAINS OF N.O.W.H.E.R.E.'S ARCTIC HOUSE OF HORRORS KNOWN AS THE COLONY.
ULP.
NICE KITTY UM THING UM WHATEVU-SAURUS?
HRRRRRKKKSSS
WAKING UP TO HIS CURRENT PREDICAMENT ISN'T WHAT KID FLASH CONSIDERS A STEP UP.

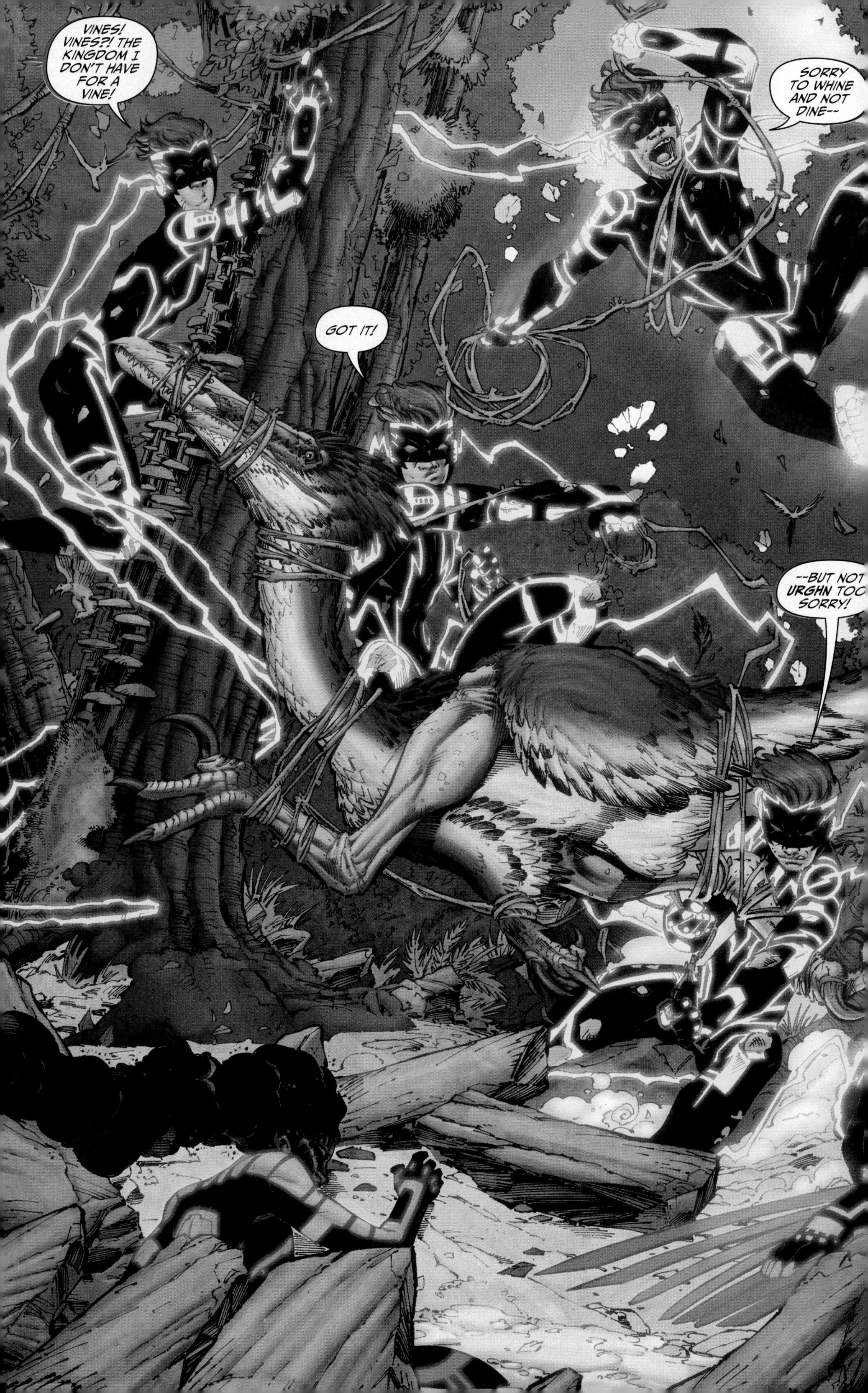
VINES! VINES?! THE KINGDOM I DON'T HAVE FOR A VINE!
SORRY TO WHINE AND NOT DINE--
GOT IT!
--BUT NOT URGHN TOO SORRY!

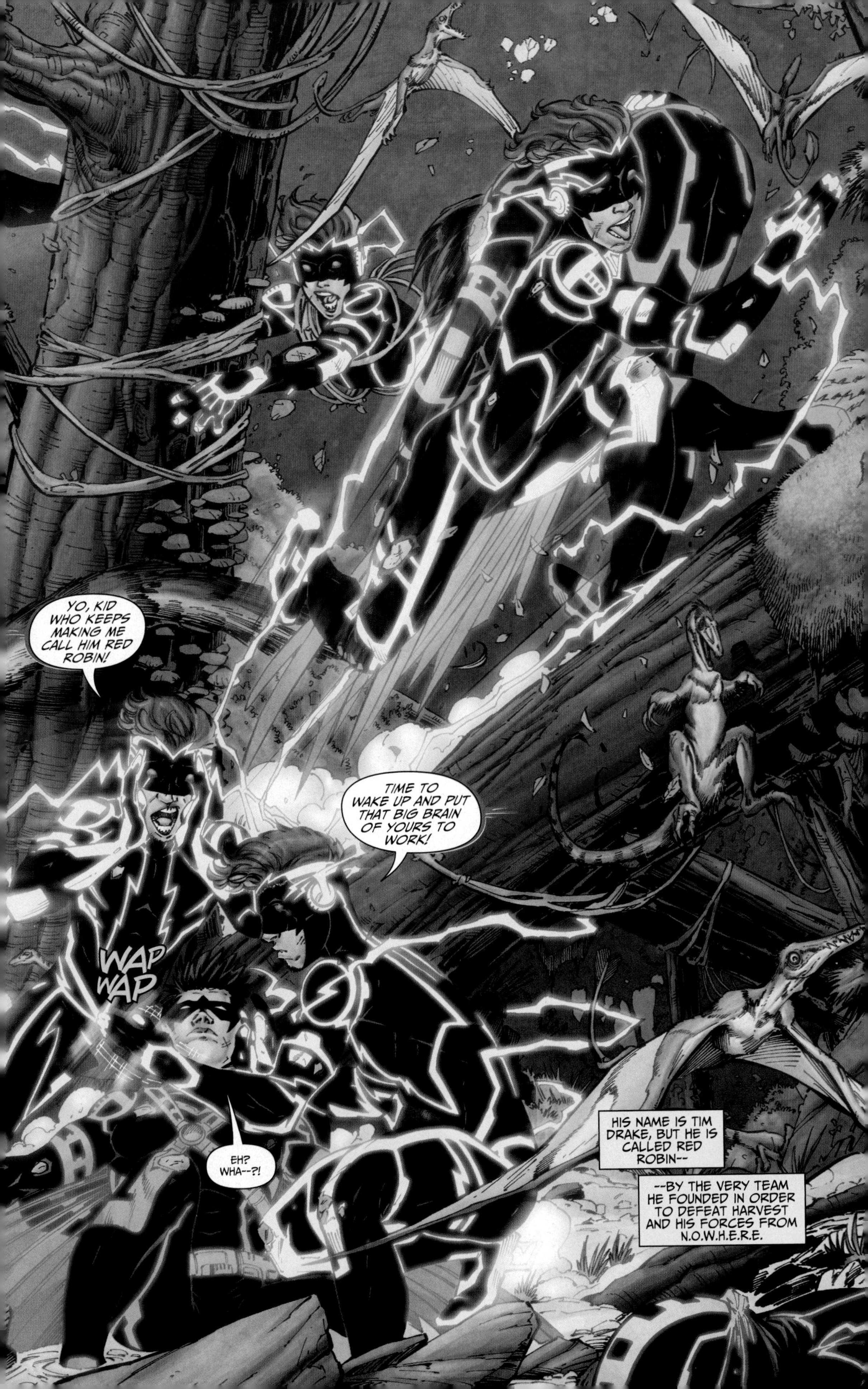
YO, KID WHO KEEPS MAKING ME CALL HIM RED ROBIN!
TIME TO WAKE UP AND PUT THAT BIG BRAIN OF YOURS TO WORK!
WAP WAP
EH? WHA--?!
HIS NAME IS TIM DRAKE, BUT HE IS CALLED RED ROBIN--
--BY THE VERY TEAM HE FOUNDED IN ORDER TO DEFEAT HARVEST AND HIS FORCES FROM N.O.W.H.E.R.E.

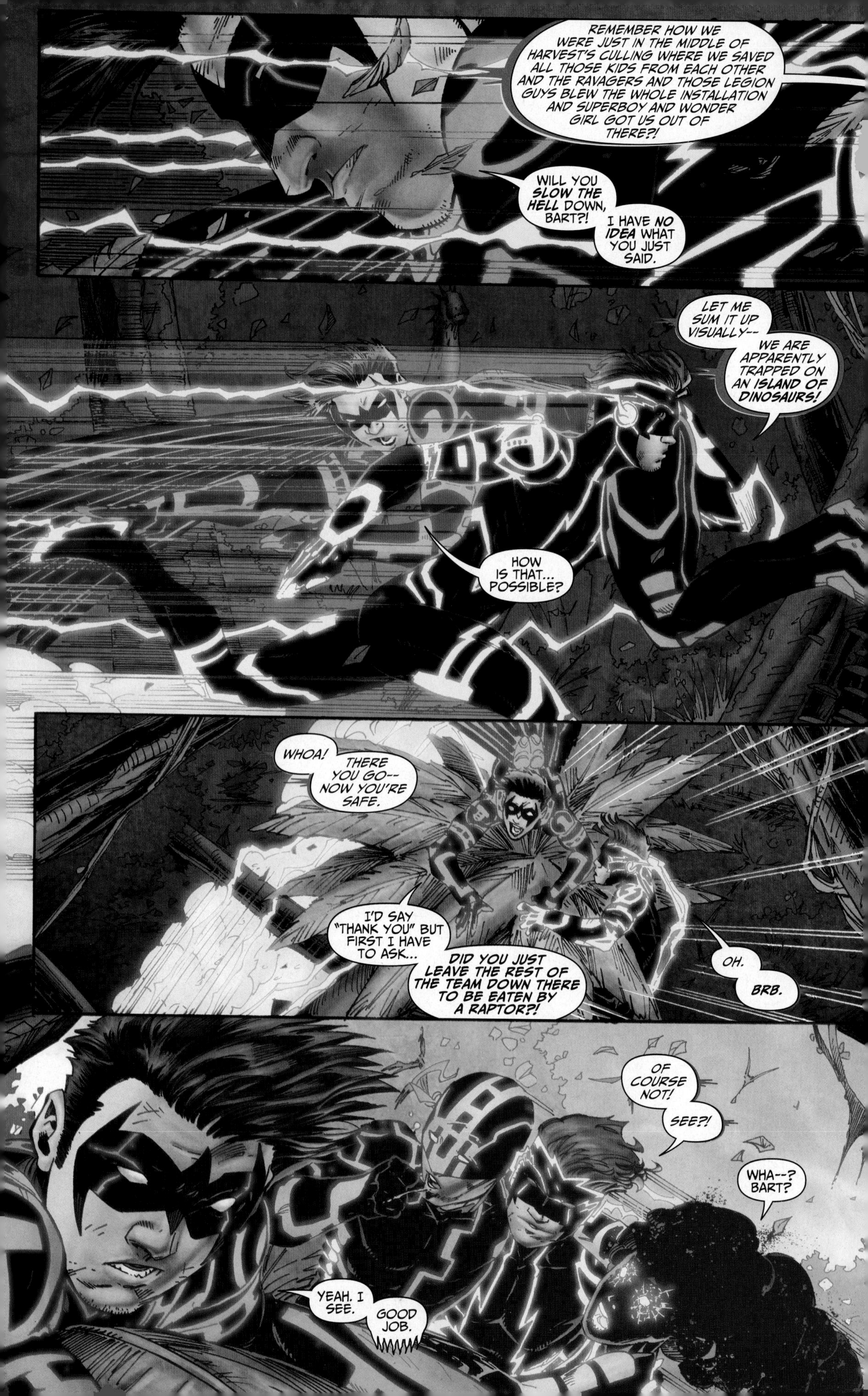
REMEMBER HOW WE WERE JUST IN THE MIDDLE OF HARVEST'S CULLING WHERE WE SAVED ALL THOSE KIDS FROM EACH OTHER AND THE RAVAGERS AND THOSE LEGION GUYS BLEW THE WHOLE INSTALLATION AND SUPERBOY AND WONDER GIRL GOT US OUT OF THERE?!
WILL YOU SLOW THE HELL DOWN, BART?!
I HAVE NO IDEA WHAT YOU JUST SAID.
LET ME SUM IT UP VISUALLY--
WE ARE APPARENTLY TRAPPED ON AN ISLAND OF DINOSAURS!
HOW IS THAT... POSSIBLE?
WHOA!
THERE YOU GO-- NOW YOU'RE SAFE.
I'D SAY "THANK YOU" BUT FIRST I HAVE TO ASK...
DID YOU JUST LEAVE THE REST OF THE TEAM DOWN THERE TO BE EATEN BY A RAPTOR?!
OH.
BRB.
OF COURSE NOT!
SEE?!
WHA--? BART?
YEAH. I SEE.
GOOD JOB.

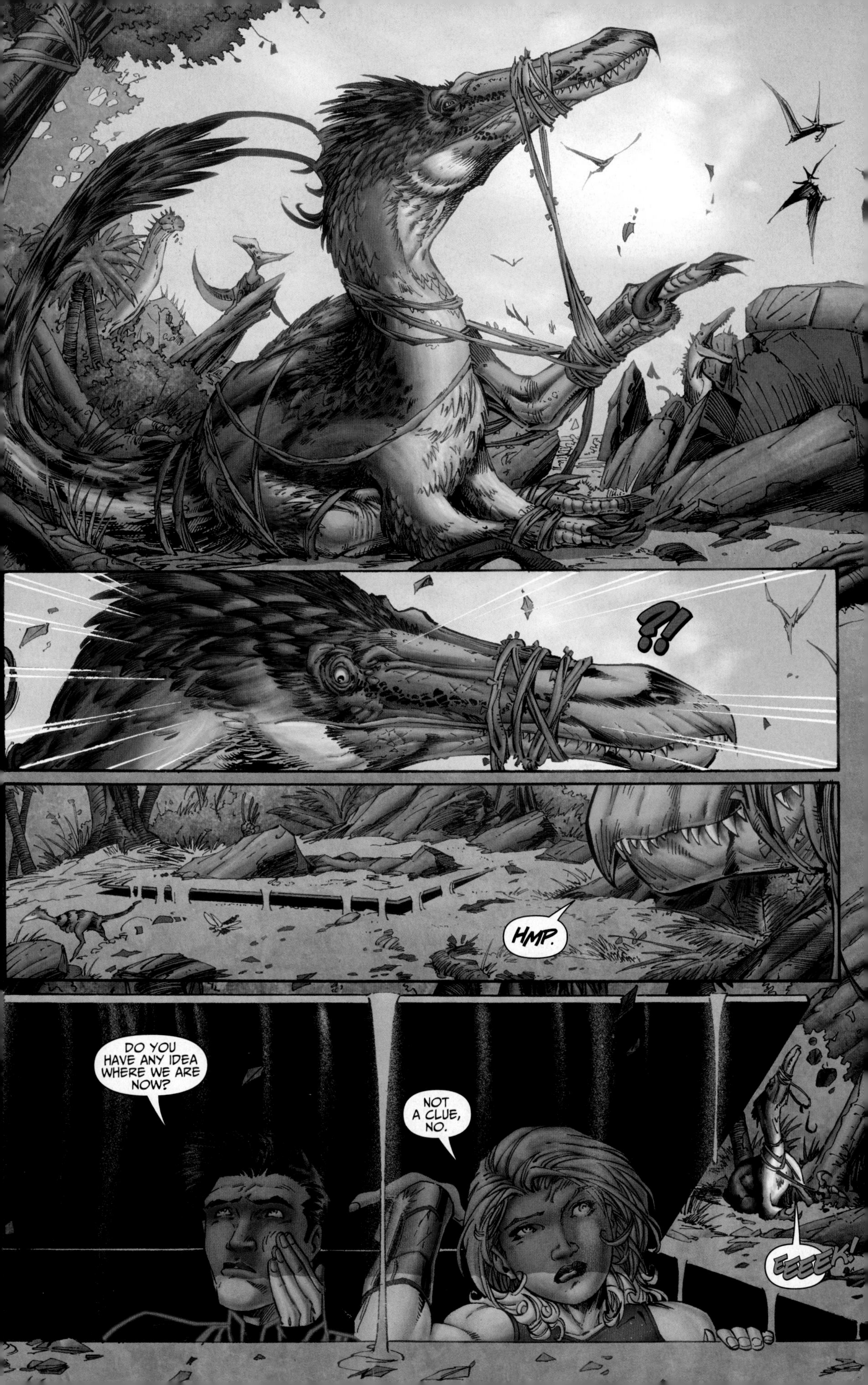
?!
HMP.
DO YOU HAVE ANY IDEA WHERE WE ARE NOW?
NOT A CLUE, NO.
EEEEK!

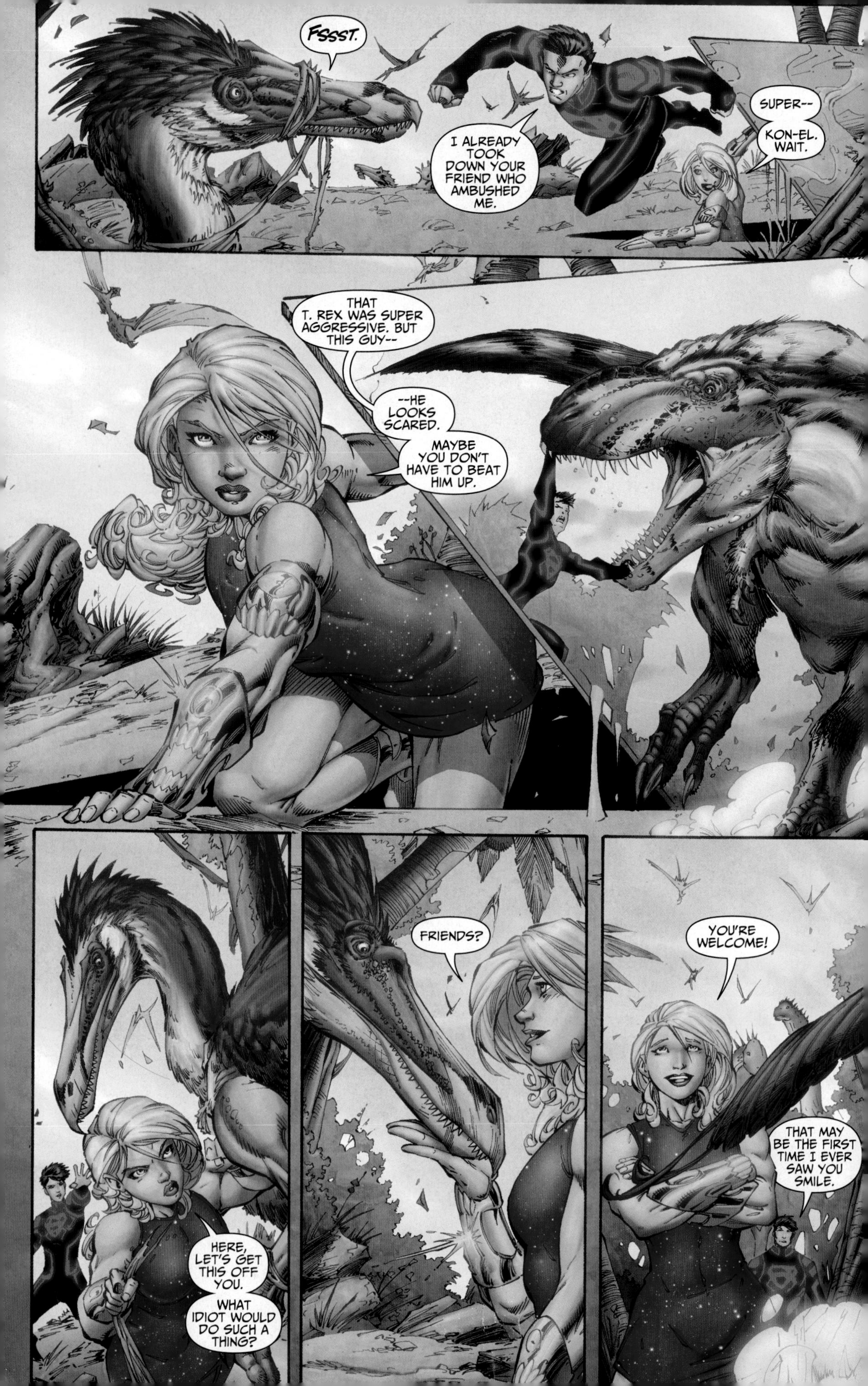
FSSST.
I ALREADY TOOK DOWN YOUR FRIEND WHO AMBUSHED ME.
SUPER--
KON-EL. WAIT.
THAT T. REX WAS SUPER AGGRESSIVE. BUT THIS GUY--
--HE LOOKS SCARED.
MAYBE YOU DON'T HAVE TO BEAT HIM UP.
HERE, LET'S GET THIS OFF YOU.
WHAT IDIOT WOULD DO SUCH A THING?
FRIENDS?
YOU'RE WELCOME!
THAT MAY BE THE FIRST TIME I EVER SAW YOU SMILE.

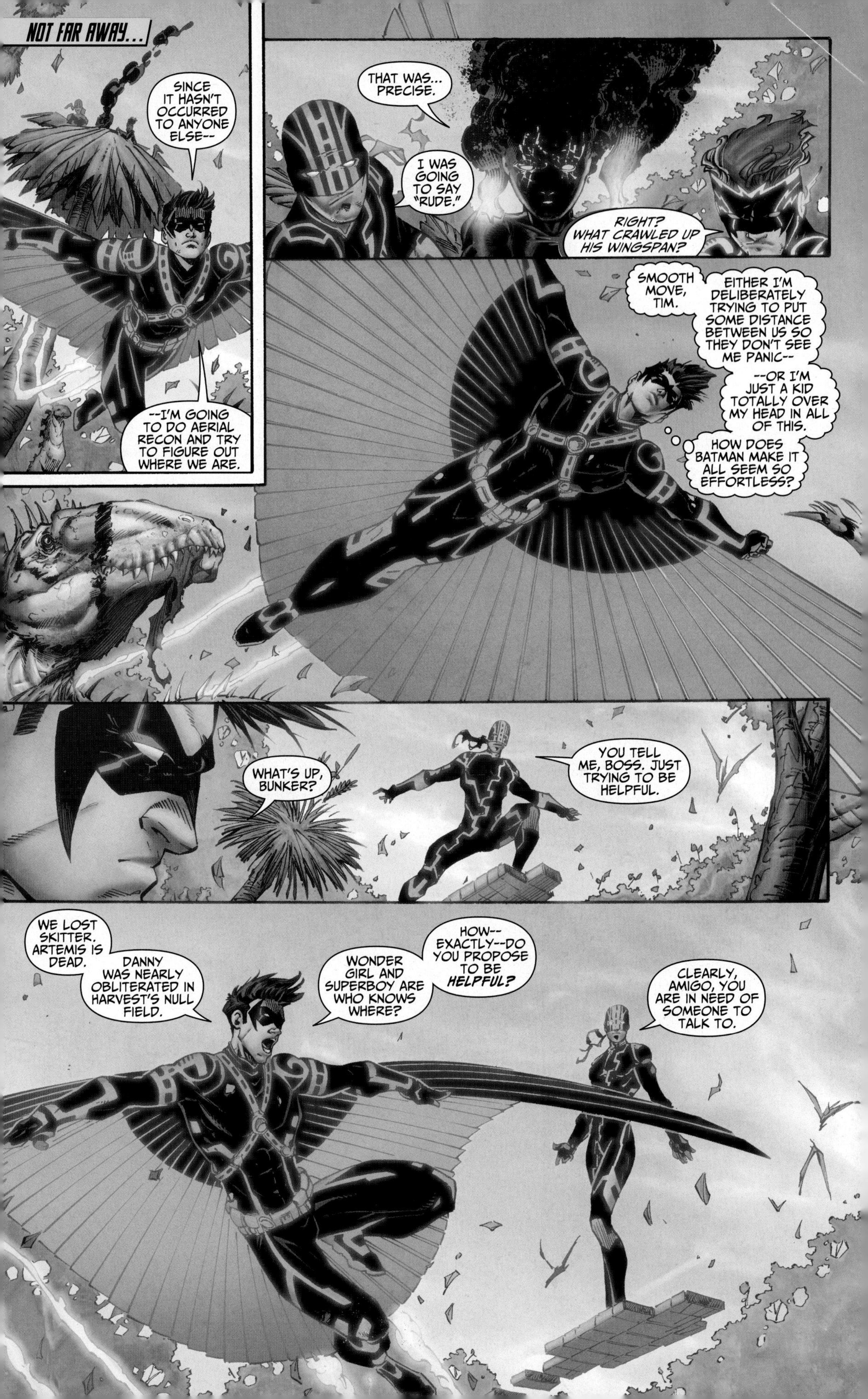
NOT FAR AWAY...
SINCE IT HASN'T OCCURRED TO ANYONE ELSE--
--I'M GOING TO DO AERIAL RECON AND TRY TO FIGURE OUT WHERE WE ARE.
THAT WAS... PRECISE.
I WAS GOING TO SAY "RUDE."
RIGHT? WHAT CRAWLED UP HIS WINGSPAN?
SMOOTH MOVE, TIM.
EITHER I'M DELIBERATELY TRYING TO PUT SOME DISTANCE BETWEEN US SO THEY DON'T SEE ME PANIC--
--OR I'M JUST A KID TOTALLY OVER MY HEAD IN ALL OF THIS.
HOW DOES BATMAN MAKE IT ALL SEEM SO EFFORTLESS?
WHAT'S UP, BUNKER?
YOU TELL ME, BOSS. JUST TRYING TO BE HELPFUL.
WE LOST SKITTER. ARTEMIS IS DEAD.
DANNY WAS NEARLY OBLITERATED IN HARVEST'S NULL FIELD.
WONDER GIRL AND SUPERBOY ARE WHO KNOWS WHERE?
HOW--EXACTLY--DO YOU PROPOSE TO BE HELPFUL?
CLEARLY, AMIGO, YOU ARE IN NEED OF SOMEONE TO TALK TO.

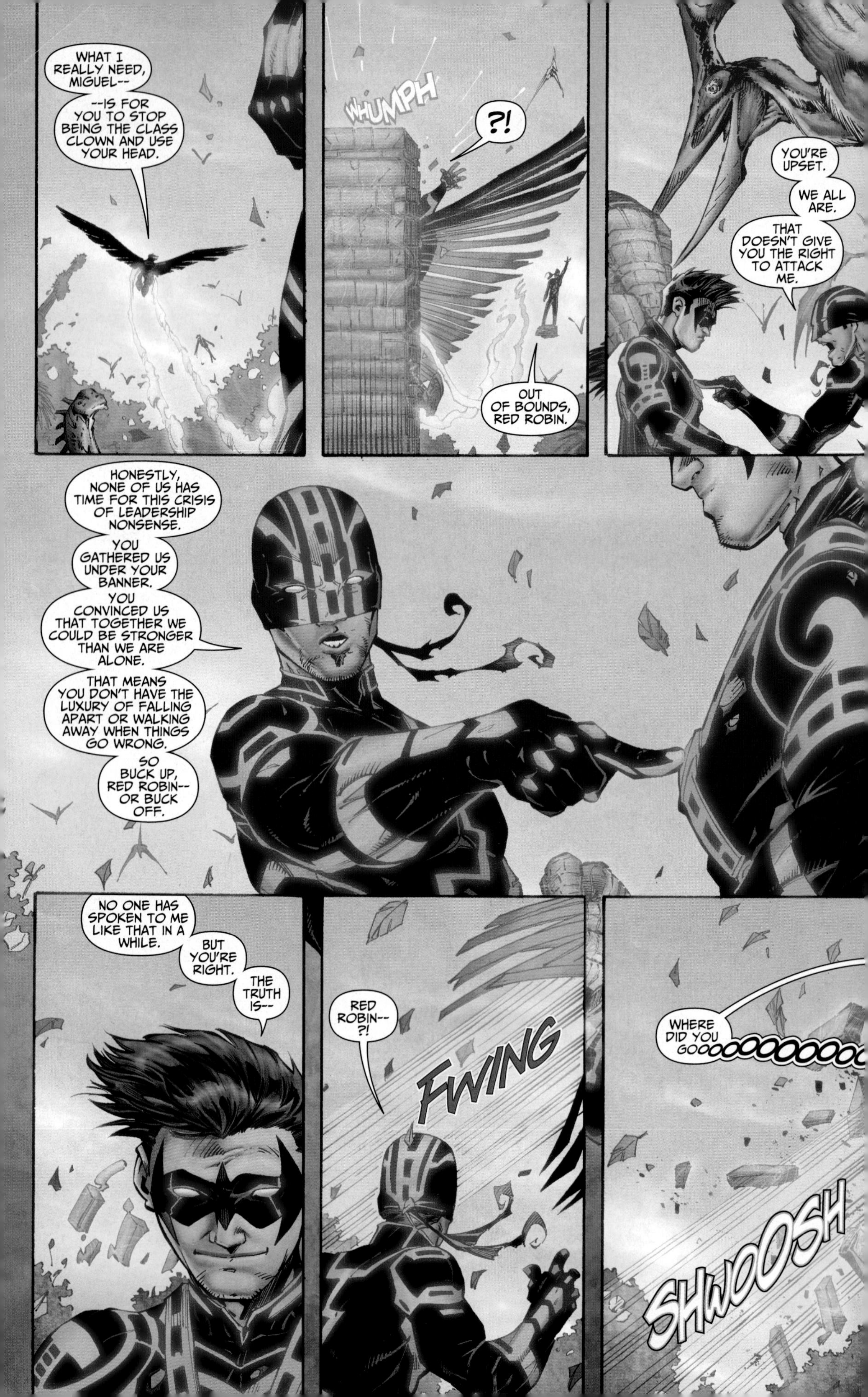
WHAT I REALLY NEED, MIGUEL--
--IS FOR YOU TO STOP BEING THE CLASS CLOWN AND USE YOUR HEAD.
WHUMPH
?!
OUT OF BOUNDS, RED ROBIN.
YOU'RE UPSET.
WE ALL ARE.
THAT DOESN'T GIVE YOU THE RIGHT TO ATTACK ME.
HONESTLY, NONE OF US HAS TIME FOR THIS CRISIS OF LEADERSHIP NONSENSE.
YOU GATHERED US UNDER YOUR BANNER.
YOU CONVINCED US THAT TOGETHER WE COULD BE STRONGER THAN WE ARE ALONE.
THAT MEANS YOU DON'T HAVE THE LUXURY OF FALLING APART OR WALKING AWAY WHEN THINGS GO WRONG.
SO BUCK UP, RED ROBIN-- OR BUCK OFF.
NO ONE HAS SPOKEN TO ME LIKE THAT IN A WHILE.
BUT YOU'RE RIGHT.
THE TRUTH IS--
RED ROBIN-- ?!
FWING
WHERE DID YOU GOOOOOOOOOOOO
SHWOOSH

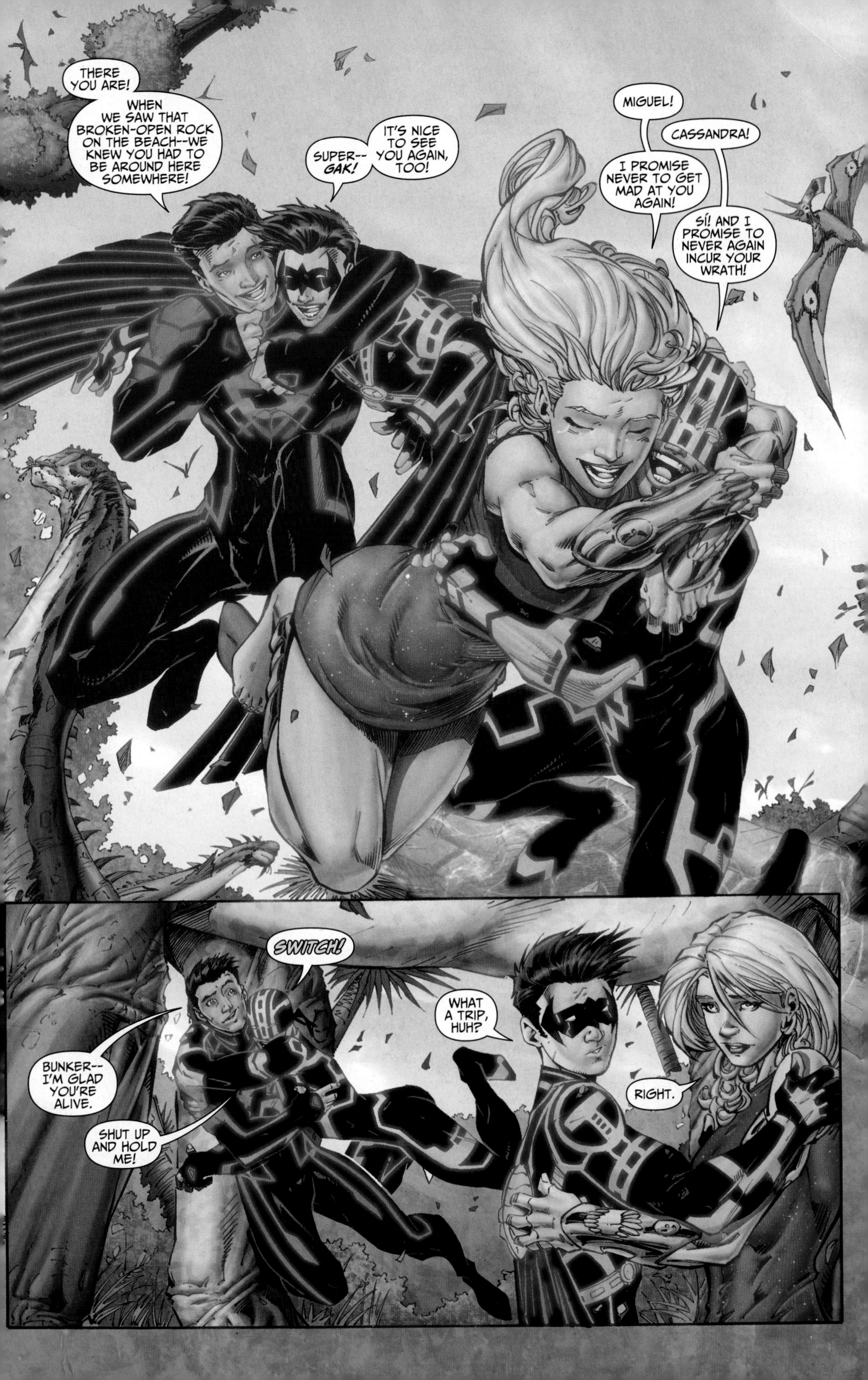
THERE YOU ARE!
WHEN WE SAW THAT BROKEN-OPEN ROCK ON THE BEACH--WE KNEW YOU HAD TO BE AROUND HERE SOMEWHERE!
SUPER-- GAK!
IT'S NICE TO SEE YOU AGAIN, TOO!
MIGUEL!
I PROMISE NEVER TO GET MAD AT YOU AGAIN!
CASSANDRA!
SÍ! AND I PROMISE TO NEVER AGAIN INCUR YOUR WRATH!
SWITCH!
BUNKER-- I'M GLAD YOU'RE ALIVE.
SHUT UP AND HOLD ME!
WHAT A TRIP, HUH?
RIGHT.

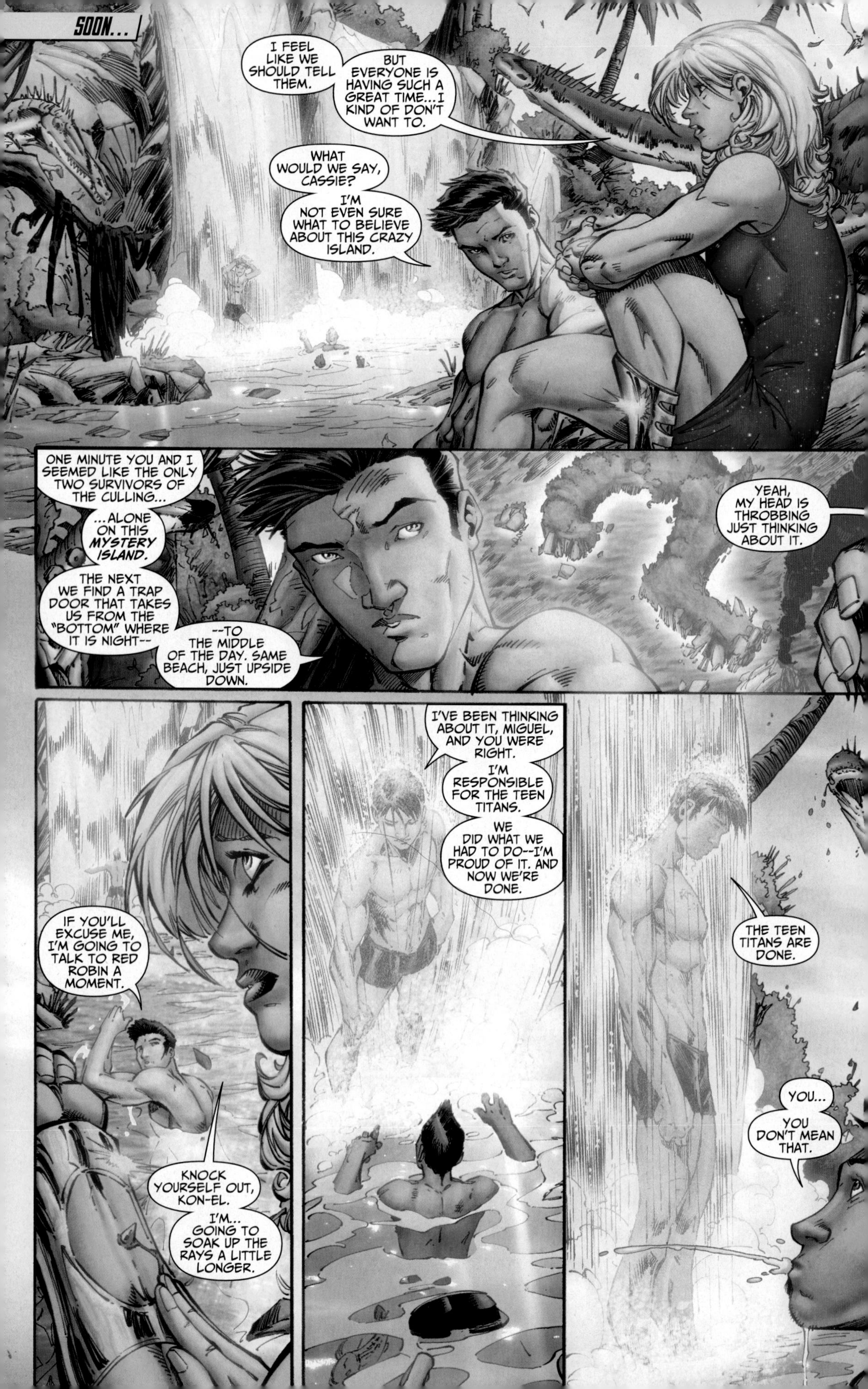
SOON...
I FEEL LIKE WE SHOULD TELL THEM.
BUT EVERYONE IS HAVING SUCH A GREAT TIME...I KIND OF DON'T WANT TO.
WHAT WOULD WE SAY, CASSIE?
I'M NOT EVEN SURE WHAT TO BELIEVE ABOUT THIS CRAZY ISLAND.
ONE MINUTE YOU AND I SEEMED LIKE THE ONLY TWO SURVIVORS OF THE CULLING...
...ALONE ON THIS MYSTERY ISLAND.
THE NEXT WE FIND A TRAP DOOR THAT TAKES US FROM THE "BOTTOM" WHERE IT IS NIGHT--
--TO THE MIDDLE OF THE DAY. SAME BEACH, JUST UPSIDE DOWN.
YEAH, MY HEAD IS THROBBING JUST THINKING ABOUT IT.
IF YOU'LL EXCUSE ME, I'M GOING TO TALK TO RED ROBIN A MOMENT.
KNOCK YOURSELF OUT, KON-EL.
I'M... GOING TO SOAK UP THE RAYS A LITTLE LONGER.
I'VE BEEN THINKING ABOUT IT, MIGUEL, AND YOU WERE RIGHT.
I'M RESPONSIBLE FOR THE TEEN TITANS.
WE DID WHAT WE HAD TO DO--I'M PROUD OF IT. AND NOW WE'RE DONE.
THE TEEN TITANS ARE DONE.
YOU...
YOU DON'T MEAN THAT.

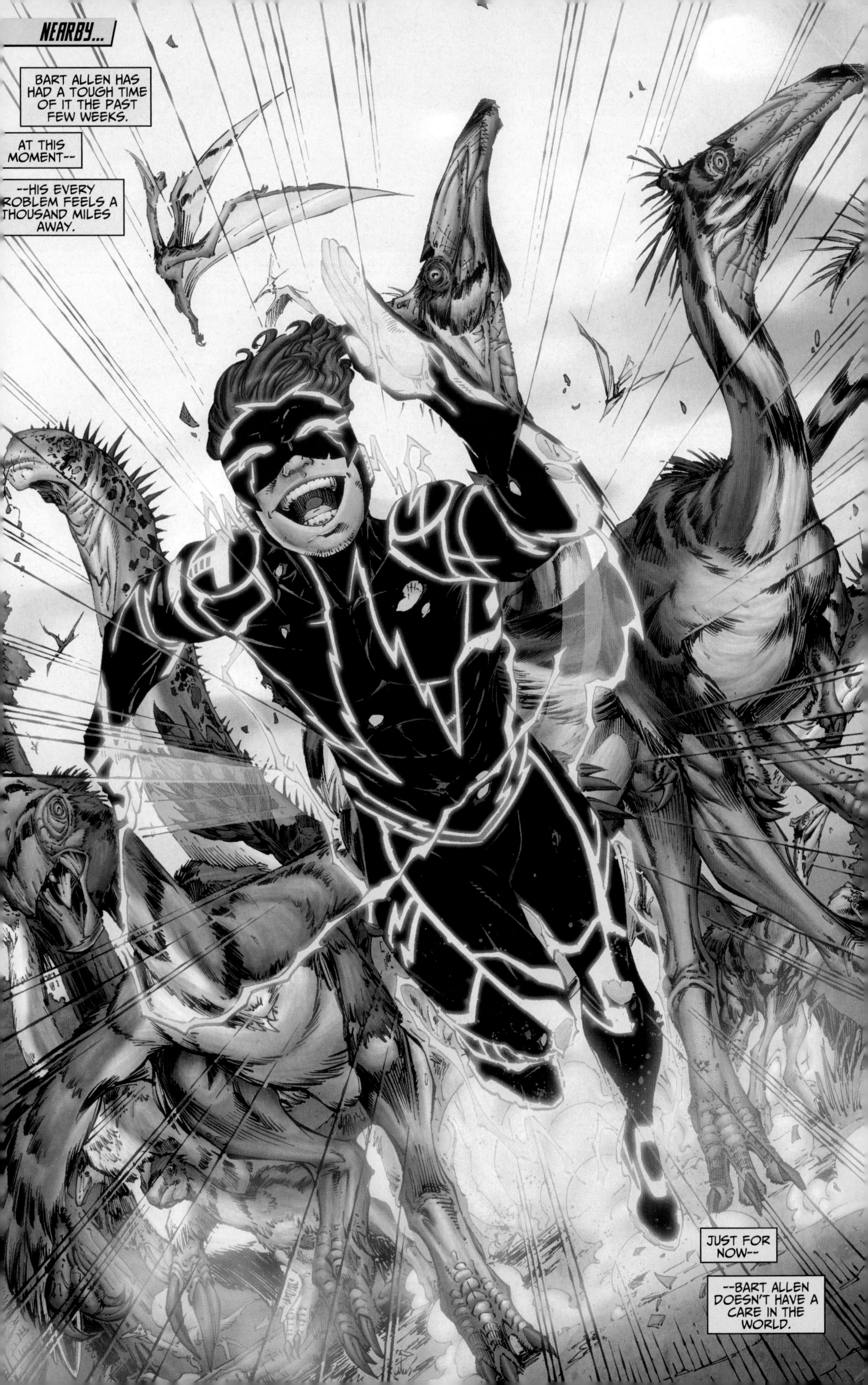
NEARBY...
BART ALLEN HAS HAD A TOUGH TIME OF IT THE PAST FEW WEEKS.
AT THIS MOMENT--
--HIS EVERY PROBLEM FEELS A THOUSAND MILES AWAY.
JUST FOR NOW--
--BART ALLEN DOESN'T HAVE A CARE IN THE WORLD.

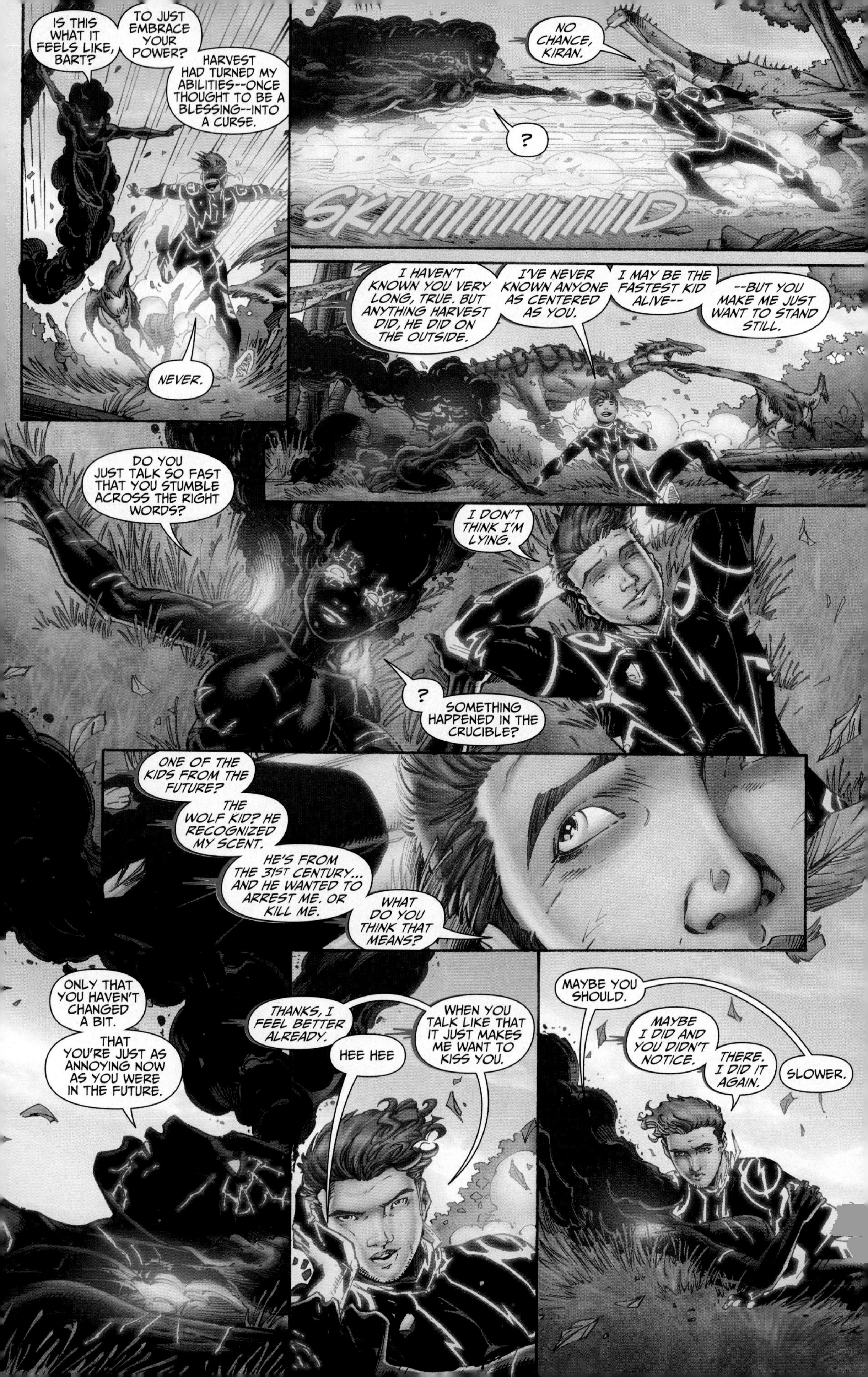
IS THIS WHAT IT FEELS LIKE, BART?
TO JUST EMBRACE YOUR POWER?
HARVEST HAD TURNED MY ABILITIES--ONCE THOUGHT TO BE A BLESSING--INTO A CURSE.
NEVER.
NO CHANCE, KIRAN.
?
SKIIIIIIIIIIIIIIIIID
I HAVEN'T KNOWN YOU VERY LONG, TRUE. BUT ANYTHING HARVEST DID, HE DID ON THE OUTSIDE.
I'VE NEVER KNOWN ANYONE AS CENTERED AS YOU.
I MAY BE THE FASTEST KID ALIVE--
--BUT YOU MAKE ME JUST WANT TO STAND STILL.
DO YOU JUST TALK SO FAST THAT YOU STUMBLE ACROSS THE RIGHT WORDS?
I DON'T THINK I'M LYING.
?
SOMETHING HAPPENED IN THE CRUCIBLE?
ONE OF THE KIDS FROM THE FUTURE?
THE WOLF KID? HE RECOGNIZED MY SCENT.
HE'S FROM THE 31ST CENTURY... AND HE WANTED TO ARREST ME. OR KILL ME.
WHAT DO YOU THINK THAT MEANS?
ONLY THAT YOU HAVEN'T CHANGED A BIT.
THAT YOU'RE JUST AS ANNOYING NOW AS YOU WERE IN THE FUTURE.
THANKS, I FEEL BETTER ALREADY.
HEE HEE
WHEN YOU TALK LIKE THAT IT JUST MAKES ME WANT TO KISS YOU.
MAYBE YOU SHOULD.
MAYBE I DID AND YOU DIDN'T NOTICE.
THERE. I DID IT AGAIN.
SLOWER.

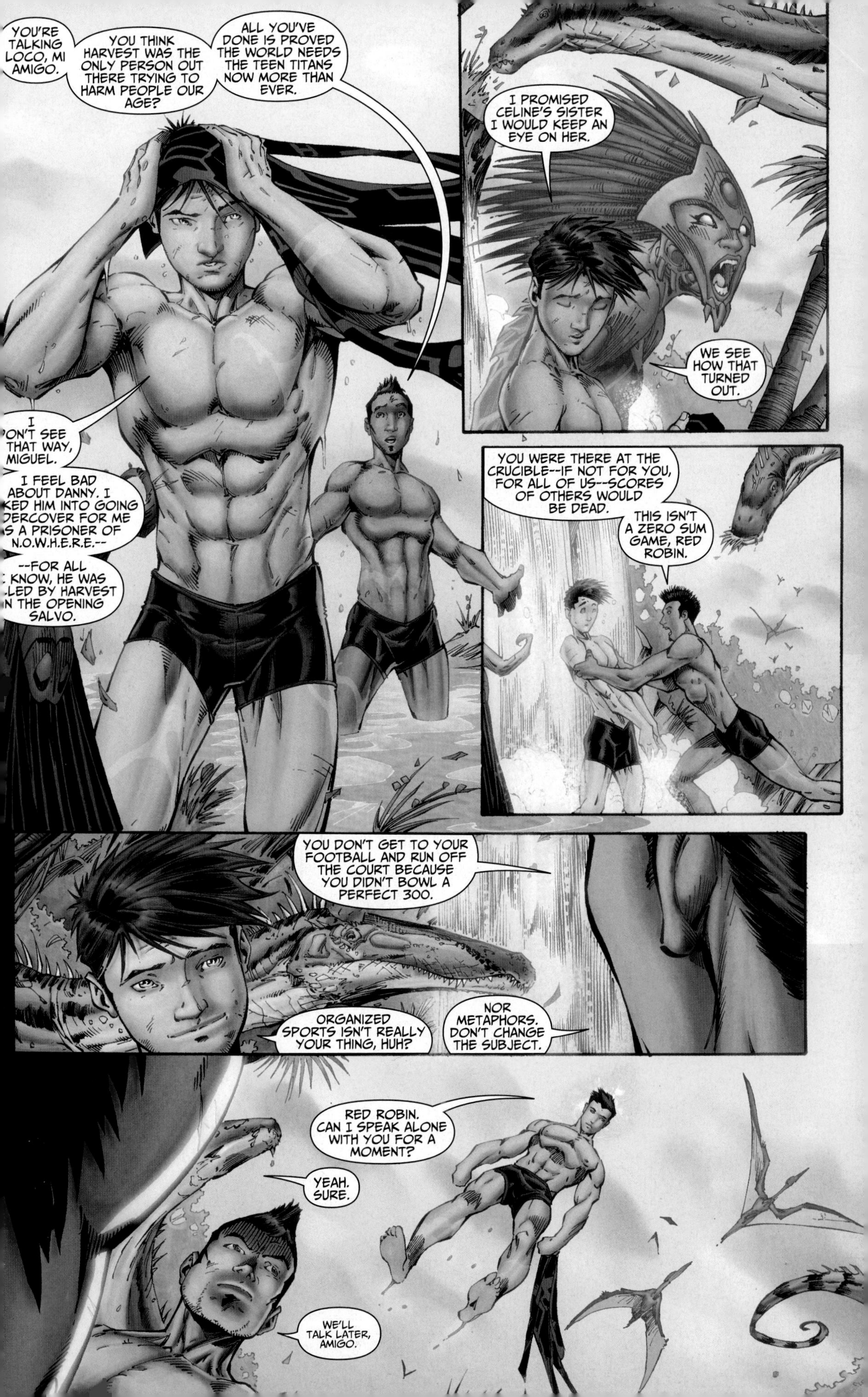
YOU'RE TALKING LOCO, MI AMIGO.
YOU THINK HARVEST WAS THE ONLY PERSON OUT THERE TRYING TO HARM PEOPLE OUR AGE?
ALL YOU'VE DONE IS PROVED THE WORLD NEEDS THE TEEN TITANS NOW MORE THAN EVER.
I PROMISED CELINE'S SISTER I WOULD KEEP AN EYE ON HER.
WE SEE HOW THAT TURNED OUT.
I ON'T SEE THAT WAY, MIGUEL.
I FEEL BAD ABOUT DANNY. I KED HIM INTO GOING DERCOVER FOR ME S A PRISONER OF N.O.W.H.E.R.E.--
--FOR ALL KNOW, HE WAS LED BY HARVEST N THE OPENING SALVO.
YOU WERE THERE AT THE CRUCIBLE--IF NOT FOR YOU, FOR ALL OF US--SCORES OF OTHERS WOULD BE DEAD.
THIS ISN'T A ZERO SUM GAME, RED ROBIN.
YOU DON'T GET TO YOUR FOOTBALL AND RUN OFF THE COURT BECAUSE YOU DIDN'T BOWL A PERFECT 300.
ORGANIZED SPORTS ISN'T REALLY YOUR THING, HUH?
NOR METAPHORS. DON'T CHANGE THE SUBJECT.
RED ROBIN. CAN I SPEAK ALONE WITH YOU FOR A MOMENT?
YEAH. SURE.
WE'LL TALK LATER, AMIGO.

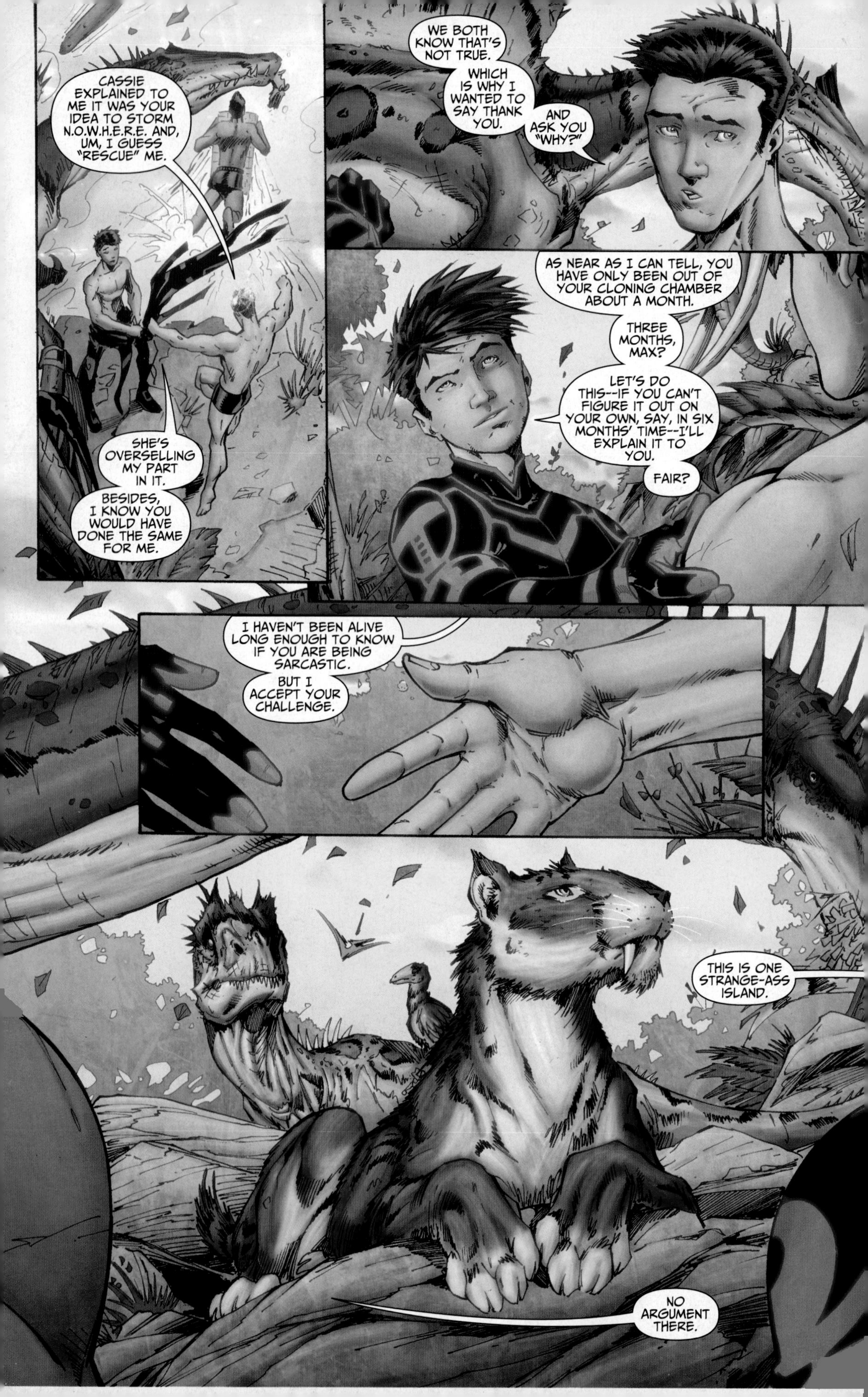

CASSIE EXPLAINED TO ME IT WAS YOUR IDEA TO STORM N.O.W.H.E.R.E. AND, UM, I GUESS "RESCUE" ME.
SHE'S OVERSELLING MY PART IN IT.
BESIDES, I KNOW YOU WOULD HAVE DONE THE SAME FOR ME.
WE BOTH KNOW THAT'S NOT TRUE.
WHICH IS WHY I WANTED TO SAY THANK YOU.
AND ASK YOU "WHY?"
AS NEAR AS I CAN TELL, YOU HAVE ONLY BEEN OUT OF YOUR CLONING CHAMBER ABOUT A MONTH.
THREE MONTHS, MAX?
LET'S DO THIS--IF YOU CAN'T FIGURE IT OUT ON YOUR OWN, SAY, IN SIX MONTHS' TIME--I'LL EXPLAIN IT TO YOU.
FAIR?
I HAVEN'T BEEN ALIVE LONG ENOUGH TO KNOW IF YOU ARE BEING SARCASTIC.
BUT I ACCEPT YOUR CHALLENGE.
THIS IS ONE STRANGE-ASS ISLAND.
NO ARGUMENT THERE.

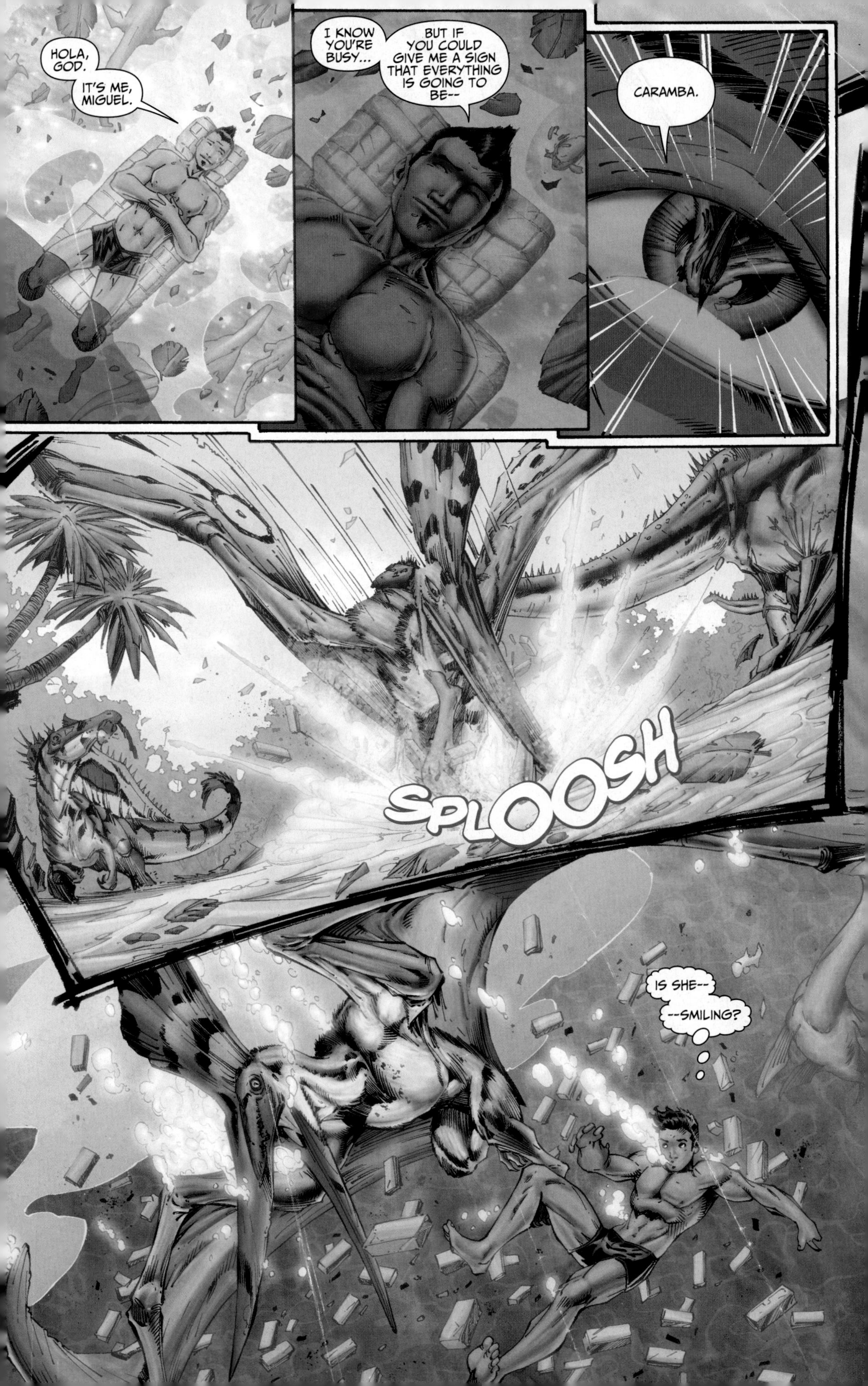
HOLA, GOD.
IT'S ME, MIGUEL.
I KNOW YOU'RE BUSY...
BUT IF YOU COULD GIVE ME A SIGN THAT EVERYTHING IS GOING TO BE--
CARAMBA.
SPLOOSH
IS SHE--
--SMILING?

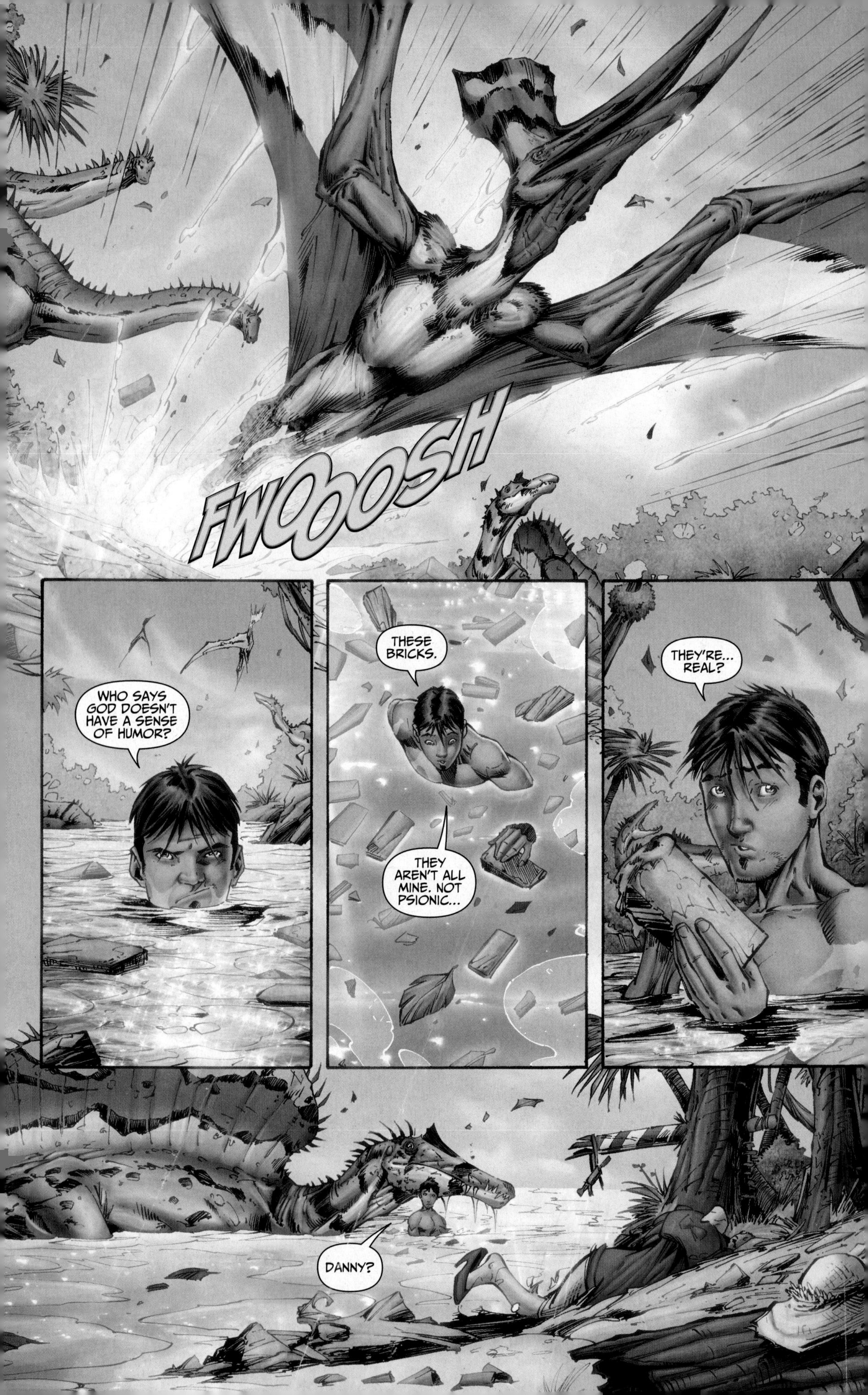
FWOOOSH
WHO SAYS GOD DOESN'T HAVE A SENSE OF HUMOR?
THESE BRICKS.
THEY AREN'T ALL MINE. NOT PSIONIC...
THEY'RE... REAL?
DANNY?

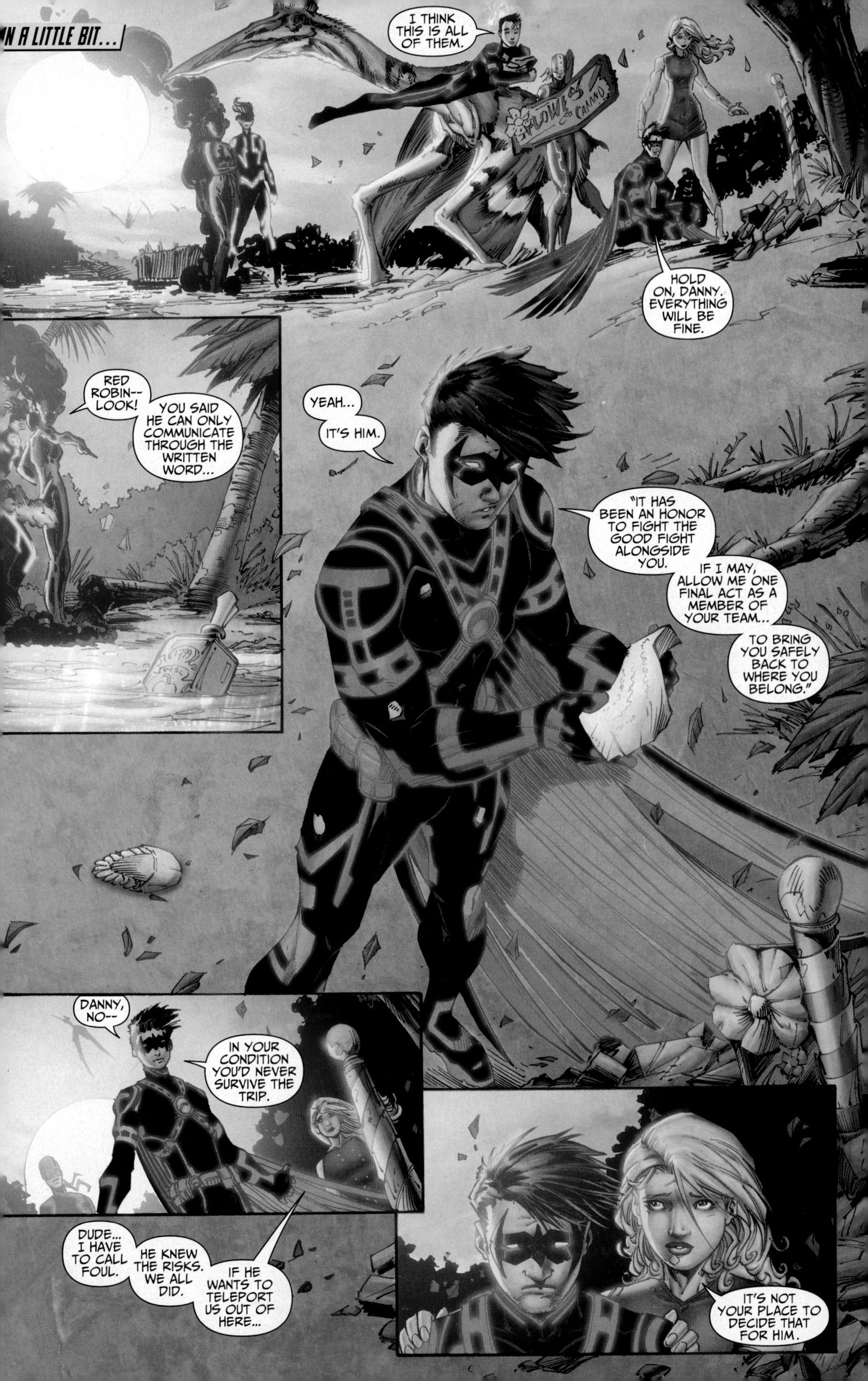
IN A LITTLE BIT...
I THINK THIS IS ALL OF THEM.
HOLD ON, DANNY. EVERYTHING WILL BE FINE.
RED ROBIN-- LOOK!
YOU SAID HE CAN ONLY COMMUNICATE THROUGH THE WRITTEN WORD...
YEAH...
IT'S HIM.
"IT HAS BEEN AN HONOR TO FIGHT THE GOOD FIGHT ALONGSIDE YOU.
IF I MAY, ALLOW ME ONE FINAL ACT AS A MEMBER OF YOUR TEAM...
TO BRING YOU SAFELY BACK TO WHERE YOU BELONG."
DANNY, NO--
IN YOUR CONDITION YOU'D NEVER SURVIVE THE TRIP.
DUDE... I HAVE TO CALL FOUL.
HE KNEW THE RISKS. WE ALL DID.
IF HE WANTS TO TELEPORT US OUT OF HERE...
IT'S NOT YOUR PLACE TO DECIDE THAT FOR HIM.

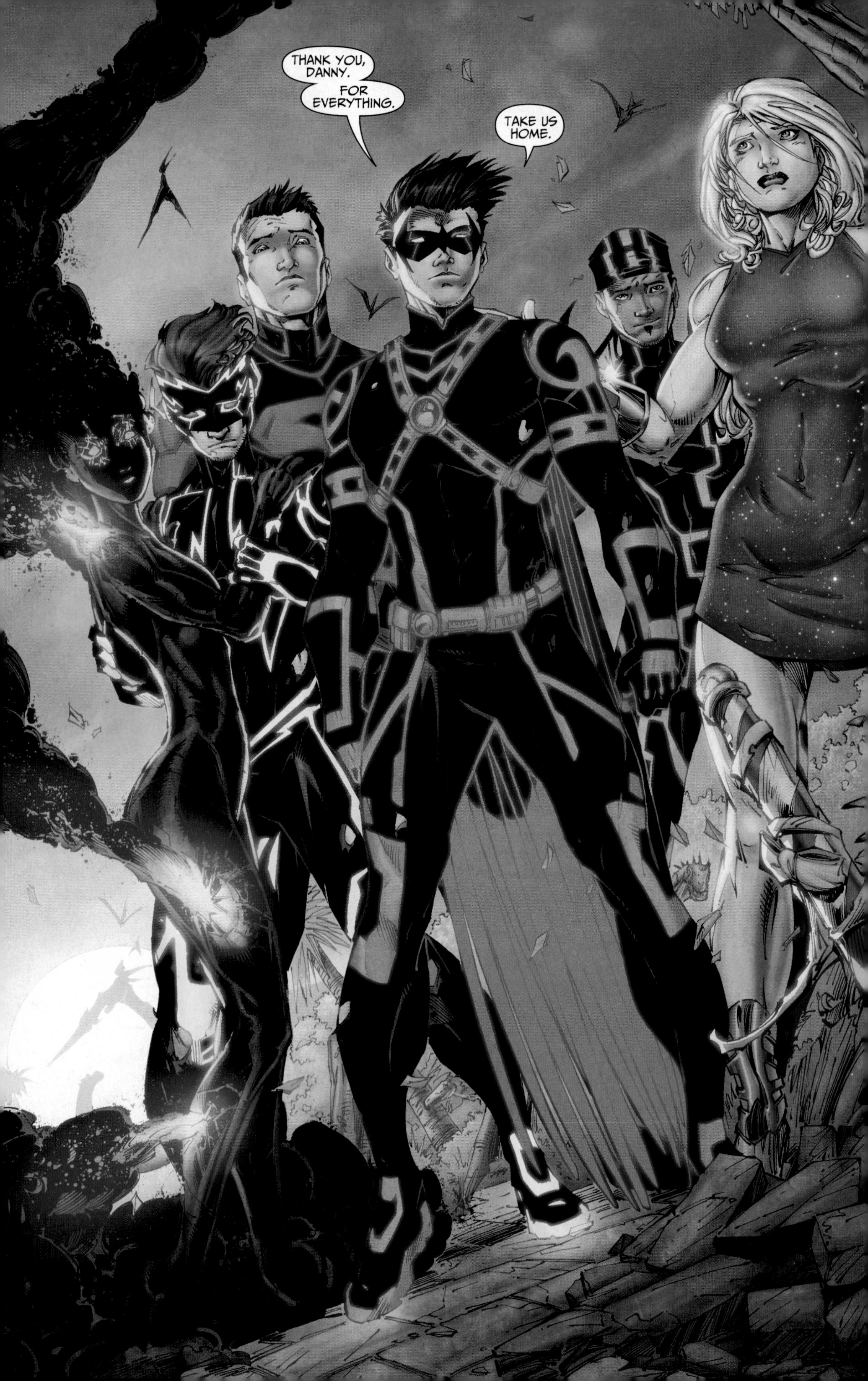
THANK YOU, DANNY. FOR EVERYTHING.
TAKE US HOME.

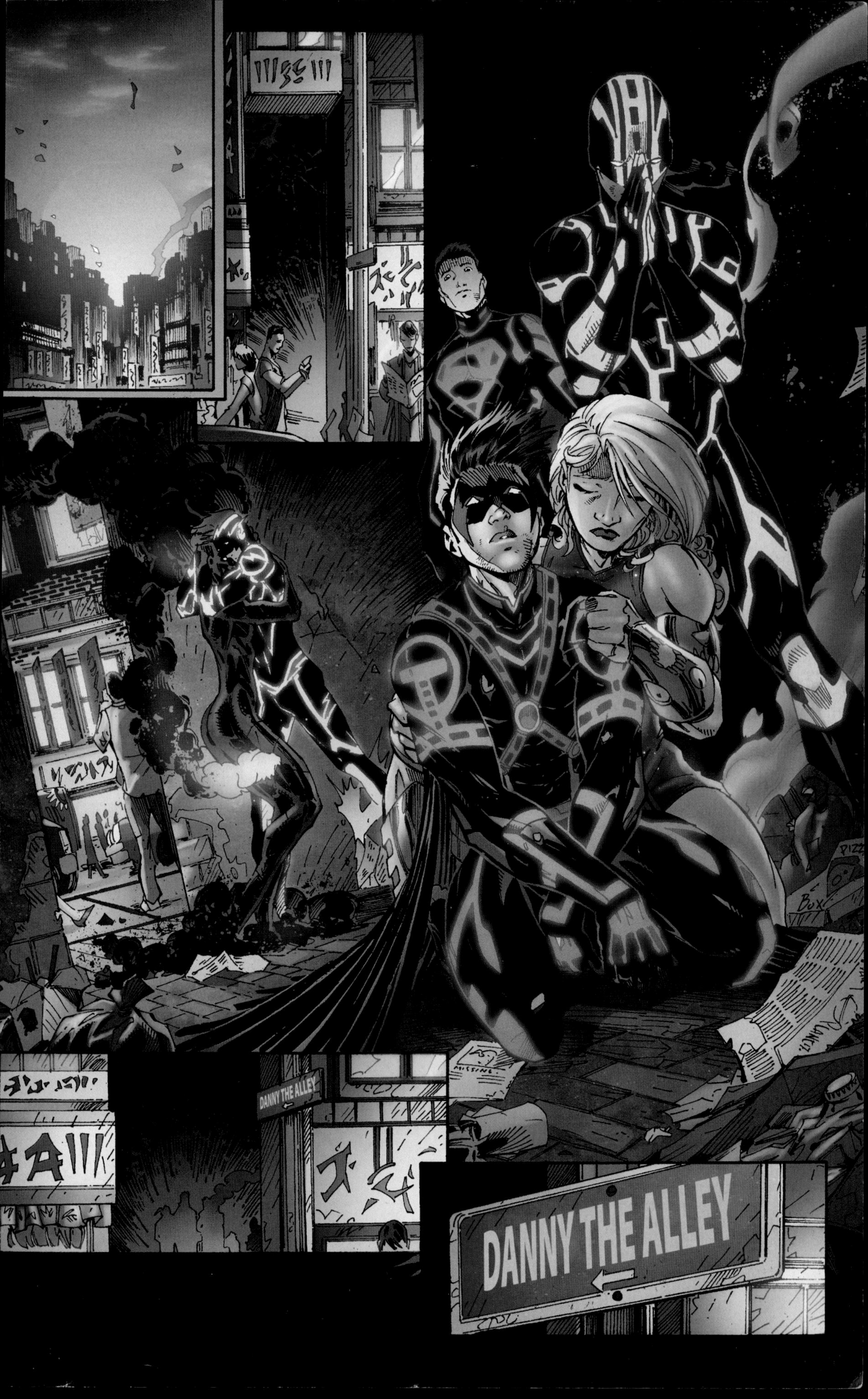
DANNY THE ALLEY
DANNY THE ALLEY

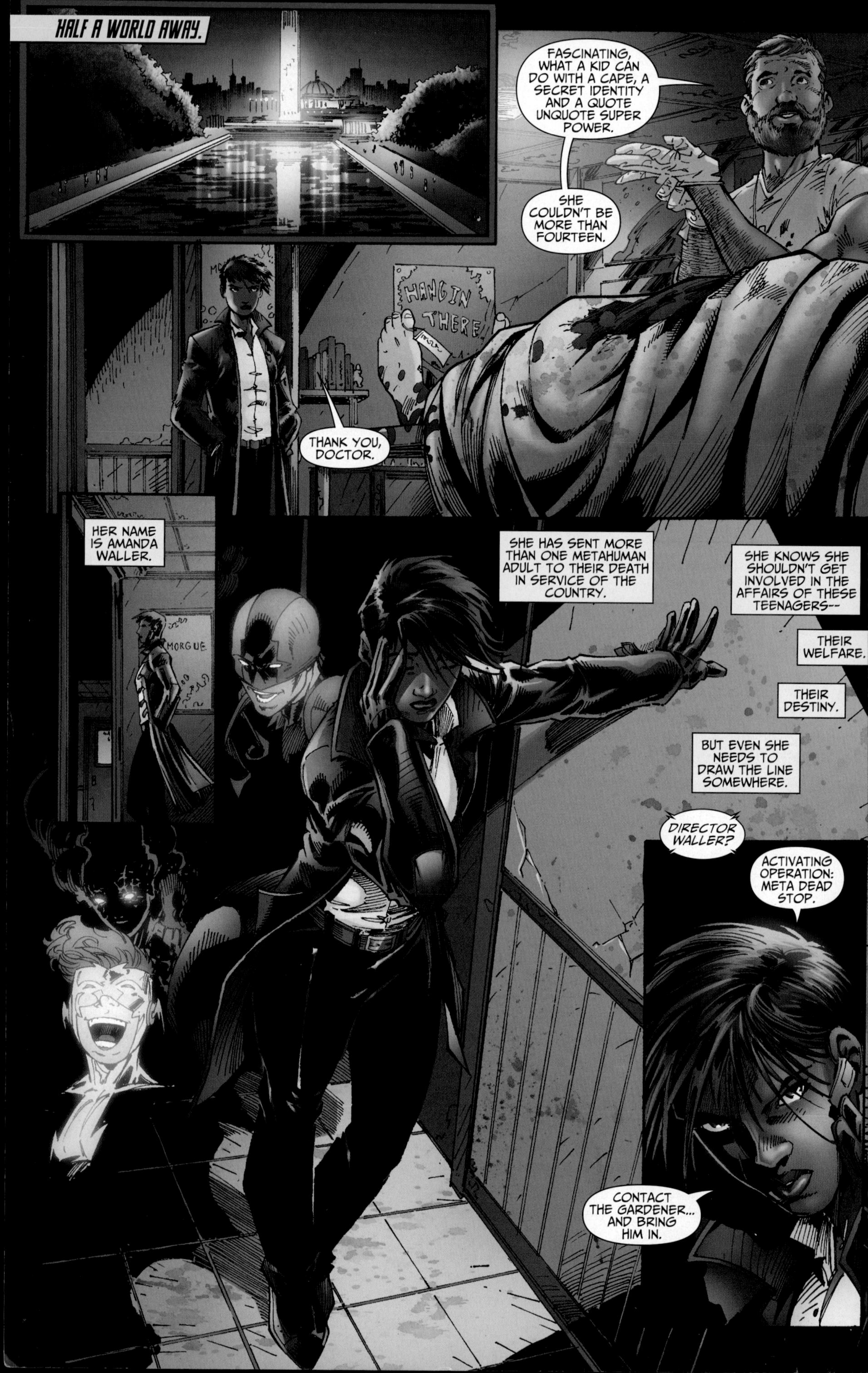
HALF A WORLD AWAY.
FASCINATING, WHAT A KID CAN DO WITH A CAPE, A SECRET IDENTITY AND A QUOTE UNQUOTE SUPER POWER.
SHE COULDN'T BE MORE THAN FOURTEEN.
HANG IN THERE
THANK YOU, DOCTOR.
HER NAME IS AMANDA WALLER.
MORGUE
SHE HAS SENT MORE THAN ONE METAHUMAN ADULT TO THEIR DEATH IN SERVICE OF THE COUNTRY.
SHE KNOWS SHE SHOULDN'T GET INVOLVED IN THE AFFAIRS OF THESE TEENAGERS--
THEIR WELFARE.
THEIR DESTINY.
BUT EVEN SHE NEEDS TO DRAW THE LINE SOMEWHERE.
DIRECTOR WALLER?
ACTIVATING OPERATION: META DEAD STOP.
CONTACT THE GARDENER... AND BRING HIM IN.

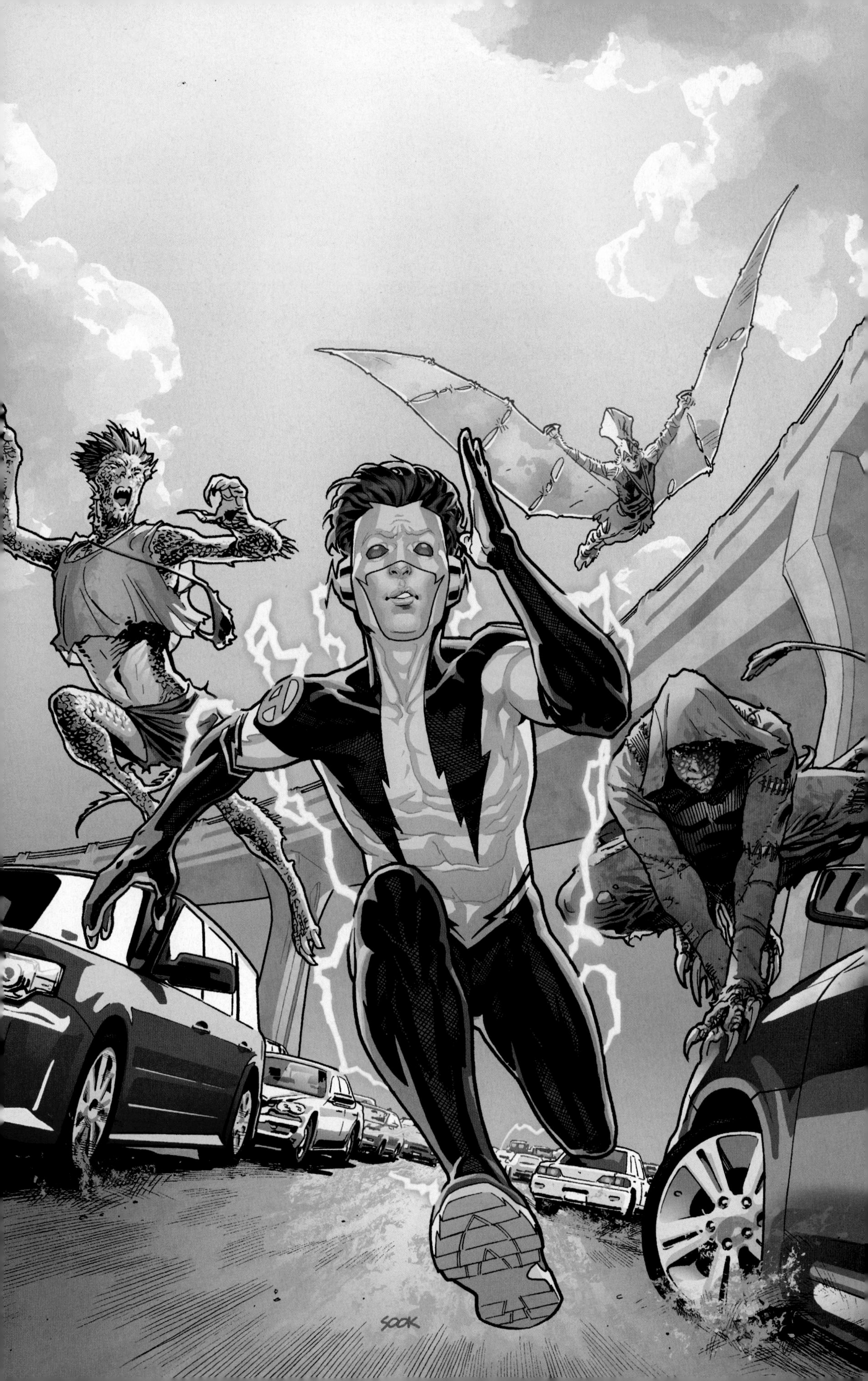
SOOK

WHEN DINOSAURS WALKED THE EARTH

FABIAN NICIEZA
writer

JORGE JIMÉNEZ
artist

cover art by
RYAN SOOK

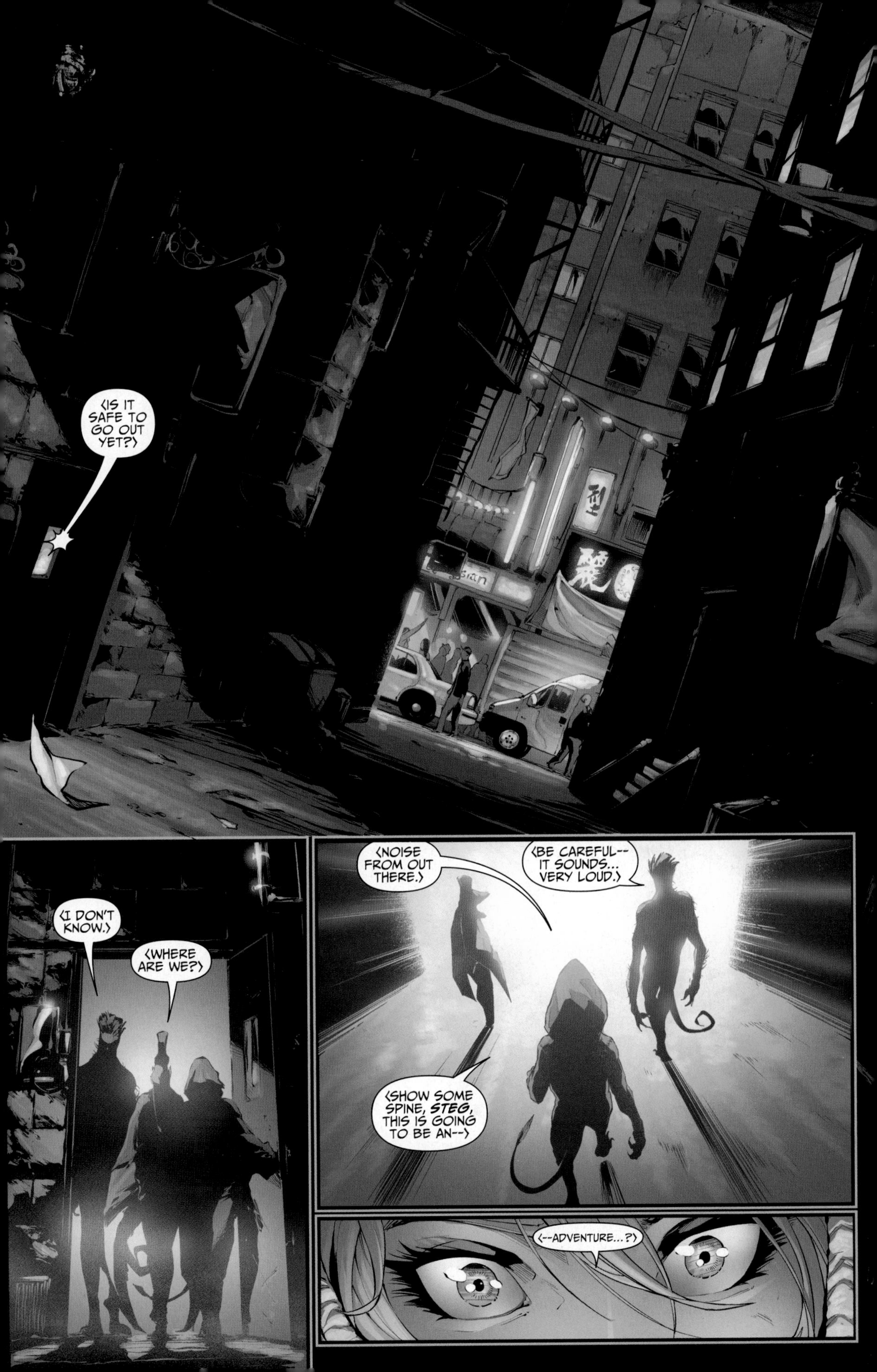
<IS IT SAFE TO GO OUT YET?>
<I DON'T KNOW.>
<WHERE ARE WE?>
<NOISE FROM OUT THERE.>
<BE CAREFUL-- IT SOUNDS... VERY LOUD.>
<SHOW SOME SPINE, STEG, THIS IS GOING TO BE AN-->
<--ADVENTURE...?>

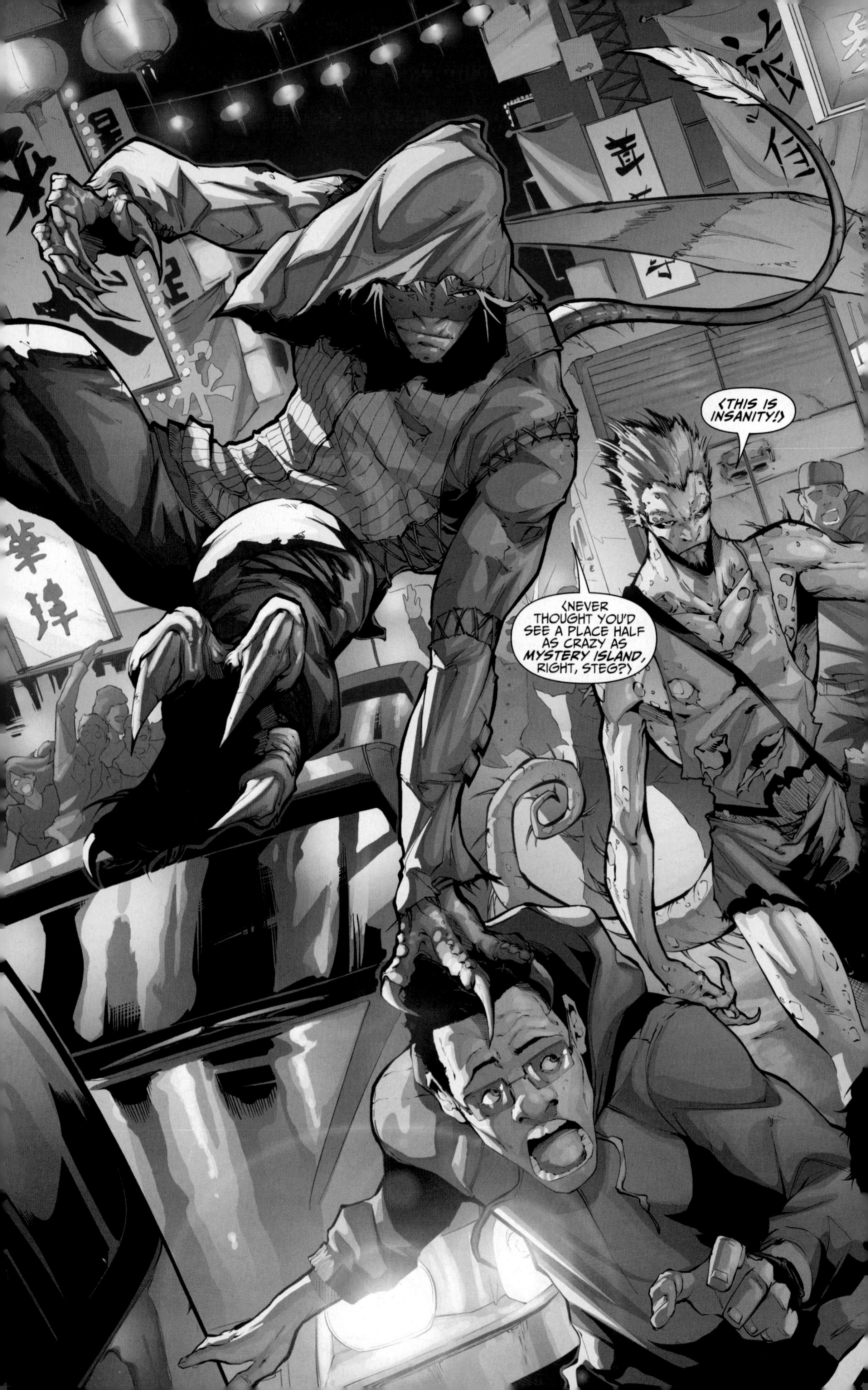

‹THIS IS INSANITY!›
‹NEVER THOUGHT YOU'D SEE A PLACE HALF AS CRAZY AS MYSTERY ISLAND, RIGHT, STEG?›

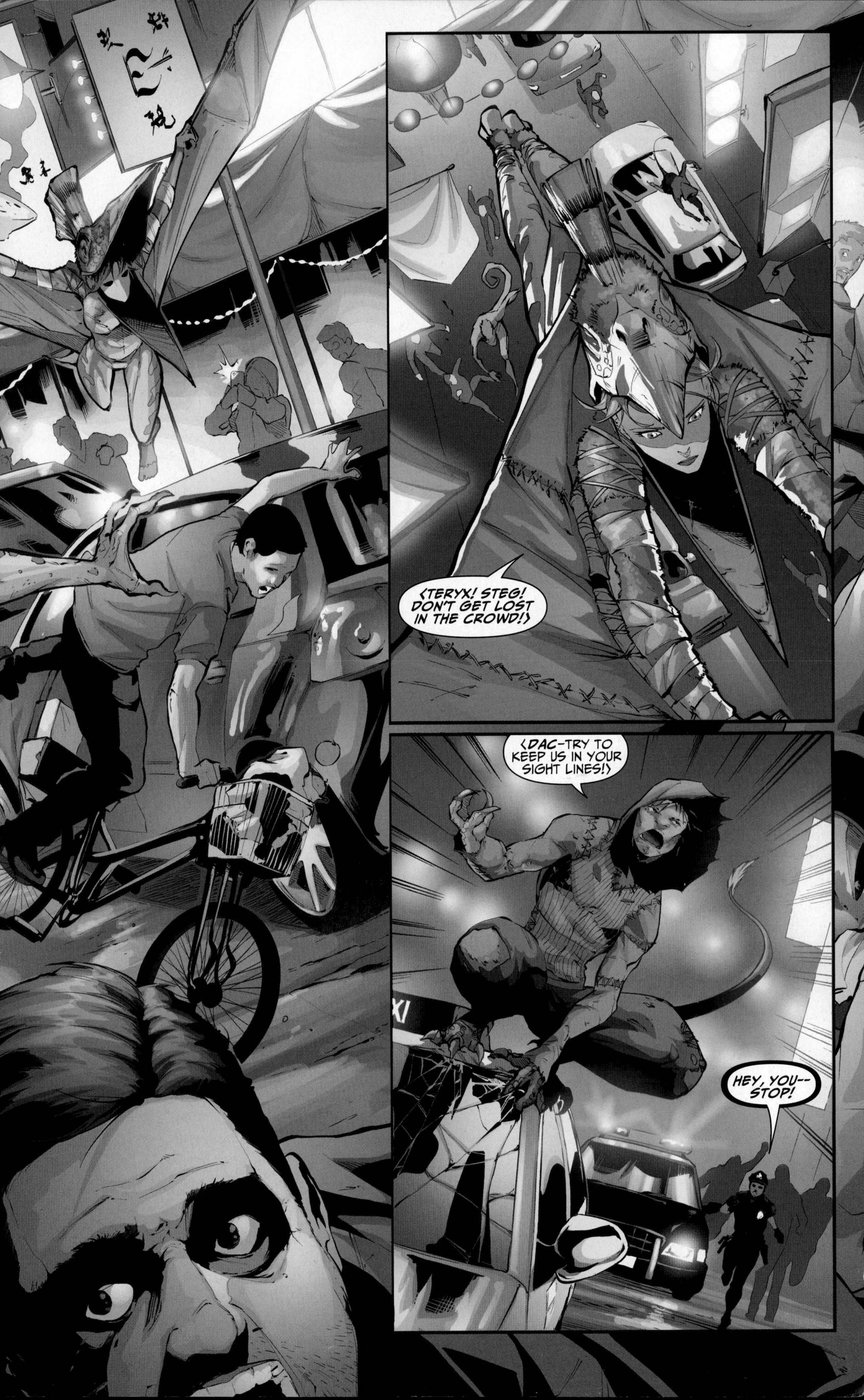
⟨TERYX! STEG! DON'T GET LOST IN THE CROWD!⟩
⟨DAC-TRY TO KEEP US IN YOUR SIGHT LINES!⟩
HEY, YOU-- STOP!

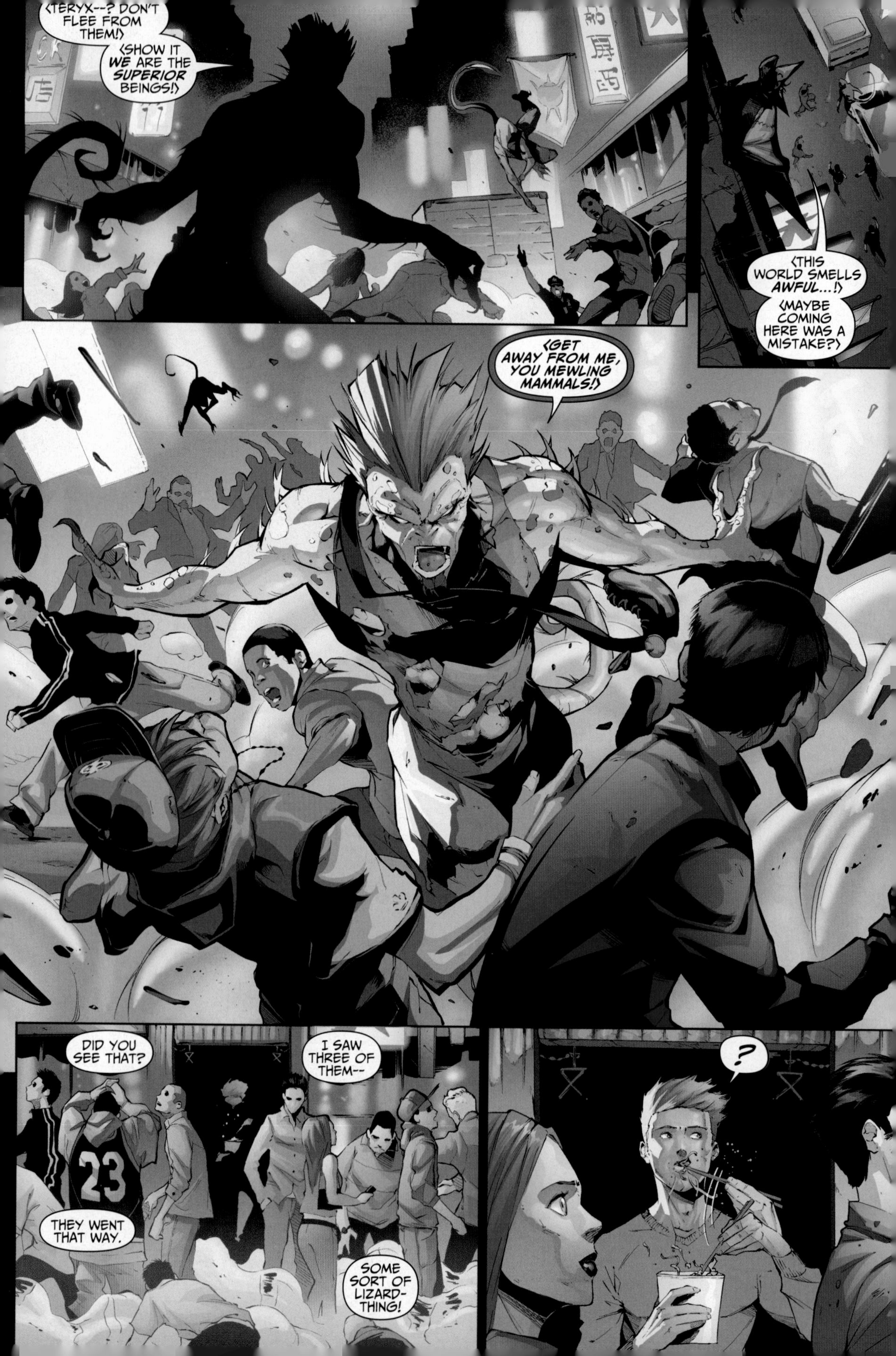
<TERYX--? DON'T FLEE FROM THEM!>
<SHOW IT WE ARE THE SUPERIOR BEINGS!>
<THIS WORLD SMELLS AWFUL...!>
<MAYBE COMING HERE WAS A MISTAKE?>
<GET AWAY FROM ME, YOU MEWLING MAMMALS!>
DID YOU SEE THAT?
I SAW THREE OF THEM--
23
THEY WENT THAT WAY.
SOME SORT OF LIZARD-THING!
?

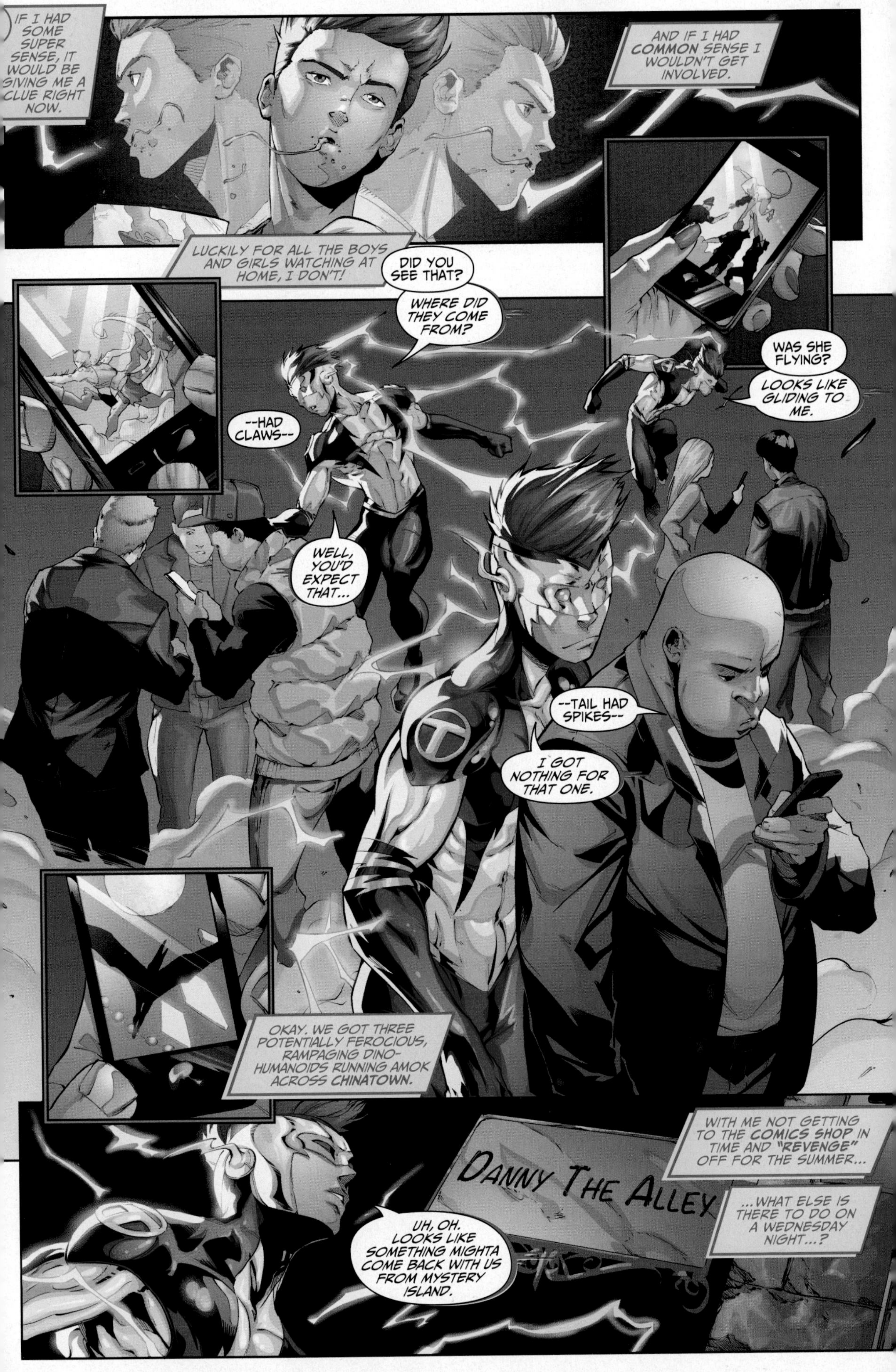
IF I HAD SOME SUPER SENSE, IT WOULD BE GIVING ME A CLUE RIGHT NOW.
AND IF I HAD COMMON SENSE I WOULDN'T GET INVOLVED.
LUCKILY FOR ALL THE BOYS AND GIRLS WATCHING AT HOME, I DON'T!
DID YOU SEE THAT?
WHERE DID THEY COME FROM?
WAS SHE FLYING?
LOOKS LIKE GLIDING TO ME.
--HAD CLAWS--
WELL, YOU'D EXPECT THAT...
--TAIL HAD SPIKES--
I GOT NOTHING FOR THAT ONE.
OKAY. WE GOT THREE POTENTIALLY FEROCIOUS, RAMPAGING DINO-HUMANOIDS RUNNING AMOK ACROSS CHINATOWN.
WITH ME NOT GETTING TO THE COMICS SHOP IN TIME AND "REVENGE" OFF FOR THE SUMMER...
DANNY THE ALLEY
...WHAT ELSE IS THERE TO DO ON A WEDNESDAY NIGHT...?
UH, OH. LOOKS LIKE SOMETHING MIGHTA COME BACK WITH US FROM MYSTERY ISLAND.

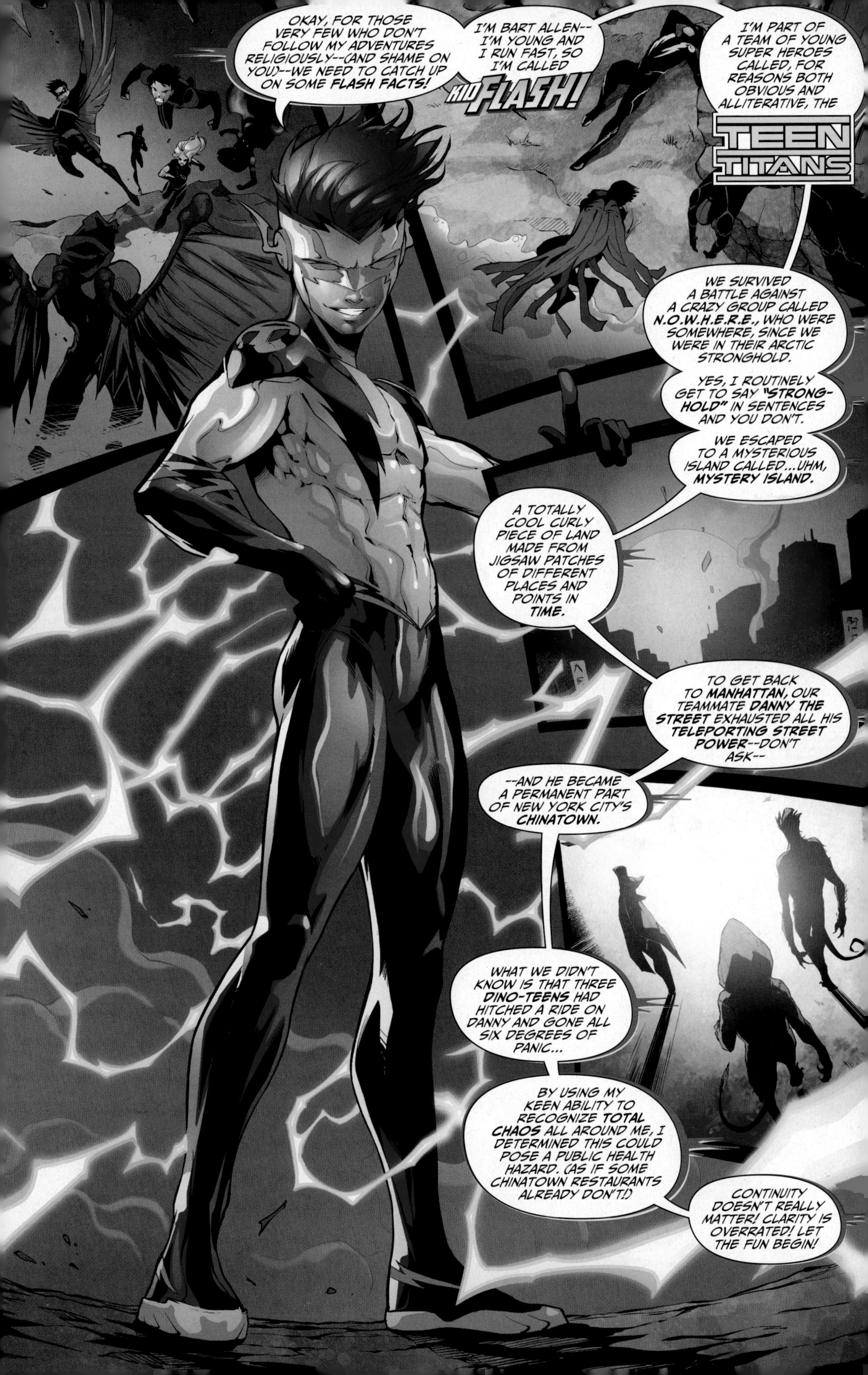
OKAY, FOR THOSE VERY FEW WHO DON'T FOLLOW MY ADVENTURES RELIGIOUSLY--(AND SHAME ON YOU)--WE NEED TO CATCH UP ON SOME FLASH FACTS!
I'M BART ALLEN-- I'M YOUNG AND I RUN FAST, SO I'M CALLED
KID FLASH!
I'M PART OF A TEAM OF YOUNG SUPER HEROES CALLED, FOR REASONS BOTH OBVIOUS AND ALLITERATIVE, THE
TEEN TITANS
WE SURVIVED A BATTLE AGAINST A CRAZY GROUP CALLED N.O.W.H.E.R.E., WHO WERE SOMEWHERE, SINCE WE WERE IN THEIR ARCTIC STRONGHOLD.
YES, I ROUTINELY GET TO SAY "STRONG-HOLD" IN SENTENCES AND YOU DON'T.
WE ESCAPED TO A MYSTERIOUS ISLAND CALLED...UHM, MYSTERY ISLAND.
A TOTALLY COOL CURLY PIECE OF LAND MADE FROM JIGSAW PATCHES OF DIFFERENT PLACES AND POINTS IN TIME.
TO GET BACK TO MANHATTAN, OUR TEAMMATE DANNY THE STREET EXHAUSTED ALL HIS TELEPORTING STREET POWER--DON'T ASK--
--AND HE BECAME A PERMANENT PART OF NEW YORK CITY'S CHINATOWN.
WHAT WE DIDN'T KNOW IS THAT THREE DINO-TEENS HAD HITCHED A RIDE ON DANNY AND GONE ALL SIX DEGREES OF PANIC...
BY USING MY KEEN ABILITY TO RECOGNIZE TOTAL CHAOS ALL AROUND ME, I DETERMINED THIS COULD POSE A PUBLIC HEALTH HAZARD. (AS IF SOME CHINATOWN RESTAURANTS ALREADY DON'T!)
CONTINUITY DOESN'T REALLY MATTER! CLARITY IS OVERRATED! LET THE FUN BEGIN!

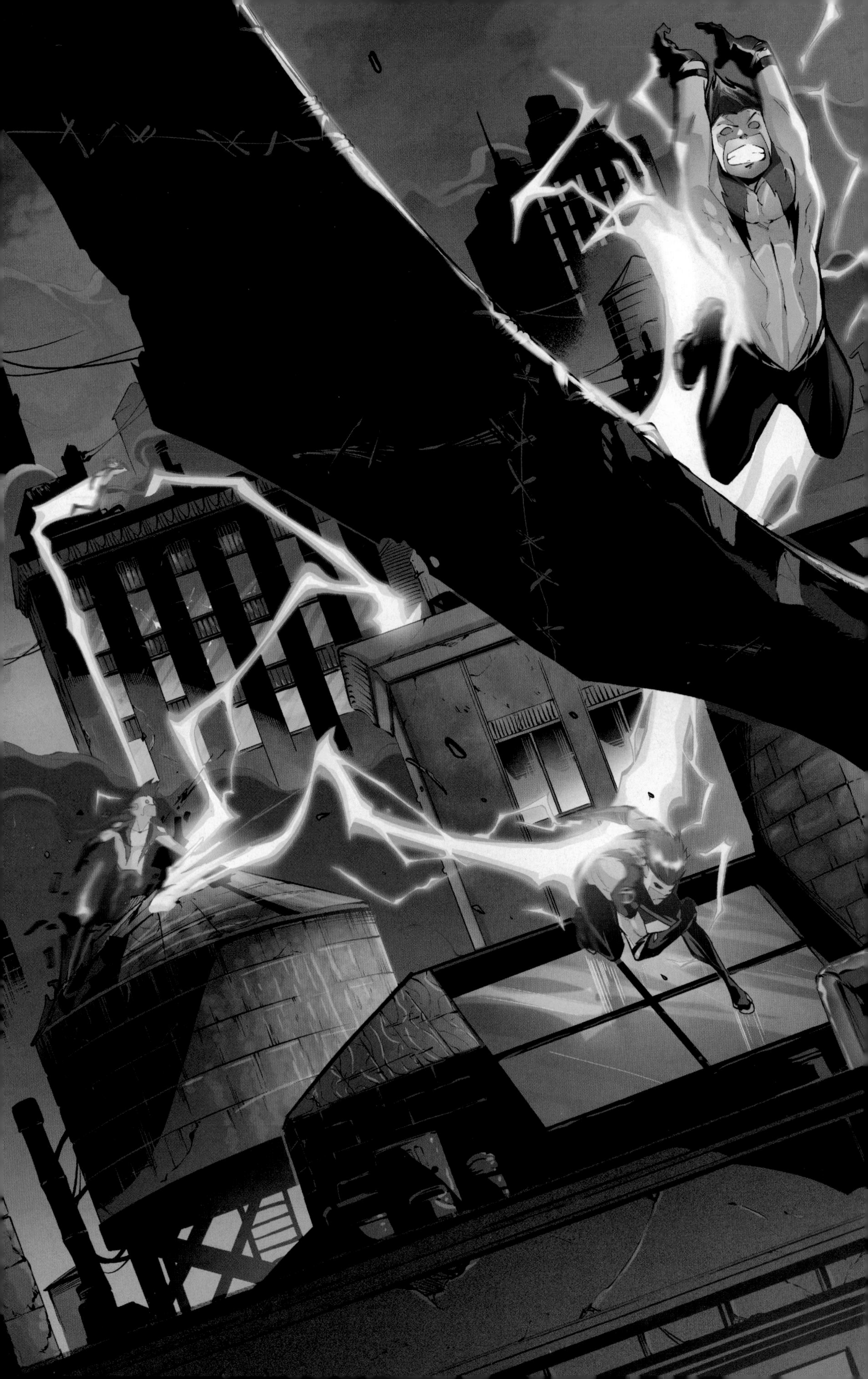

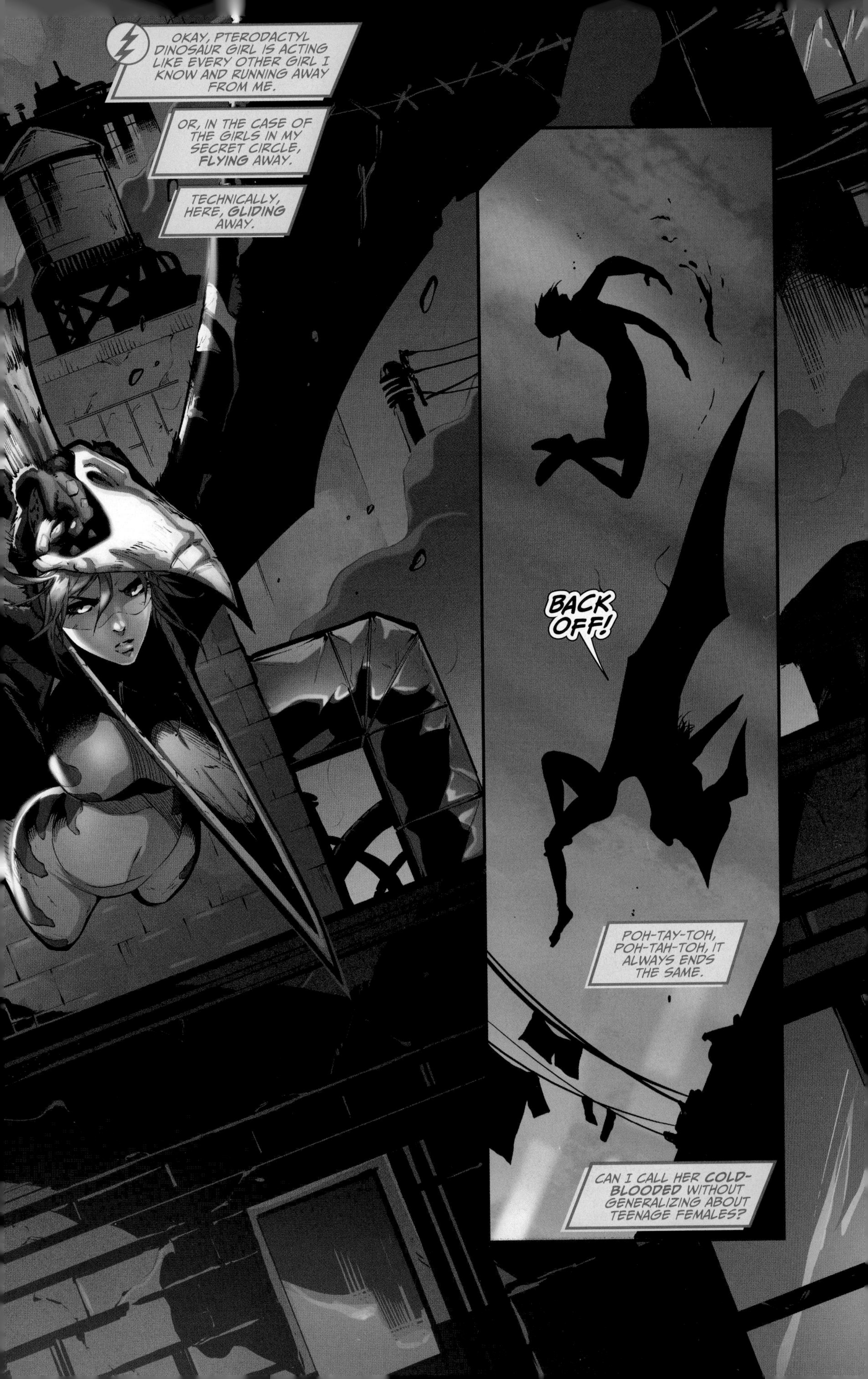
OKAY, PTERODACTYL DINOSAUR GIRL IS ACTING LIKE EVERY OTHER GIRL I KNOW AND RUNNING AWAY FROM ME.
OR, IN THE CASE OF THE GIRLS IN MY SECRET CIRCLE, FLYING AWAY.
TECHNICALLY, HERE, GLIDING AWAY.
BACK OFF!
POH-TAY-TOH, POH-TAH-TOH, IT ALWAYS ENDS THE SAME.
CAN I CALL HER COLD-BLOODED WITHOUT GENERALIZING ABOUT TEENAGE FEMALES?

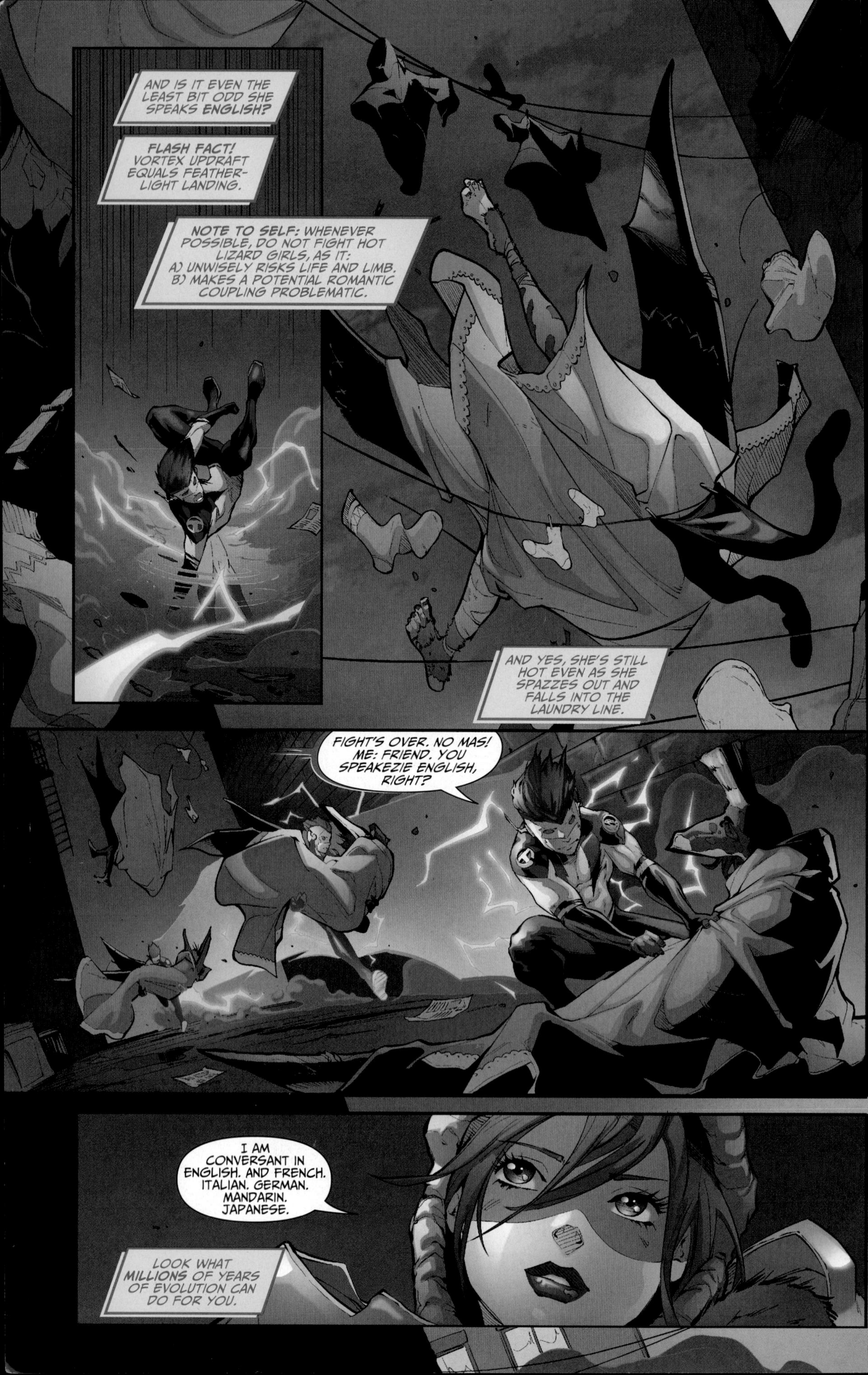
AND IS IT EVEN THE LEAST BIT ODD SHE SPEAKS ENGLISH?
FLASH FACT! VORTEX UPDRAFT EQUALS FEATHER-LIGHT LANDING.
NOTE TO SELF: WHENEVER POSSIBLE, DO NOT FIGHT HOT LIZARD GIRLS, AS IT: A) UNWISELY RISKS LIFE AND LIMB. B) MAKES A POTENTIAL ROMANTIC COUPLING PROBLEMATIC.
AND YES, SHE'S STILL HOT EVEN AS SHE SPAZZES OUT AND FALLS INTO THE LAUNDRY LINE.
FIGHT'S OVER. NO MAS! ME: FRIEND. YOU SPEAKEZIE ENGLISH, RIGHT?
I AM CONVERSANT IN ENGLISH. AND FRENCH. ITALIAN. GERMAN. MANDARIN. JAPANESE.
LOOK WHAT MILLIONS OF YEARS OF EVOLUTION CAN DO FOR YOU.

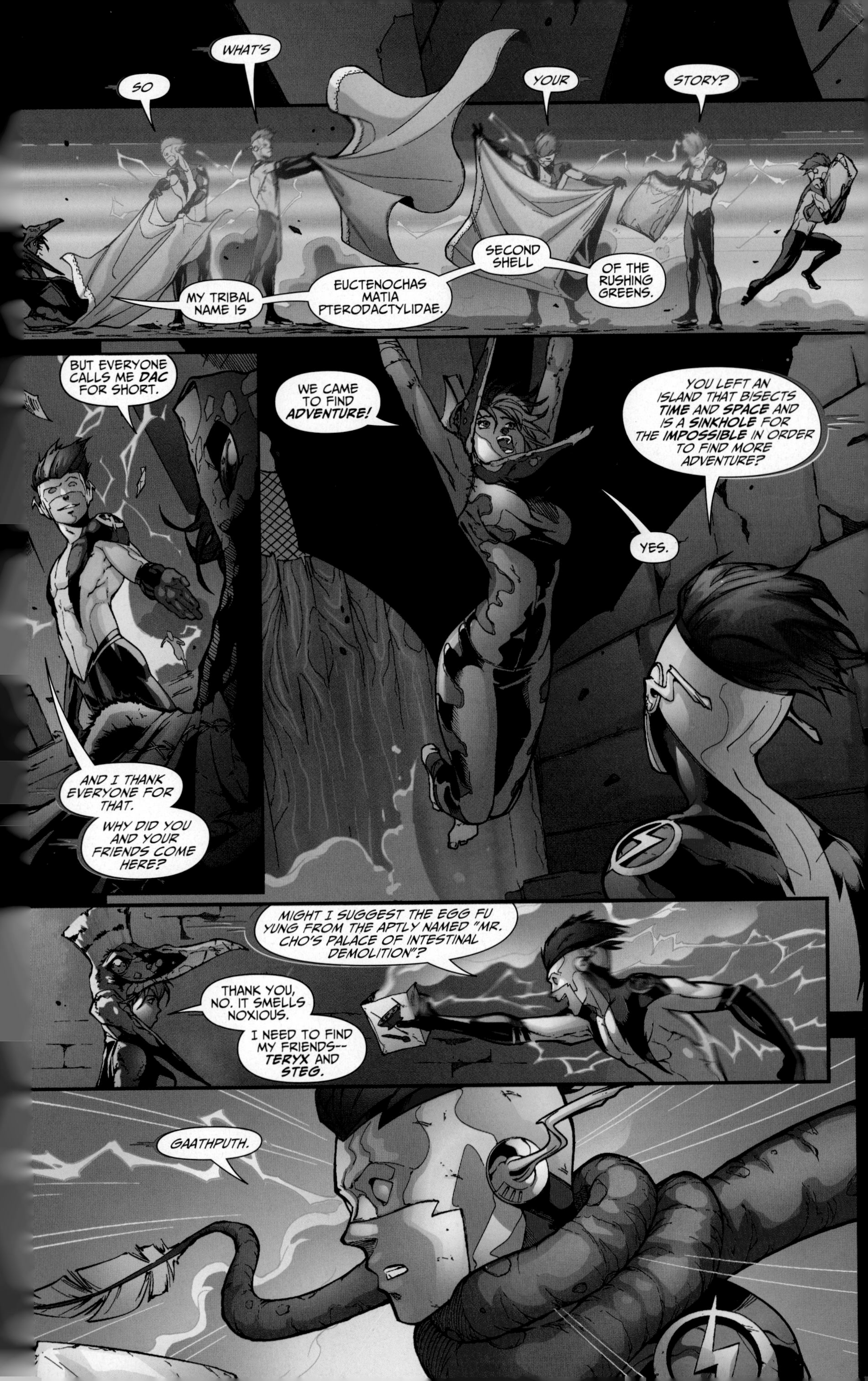
SO
WHAT'S
YOUR
STORY?
MY TRIBAL NAME IS
EUCTENOCHAS MATIA PTERODACTYLIDAE.
SECOND SHELL
OF THE RUSHING GREENS.
BUT EVERYONE CALLS ME DAC FOR SHORT.
AND I THANK EVERYONE FOR THAT.
WHY DID YOU AND YOUR FRIENDS COME HERE?
WE CAME TO FIND ADVENTURE!
YOU LEFT AN ISLAND THAT BISECTS TIME AND SPACE AND IS A SINKHOLE FOR THE IMPOSSIBLE IN ORDER TO FIND MORE ADVENTURE?
YES.
MIGHT I SUGGEST THE EGG FU YUNG FROM THE APTLY NAMED "MR. CHO'S PALACE OF INTESTINAL DEMOLITION"?
THANK YOU, NO. IT SMELLS NOXIOUS.
I NEED TO FIND MY FRIENDS-- TERYX AND STEG.
GAATHPUTH.

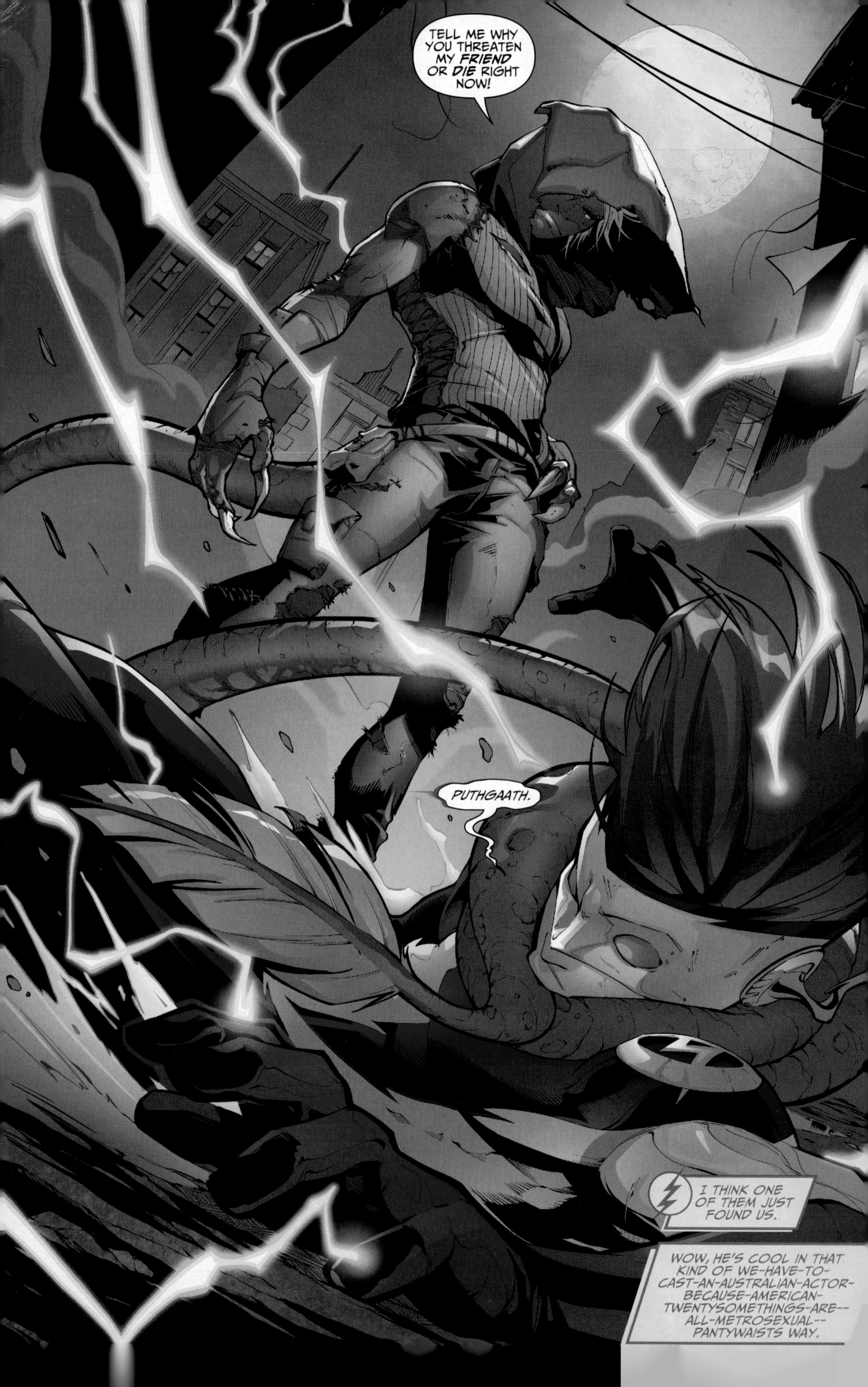

TELL ME WHY YOU THREATEN MY *FRIEND* OR *DIE* RIGHT NOW!
PUTHGAATH.
I THINK ONE OF THEM JUST FOUND US.
WOW, HE'S COOL IN THAT KIND OF WE-HAVE-TO-CAST-AN-AUSTRALIAN-ACTOR-BECAUSE-AMERICAN-TWENTYSOMETHINGS-ARE--ALL-METROSEXUAL--PANTYWAISTS WAY.

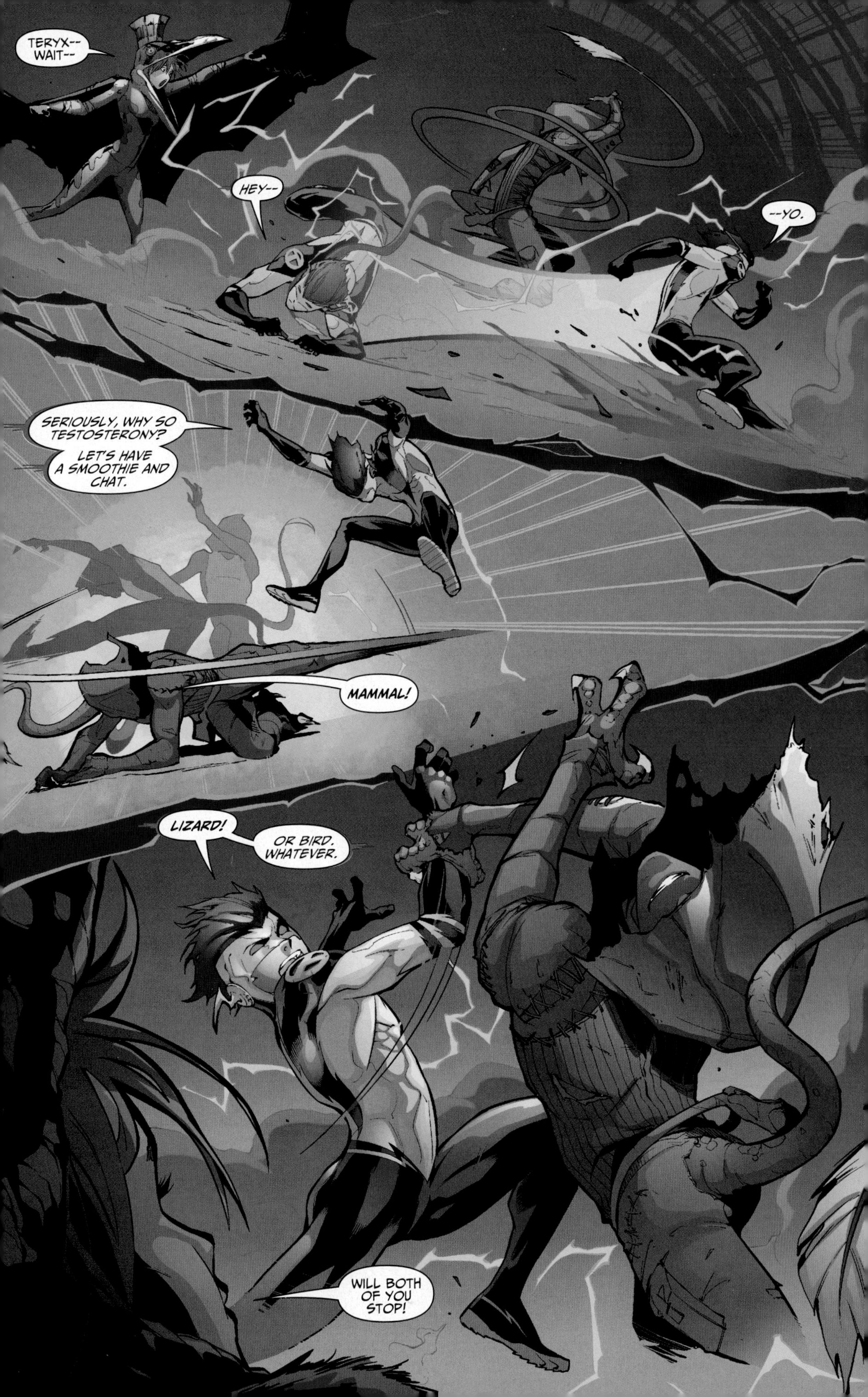
TERYX--
WAIT--
HEY--
--YO.
SERIOUSLY, WHY SO TESTOSTERONY?
LET'S HAVE A SMOOTHIE AND CHAT.
MAMMAL!
LIZARD!
OR BIRD. WHATEVER.
WILL BOTH OF YOU STOP!

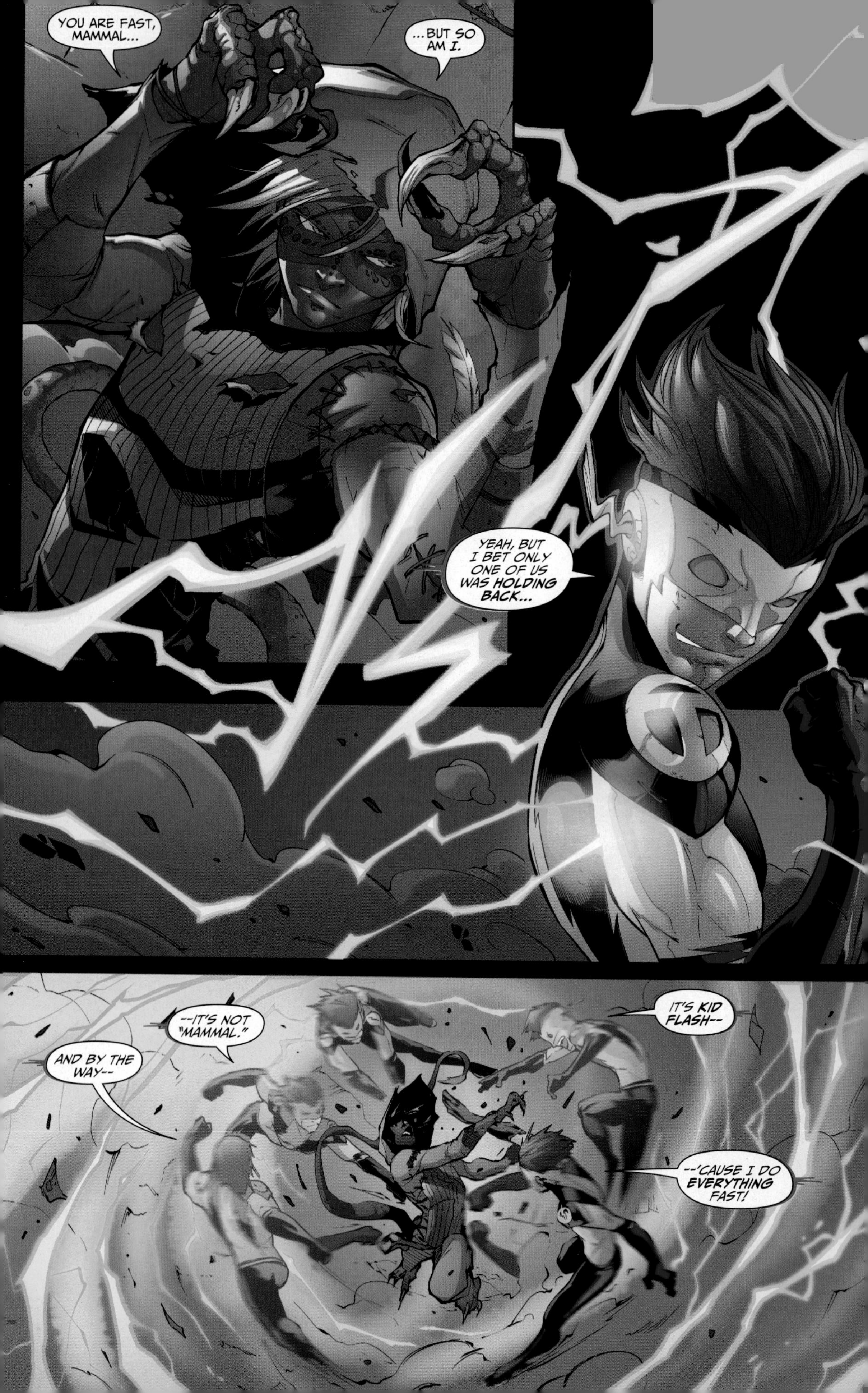
YOU ARE FAST, MAMMAL...
...BUT SO AM I.
YEAH, BUT I BET ONLY ONE OF US WAS HOLDING BACK...
AND BY THE WAY--
--IT'S NOT "MAMMAL."
IT'S KID FLASH--
--'CAUSE I DO EVERYTHING FAST!

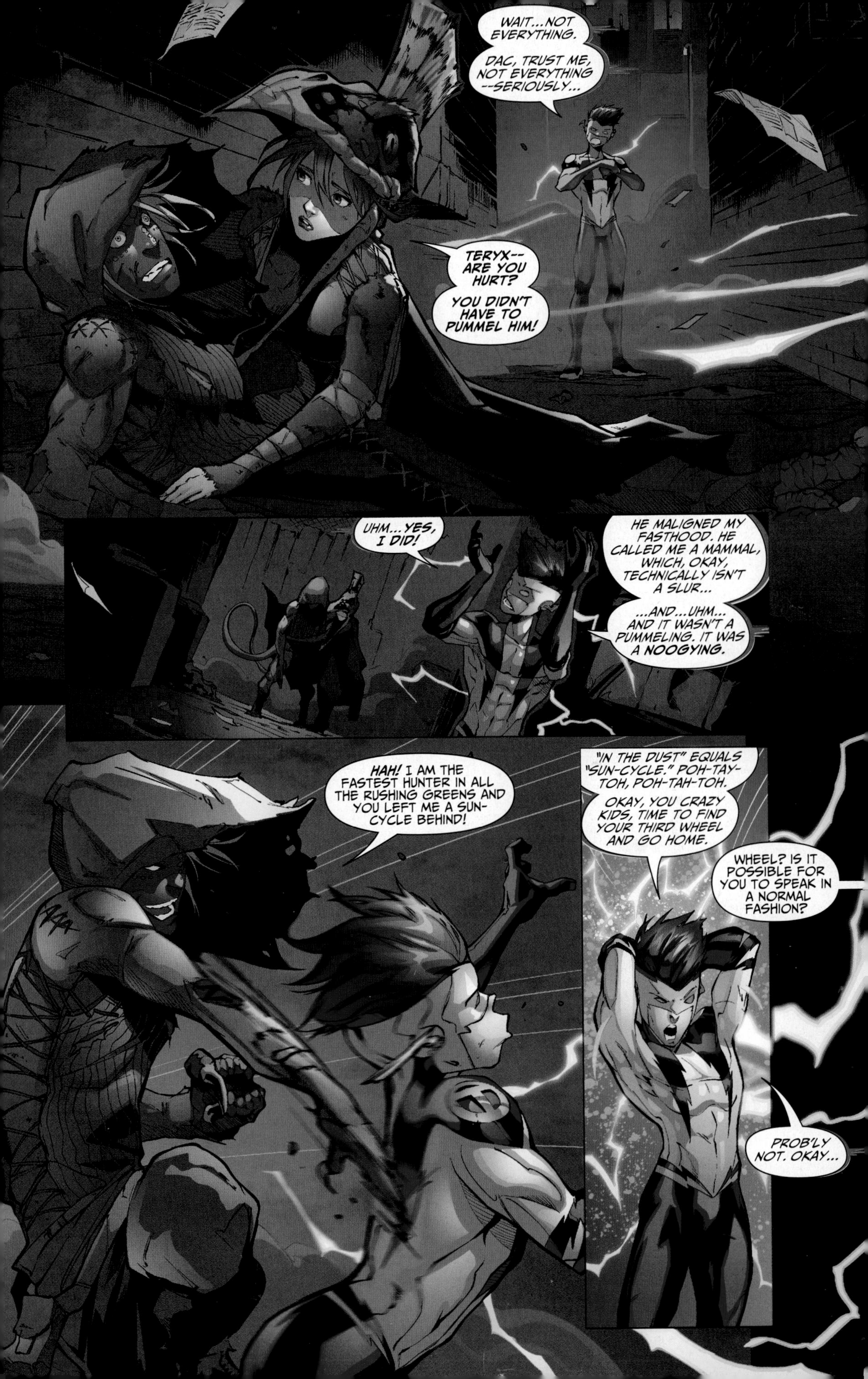
WAIT...NOT EVERYTHING.
DAC, TRUST ME, NOT EVERYTHING --SERIOUSLY...
TERYX-- ARE YOU HURT?
YOU DIDN'T HAVE TO PUMMEL HIM!
UHM...YES, I DID!
HE MALIGNED MY FASTHOOD. HE CALLED ME A MAMMAL, WHICH, OKAY, TECHNICALLY ISN'T A SLUR...
...AND...UHM... AND IT WASN'T A PUMMELING. IT WAS A NOOGYING.
HAH! I AM THE FASTEST HUNTER IN ALL THE RUSHING GREENS AND YOU LEFT ME A SUN-CYCLE BEHIND!
"IN THE DUST" EQUALS "SUN-CYCLE." POH-TAY-TOH, POH-TAH-TOH.
OKAY, YOU CRAZY KIDS, TIME TO FIND YOUR THIRD WHEEL AND GO HOME.
WHEEL? IS IT POSSIBLE FOR YOU TO SPEAK IN A NORMAL FASHION?
PROB'LY NOT. OKAY...

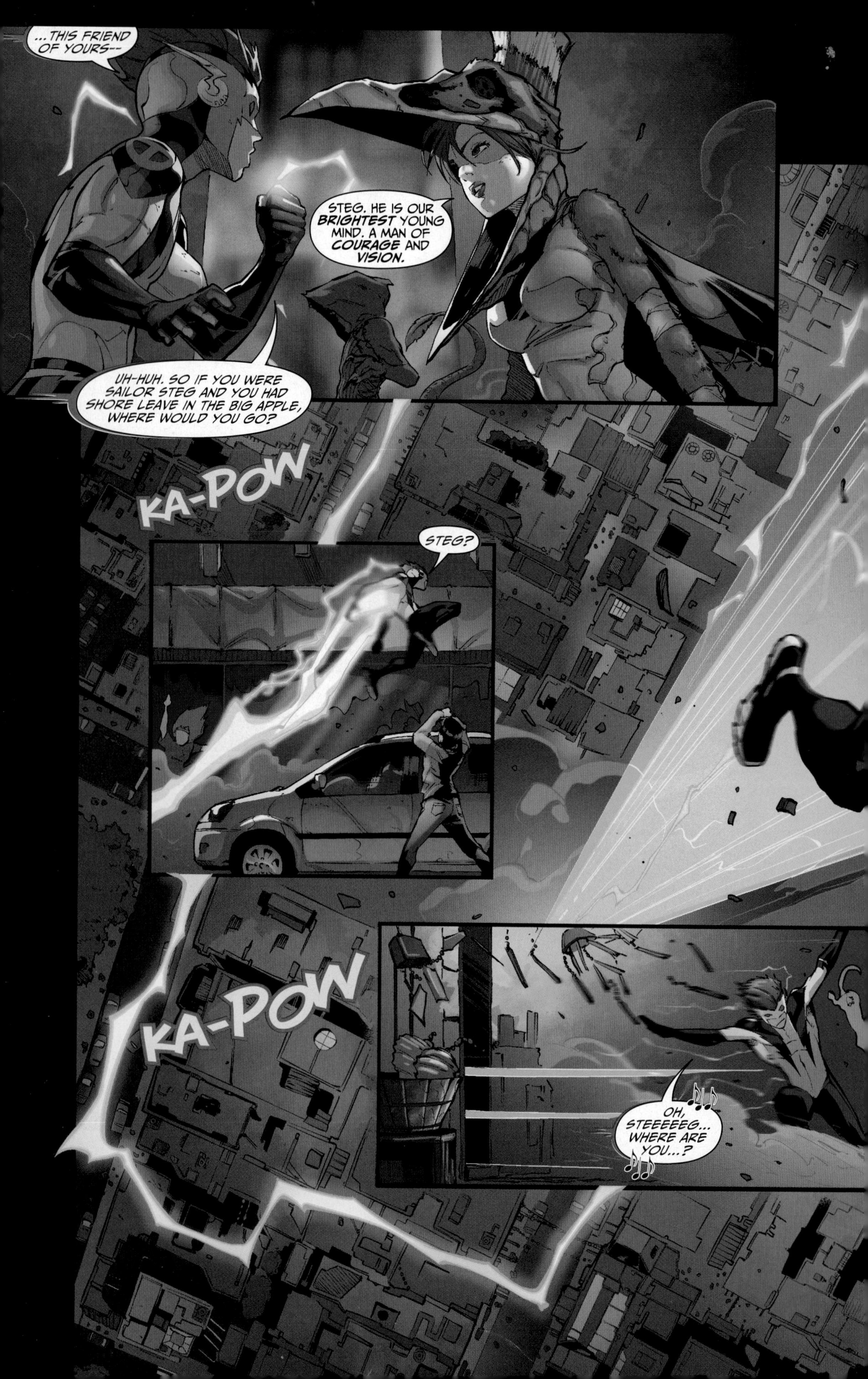
...THIS FRIEND OF YOURS--
STEG. HE IS OUR BRIGHTEST YOUNG MIND. A MAN OF COURAGE AND VISION.
UH-HUH. SO IF YOU WERE SAILOR STEG AND YOU HAD SHORE LEAVE IN THE BIG APPLE, WHERE WOULD YOU GO?
KA-POW
STEG?
KA-POW
OH, STEEEEEG... WHERE ARE YOU...?

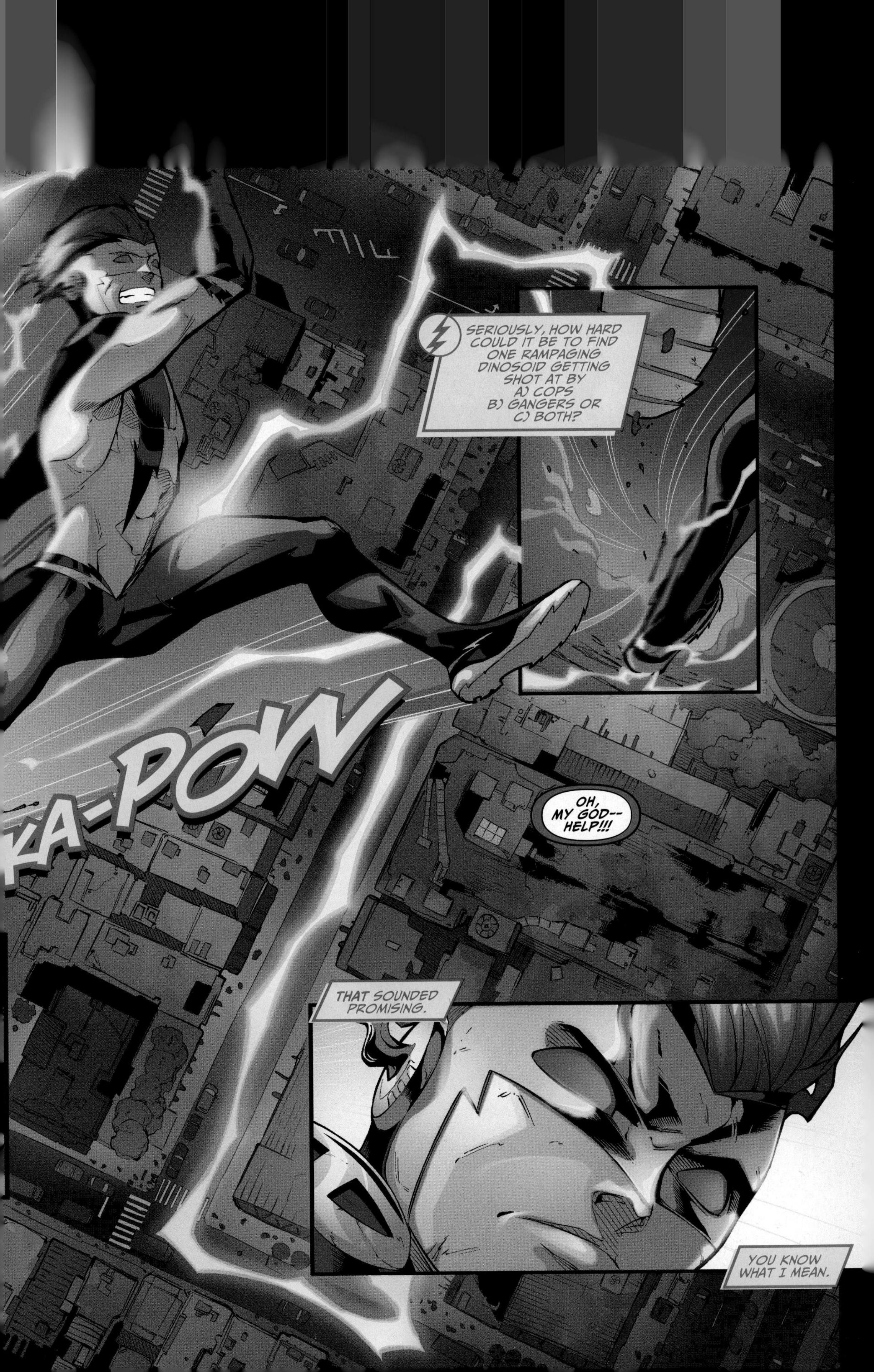
SERIOUSLY, HOW HARD COULD IT BE TO FIND ONE RAMPAGING DINOSOID GETTING SHOT AT BY
A) COPS
B) GANGERS OR
C) BOTH?
KA-POW
OH, MY GOD-- HELP!!!
THAT SOUNDED PROMISING.
YOU KNOW WHAT I MEAN.

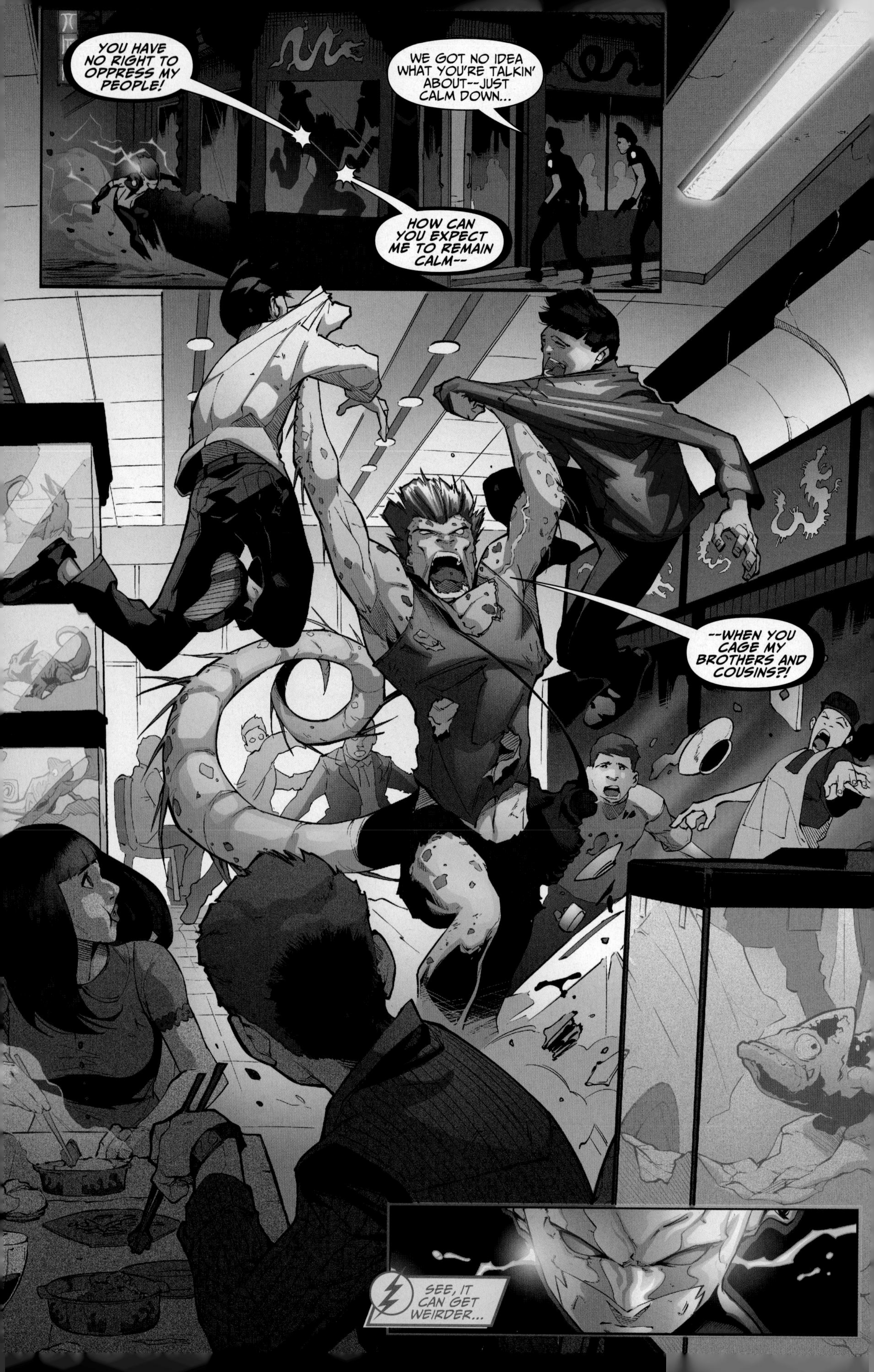
YOU HAVE NO RIGHT TO OPPRESS MY PEOPLE!
WE GOT NO IDEA WHAT YOU'RE TALKIN' ABOUT--JUST CALM DOWN...
HOW CAN YOU EXPECT ME TO REMAIN CALM--
--WHEN YOU CAGE MY BROTHERS AND COUSINS?!
SEE, IT CAN GET WEIRDER...

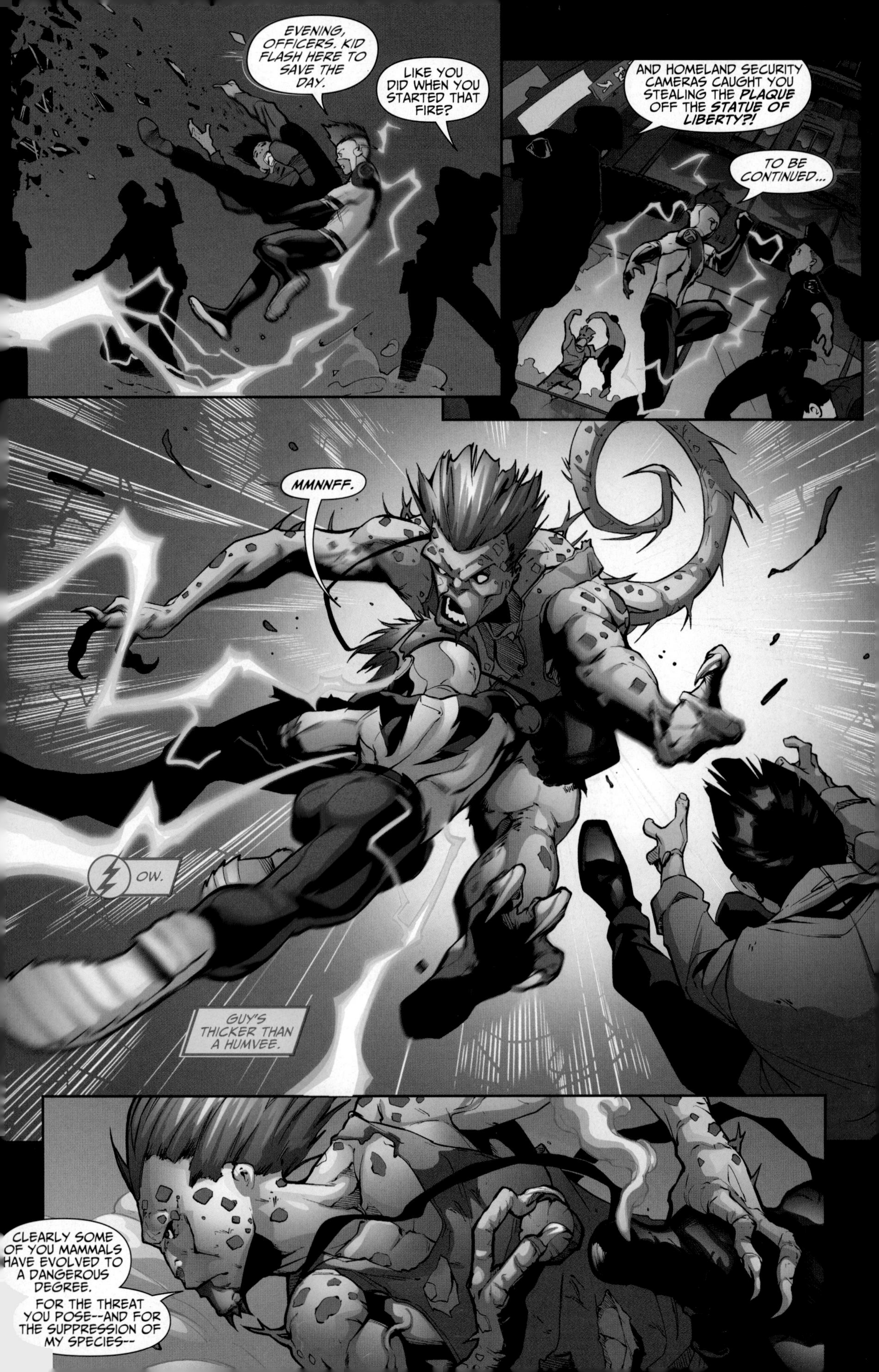
EVENING, OFFICERS. KID FLASH HERE TO SAVE THE DAY.
LIKE YOU DID WHEN YOU STARTED THAT FIRE?
AND HOMELAND SECURITY CAMERAS CAUGHT YOU STEALING THE PLAQUE OFF THE STATUE OF LIBERTY?!
TO BE CONTINUED...
MMNNFF.
OW.
GUY'S THICKER THAN A HUMVEE.
CLEARLY SOME OF YOU MAMMALS HAVE EVOLVED TO A DANGEROUS DEGREE.
FOR THE THREAT YOU POSE--AND FOR THE SUPPRESSION OF MY SPECIES--

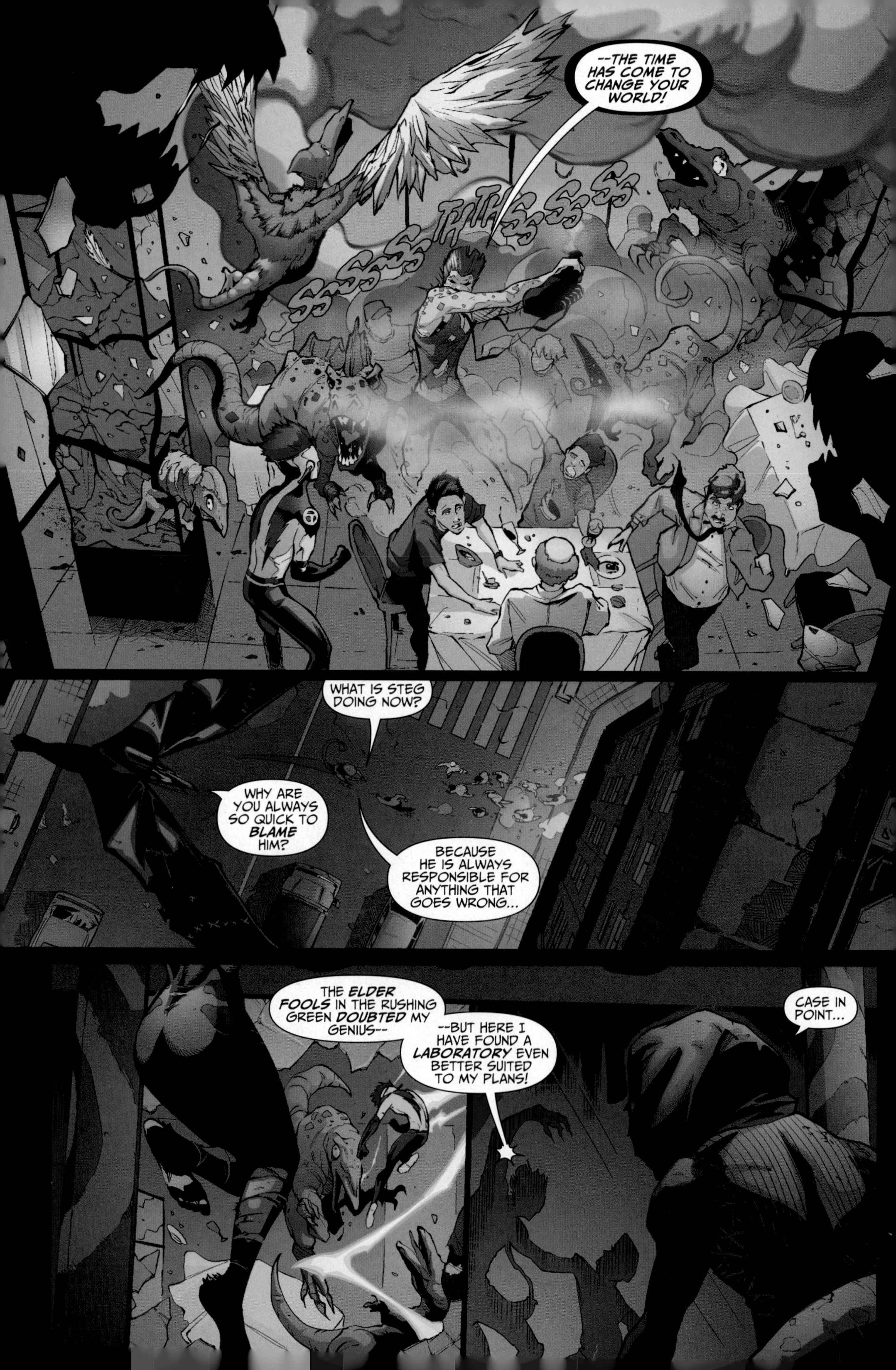
--THE TIME HAS COME TO CHANGE YOUR WORLD!
SSSSSTHTHSSSSS
WHAT IS STEG DOING NOW?
WHY ARE YOU ALWAYS SO QUICK TO BLAME HIM?
BECAUSE HE IS ALWAYS RESPONSIBLE FOR ANYTHING THAT GOES WRONG...
THE ELDER FOOLS IN THE RUSHING GREEN DOUBTED MY GENIUS--
--BUT HERE I HAVE FOUND A LABORATORY EVEN BETTER SUITED TO MY PLANS!
CASE IN POINT...

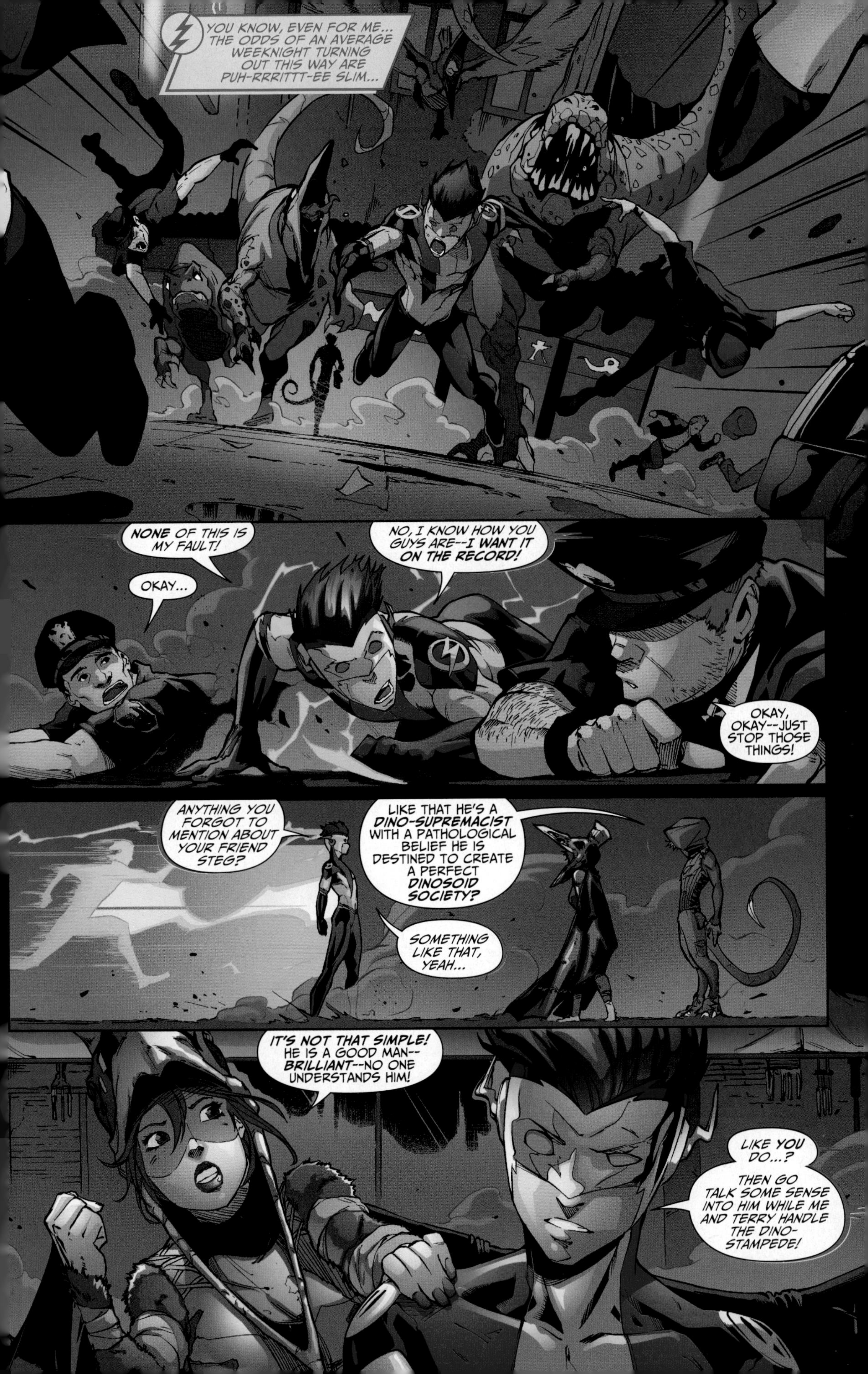
YOU KNOW, EVEN FOR ME... THE ODDS OF AN AVERAGE WEEKNIGHT TURNING OUT THIS WAY ARE PUH-RRRITTT-EE SLIM...
NONE OF THIS IS MY FAULT!
OKAY...
NO, I KNOW HOW YOU GUYS ARE--I WANT IT ON THE RECORD!
OKAY, OKAY--JUST STOP THOSE THINGS!
ANYTHING YOU FORGOT TO MENTION ABOUT YOUR FRIEND STEG?
LIKE THAT HE'S A DINO-SUPREMACIST WITH A PATHOLOGICAL BELIEF HE IS DESTINED TO CREATE A PERFECT DINOSOID SOCIETY?
SOMETHING LIKE THAT, YEAH...
IT'S NOT THAT SIMPLE! HE IS A GOOD MAN--BRILLIANT--NO ONE UNDERSTANDS HIM!
LIKE YOU DO...?
THEN GO TALK SOME SENSE INTO HIM WHILE ME AND TERRY HANDLE THE DINO-STAMPEDE!

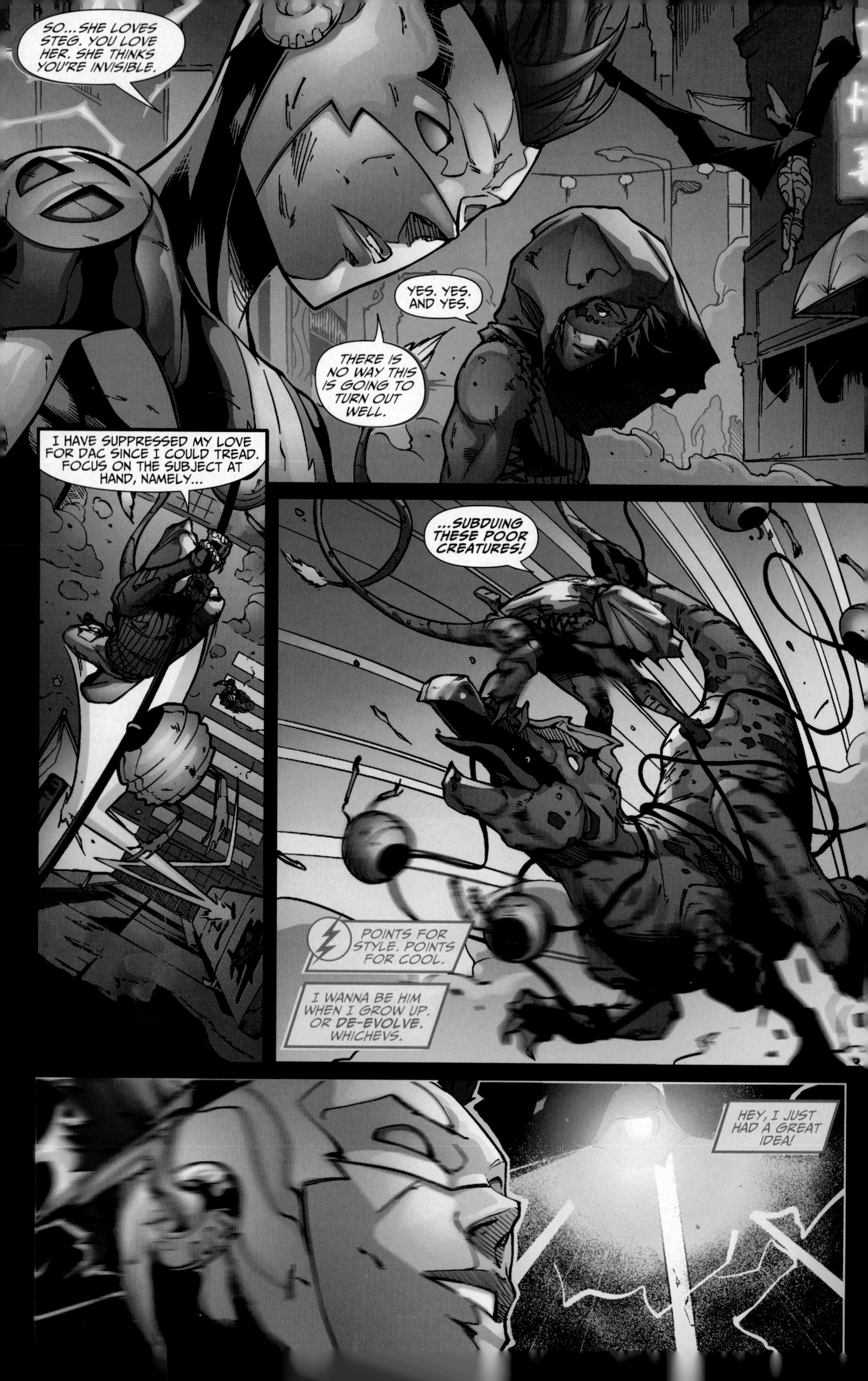
SO...SHE LOVES STEG. YOU LOVE HER. SHE THINKS YOU'RE INVISIBLE.
YES. YES. AND YES.
THERE IS NO WAY THIS IS GOING TO TURN OUT WELL.
I HAVE SUPPRESSED MY LOVE FOR DAC SINCE I COULD TREAD. FOCUS ON THE SUBJECT AT HAND, NAMELY...
...SUBDUING THESE POOR CREATURES!
POINTS FOR STYLE. POINTS FOR COOL.
I WANNA BE HIM WHEN I GROW UP. OR DE-EVOLVE. WHICHEVS.
HEY, I JUST HAD A GREAT IDEA!

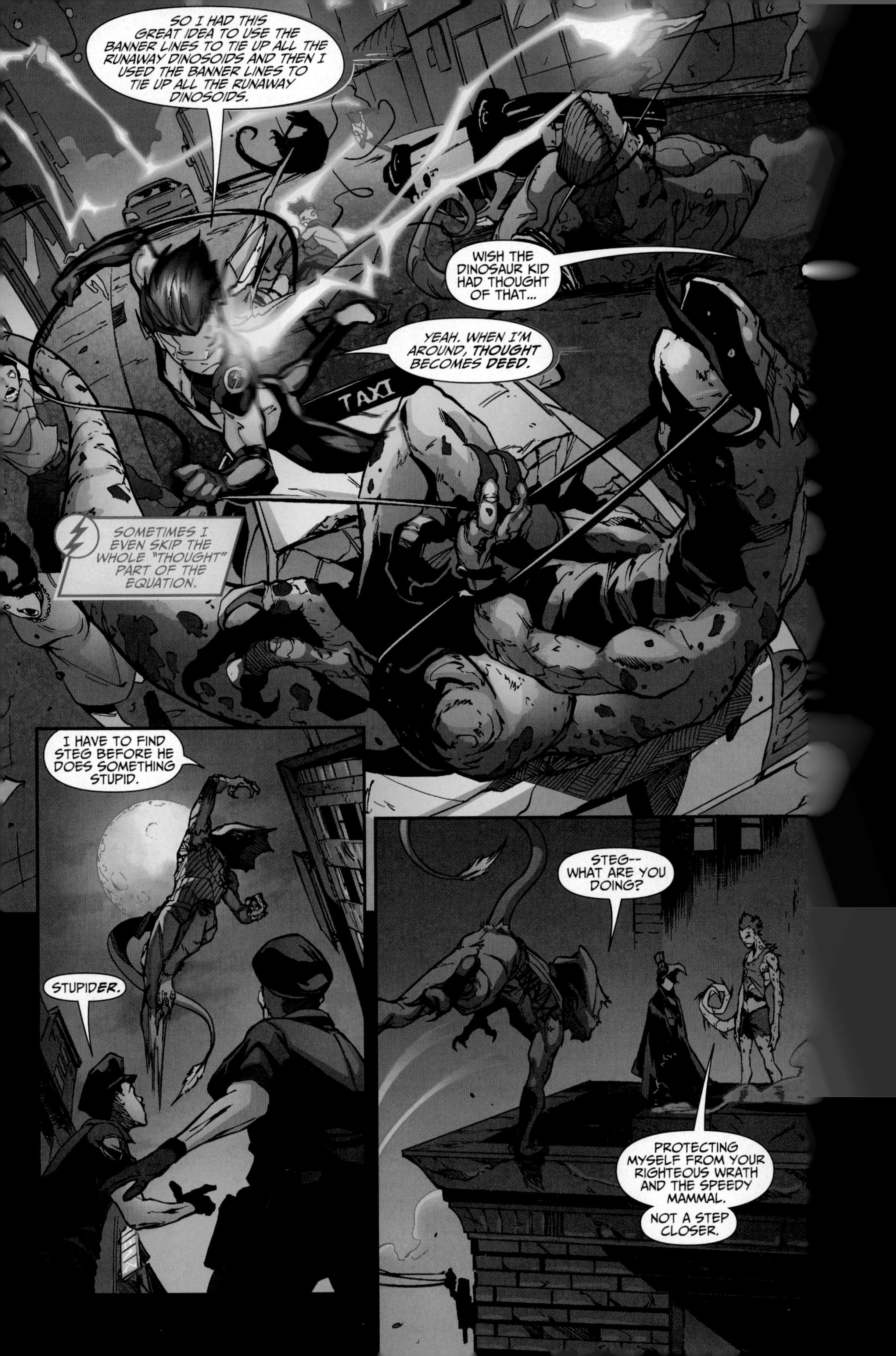
SO I HAD THIS GREAT IDEA TO USE THE BANNER LINES TO TIE UP ALL THE RUNAWAY DINOSOIDS AND THEN I USED THE BANNER LINES TO TIE UP ALL THE RUNAWAY DINOSOIDS.
WISH THE DINOSAUR KID HAD THOUGHT OF THAT...
YEAH. WHEN I'M AROUND, **THOUGHT** BECOMES **DEED.**
TAXI
SOMETIMES I EVEN SKIP THE WHOLE "THOUGHT" PART OF THE EQUATION.
I HAVE TO FIND STEG BEFORE HE DOES SOMETHING STUPID.
STUPID**ER.**
STEG-- WHAT ARE YOU DOING?
PROTECTING MYSELF FROM YOUR RIGHTEOUS WRATH AND THE SPEEDY MAMMAL.
NOT A STEP CLOSER.

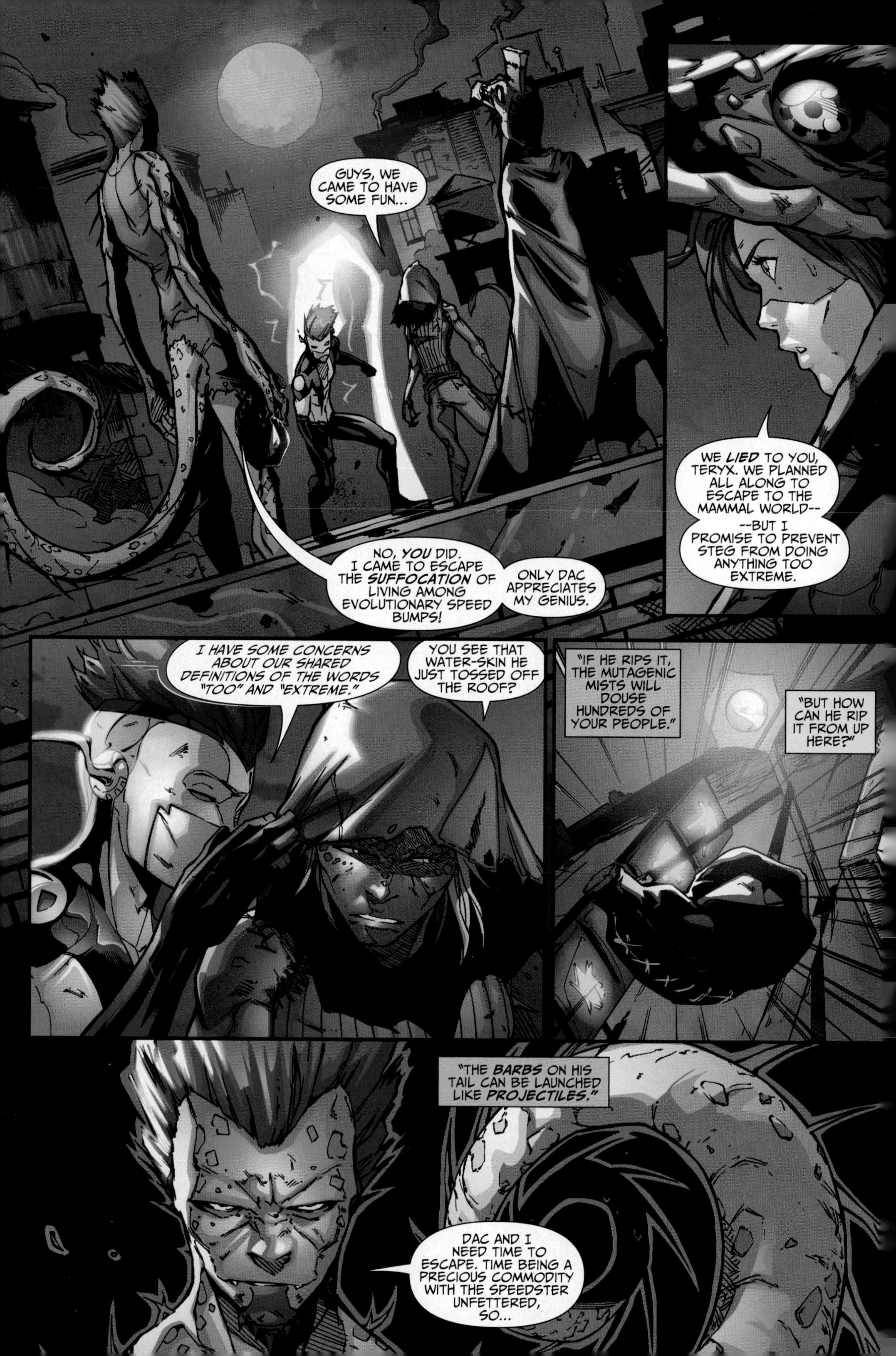
GUYS, WE CAME TO HAVE SOME FUN...
NO, YOU DID. I CAME TO ESCAPE THE SUFFOCATION OF LIVING AMONG EVOLUTIONARY SPEED BUMPS!
ONLY DAC APPRECIATES MY GENIUS.
WE LIED TO YOU, TERYX. WE PLANNED ALL ALONG TO ESCAPE TO THE MAMMAL WORLD--
--BUT I PROMISE TO PREVENT STEG FROM DOING ANYTHING TOO EXTREME.
I HAVE SOME CONCERNS ABOUT OUR SHARED DEFINITIONS OF THE WORDS "TOO" AND "EXTREME."
YOU SEE THAT WATER-SKIN HE JUST TOSSED OFF THE ROOF?
"IF HE RIPS IT, THE MUTAGENIC MISTS WILL DOUSE HUNDREDS OF YOUR PEOPLE."
"BUT HOW CAN HE RIP IT FROM UP HERE?"
"THE BARBS ON HIS TAIL CAN BE LAUNCHED LIKE PROJECTILES."
DAC AND I NEED TIME TO ESCAPE. TIME BEING A PRECIOUS COMMODITY WITH THE SPEEDSTER UNFETTERED, SO...

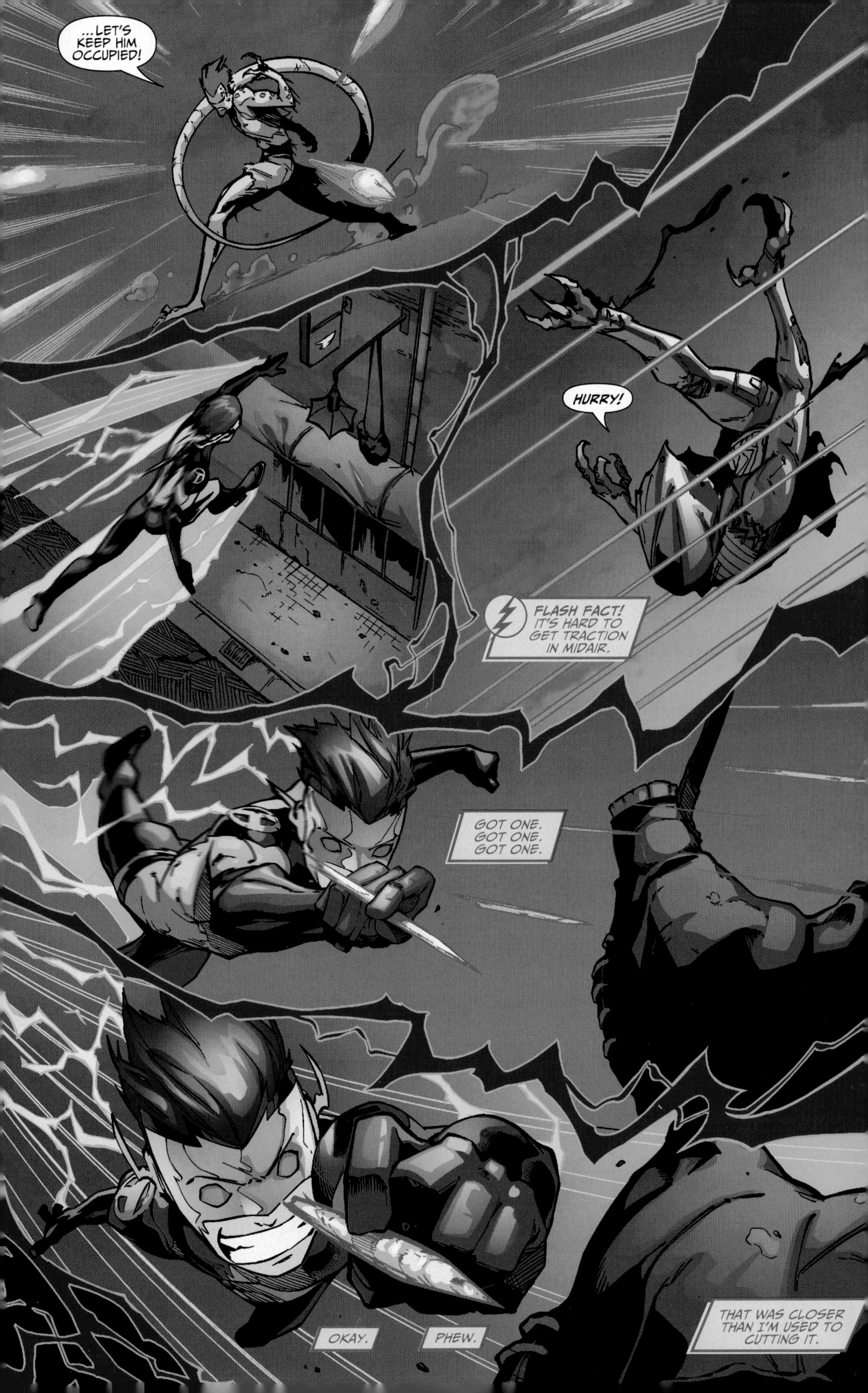
...LET'S KEEP HIM OCCUPIED!
HURRY!
FLASH FACT! IT'S HARD TO GET TRACTION IN MIDAIR.
GOT ONE. GOT ONE. GOT ONE.
OKAY.
PHEW.
THAT WAS CLOSER THAN I'M USED TO CUTTING IT.

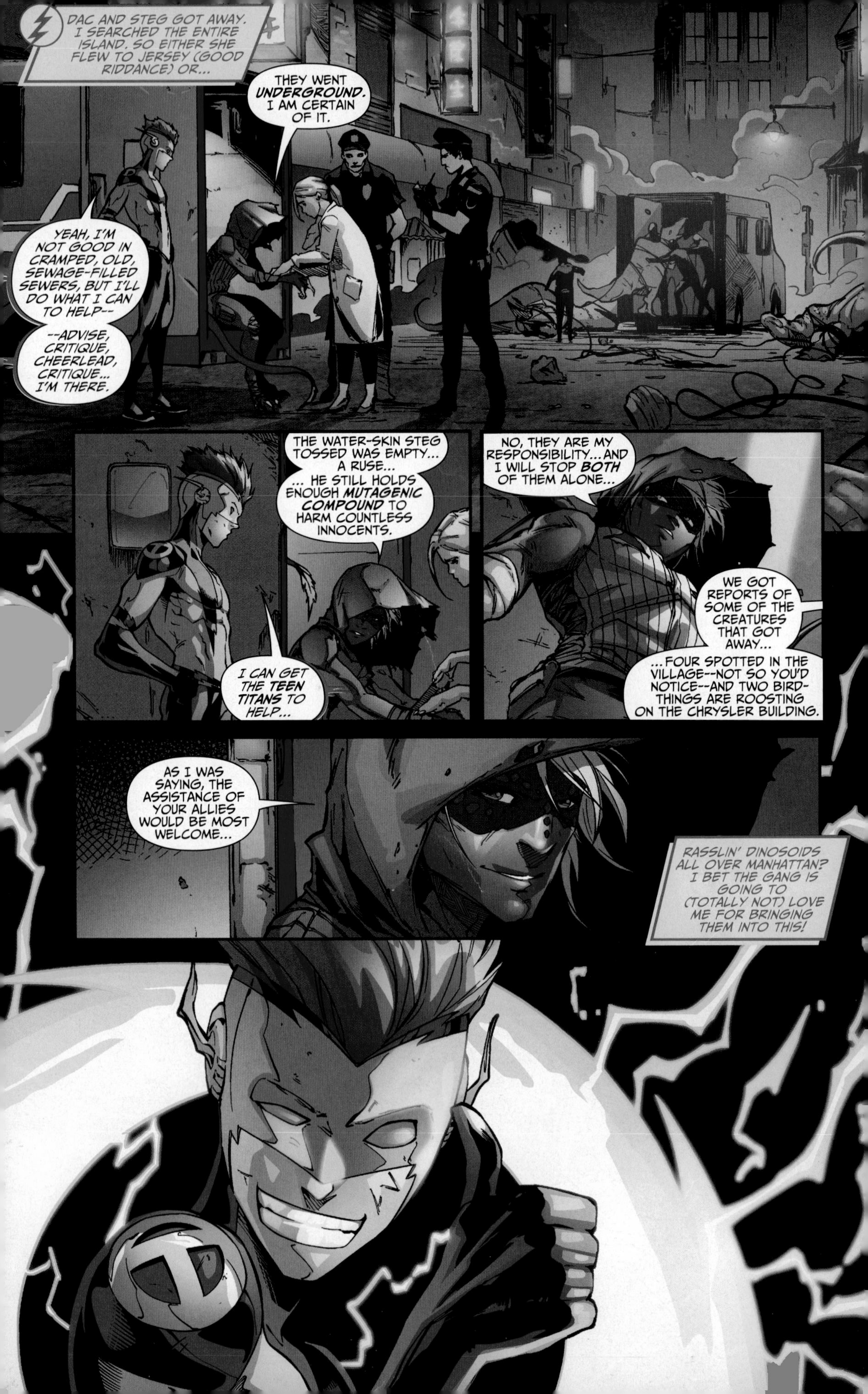
DAC AND STEG GOT AWAY. I SEARCHED THE ENTIRE ISLAND. SO EITHER SHE FLEW TO JERSEY (GOOD RIDDANCE) OR...
THEY WENT UNDERGROUND. I AM CERTAIN OF IT.
YEAH, I'M NOT GOOD IN CRAMPED, OLD, SEWAGE-FILLED SEWERS, BUT I'LL DO WHAT I CAN TO HELP--
--ADVISE, CRITIQUE, CHEERLEAD, CRITIQUE... I'M THERE.
THE WATER-SKIN STEG TOSSED WAS EMPTY... A RUSE...
... HE STILL HOLDS ENOUGH MUTAGENIC COMPOUND TO HARM COUNTLESS INNOCENTS.
I CAN GET THE TEEN TITANS TO HELP...
NO, THEY ARE MY RESPONSIBILITY... AND I WILL STOP BOTH OF THEM ALONE...
WE GOT REPORTS OF SOME OF THE CREATURES THAT GOT AWAY...
...FOUR SPOTTED IN THE VILLAGE--NOT SO YOU'D NOTICE--AND TWO BIRD-THINGS ARE ROOSTING ON THE CHRYSLER BUILDING.
AS I WAS SAYING, THE ASSISTANCE OF YOUR ALLIES WOULD BE MOST WELCOME...
RASSLIN' DINOSOIDS ALL OVER MANHATTAN? I BET THE GANG IS GOING TO (TOTALLY NOT) LOVE ME FOR BRINGING THEM INTO THIS!

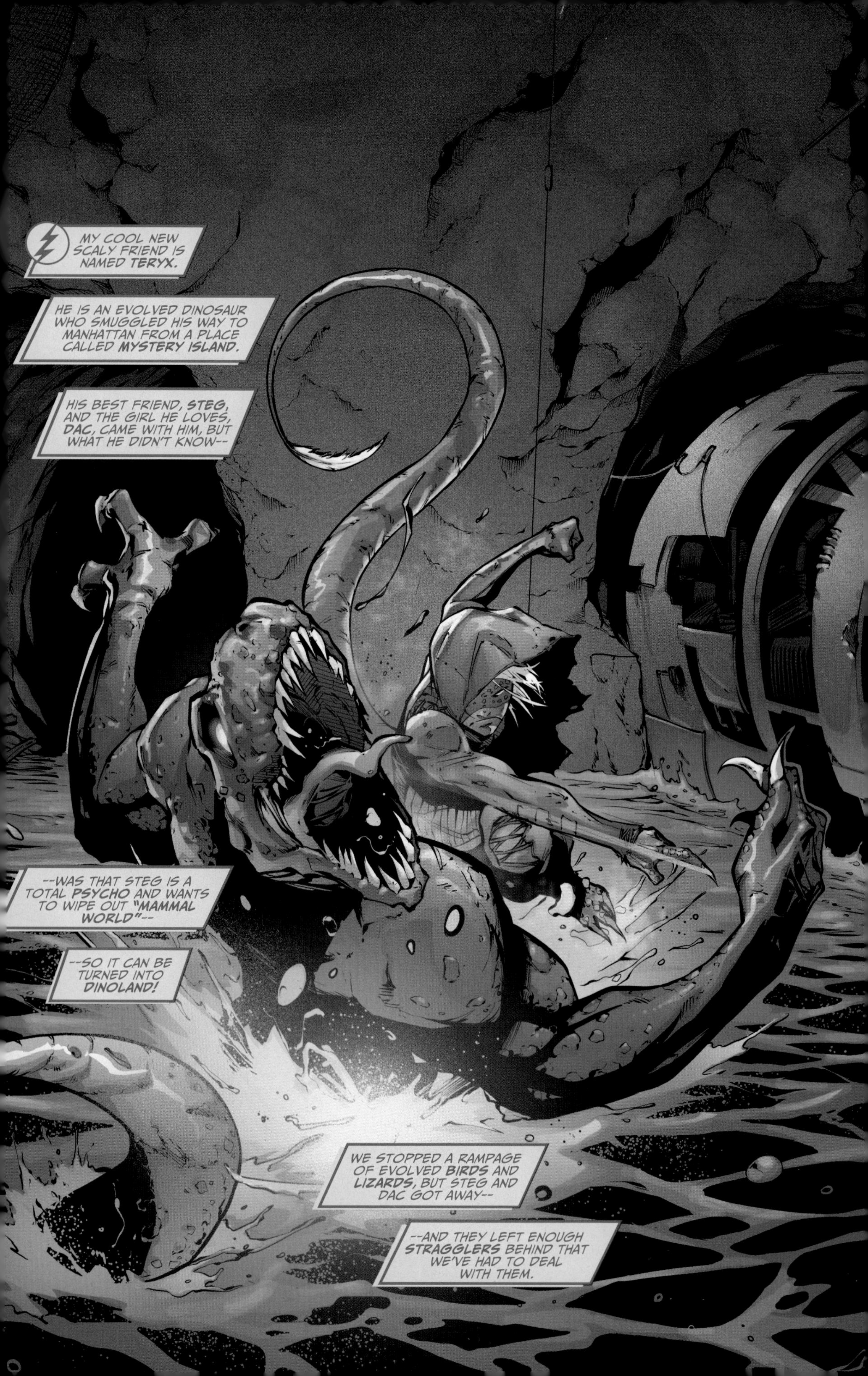
MY COOL NEW SCALY FRIEND IS NAMED TERYX.
HE IS AN EVOLVED DINOSAUR WHO SMUGGLED HIS WAY TO MANHATTAN FROM A PLACE CALLED MYSTERY ISLAND.
HIS BEST FRIEND, STEG, AND THE GIRL HE LOVES, DAC, CAME WITH HIM, BUT WHAT HE DIDN'T KNOW--
--WAS THAT STEG IS A TOTAL PSYCHO AND WANTS TO WIPE OUT "MAMMAL WORLD"--
--SO IT CAN BE TURNED INTO DINOLAND!
WE STOPPED A RAMPAGE OF EVOLVED BIRDS AND LIZARDS, BUT STEG AND DAC GOT AWAY--
--AND THEY LEFT ENOUGH STRAGGLERS BEHIND THAT WE'VE HAD TO DEAL WITH THEM.

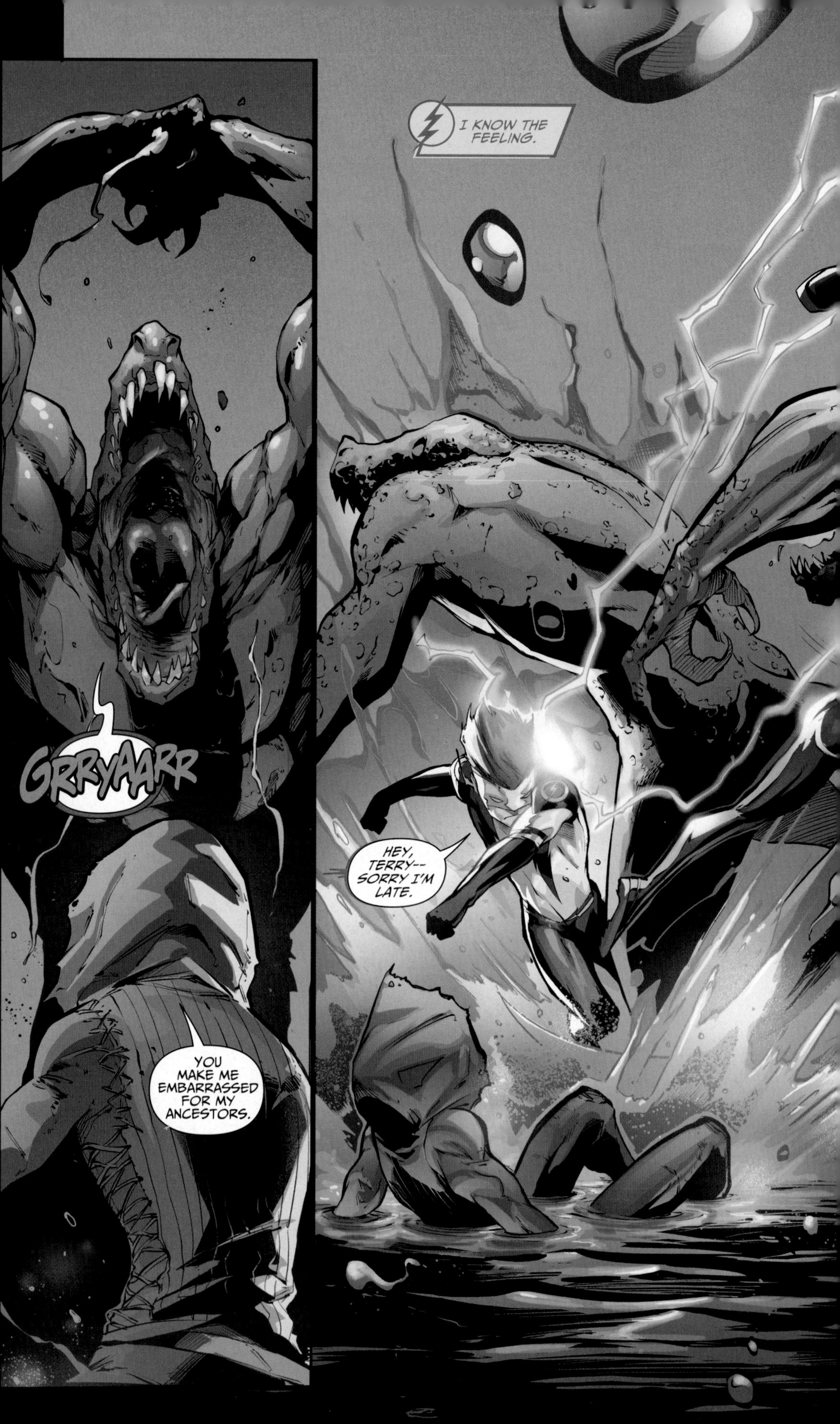
GRRYAARR
YOU MAKE ME EMBARRASSED FOR MY ANCESTORS.
I KNOW THE FEELING.
HEY, TERRY-- SORRY I'M LATE.

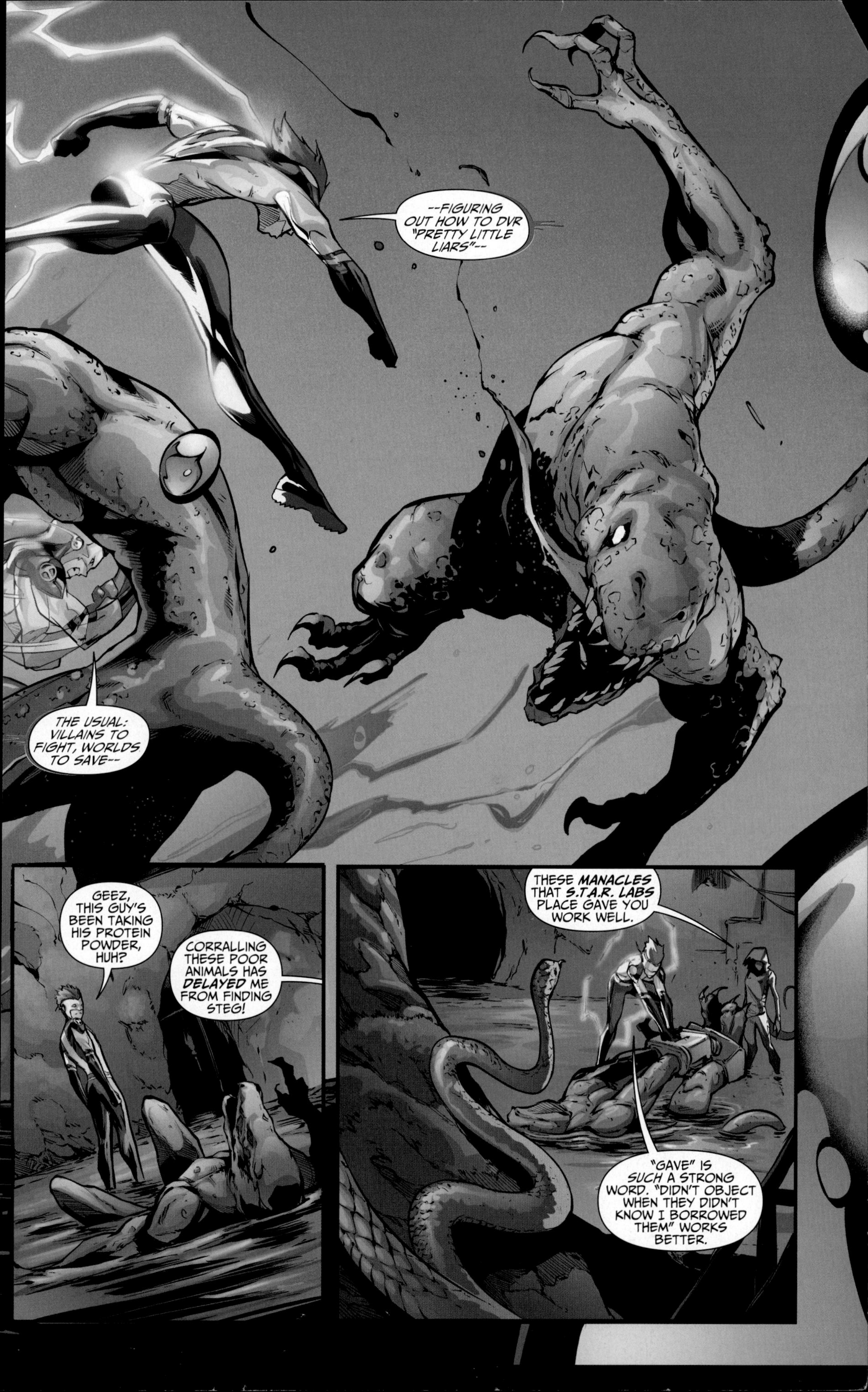
--FIGURING OUT HOW TO DVR "PRETTY LITTLE LIARS"--
THE USUAL: VILLAINS TO FIGHT, WORLDS TO SAVE--
GEEZ, THIS GUY'S BEEN TAKING HIS PROTEIN POWDER, HUH?
CORRALLING THESE POOR ANIMALS HAS DELAYED ME FROM FINDING STEG!
THESE MANACLES THAT S.T.A.R. LABS PLACE GAVE YOU WORK WELL.
"GAVE" IS SUCH A STRONG WORD. "DIDN'T OBJECT WHEN THEY DIDN'T KNOW I BORROWED THEM" WORKS BETTER.

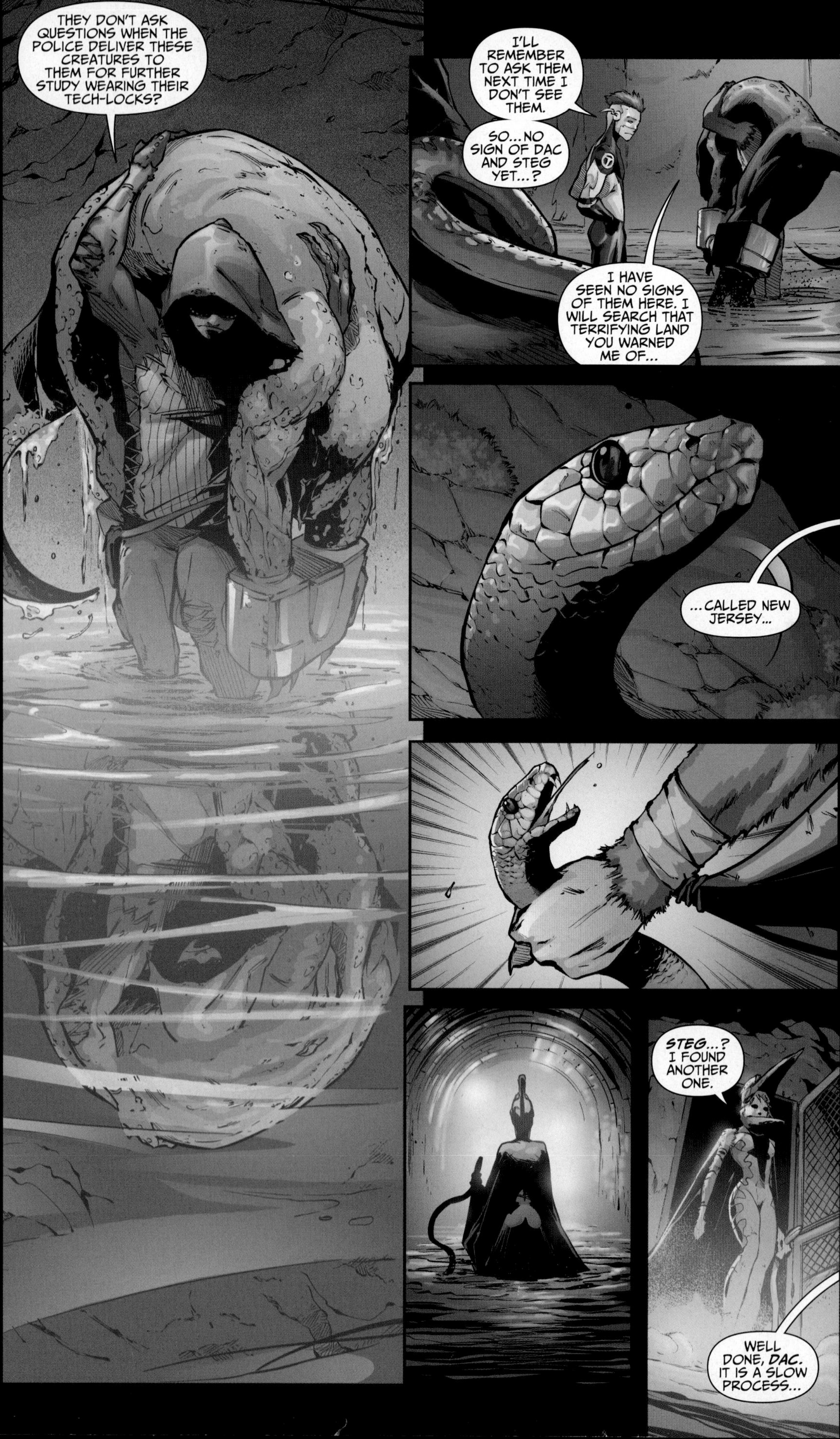
THEY DON'T ASK QUESTIONS WHEN THE POLICE DELIVER THESE CREATURES TO THEM FOR FURTHER STUDY WEARING THEIR TECH-LOCKS?
I'LL REMEMBER TO ASK THEM NEXT TIME I DON'T SEE THEM.
SO...NO SIGN OF DAC AND STEG YET...?
I HAVE SEEN NO SIGNS OF THEM HERE. I WILL SEARCH THAT TERRIFYING LAND YOU WARNED ME OF...
...CALLED NEW JERSEY...
STEG...? I FOUND ANOTHER ONE.
WELL DONE, DAC. IT IS A SLOW PROCESS...

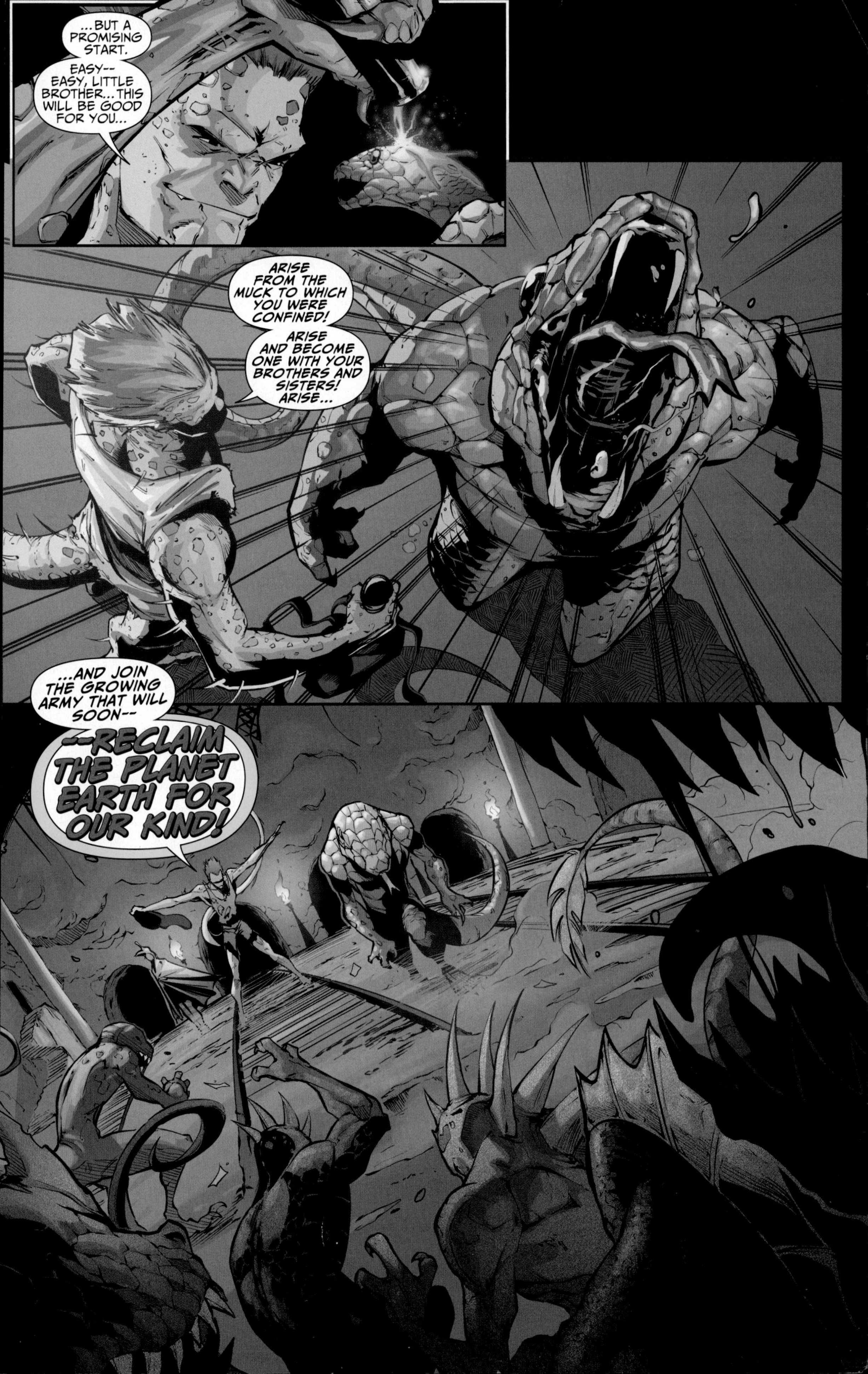
...BUT A PROMISING START.
EASY-- EASY, LITTLE BROTHER...THIS WILL BE GOOD FOR YOU...
ARISE FROM THE MUCK TO WHICH YOU WERE CONFINED!
ARISE AND BECOME ONE WITH YOUR BROTHERS AND SISTERS! ARISE...
...AND JOIN THE GROWING ARMY THAT WILL SOON--
--RECLAIM THE PLANET EARTH FOR OUR KIND!

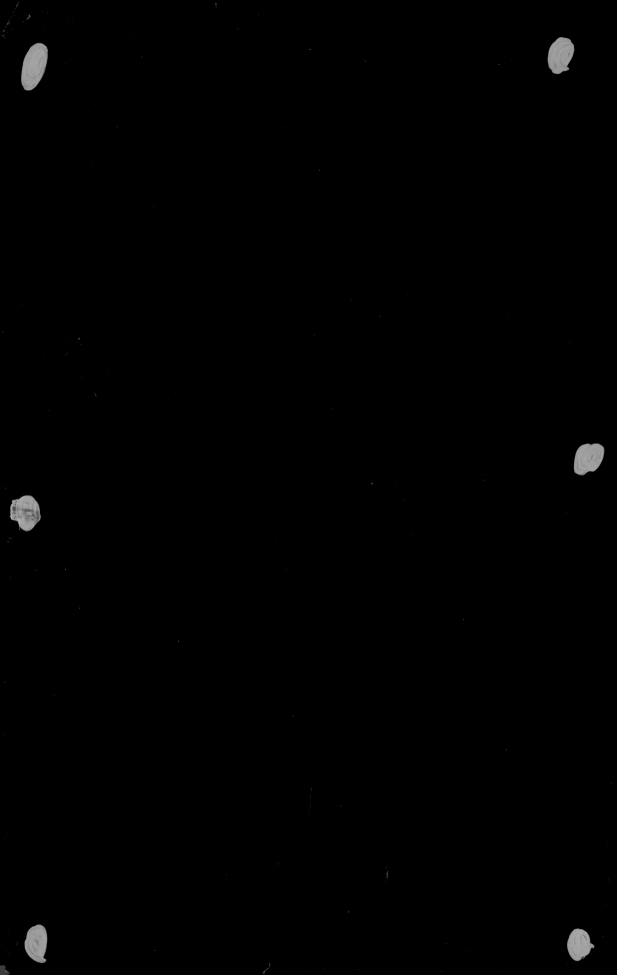

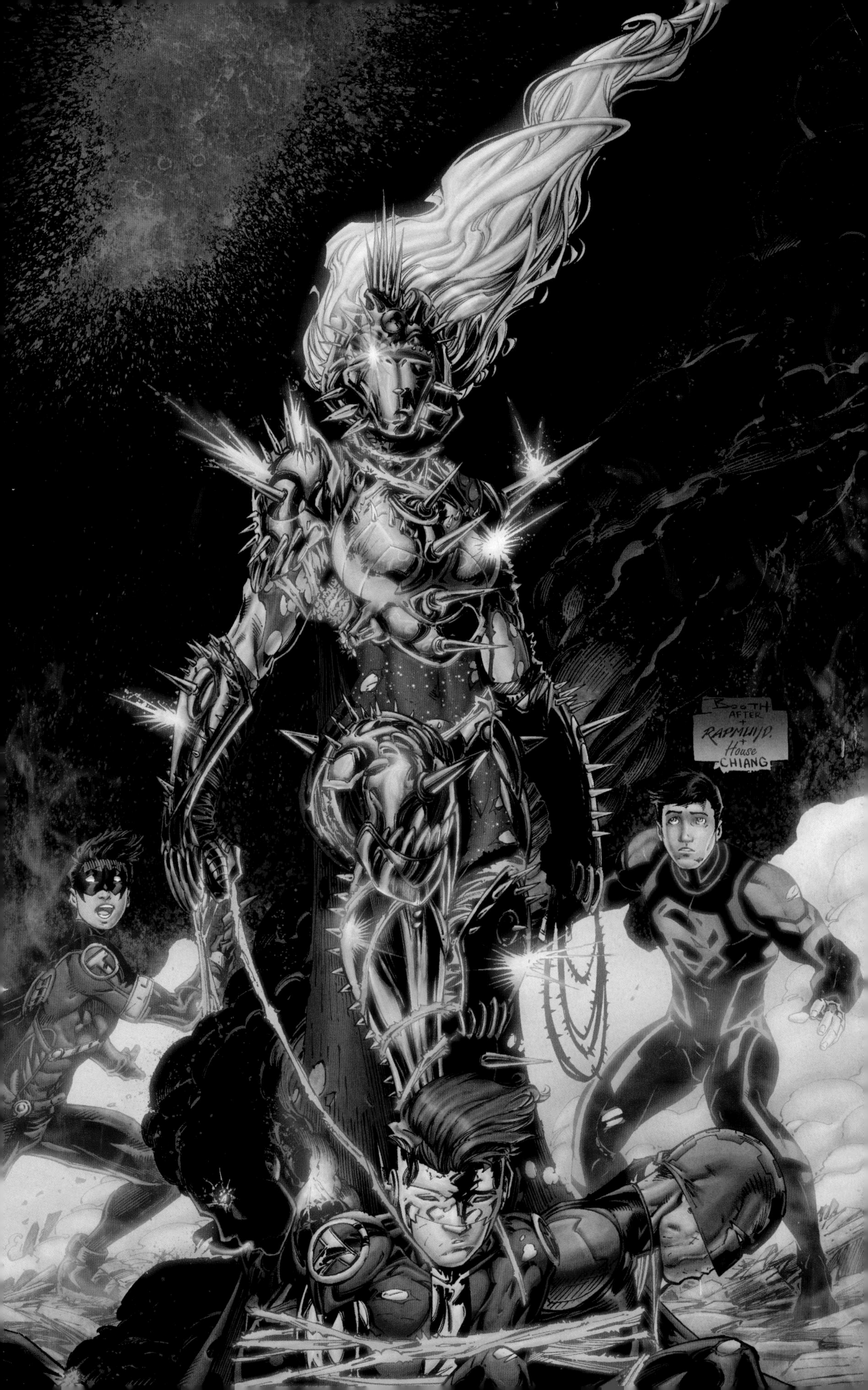
BOOTH
AFTER
+
RAPMUND.
+
House
CHIANG

WONDER WONDER WHO

SCOTT LOBDELL
writer

BRETT BOOTH
penciller

NORM RAPMUND
inker

cover art by
BRETT BOOTH, NORM RAPMUND & ANDREW DALHOUSE

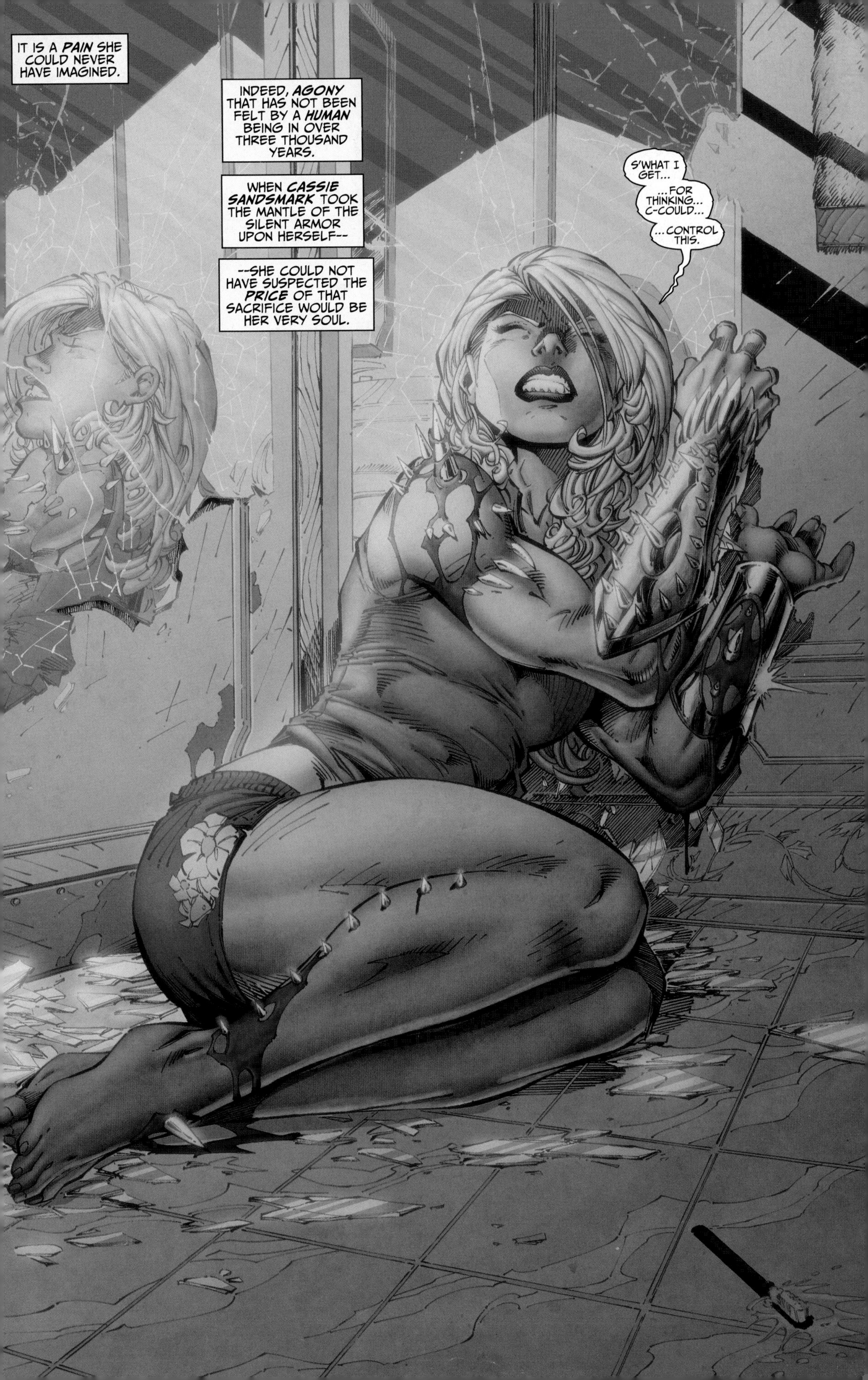
IT IS A *PAIN* SHE COULD NEVER HAVE IMAGINED.
INDEED, *AGONY* THAT HAS NOT BEEN FELT BY A *HUMAN* BEING IN OVER THREE THOUSAND YEARS.
WHEN *CASSIE SANDSMARK* TOOK THE MANTLE OF THE SILENT ARMOR UPON HERSELF--
--SHE COULD NOT HAVE SUSPECTED THE *PRICE* OF THAT SACRIFICE WOULD BE HER VERY SOUL.
S'WHAT I GET... ...FOR THINKING... C-COULD... ...CONTROL THIS.

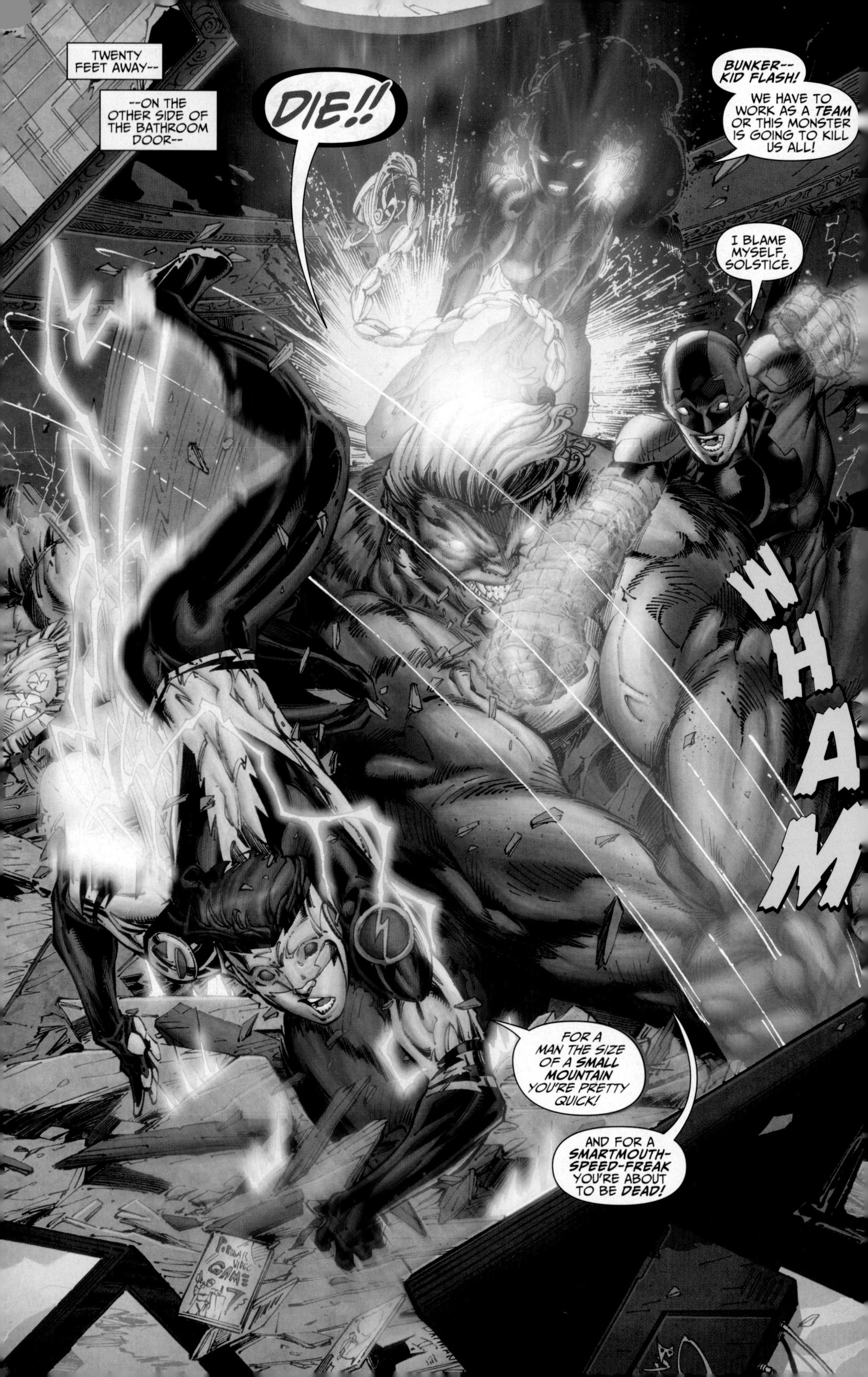
TWENTY FEET AWAY--
--ON THE OTHER SIDE OF THE BATHROOM DOOR--
DIE!!
BUNKER-- KID FLASH!
WE HAVE TO WORK AS A TEAM OR THIS MONSTER IS GOING TO KILL US ALL!
I BLAME MYSELF, SOLSTICE.
WHAM
FOR A MAN THE SIZE OF A SMALL MOUNTAIN YOU'RE PRETTY QUICK!
AND FOR A SMARTMOUTH-SPEED-FREAK YOU'RE ABOUT TO BE DEAD!

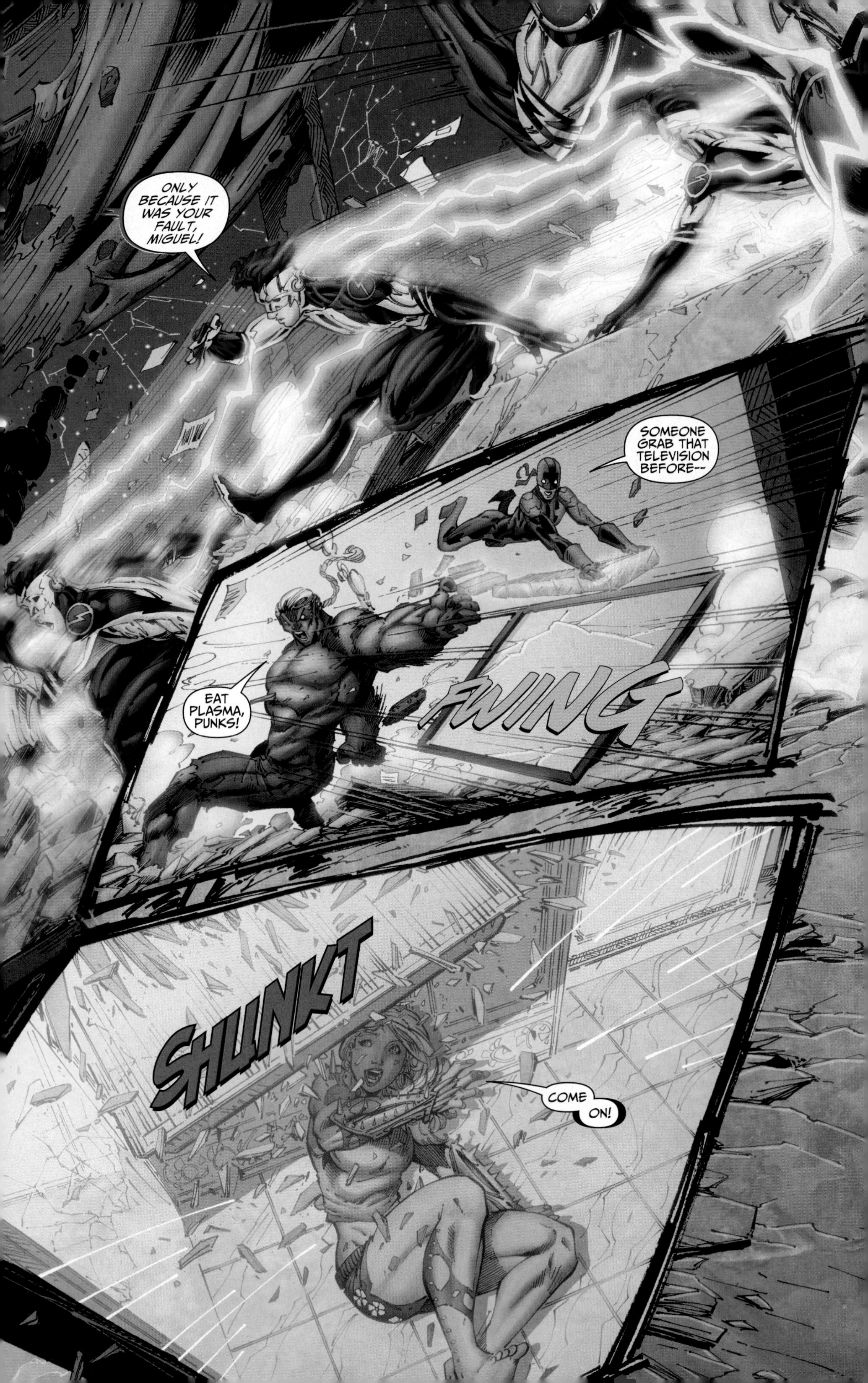
ONLY BECAUSE IT WAS YOUR FAULT, MIGUEL!
SOMEONE GRAB THAT TELEVISION BEFORE--
EAT PLASMA, PUNKS!
FWING
SHUNKT
COME ON!

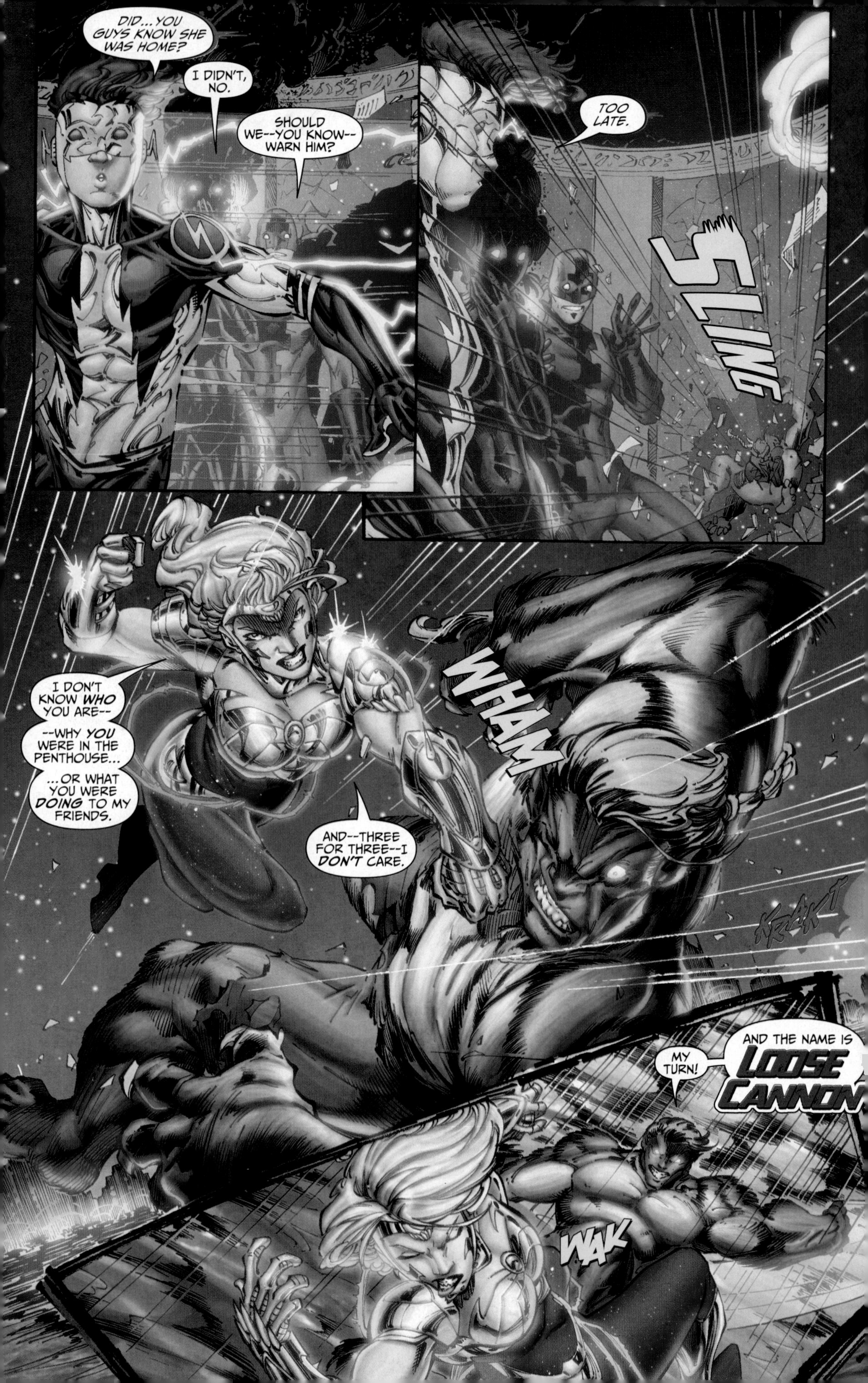

DID...YOU GUYS KNOW SHE WAS HOME?
I DIDN'T, NO.
SHOULD WE--YOU KNOW--WARN HIM?
TOO LATE.
SLING
I DON'T KNOW WHO YOU ARE--
--WHY YOU WERE IN THE PENTHOUSE...
...OR WHAT YOU WERE DOING TO MY FRIENDS.
WHAM
AND--THREE FOR THREE--I DON'T CARE.
KRAKT
MY TURN!
AND THE NAME IS LOOSE CANNON
WAK

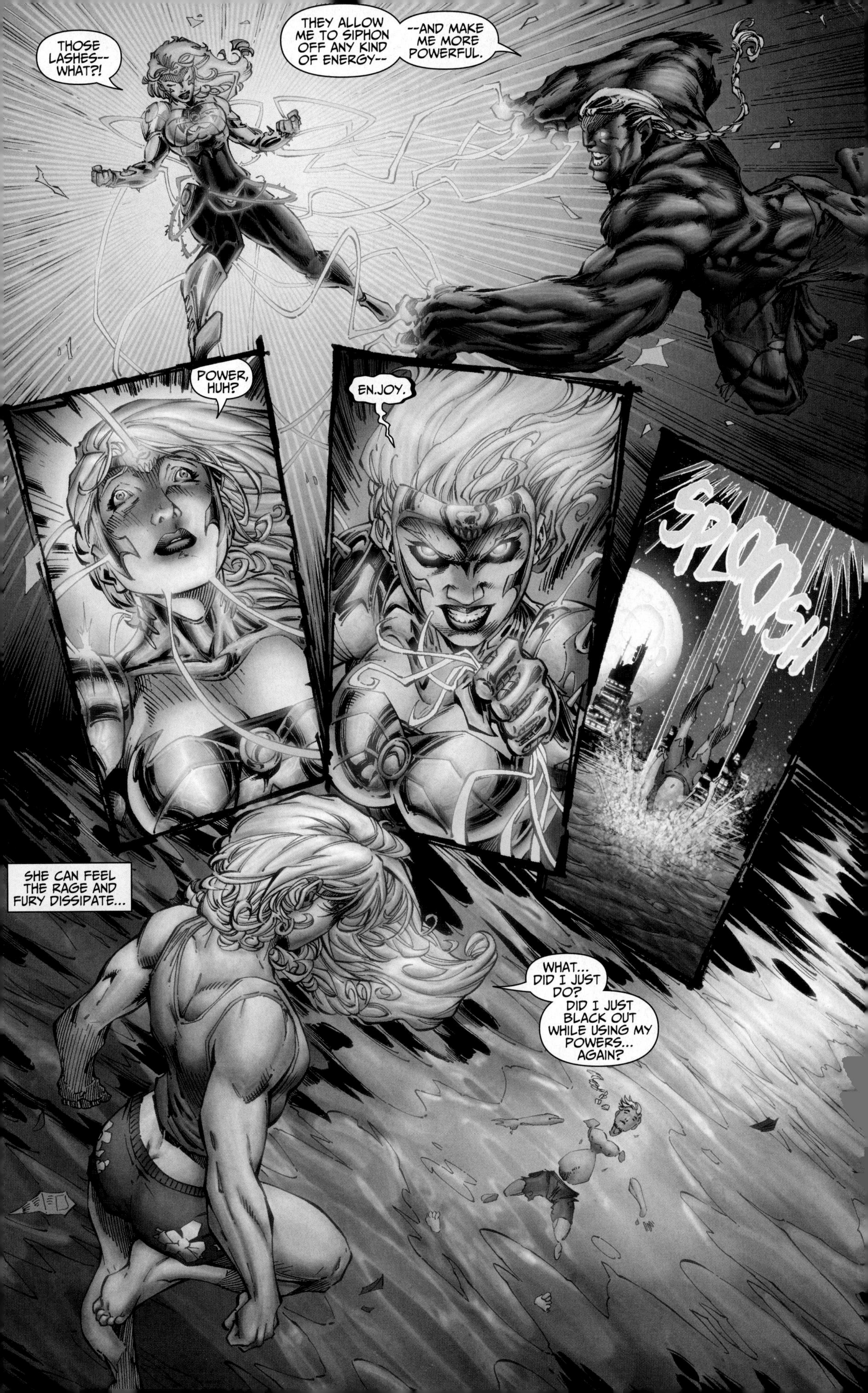
THOSE LASHES-- WHAT?!
THEY ALLOW ME TO SIPHON OFF ANY KIND OF ENERGY--
--AND MAKE ME MORE POWERFUL.
POWER, HUH?
ENJOY.
SPLOOSH
SHE CAN FEEL THE RAGE AND FURY DISSIPATE...
WHAT... DID I JUST DO?
DID I JUST BLACK OUT WHILE USING MY POWERS... AGAIN?

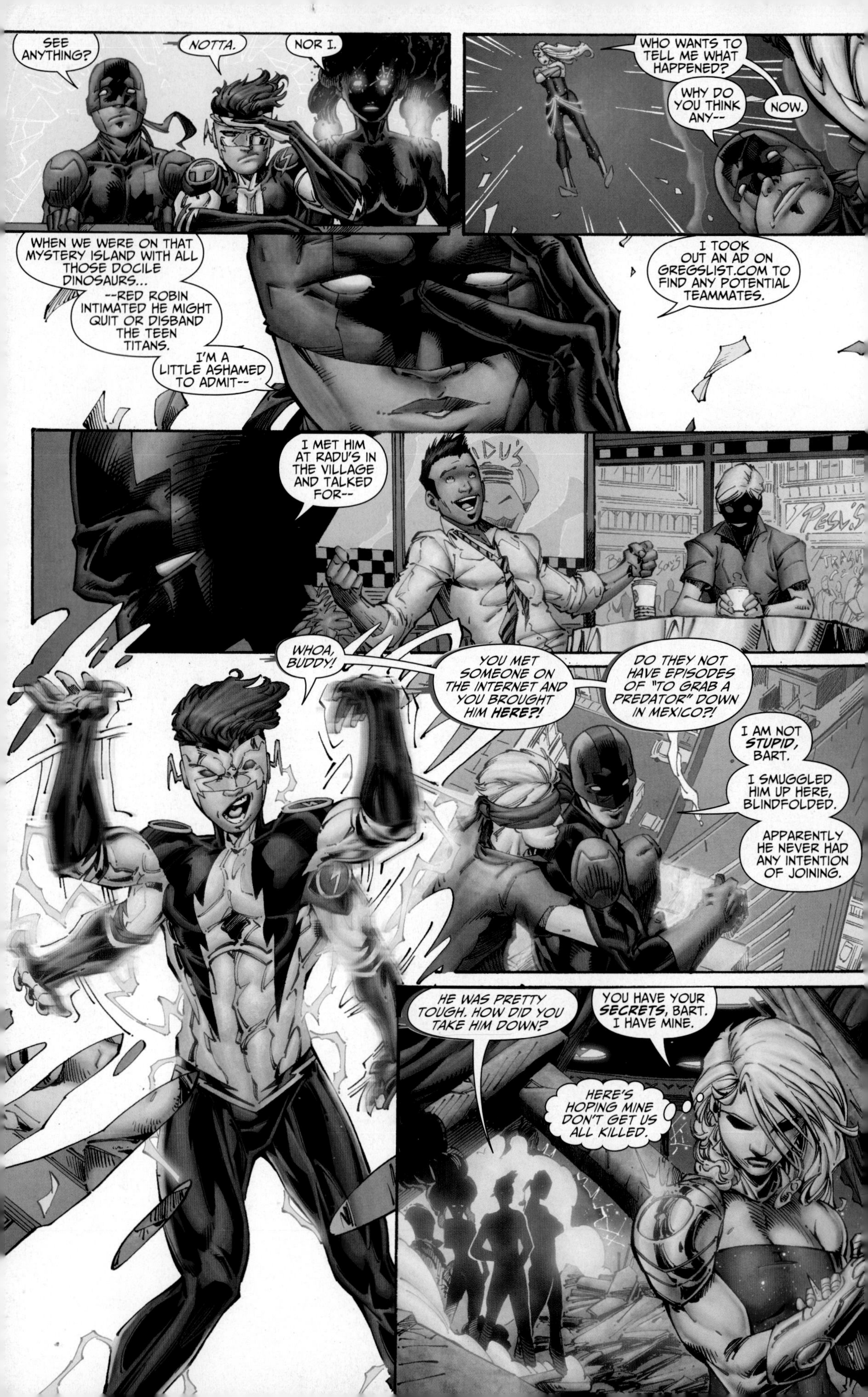
SEE ANYTHING?
NOTTA.
NOR I.
WHO WANTS TO TELL ME WHAT HAPPENED?
WHY DO YOU THINK ANY--
NOW.
WHEN WE WERE ON THAT MYSTERY ISLAND WITH ALL THOSE DOCILE DINOSAURS...
--RED ROBIN INTIMATED HE MIGHT QUIT OR DISBAND THE TEEN TITANS.
I'M A LITTLE ASHAMED TO ADMIT--
I TOOK OUT AN AD ON GREGSLIST.COM TO FIND ANY POTENTIAL TEAMMATES.
I MET HIM AT RADU'S IN THE VILLAGE AND TALKED FOR--
WHOA, BUDDY!
YOU MET SOMEONE ON THE INTERNET AND YOU BROUGHT HIM HERE?!
DO THEY NOT HAVE EPISODES OF "TO GRAB A PREDATOR" DOWN IN MEXICO?!
I AM NOT STUPID, BART.
I SMUGGLED HIM UP HERE, BLINDFOLDED.
APPARENTLY HE NEVER HAD ANY INTENTION OF JOINING.
HE WAS PRETTY TOUGH. HOW DID YOU TAKE HIM DOWN?
YOU HAVE YOUR SECRETS, BART. I HAVE MINE.
HERE'S HOPING MINE DON'T GET US ALL KILLED.

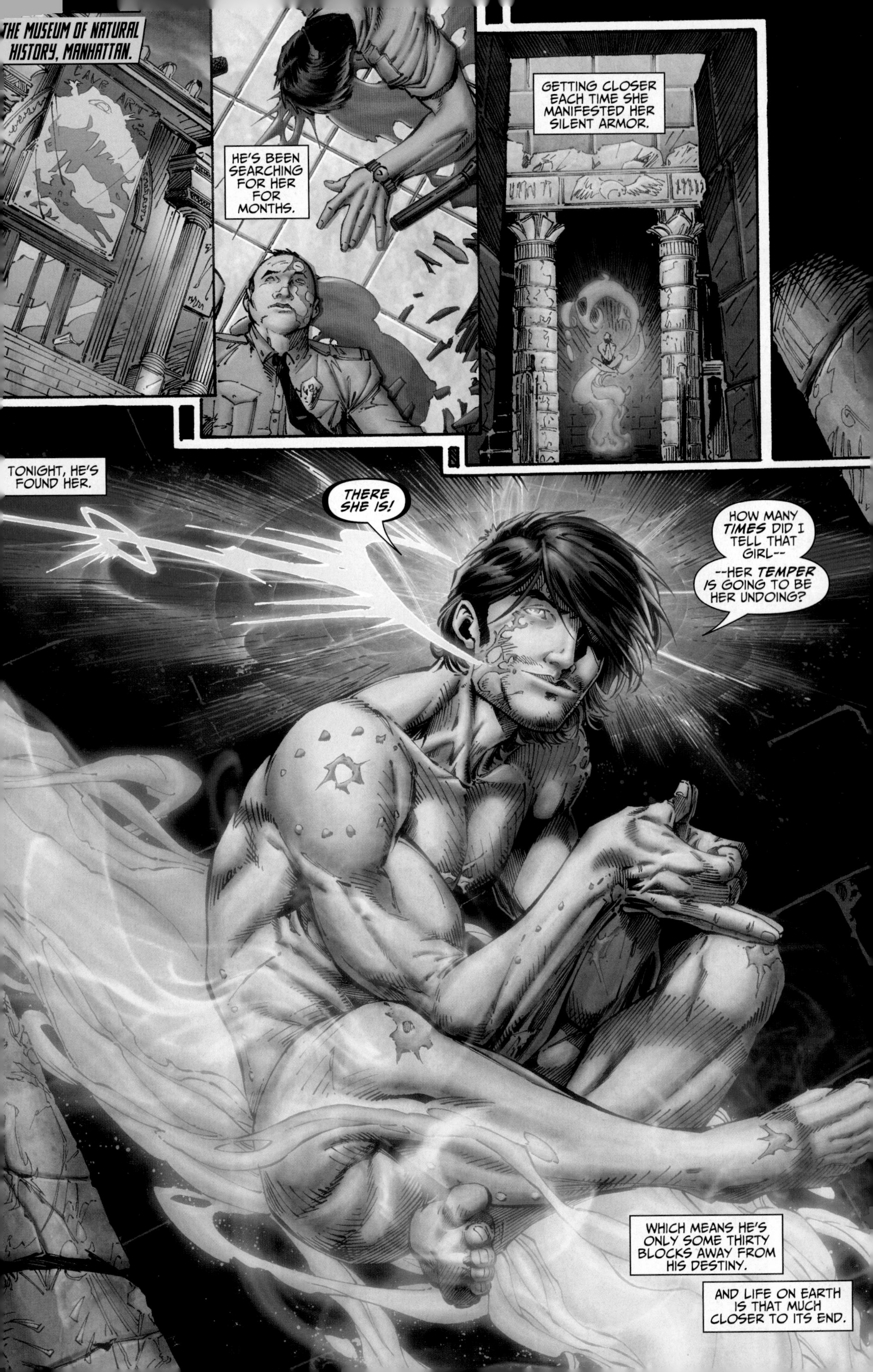
THE MUSEUM OF NATURAL HISTORY, MANHATTAN.
CAVE ART
HE'S BEEN SEARCHING FOR HER FOR MONTHS.
GETTING CLOSER EACH TIME SHE MANIFESTED HER SILENT ARMOR.
TONIGHT, HE'S FOUND HER.
THERE SHE IS!
HOW MANY TIMES DID I TELL THAT GIRL--
--HER TEMPER IS GOING TO BE HER UNDOING?
WHICH MEANS HE'S ONLY SOME THIRTY BLOCKS AWAY FROM HIS DESTINY.
AND LIFE ON EARTH IS THAT MUCH CLOSER TO ITS END.

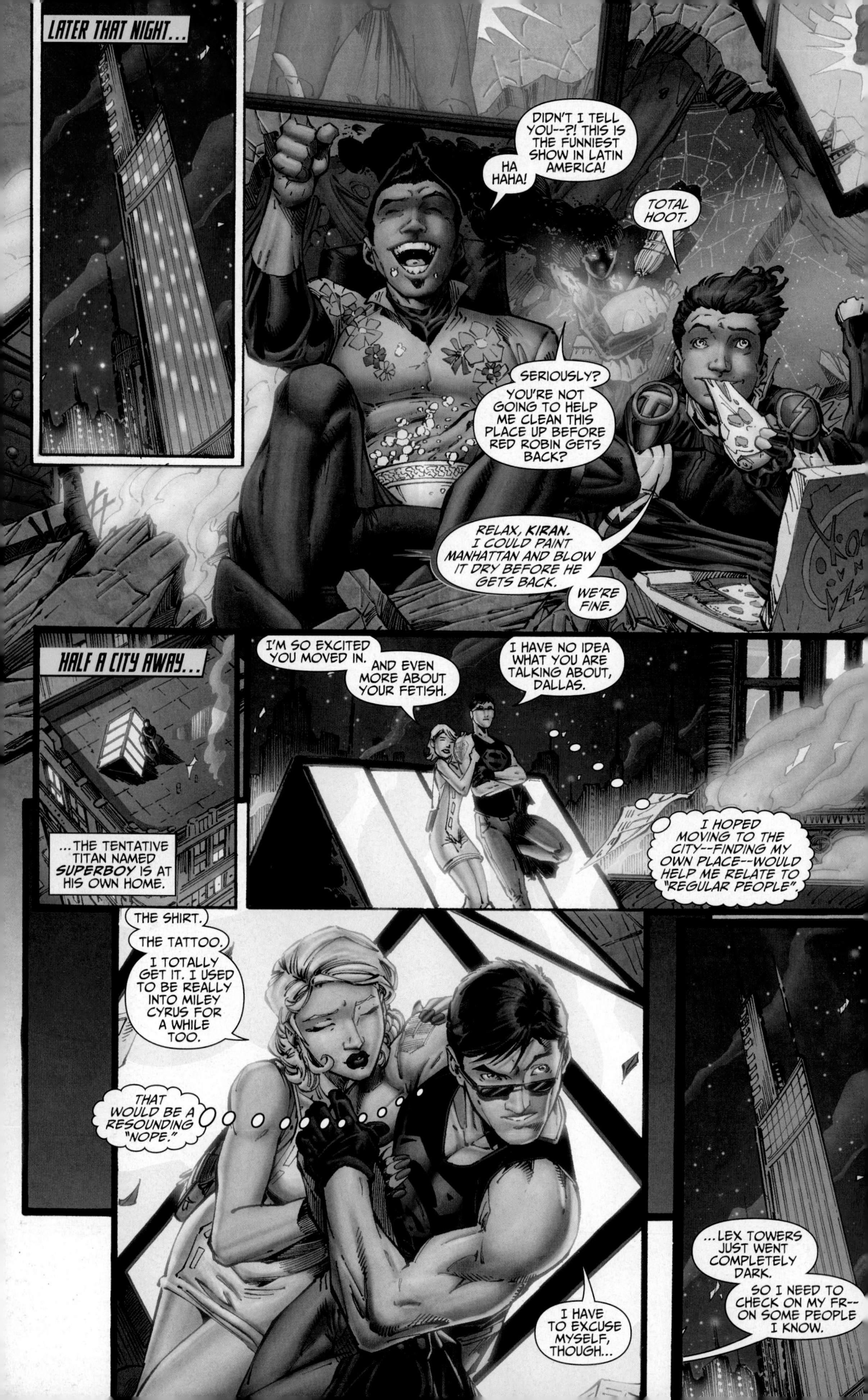
LATER THAT NIGHT...
HA HAHA!
DIDN'T I TELL YOU--?! THIS IS THE FUNNIEST SHOW IN LATIN AMERICA!
TOTAL HOOT.
SERIOUSLY?
YOU'RE NOT GOING TO HELP ME CLEAN THIS PLACE UP BEFORE RED ROBIN GETS BACK?
RELAX, KIRAN. I COULD PAINT MANHATTAN AND BLOW IT DRY BEFORE HE GETS BACK.
WE'RE FINE.
HALF A CITY AWAY...
...THE TENTATIVE TITAN NAMED SUPERBOY IS AT HIS OWN HOME.
I'M SO EXCITED YOU MOVED IN.
AND EVEN MORE ABOUT YOUR FETISH.
I HAVE NO IDEA WHAT YOU ARE TALKING ABOUT, DALLAS.
I HOPED MOVING TO THE CITY--FINDING MY OWN PLACE--WOULD HELP ME RELATE TO "REGULAR PEOPLE".
THE SHIRT.
THE TATTOO.
I TOTALLY GET IT. I USED TO BE REALLY INTO MILEY CYRUS FOR A WHILE TOO.
THAT WOULD BE A RESOUNDING "NOPE."
I HAVE TO EXCUSE MYSELF, THOUGH...
...LEX TOWERS JUST WENT COMPLETELY DARK.
SO I NEED TO CHECK ON MY FR-- ON SOME PEOPLE I KNOW.

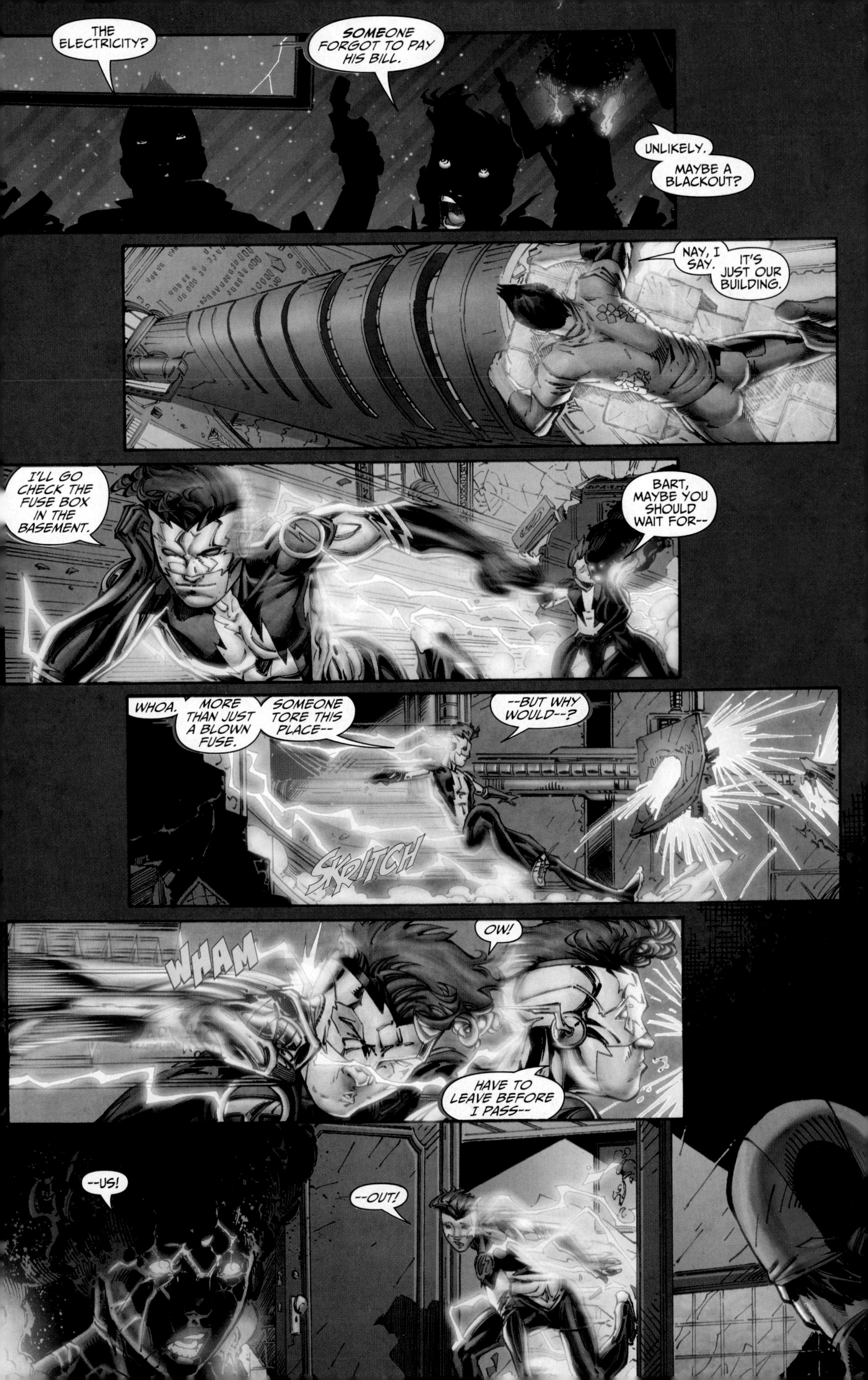
THE ELECTRICITY?
SOMEONE FORGOT TO PAY HIS BILL.
UNLIKELY.
MAYBE A BLACKOUT?
NAY, I SAY.
IT'S JUST OUR BUILDING.
I'LL GO CHECK THE FUSE BOX IN THE BASEMENT.
BART, MAYBE YOU SHOULD WAIT FOR--
WHOA.
MORE THAN JUST A BLOWN FUSE.
SOMEONE TORE THIS PLACE--
--BUT WHY WOULD--?
SKRITCH
WHAM
OW!
HAVE TO LEAVE BEFORE I PASS--
--US!
--OUT!

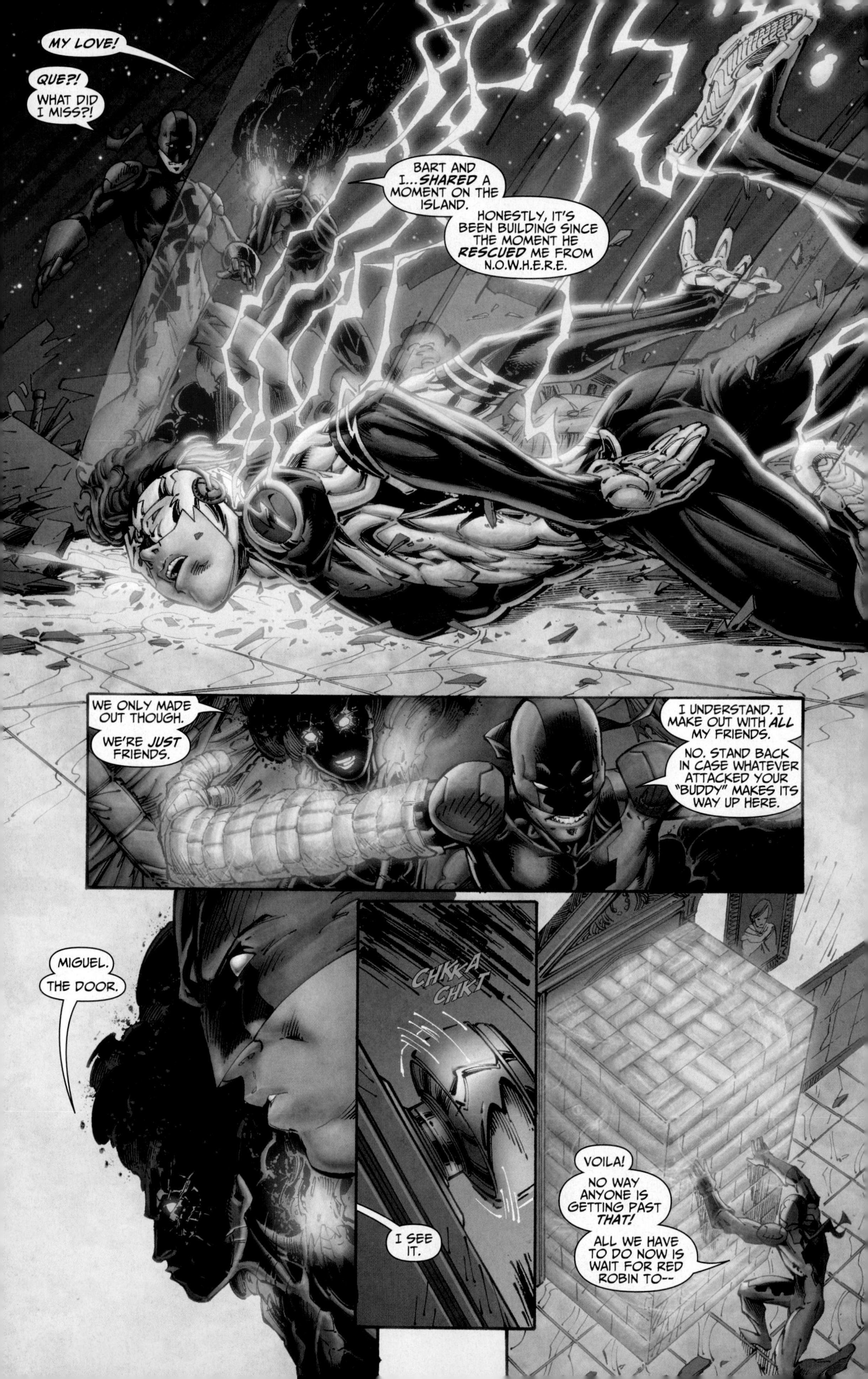
MY LOVE!
QUE?! WHAT DID I MISS?!
BART AND I...SHARED A MOMENT ON THE ISLAND.
HONESTLY, IT'S BEEN BUILDING SINCE THE MOMENT HE RESCUED ME FROM N.O.W.H.E.R.E.
WE ONLY MADE OUT THOUGH.
WE'RE JUST FRIENDS.
I UNDERSTAND. I MAKE OUT WITH ALL MY FRIENDS.
NO. STAND BACK IN CASE WHATEVER ATTACKED YOUR "BUDDY" MAKES ITS WAY UP HERE.
MIGUEL.
THE DOOR.
CHKKA CHKT
I SEE IT.
VOILA!
NO WAY ANYONE IS GETTING PAST THAT!
ALL WE HAVE TO DO NOW IS WAIT FOR RED ROBIN TO--

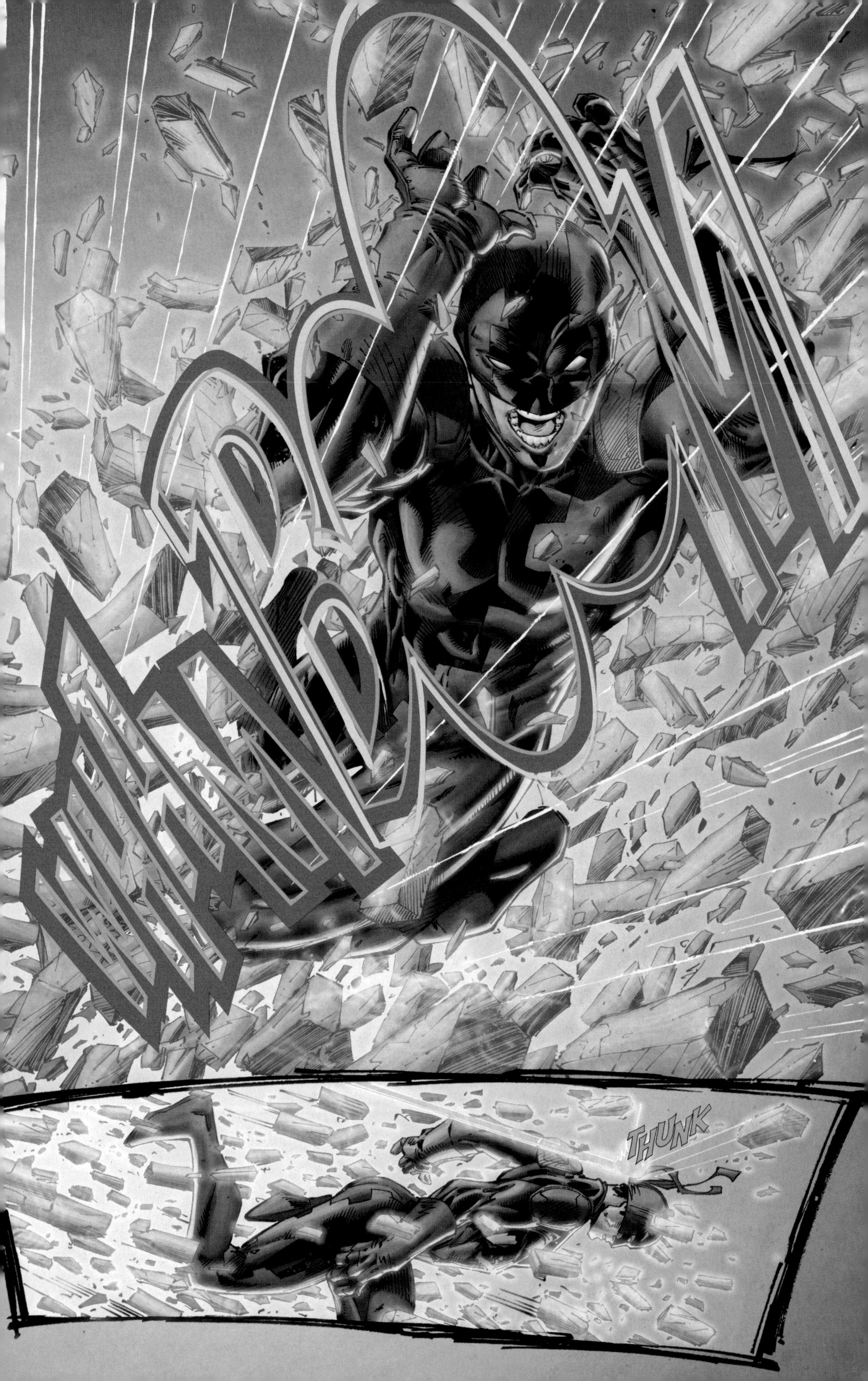
THUNK

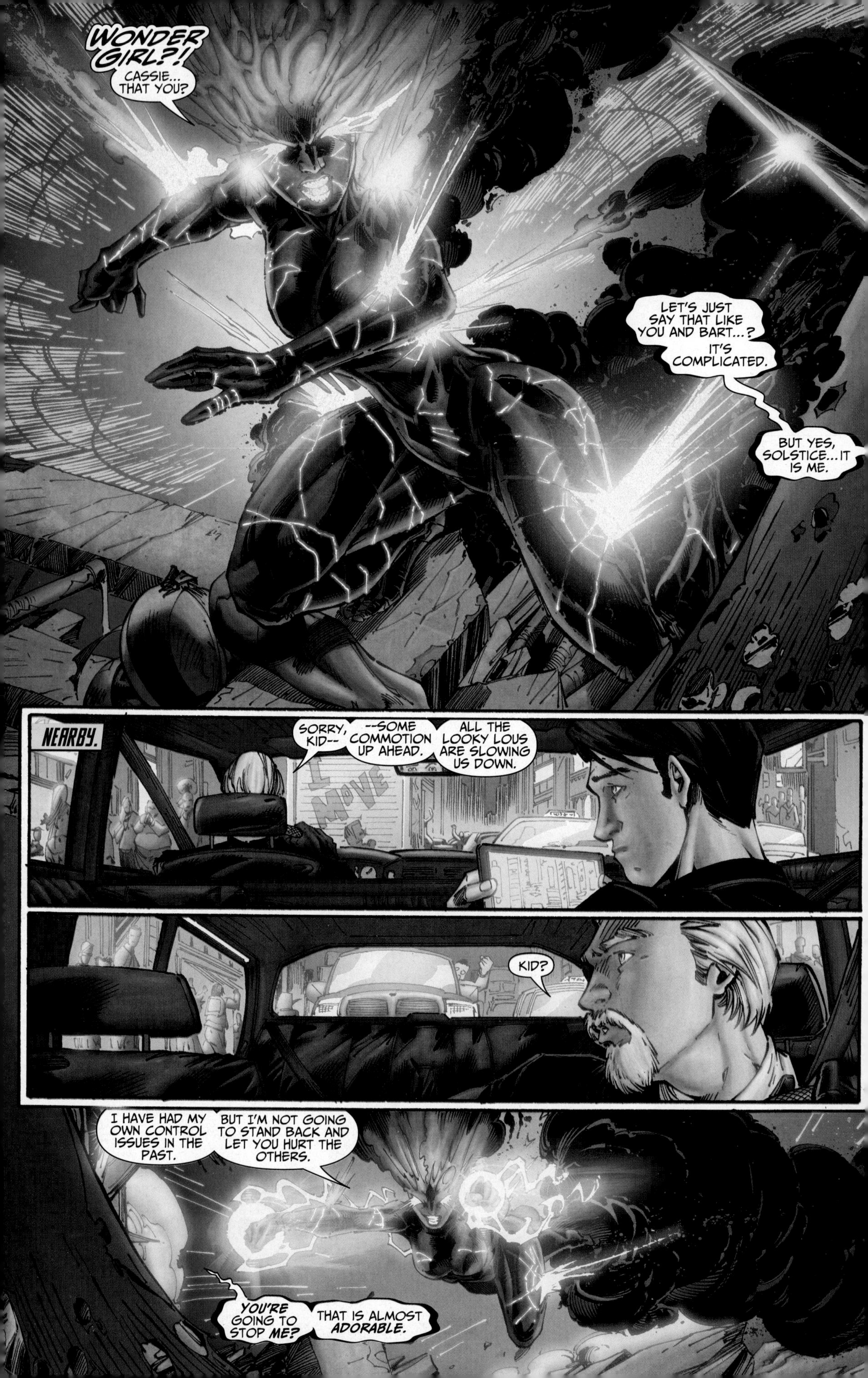
WONDER GIRL?!
CASSIE... THAT YOU?
LET'S JUST SAY THAT LIKE YOU AND BART...?
IT'S COMPLICATED.
BUT YES, SOLSTICE...IT IS ME.
NEARBY.
SORRY, KID--
--SOME COMMOTION UP AHEAD.
ALL THE LOOKY LOUS ARE SLOWING US DOWN.
KID?
I HAVE HAD MY OWN CONTROL ISSUES IN THE PAST.
BUT I'M NOT GOING TO STAND BACK AND LET YOU HURT THE OTHERS.
YOU'RE GOING TO STOP ME?
THAT IS ALMOST ADORABLE.

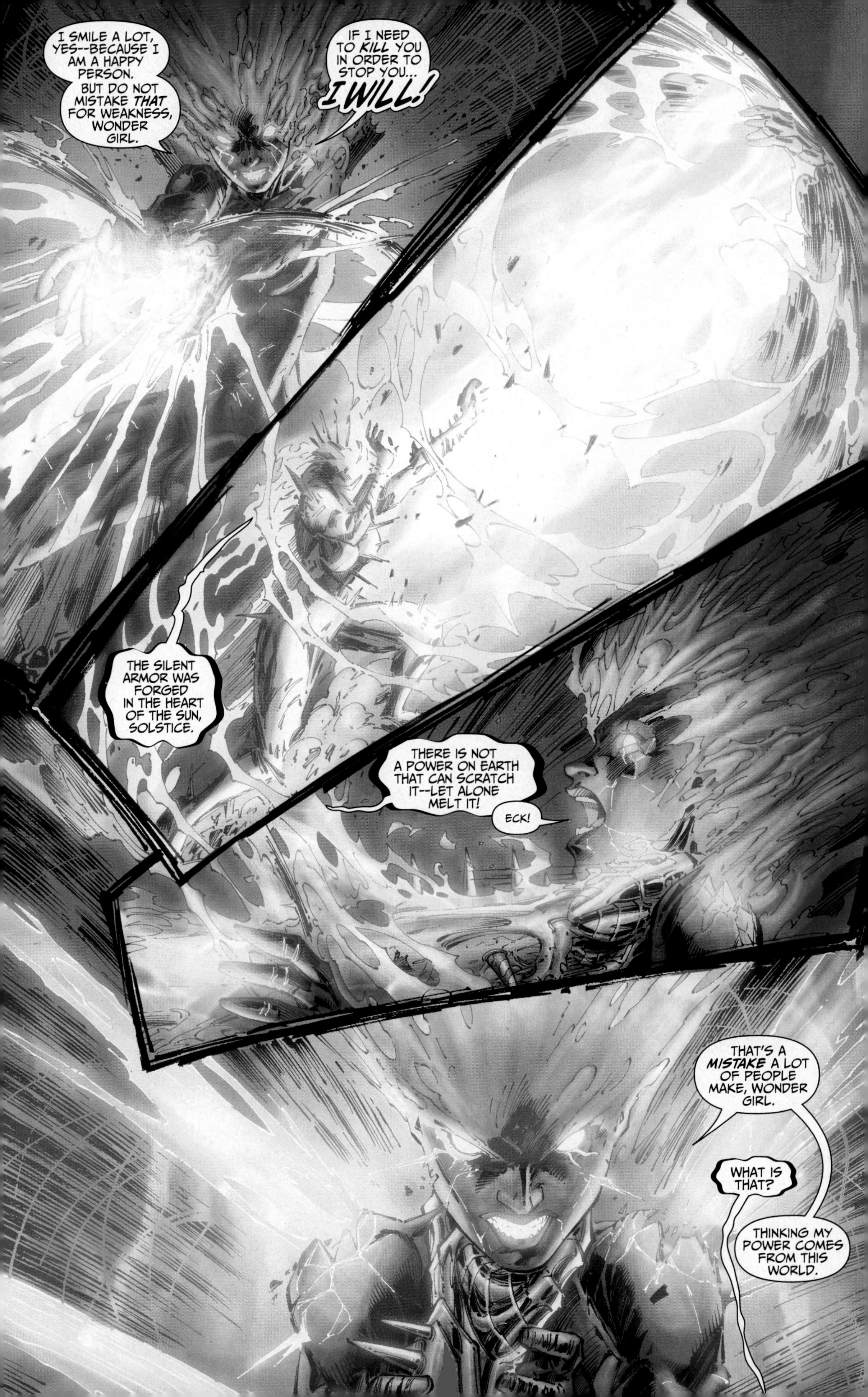
I SMILE A LOT, YES--BECAUSE I AM A HAPPY PERSON.
BUT DO NOT MISTAKE *THAT* FOR WEAKNESS, WONDER GIRL.
IF I NEED TO *KILL* YOU IN ORDER TO STOP YOU... *I WILL!*
THE SILENT ARMOR WAS FORGED IN THE HEART OF THE SUN, SOLSTICE.
THERE IS NOT A POWER ON EARTH THAT CAN SCRATCH IT--LET ALONE MELT IT!
ECK!
THAT'S A *MISTAKE* A LOT OF PEOPLE MAKE, WONDER GIRL.
WHAT IS THAT?
THINKING MY POWER COMES FROM THIS WORLD.

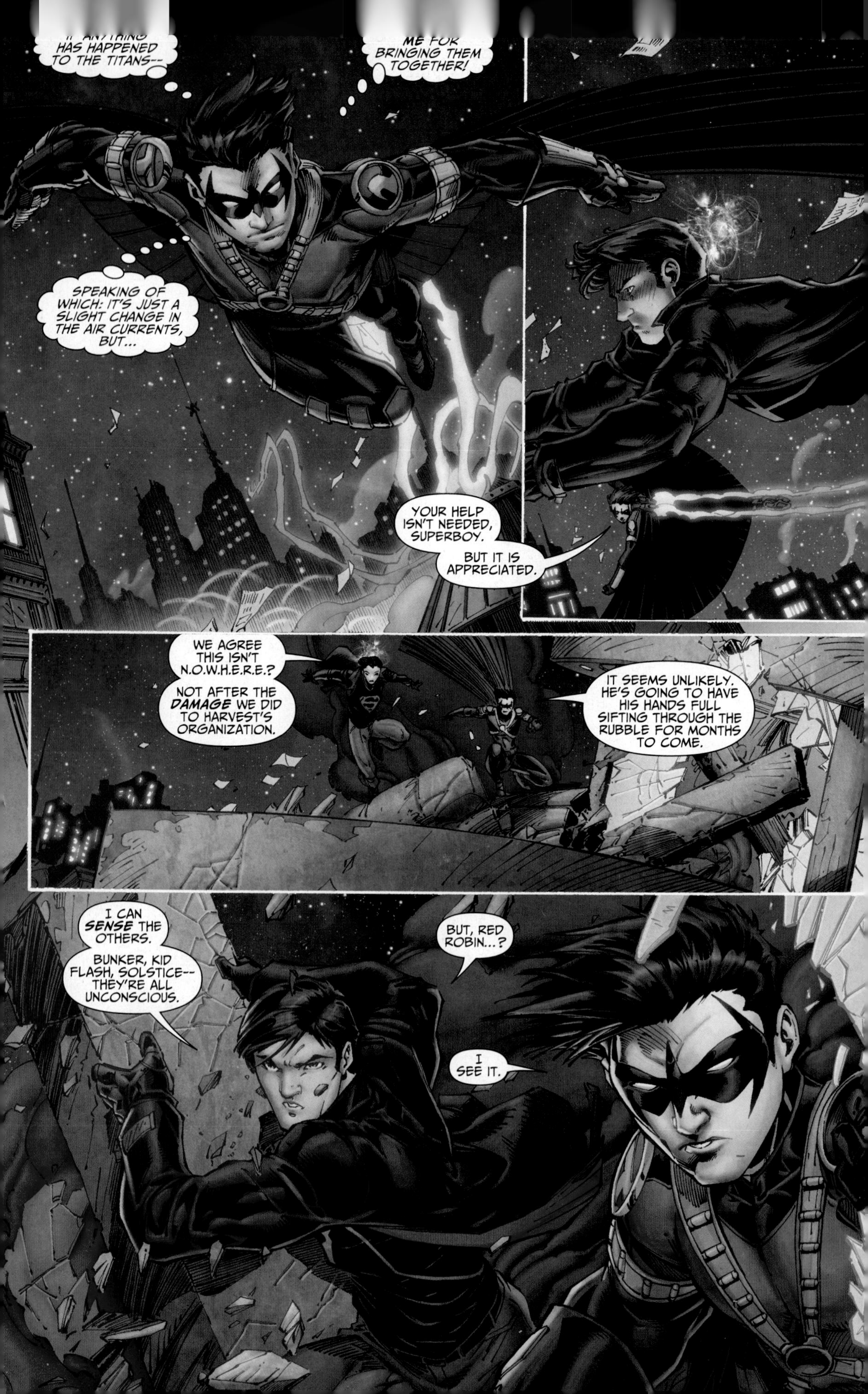
HAS HAPPENED TO THE TITANS--
ME FOR BRINGING THEM TOGETHER!
SPEAKING OF WHICH: IT'S JUST A SLIGHT CHANGE IN THE AIR CURRENTS, BUT...
YOUR HELP ISN'T NEEDED, SUPERBOY.
BUT IT IS APPRECIATED.
WE AGREE THIS ISN'T N.O.W.H.E.R.E.?
NOT AFTER THE DAMAGE WE DID TO HARVEST'S ORGANIZATION.
IT SEEMS UNLIKELY. HE'S GOING TO HAVE HIS HANDS FULL SIFTING THROUGH THE RUBBLE FOR MONTHS TO COME.
I CAN SENSE THE OTHERS.
BUNKER, KID FLASH, SOLSTICE-- THEY'RE ALL UNCONSCIOUS.
BUT, RED ROBIN...?
I SEE IT.

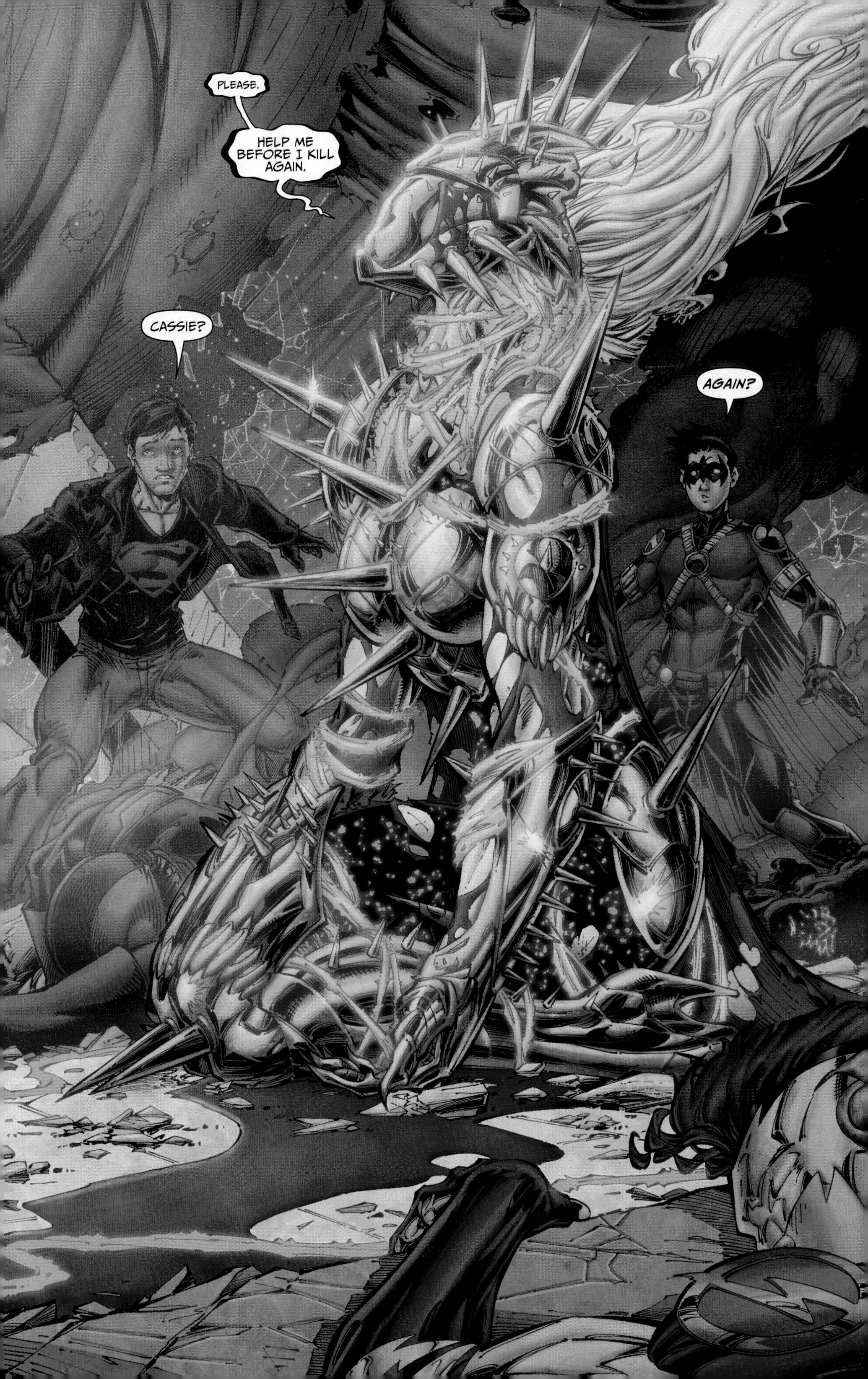
PLEASE.
HELP ME BEFORE I KILL AGAIN.
CASSIE?
AGAIN?

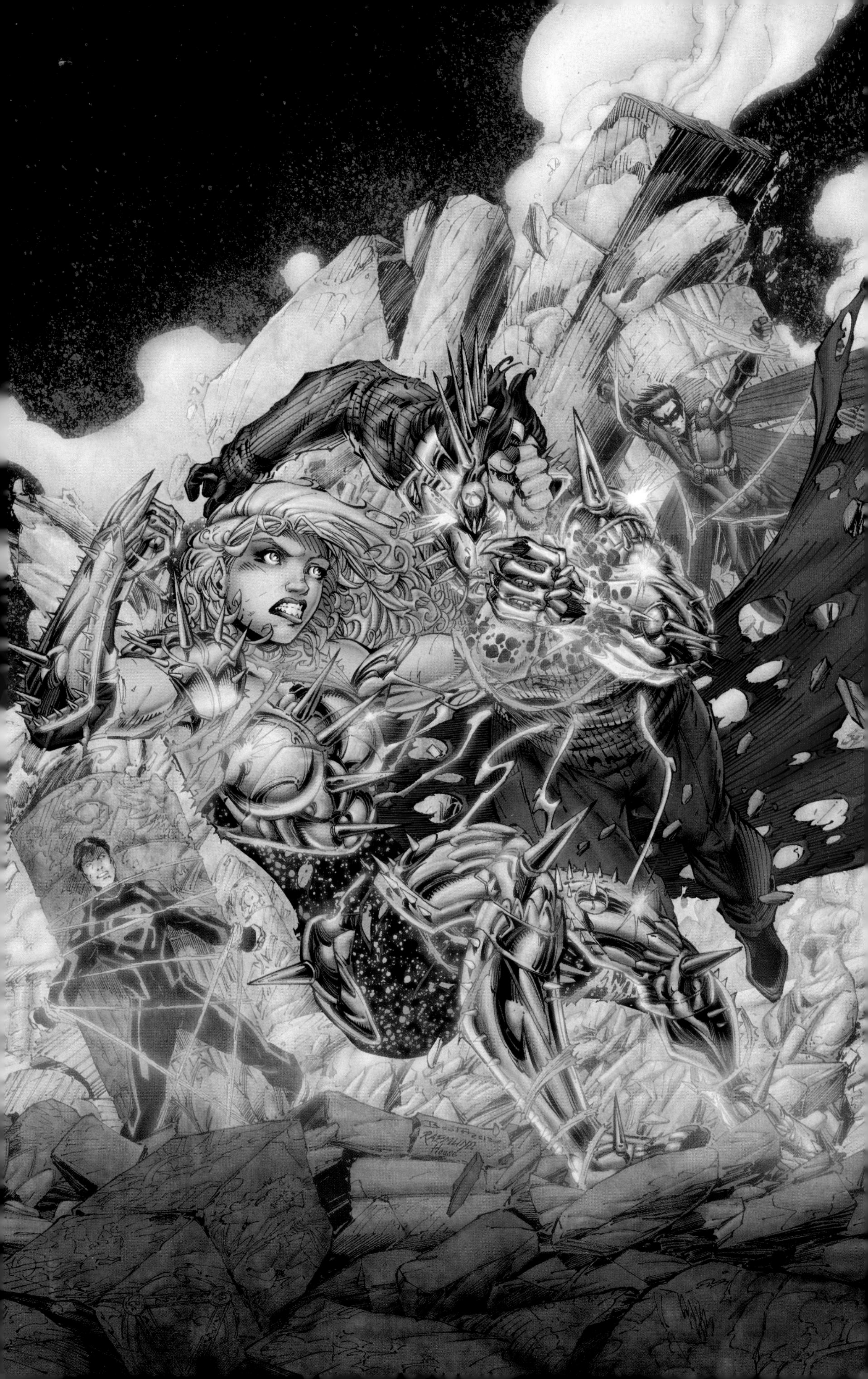

ARMORED UP AND OUT

SCOTT LOBDELL
writer

BRETT BOOTH
penciller

NORM RAPMUND
inker

cover art by
BRETT BOOTH, NORM RAPMUND & ANDREW DALHOUSE

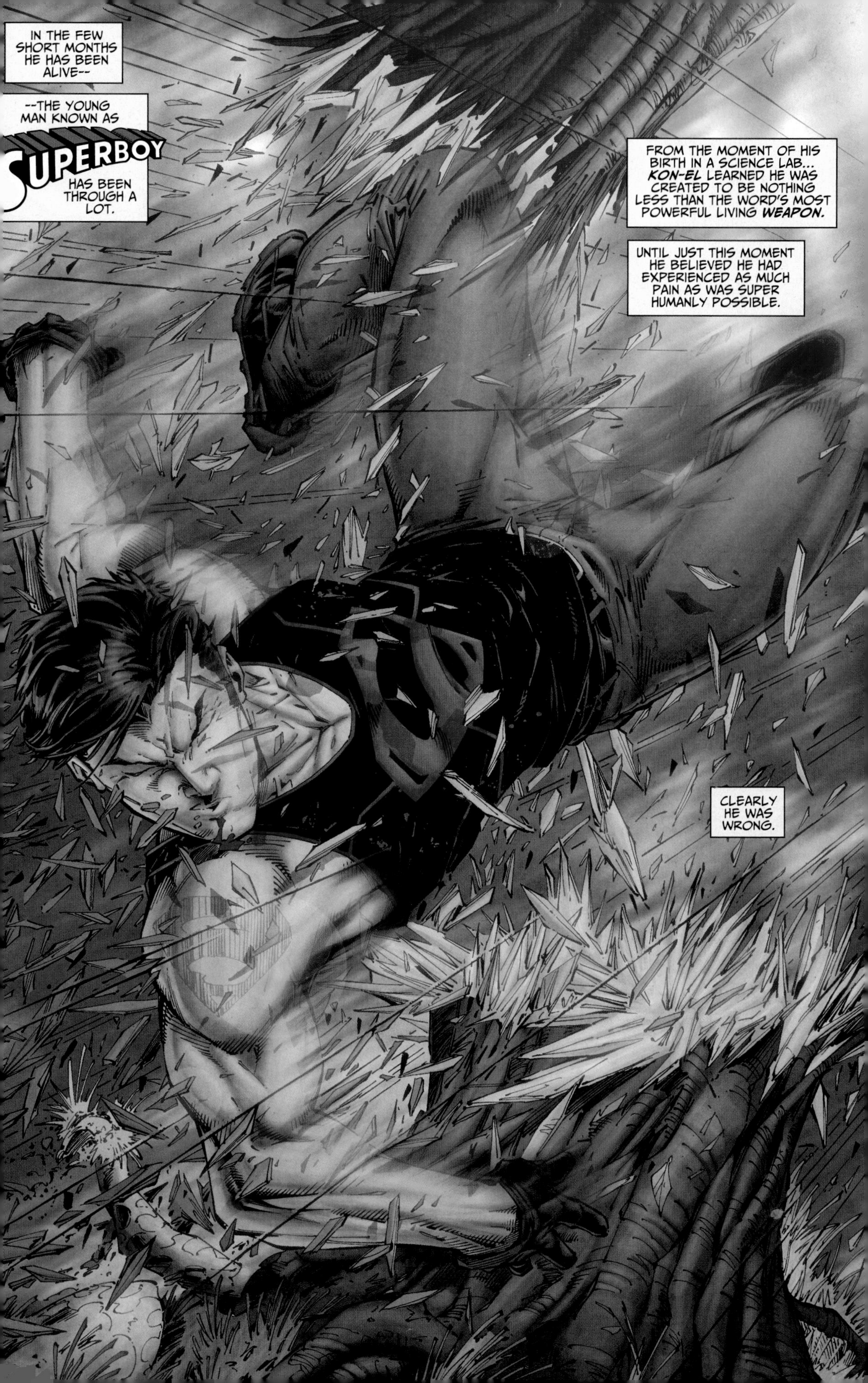
IN THE FEW SHORT MONTHS HE HAS BEEN ALIVE--
--THE YOUNG MAN KNOWN AS
SUPERBOY
HAS BEEN THROUGH A LOT.
FROM THE MOMENT OF HIS BIRTH IN A SCIENCE LAB... KON-EL LEARNED HE WAS CREATED TO BE NOTHING LESS THAN THE WORD'S MOST POWERFUL LIVING WEAPON.
UNTIL JUST THIS MOMENT HE BELIEVED HE HAD EXPERIENCED AS MUCH PAIN AS WAS SUPER HUMANLY POSSIBLE.
CLEARLY HE WAS WRONG.

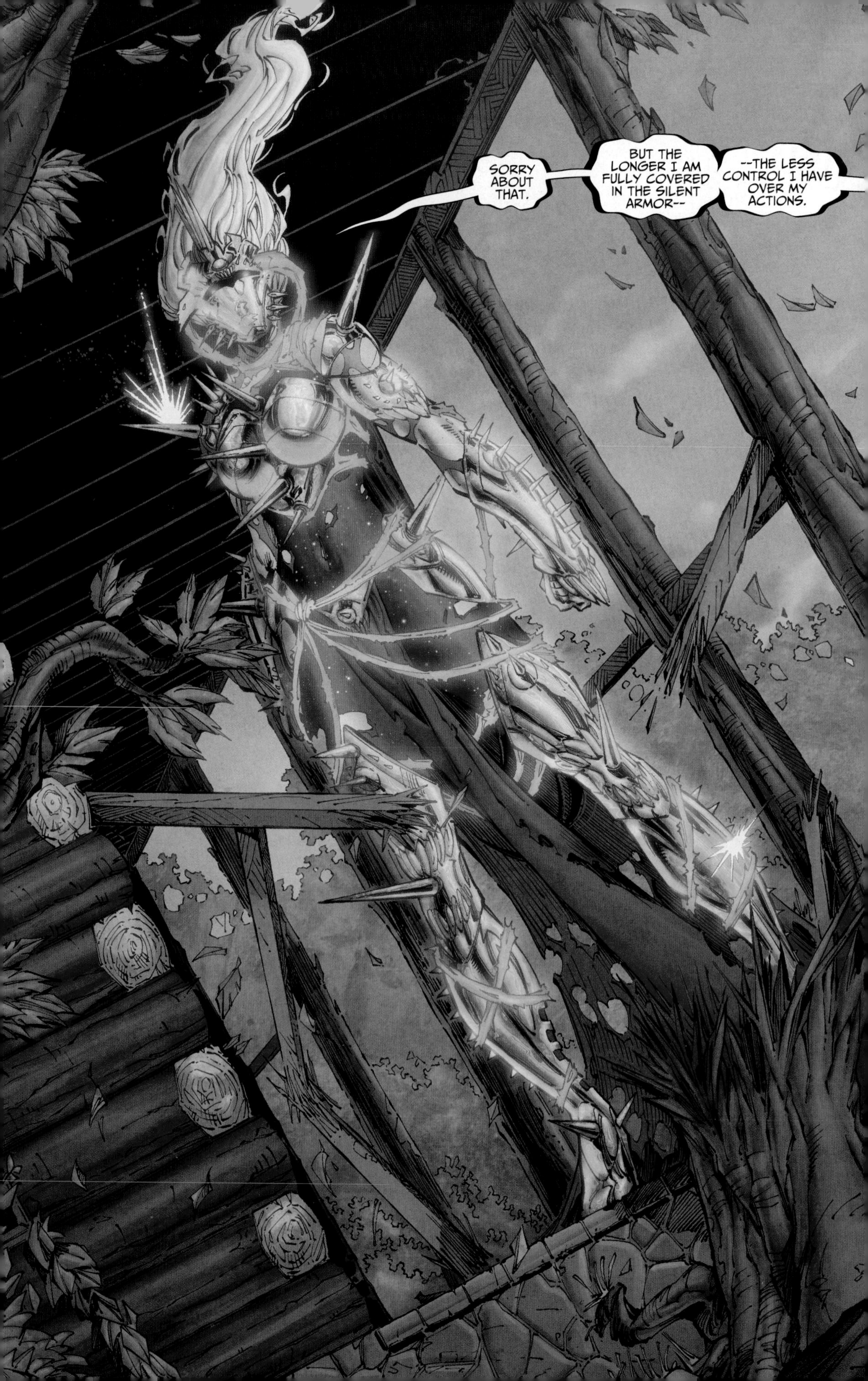
SORRY ABOUT THAT.
BUT THE LONGER I AM FULLY COVERED IN THE SILENT ARMOR--
--THE LESS CONTROL I HAVE OVER MY ACTIONS.

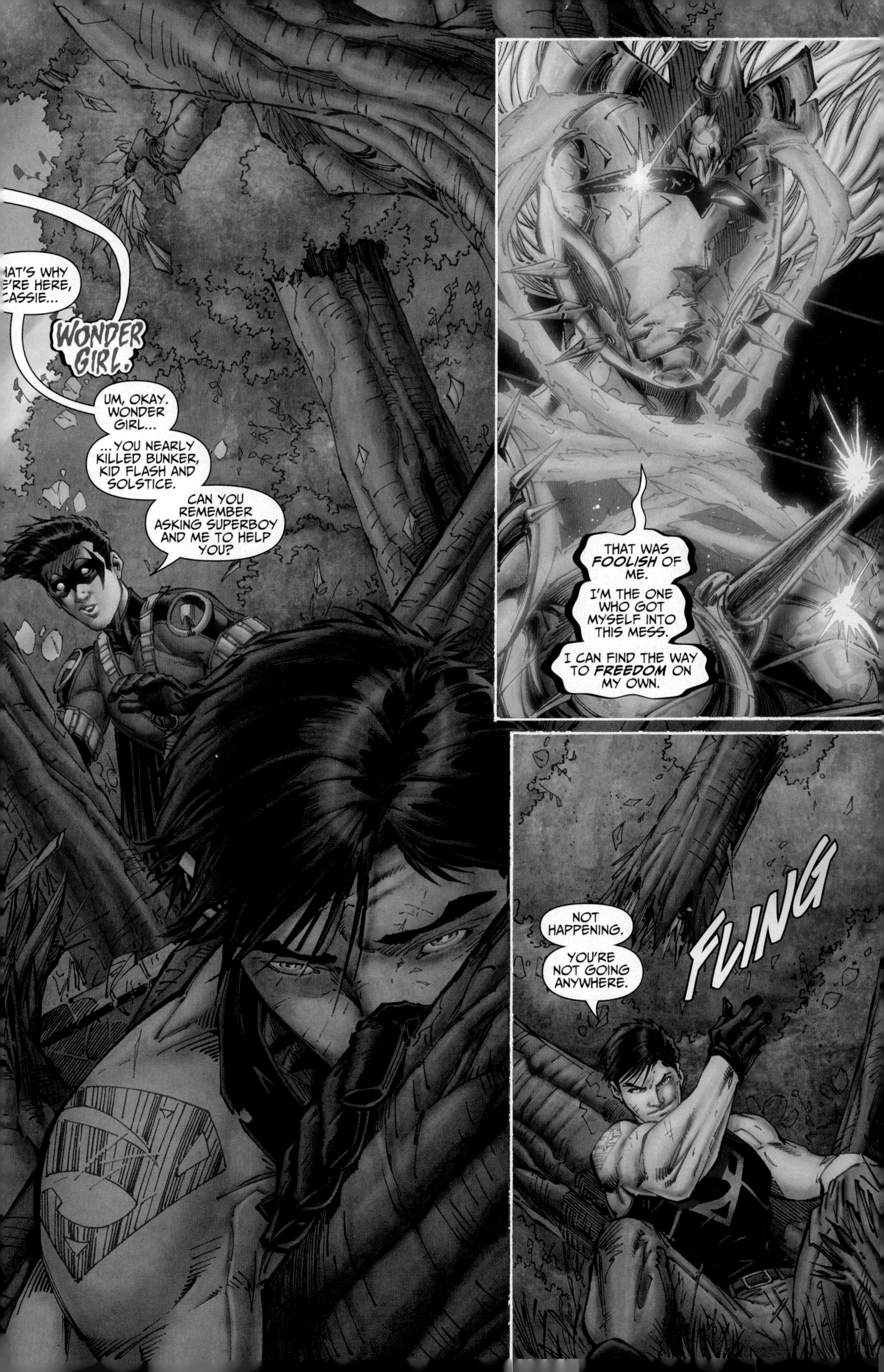

HAT'S WHY
E'RE HERE,
CASSIE...
WONDER GIRL.
UM, OKAY. WONDER GIRL...
...YOU NEARLY KILLED BUNKER, KID FLASH AND SOLSTICE.
CAN YOU REMEMBER ASKING SUPERBOY AND ME TO HELP YOU?
THAT WAS FOOLISH OF ME.
I'M THE ONE WHO GOT MYSELF INTO THIS MESS.
I CAN FIND THE WAY TO FREEDOM ON MY OWN.
NOT HAPPENING.
YOU'RE NOT GOING ANYWHERE.
FLING

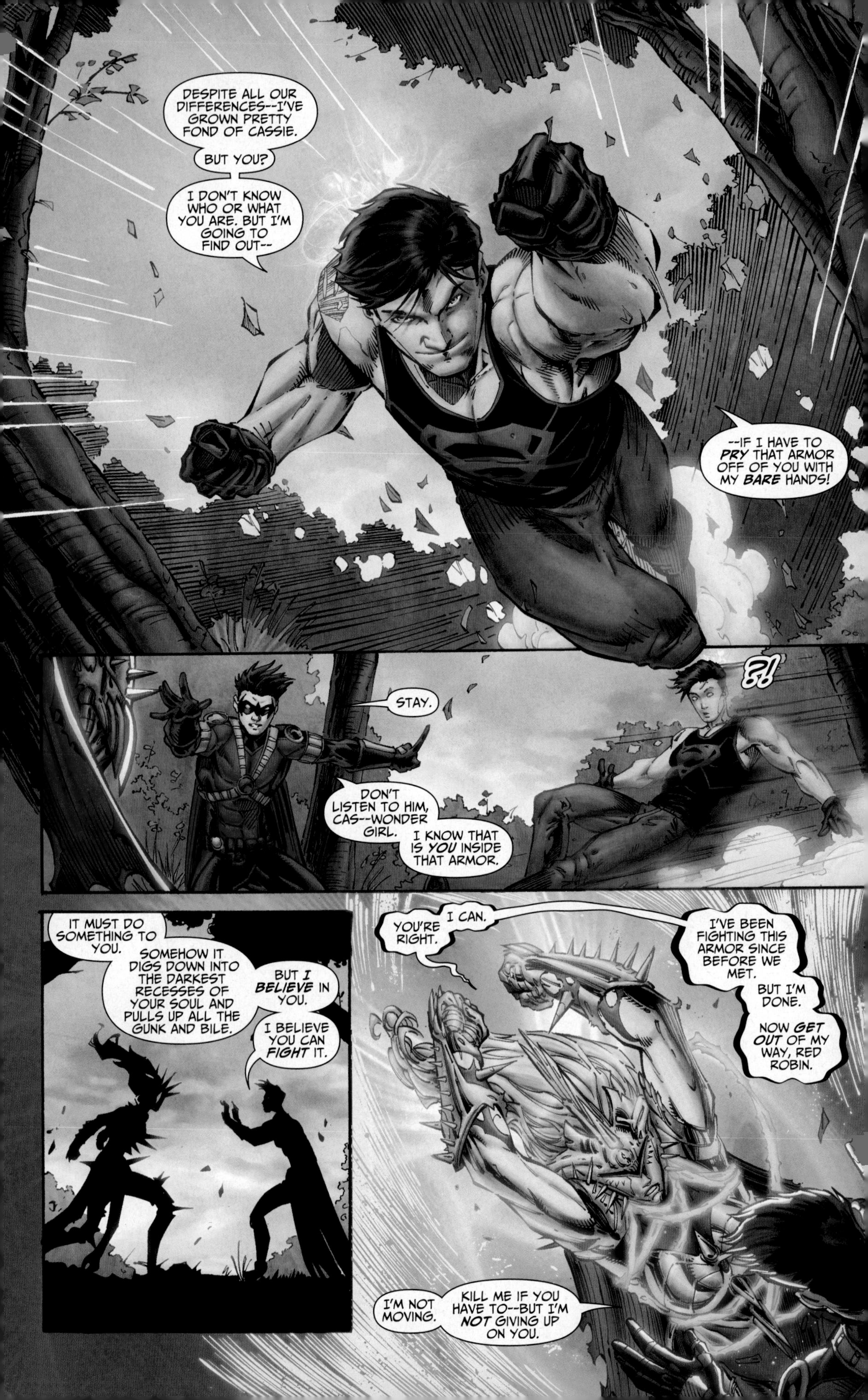
DESPITE ALL OUR DIFFERENCES--I'VE GROWN PRETTY FOND OF CASSIE.
BUT YOU?
I DON'T KNOW WHO OR WHAT YOU ARE. BUT I'M GOING TO FIND OUT--
--IF I HAVE TO PRY THAT ARMOR OFF OF YOU WITH MY BARE HANDS!
STAY.
?!
DON'T LISTEN TO HIM, CAS--WONDER GIRL.
I KNOW THAT IS YOU INSIDE THAT ARMOR.
IT MUST DO SOMETHING TO YOU.
SOMEHOW IT DIGS DOWN INTO THE DARKEST RECESSES OF YOUR SOUL AND PULLS UP ALL THE GUNK AND BILE.
BUT I BELIEVE IN YOU.
I BELIEVE YOU CAN FIGHT IT.
YOU'RE RIGHT.
I CAN.
I'VE BEEN FIGHTING THIS ARMOR SINCE BEFORE WE MET.
BUT I'M DONE.
NOW GET OUT OF MY WAY, RED ROBIN.
I'M NOT MOVING.
KILL ME IF YOU HAVE TO--BUT I'M NOT GIVING UP ON YOU.

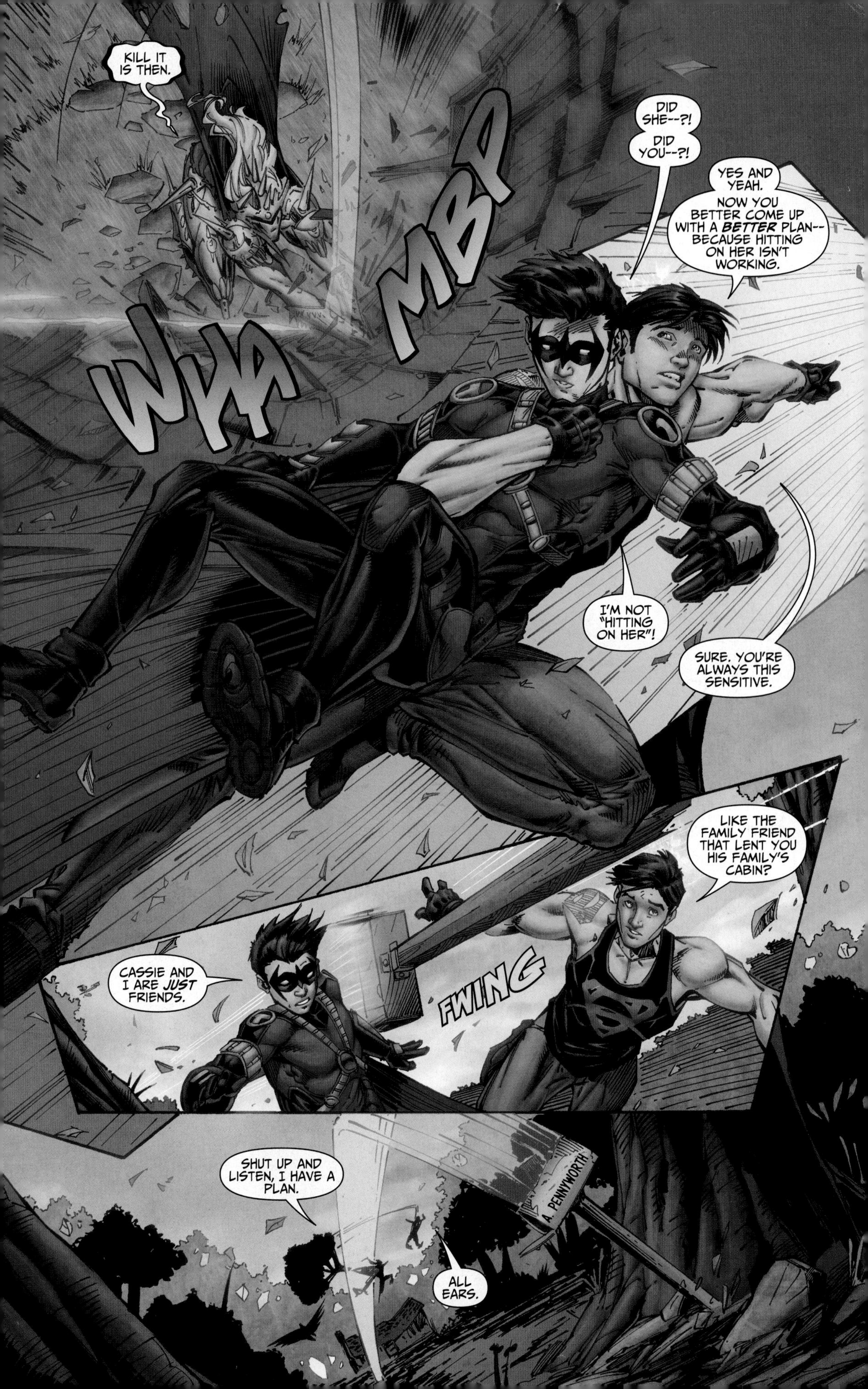
KILL IT IS THEN.
DID SHE--?!
DID YOU--?!
YES AND YEAH.
NOW YOU BETTER COME UP WITH A BETTER PLAN--BECAUSE HITTING ON HER ISN'T WORKING.
WHAMBP
I'M NOT "HITTING ON HER"!
SURE. YOU'RE ALWAYS THIS SENSITIVE.
CASSIE AND I ARE JUST FRIENDS.
LIKE THE FAMILY FRIEND THAT LENT YOU HIS FAMILY'S CABIN?
FWING
SHUT UP AND LISTEN, I HAVE A PLAN.
A. PENNYWORTH
ALL EARS.

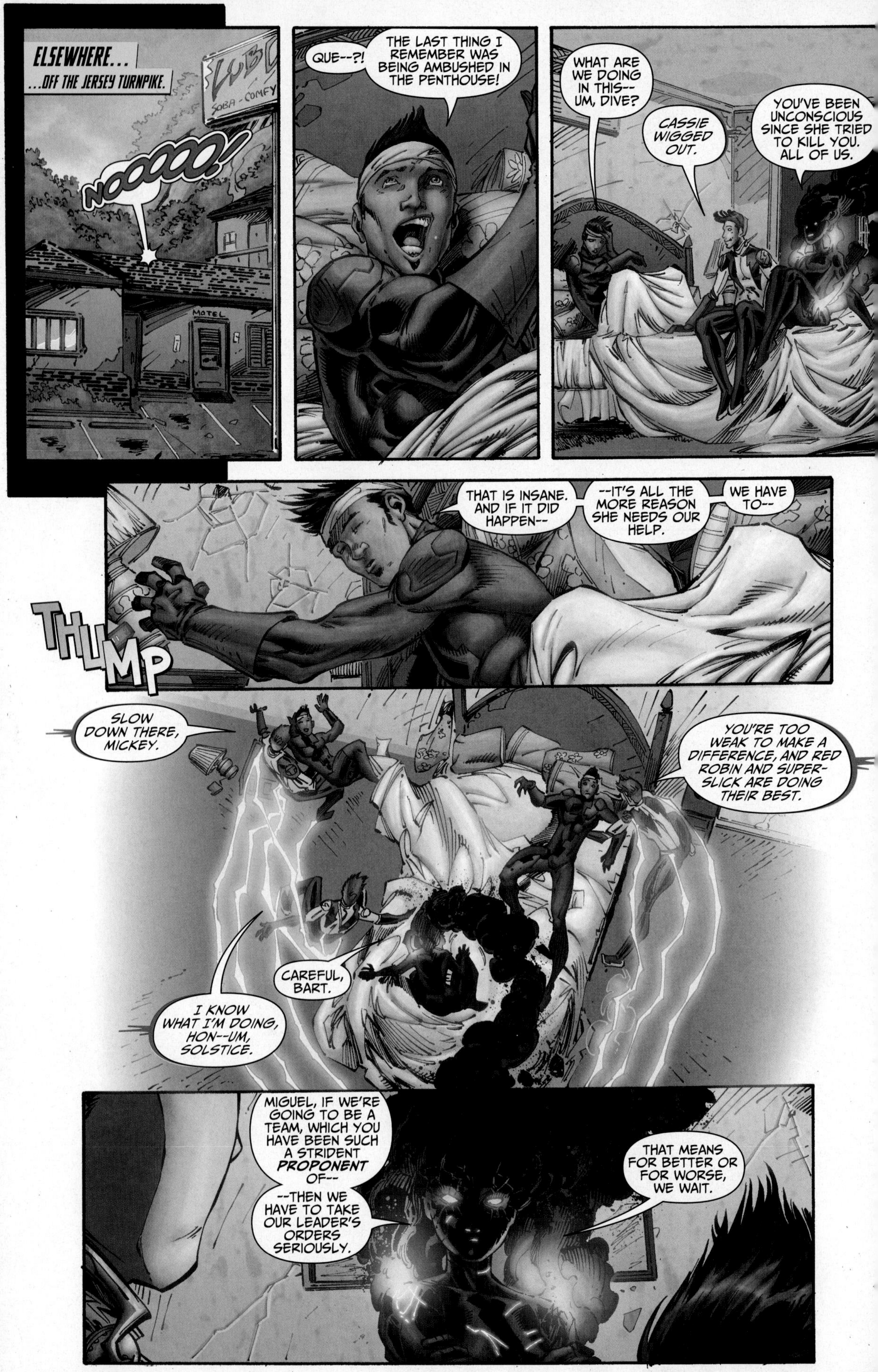
ELSEWHERE...
...OFF THE JERSEY TURNPIKE.
LOBO
SOBA - COMEY
NOOOOO!
MOTEL
QUE--?!
THE LAST THING I REMEMBER WAS BEING AMBUSHED IN THE PENTHOUSE!
WHAT ARE WE DOING IN THIS-- UM, DIVE?
CASSIE WIGGED OUT.
YOU'VE BEEN UNCONSCIOUS SINCE SHE TRIED TO KILL YOU. ALL OF US.
THAT IS INSANE. AND IF IT DID HAPPEN--
--IT'S ALL THE MORE REASON SHE NEEDS OUR HELP.
WE HAVE TO--
THUMP
SLOW DOWN THERE, MICKEY.
YOU'RE TOO WEAK TO MAKE A DIFFERENCE, AND RED ROBIN AND SUPER-SLICK ARE DOING THEIR BEST.
CAREFUL, BART.
I KNOW WHAT I'M DOING, HON--UM, SOLSTICE.
MIGUEL, IF WE'RE GOING TO BE A TEAM, WHICH YOU HAVE BEEN SUCH A STRIDENT PROPONENT OF--
--THEN WE HAVE TO TAKE OUR LEADER'S ORDERS SERIOUSLY.
THAT MEANS FOR BETTER OR FOR WORSE, WE WAIT.

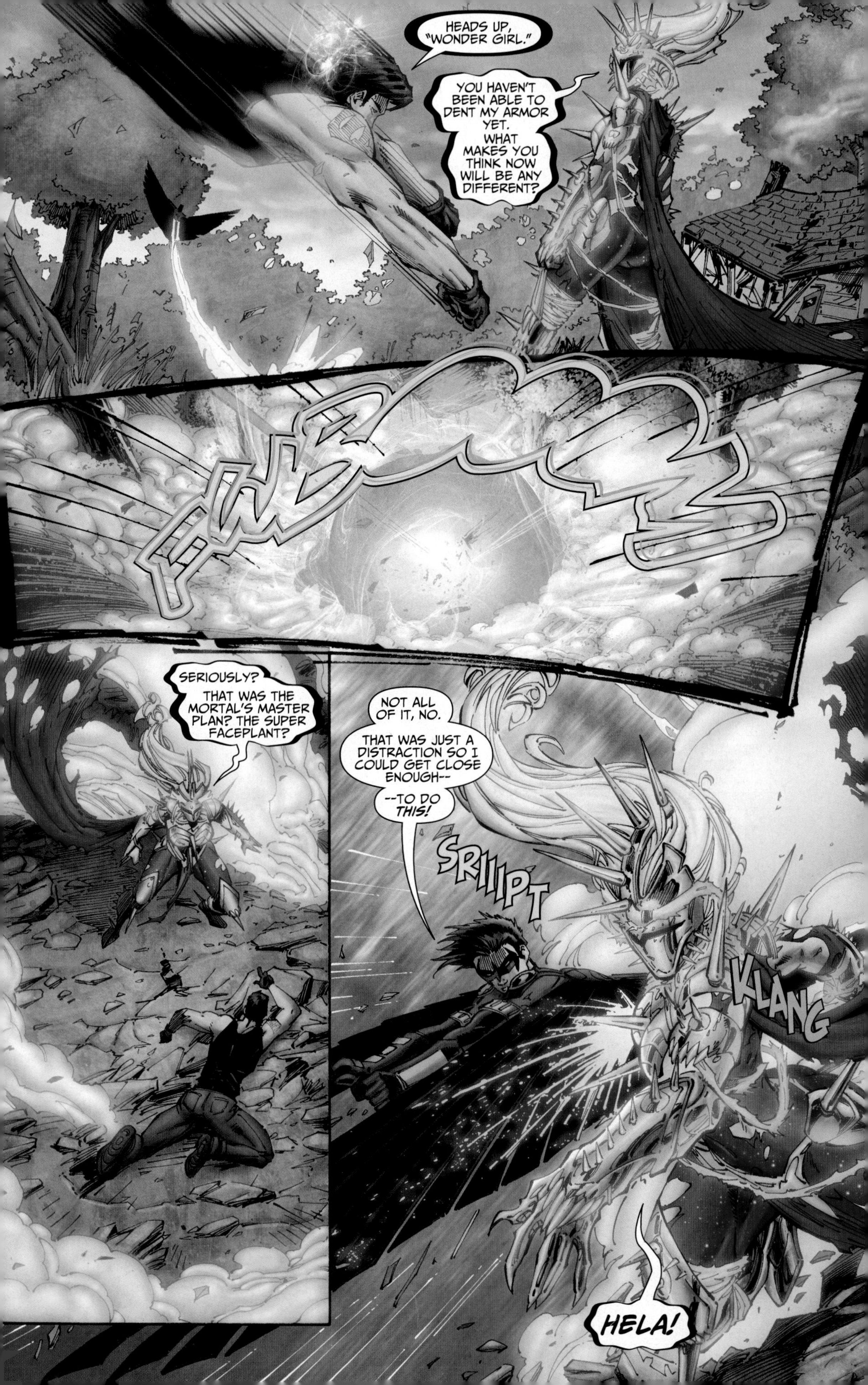
HEADS UP, "WONDER GIRL."
YOU HAVEN'T BEEN ABLE TO DENT MY ARMOR YET. WHAT MAKES YOU THINK NOW WILL BE ANY DIFFERENT?
SERIOUSLY? THAT WAS THE MORTAL'S MASTER PLAN? THE SUPER FACEPLANT?
NOT ALL OF IT, NO.
THAT WAS JUST A DISTRACTION SO I COULD GET CLOSE ENOUGH--
--TO DO *THIS!*
SRIIIPT
KLANG
HELA!

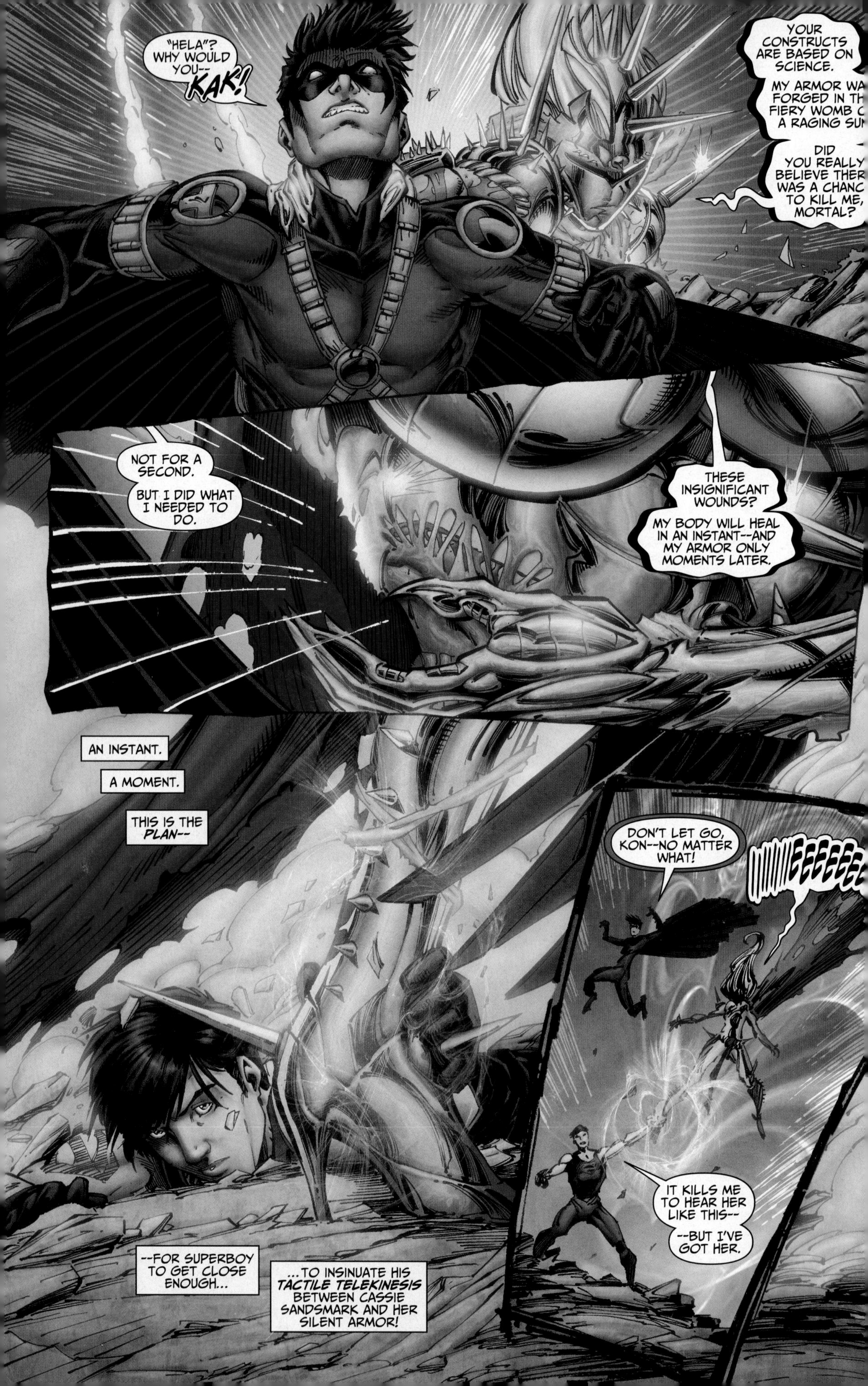

"HELA"? WHY WOULD YOU-- KAK!
YOUR CONSTRUCTS ARE BASED ON SCIENCE.
MY ARMOR WA FORGED IN TH FIERY WOMB O A RAGING SU
DID YOU REALLY BELIEVE THER WAS A CHANC TO KILL ME, MORTAL?
NOT FOR A SECOND.
BUT I DID WHAT I NEEDED TO DO.
THESE INSIGNIFICANT WOUNDS?
MY BODY WILL HEAL IN AN INSTANT--AND MY ARMOR ONLY MOMENTS LATER.
AN INSTANT.
A MOMENT.
THIS IS THE PLAN--
DON'T LET GO, KON--NO MATTER WHAT!
IIIIIIEEEEEEE
IT KILLS ME TO HEAR HER LIKE THIS--
--BUT I'VE GOT HER.
--FOR SUPERBOY TO GET CLOSE ENOUGH...
...TO INSINUATE HIS TACTILE TELEKINESIS BETWEEN CASSIE SANDSMARK AND HER SILENT ARMOR!

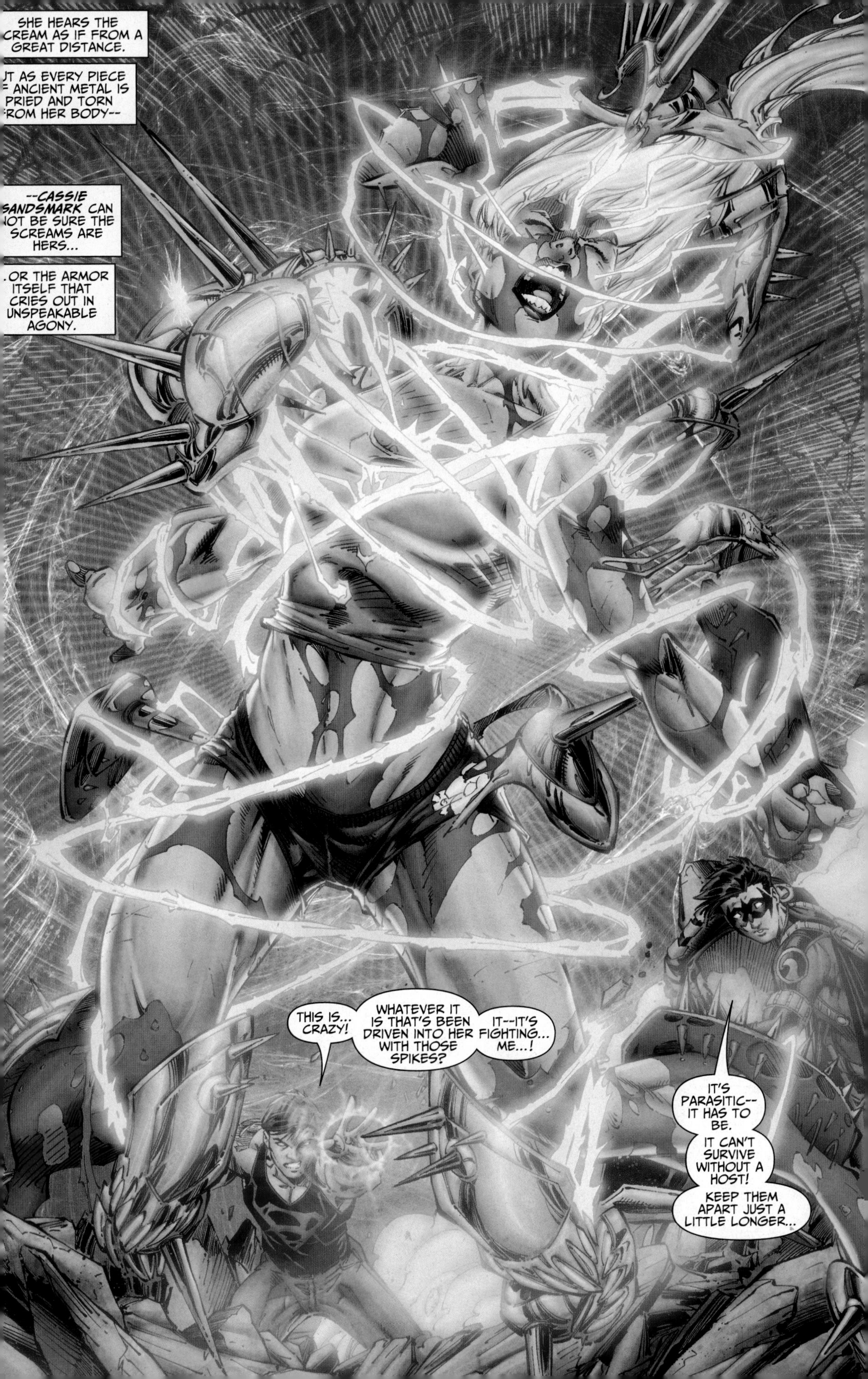
SHE HEARS THE CREAM AS IF FROM A GREAT DISTANCE.
UT AS EVERY PIECE F ANCIENT METAL IS PRIED AND TORN FROM HER BODY--
--CASSIE SANDSMARK CAN NOT BE SURE THE SCREAMS ARE HERS...
.OR THE ARMOR ITSELF THAT CRIES OUT IN UNSPEAKABLE AGONY.
THIS IS... CRAZY!
WHATEVER IT IS THAT'S BEEN DRIVEN INTO HER WITH THOSE SPIKES?
IT--IT'S FIGHTING... ME...!
IT'S PARASITIC-- IT HAS TO BE.
IT CAN'T SURVIVE WITHOUT A HOST!
KEEP THEM APART JUST A LITTLE LONGER...

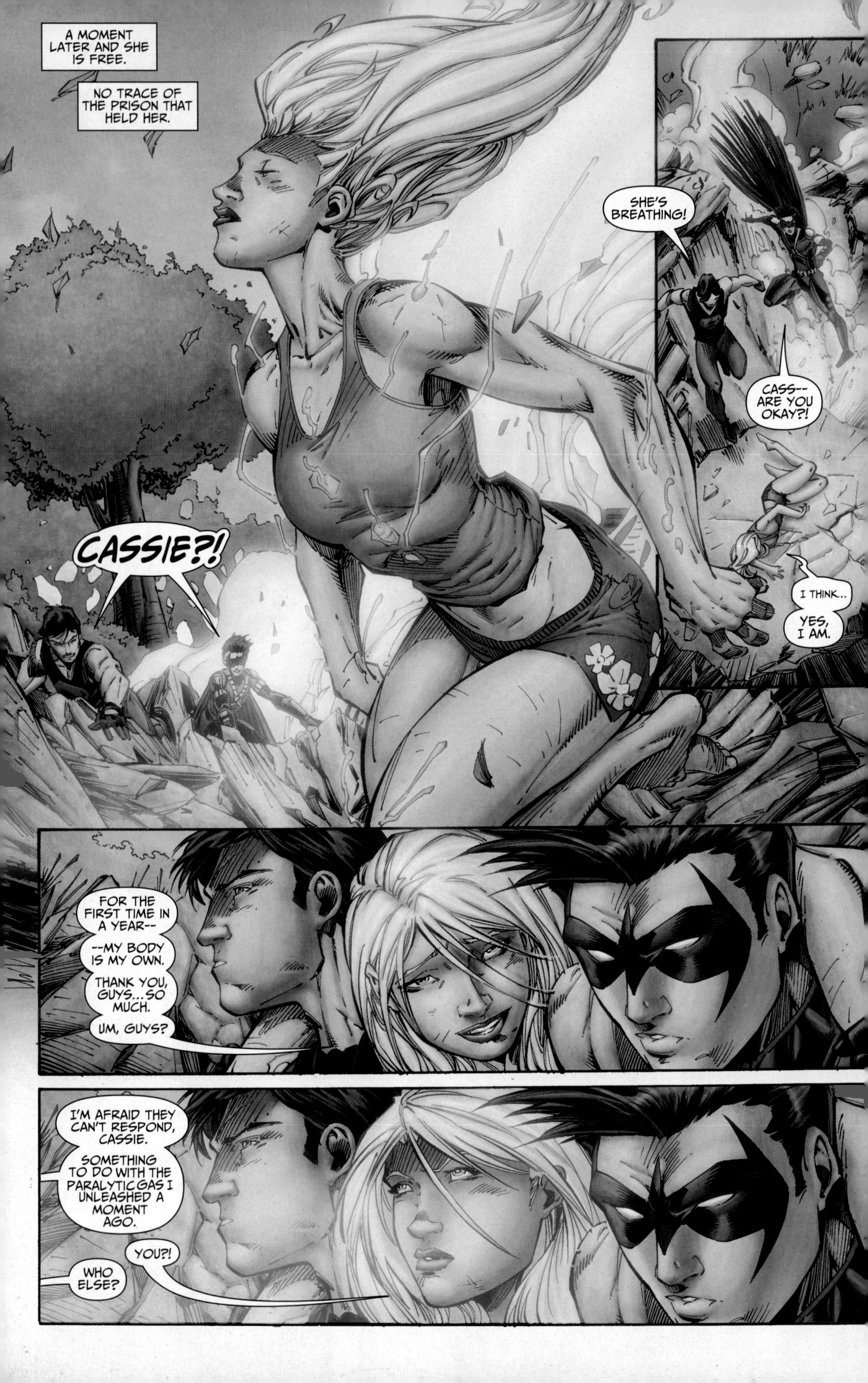
A MOMENT LATER AND SHE IS FREE.
NO TRACE OF THE PRISON THAT HELD HER.
CASSIE?!
SHE'S BREATHING!
CASS-- ARE YOU OKAY?!
I THINK...
YES, I AM.
FOR THE FIRST TIME IN A YEAR--
--MY BODY IS MY OWN.
THANK YOU, GUYS...SO MUCH.
UM, GUYS?
I'M AFRAID THEY CAN'T RESPOND, CASSIE.
SOMETHING TO DO WITH THE PARALYTIC GAS I UNLEASHED A MOMENT AGO.
YOU?!
WHO ELSE?

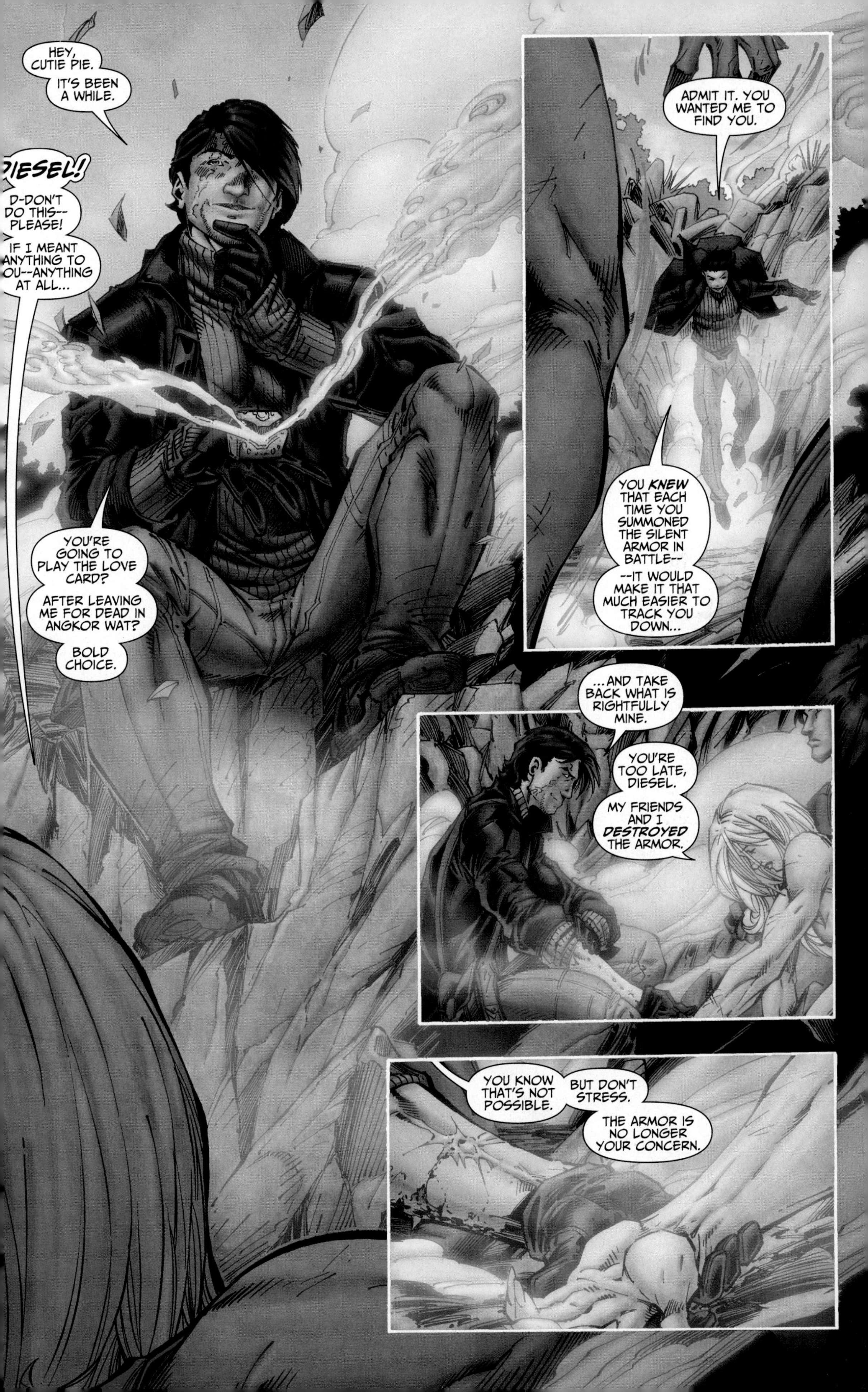
HEY, CUTIE PIE.
IT'S BEEN A WHILE.
DIESEL!
D-DON'T DO THIS-- PLEASE!
IF I MEANT ANYTHING TO YOU--ANYTHING AT ALL...
YOU'RE GOING TO PLAY THE LOVE CARD?
AFTER LEAVING ME FOR DEAD IN ANGKOR WAT?
BOLD CHOICE.
ADMIT IT. YOU WANTED ME TO FIND YOU.
YOU *KNEW* THAT EACH TIME YOU SUMMONED THE SILENT ARMOR IN BATTLE--
--IT WOULD MAKE IT THAT MUCH EASIER TO TRACK YOU DOWN...
...AND TAKE BACK WHAT IS RIGHTFULLY MINE.
YOU'RE TOO LATE, DIESEL.
MY FRIENDS AND I *DESTROYED* THE ARMOR.
YOU KNOW THAT'S NOT POSSIBLE.
BUT DON'T STRESS.
THE ARMOR IS NO LONGER YOUR CONCERN.

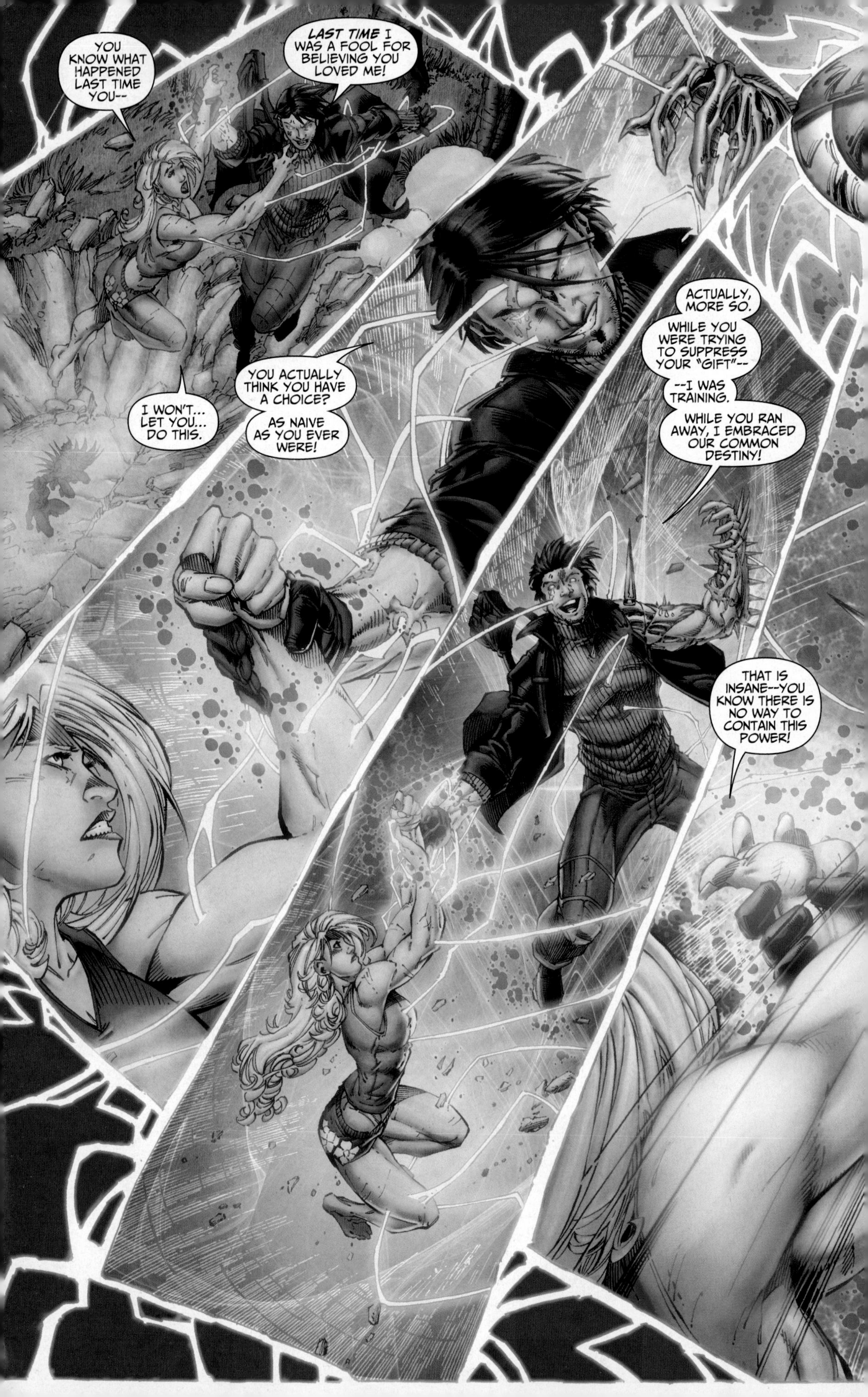
YOU KNOW WHAT HAPPENED LAST TIME YOU--
LAST TIME I WAS A FOOL FOR BELIEVING YOU LOVED ME!
I WON'T... LET YOU... DO THIS.
YOU ACTUALLY THINK YOU HAVE A CHOICE?
AS NAIVE AS YOU EVER WERE!
ACTUALLY, MORE SO.
WHILE YOU WERE TRYING TO SUPPRESS YOUR "GIFT"--
--I WAS TRAINING.
WHILE YOU RAN AWAY, I EMBRACED OUR COMMON DESTINY!
THAT IS INSANE--YOU KNOW THERE IS NO WAY TO CONTAIN THIS POWER!

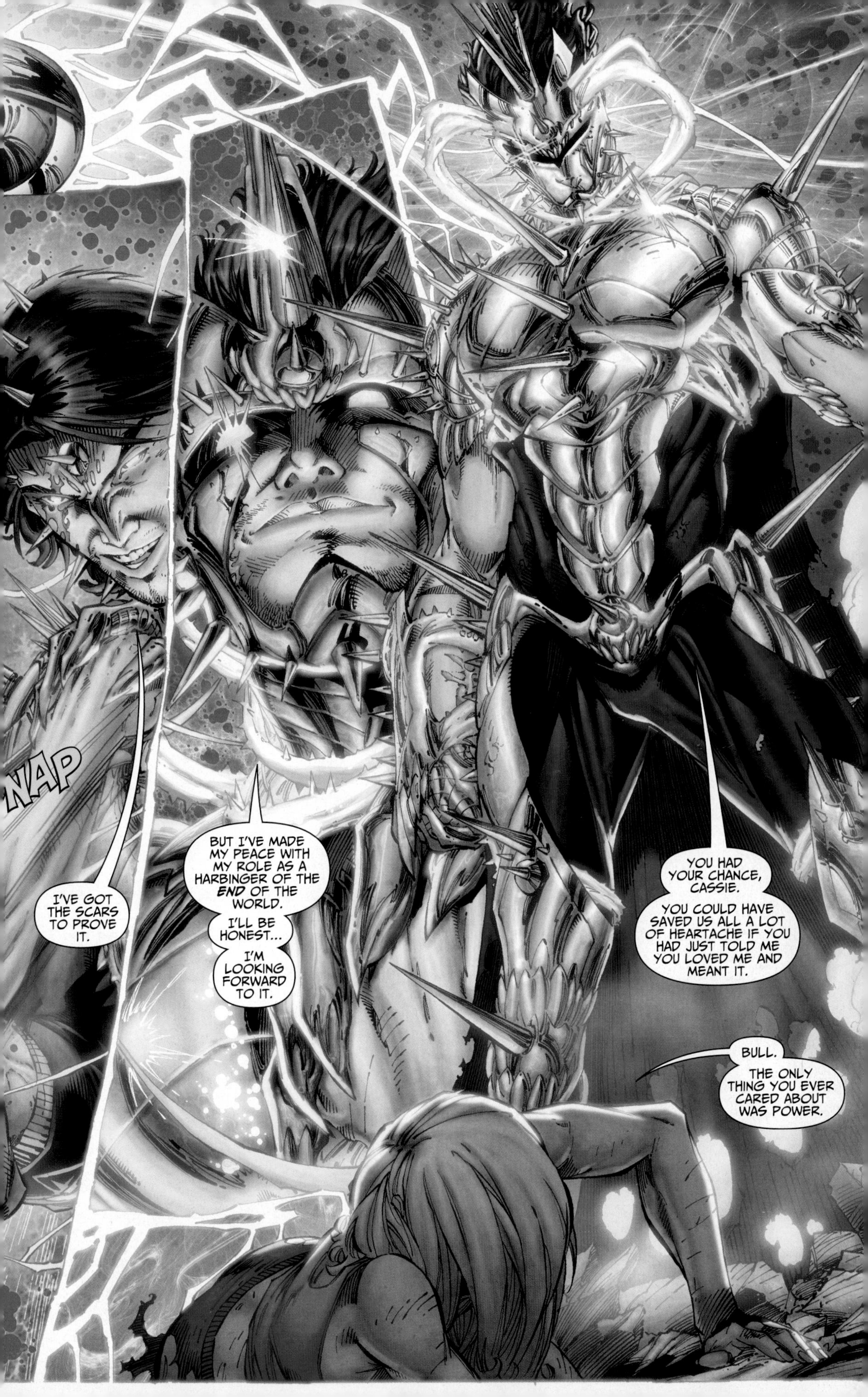
NAP
I'VE GOT THE SCARS TO PROVE IT.
BUT I'VE MADE MY PEACE WITH MY ROLE AS A HARBINGER OF THE END OF THE WORLD.
I'LL BE HONEST...
I'M LOOKING FORWARD TO IT.
YOU HAD YOUR CHANCE, CASSIE.
YOU COULD HAVE SAVED US ALL A LOT OF HEARTACHE IF YOU HAD JUST TOLD ME YOU LOVED ME AND MEANT IT.
BULL.
THE ONLY THING YOU EVER CARED ABOUT WAS POWER.

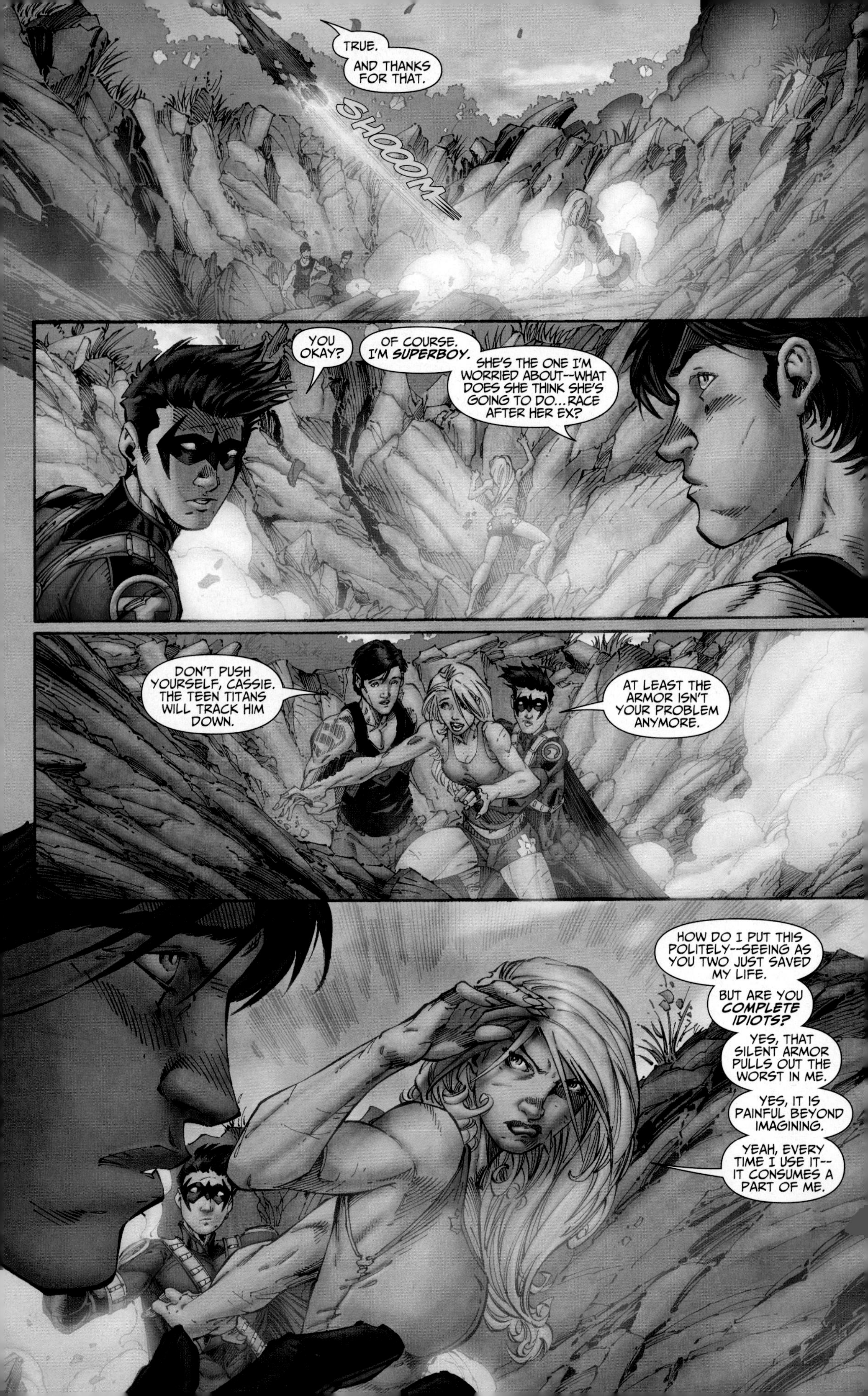

TRUE.
AND THANKS FOR THAT.
SHOOOM
YOU OKAY?
OF COURSE. I'M SUPERBOY.
SHE'S THE ONE I'M WORRIED ABOUT--WHAT DOES SHE THINK SHE'S GOING TO DO...RACE AFTER HER EX?
DON'T PUSH YOURSELF, CASSIE. THE TEEN TITANS WILL TRACK HIM DOWN.
AT LEAST THE ARMOR ISN'T YOUR PROBLEM ANYMORE.
HOW DO I PUT THIS POLITELY--SEEING AS YOU TWO JUST SAVED MY LIFE.
BUT ARE YOU COMPLETE IDIOTS?
YES, THAT SILENT ARMOR PULLS OUT THE WORST IN ME.
YES, IT IS PAINFUL BEYOND IMAGINING.
YEAH, EVERY TIME I USE IT--IT CONSUMES A PART OF ME.

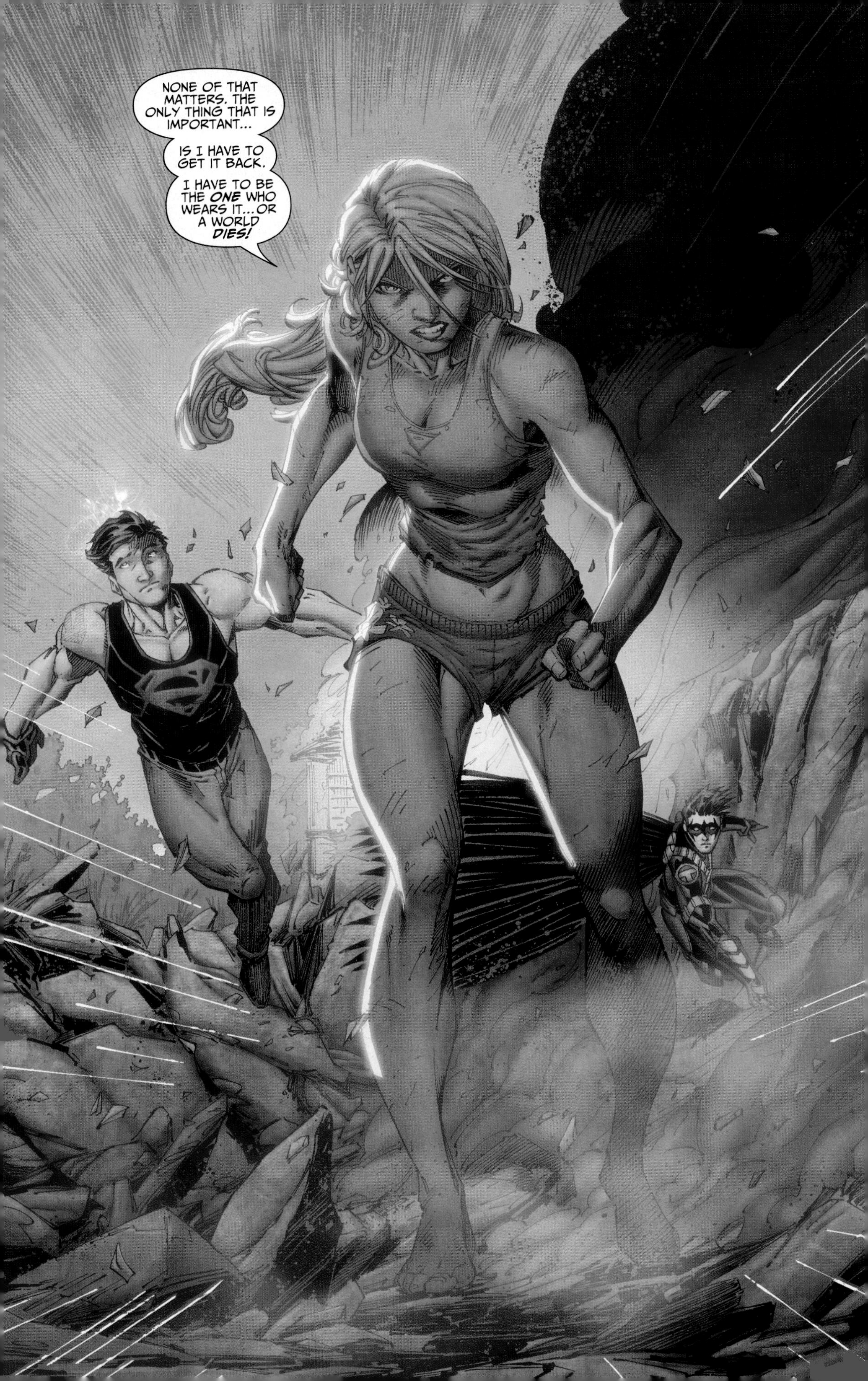
NONE OF THAT MATTERS. THE ONLY THING THAT IS IMPORTANT...
IS I HAVE TO GET IT BACK.
I HAVE TO BE THE ONE WHO WEARS IT...OR A WORLD DIES!

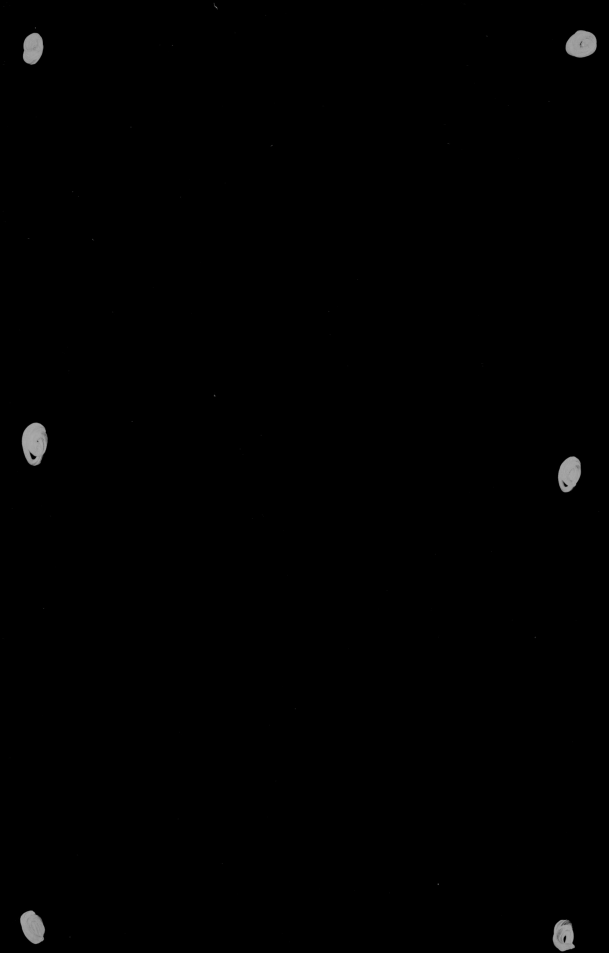

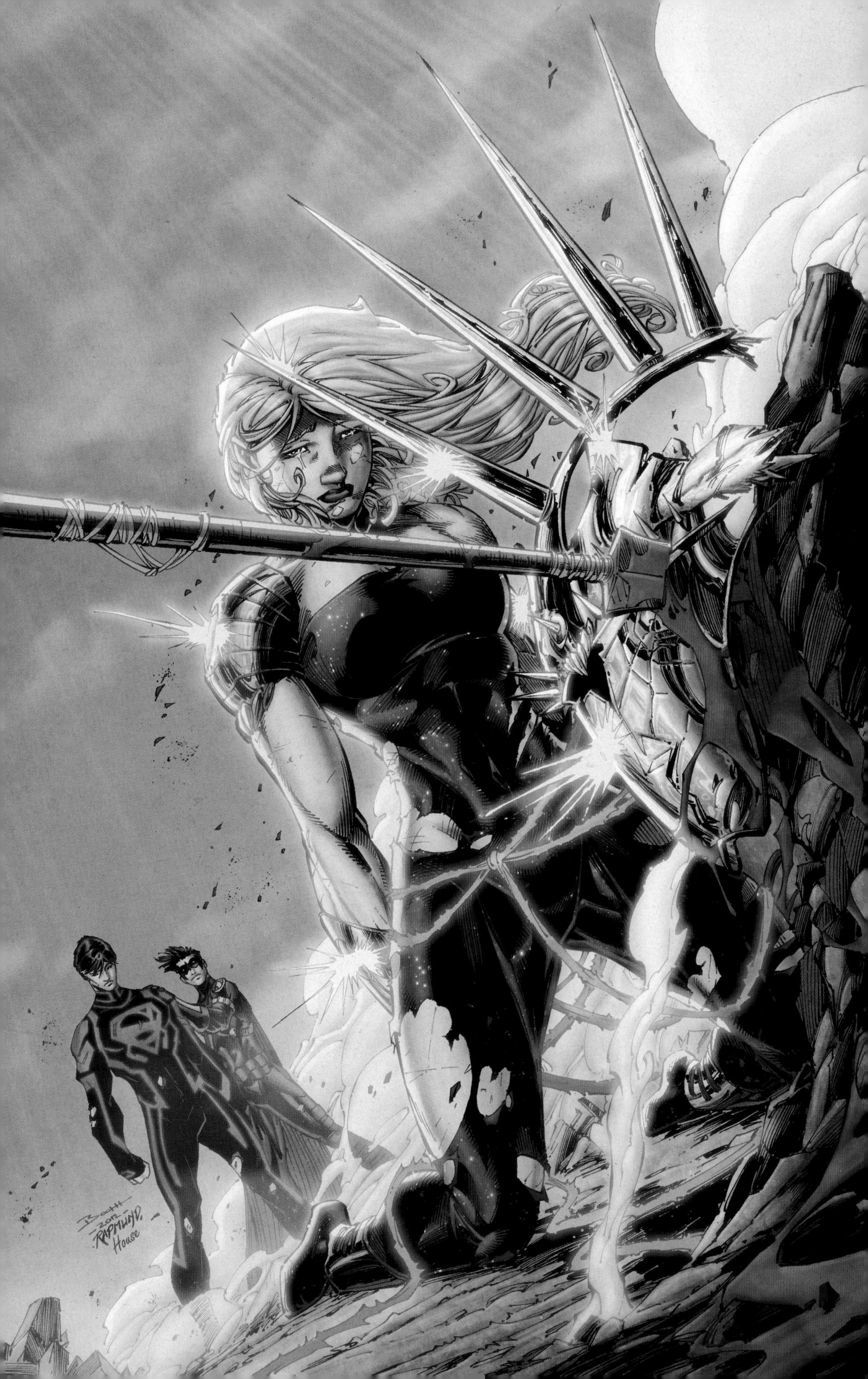
Booth
2012
RAPMUND.
House

THE ORIGIN OF WONDER GIRL part one

SCOTT LOBDELL
writer

FABIAN NICIEZA
scripter

ALÉ GARZA
artist

cover art by
BRETT BOOTH, NORM RAPMUND & ANDREW DALHOUSE

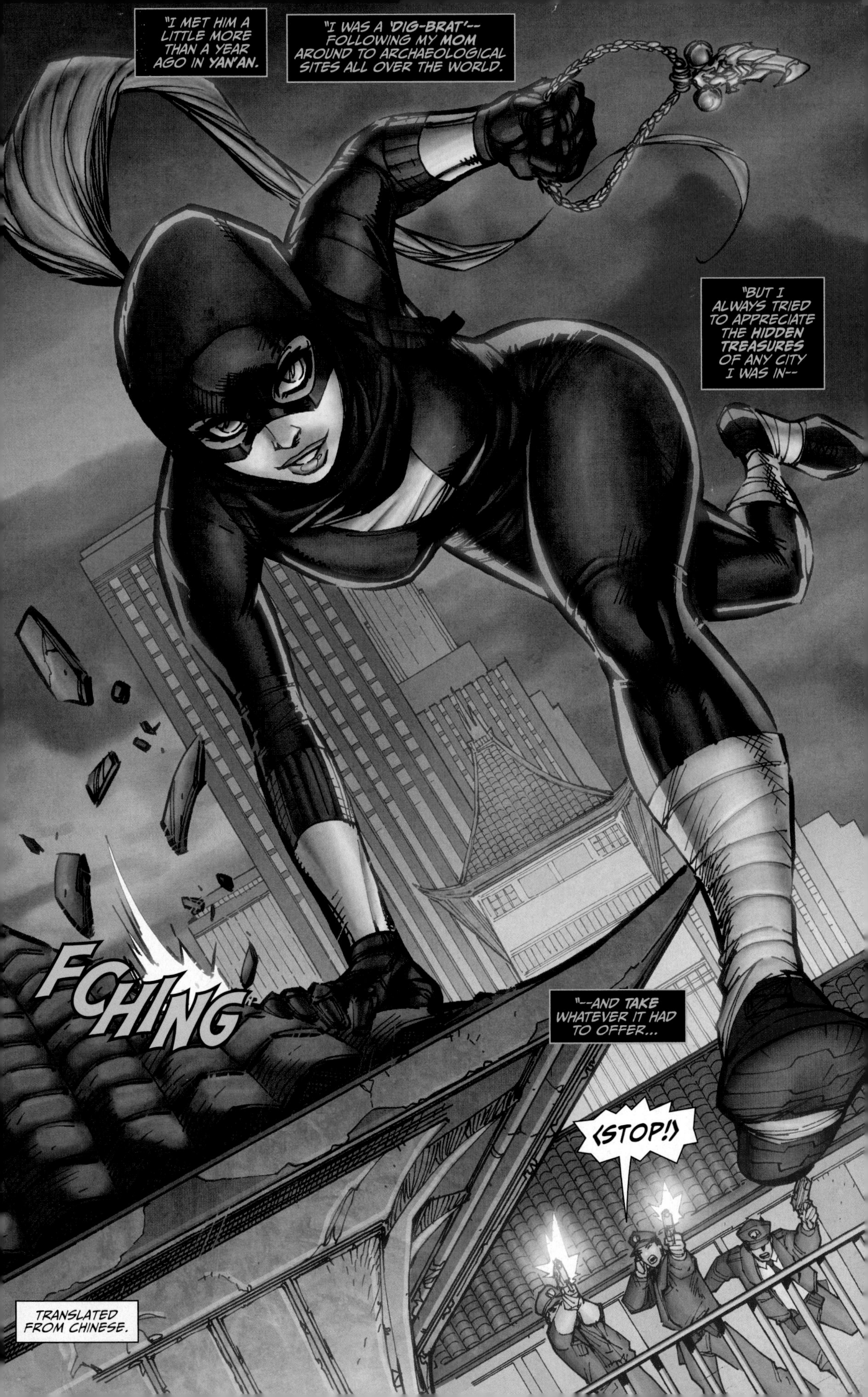
"I MET HIM A LITTLE MORE THAN A YEAR AGO IN YAN'AN.
"I WAS A 'DIG-BRAT'-- FOLLOWING MY MOM AROUND TO ARCHAEOLOGICAL SITES ALL OVER THE WORLD.
"BUT I ALWAYS TRIED TO APPRECIATE THE HIDDEN TREASURES OF ANY CITY I WAS IN--
FCHING
"--AND TAKE WHATEVER IT HAD TO OFFER...
⟨STOP!⟩
TRANSLATED FROM CHINESE.

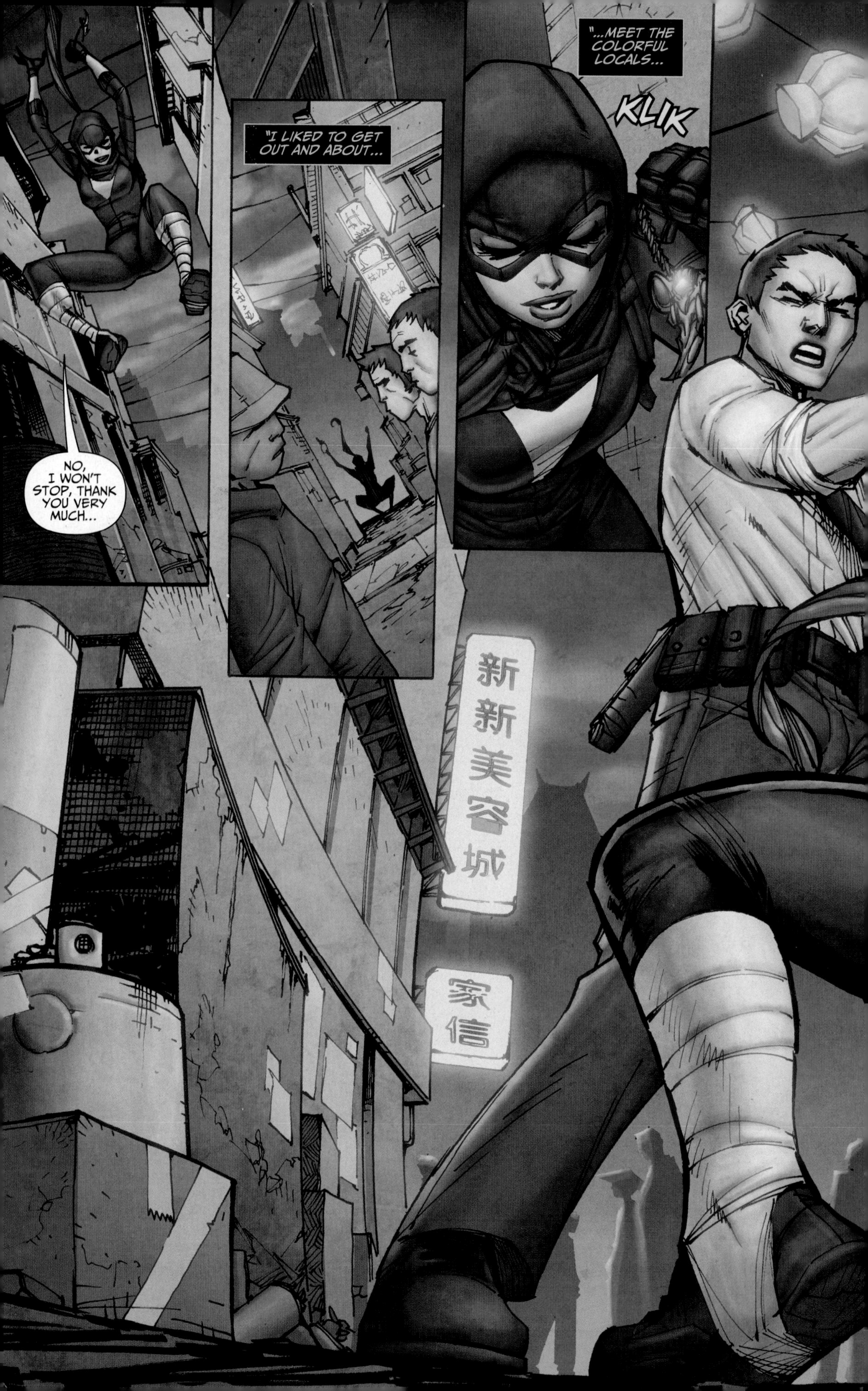

NO, I WON'T STOP, THANK YOU VERY MUCH...
"I LIKED TO GET OUT AND ABOUT...
"...MEET THE COLORFUL LOCALS...
KLIK
新新美容城
家信

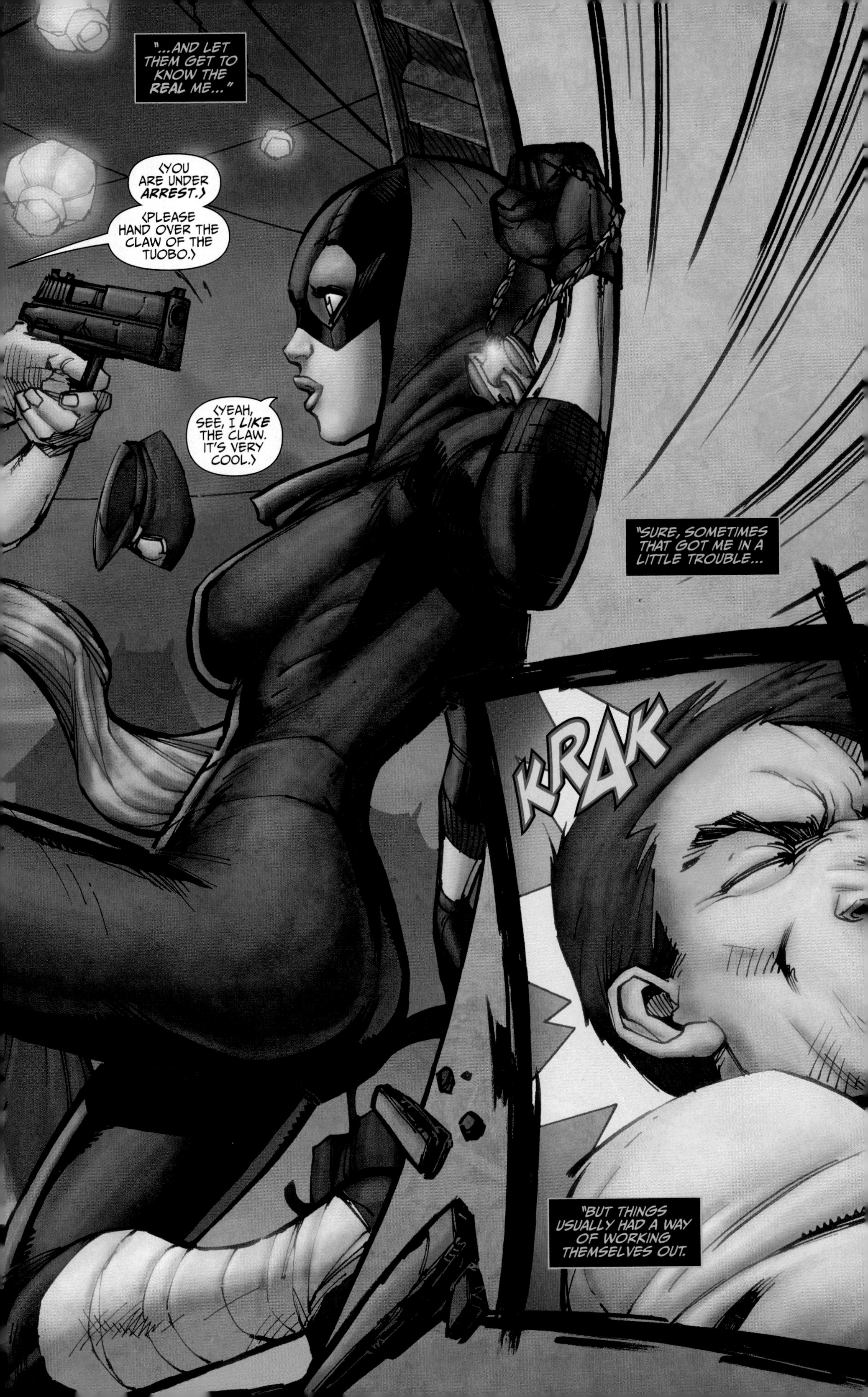
"...AND LET THEM GET TO KNOW THE REAL ME..."
⟨YOU ARE UNDER ARREST.⟩
⟨PLEASE HAND OVER THE CLAW OF THE TUOBO.⟩
⟨YEAH, SEE, I LIKE THE CLAW. IT'S VERY COOL.⟩
"SURE, SOMETIMES THAT GOT ME IN A LITTLE TROUBLE...
KRAK
"BUT THINGS USUALLY HAD A WAY OF WORKING THEMSELVES OUT.

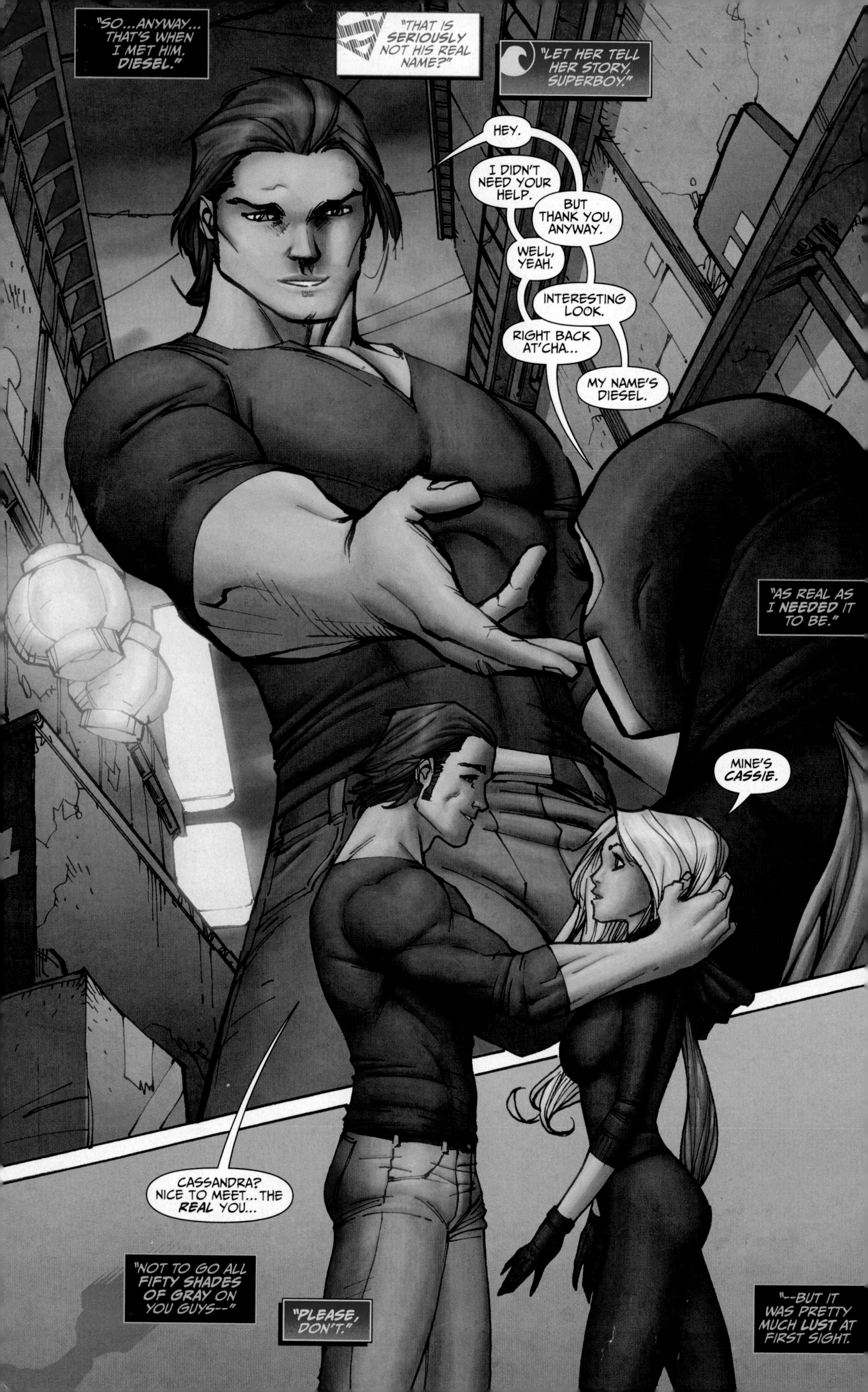
"SO...ANYWAY... THAT'S WHEN I MET HIM. DIESEL."
"THAT IS SERIOUSLY NOT HIS REAL NAME?"
"LET HER TELL HER STORY, SUPERBOY."
HEY.
I DIDN'T NEED YOUR HELP.
BUT THANK YOU, ANYWAY.
WELL, YEAH.
INTERESTING LOOK.
RIGHT BACK AT'CHA...
MY NAME'S DIESEL.
"AS REAL AS I NEEDED IT TO BE."
MINE'S CASSIE.
CASSANDRA? NICE TO MEET...THE REAL YOU...
"NOT TO GO ALL FIFTY SHADES OF GRAY ON YOU GUYS--"
"PLEASE, DON'T."
"--BUT IT WAS PRETTY MUCH LUST AT FIRST SIGHT.

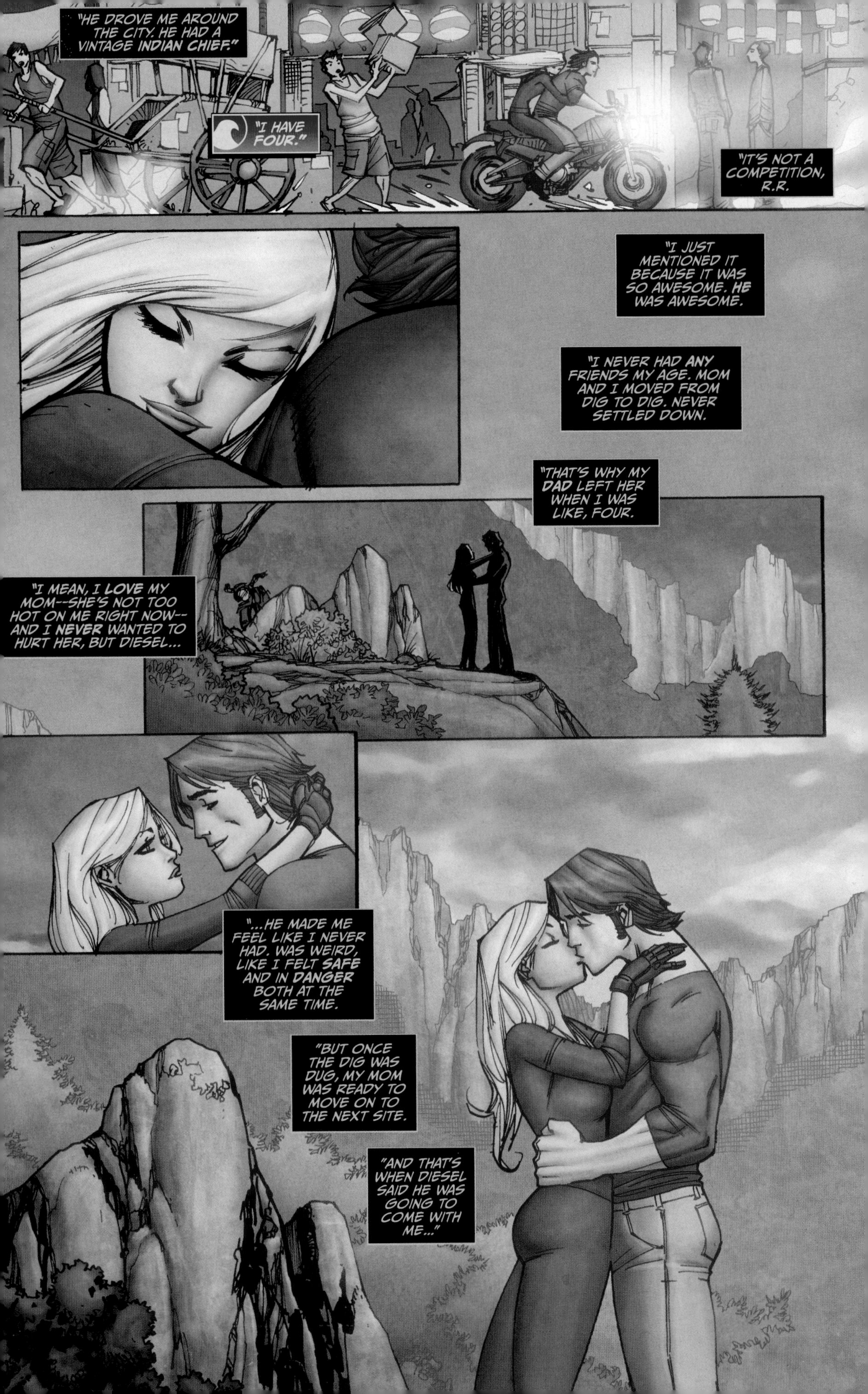
"HE DROVE ME AROUND THE CITY. HE HAD A VINTAGE INDIAN CHIEF."
"I HAVE FOUR."
"IT'S NOT A COMPETITION, R.R.
"I JUST MENTIONED IT BECAUSE IT WAS SO AWESOME. HE WAS AWESOME.
"I NEVER HAD ANY FRIENDS MY AGE. MOM AND I MOVED FROM DIG TO DIG. NEVER SETTLED DOWN.
"THAT'S WHY MY DAD LEFT HER WHEN I WAS LIKE, FOUR.
"I MEAN, I LOVE MY MOM--SHE'S NOT TOO HOT ON ME RIGHT NOW--AND I NEVER WANTED TO HURT HER, BUT DIESEL...
"...HE MADE ME FEEL LIKE I NEVER HAD. WAS WEIRD, LIKE I FELT SAFE AND IN DANGER BOTH AT THE SAME TIME.
"BUT ONCE THE DIG WAS DUG, MY MOM WAS READY TO MOVE ON TO THE NEXT SITE.
"AND THAT'S WHEN DIESEL SAID HE WAS GOING TO COME WITH ME..."

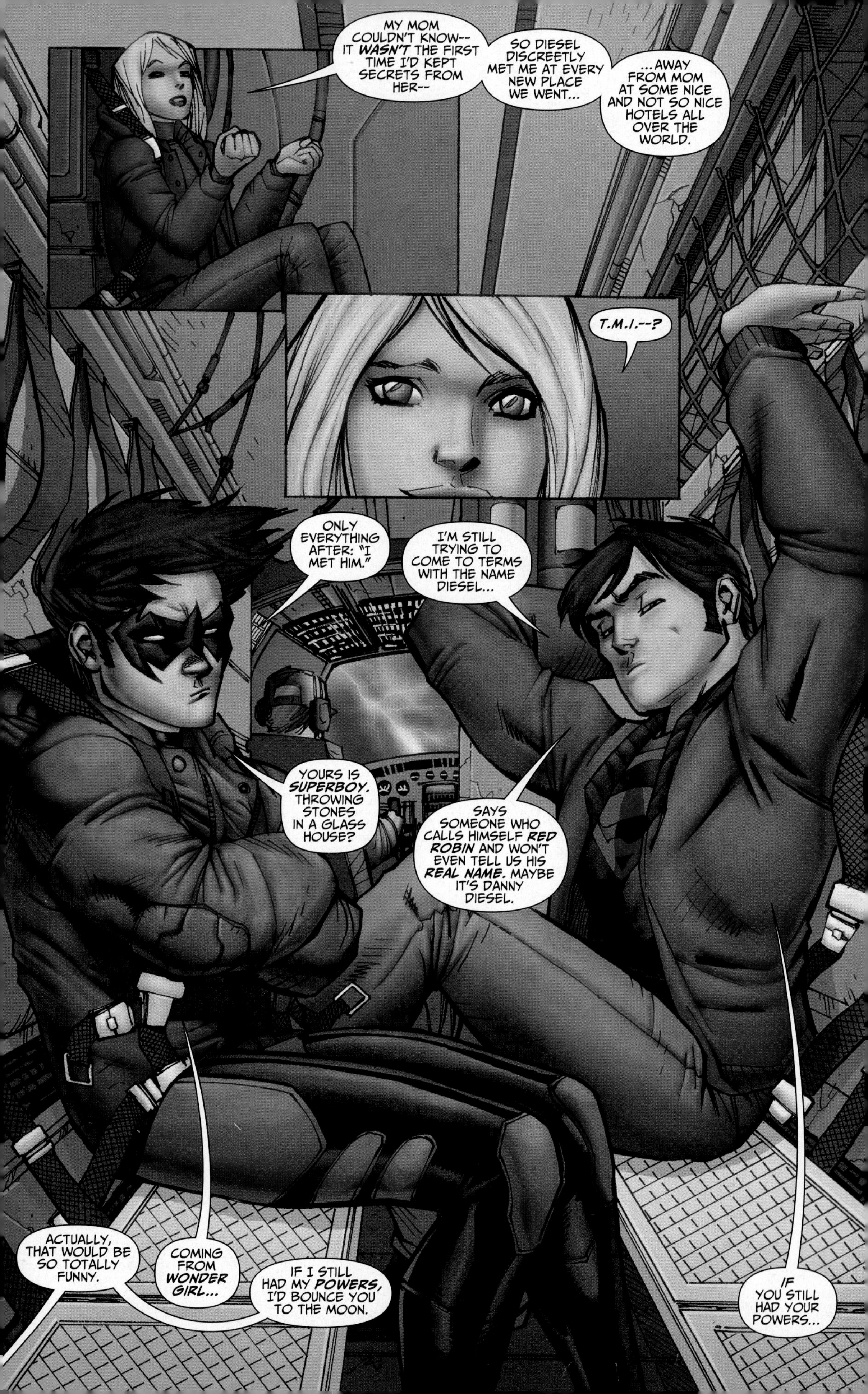
MY MOM COULDN'T KNOW-- IT ***WASN'T*** THE FIRST TIME I'D KEPT SECRETS FROM HER--
SO DIESEL DISCREETLY MET ME AT EVERY NEW PLACE WE WENT...
...AWAY FROM MOM AT SOME NICE AND NOT SO NICE HOTELS ALL OVER THE WORLD.
T.M.I.--?
ONLY EVERYTHING AFTER: "I MET HIM."
I'M STILL TRYING TO COME TO TERMS WITH THE NAME DIESEL...
YOURS IS ***SUPERBOY.*** THROWING STONES IN A GLASS HOUSE?
SAYS SOMEONE WHO CALLS HIMSELF ***RED ROBIN*** AND WON'T EVEN TELL US HIS ***REAL NAME.*** MAYBE IT'S DANNY DIESEL.
IF I STILL HAD MY ***POWERS,*** I'D BOUNCE YOU TO THE MOON.
IF YOU STILL HAD YOUR POWERS...
COMING FROM ***WONDER GIRL***...
ACTUALLY, THAT WOULD BE SO TOTALLY FUNNY.

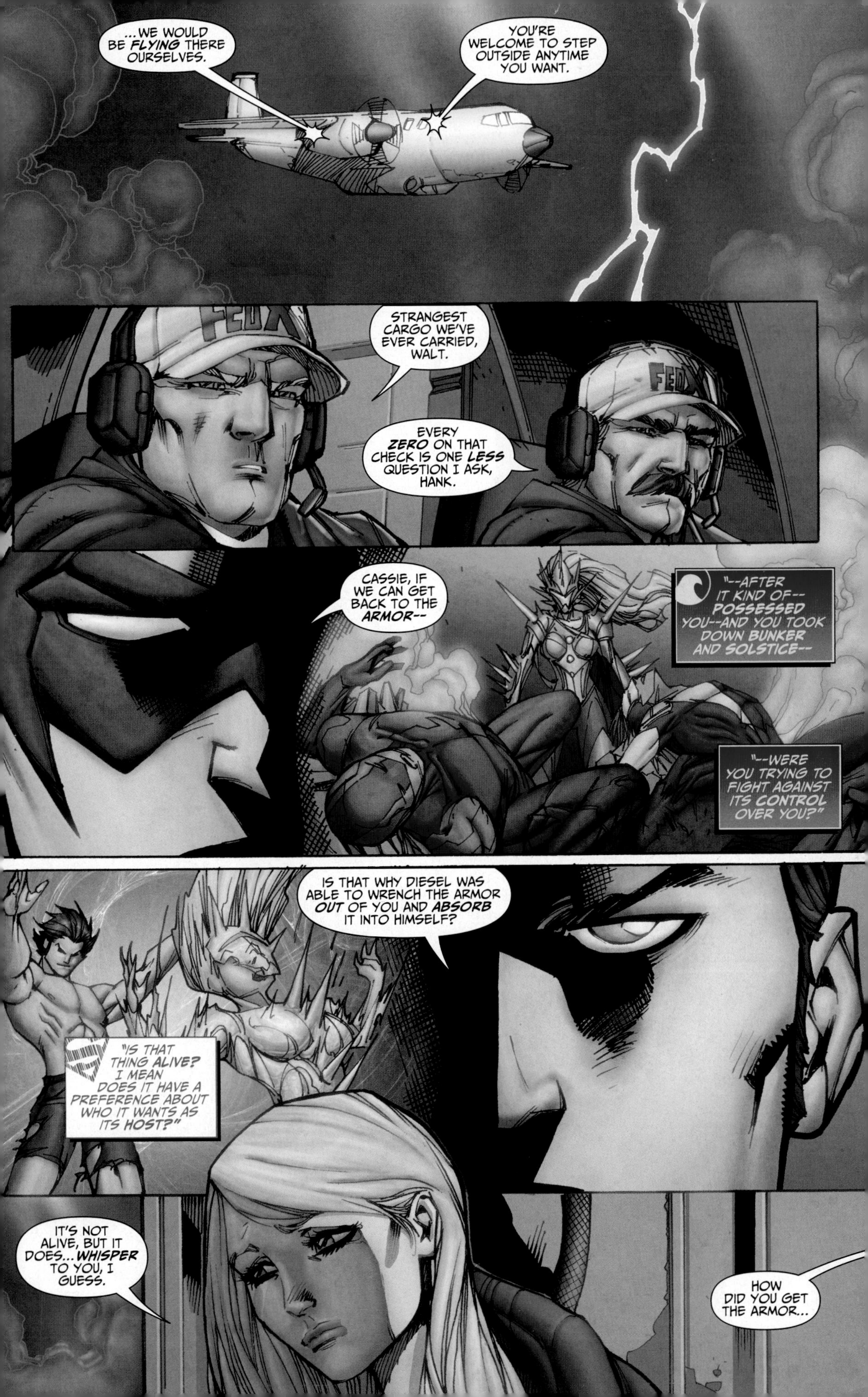
...WE WOULD BE FLYING THERE OURSELVES.
YOU'RE WELCOME TO STEP OUTSIDE ANYTIME YOU WANT.
STRANGEST CARGO WE'VE EVER CARRIED, WALT.
EVERY ZERO ON THAT CHECK IS ONE LESS QUESTION I ASK, HANK.
CASSIE, IF WE CAN GET BACK TO THE ARMOR--
"--AFTER IT KIND OF--POSSESSED YOU--AND YOU TOOK DOWN BUNKER AND SOLSTICE--
"--WERE YOU TRYING TO FIGHT AGAINST ITS CONTROL OVER YOU?"
IS THAT WHY DIESEL WAS ABLE TO WRENCH THE ARMOR OUT OF YOU AND ABSORB IT INTO HIMSELF?
"IS THAT THING ALIVE? I MEAN DOES IT HAVE A PREFERENCE ABOUT WHO IT WANTS AS ITS HOST?"
IT'S NOT ALIVE, BUT IT DOES... WHISPER TO YOU, I GUESS.
HOW DID YOU GET THE ARMOR...

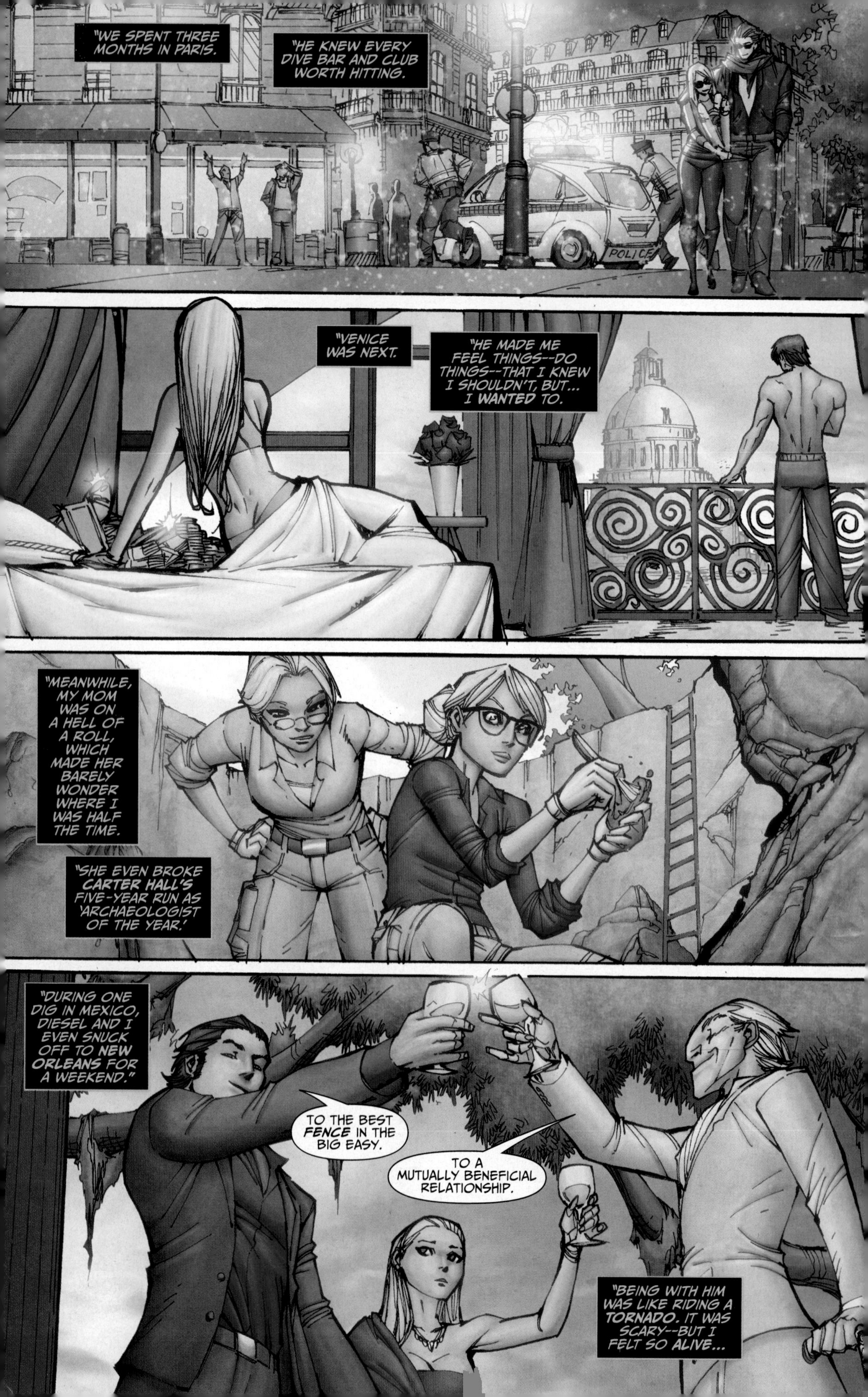
"WE SPENT THREE MONTHS IN PARIS.
"HE KNEW EVERY DIVE BAR AND CLUB WORTH HITTING.
POLICE
"VENICE WAS NEXT.
"HE MADE ME FEEL THINGS--DO THINGS--THAT I KNEW I SHOULDN'T, BUT... I WANTED TO.
"MEANWHILE, MY MOM WAS ON A HELL OF A ROLL, WHICH MADE HER BARELY WONDER WHERE I WAS HALF THE TIME.
"SHE EVEN BROKE CARTER HALL'S FIVE-YEAR RUN AS 'ARCHAEOLOGIST OF THE YEAR.'
"DURING ONE DIG IN MEXICO, DIESEL AND I EVEN SNUCK OFF TO NEW ORLEANS FOR A WEEKEND."
TO THE BEST FENCE IN THE BIG EASY.
TO A MUTUALLY BENEFICIAL RELATIONSHIP.
"BEING WITH HIM WAS LIKE RIDING A TORNADO. IT WAS SCARY--BUT I FELT SO ALIVE...

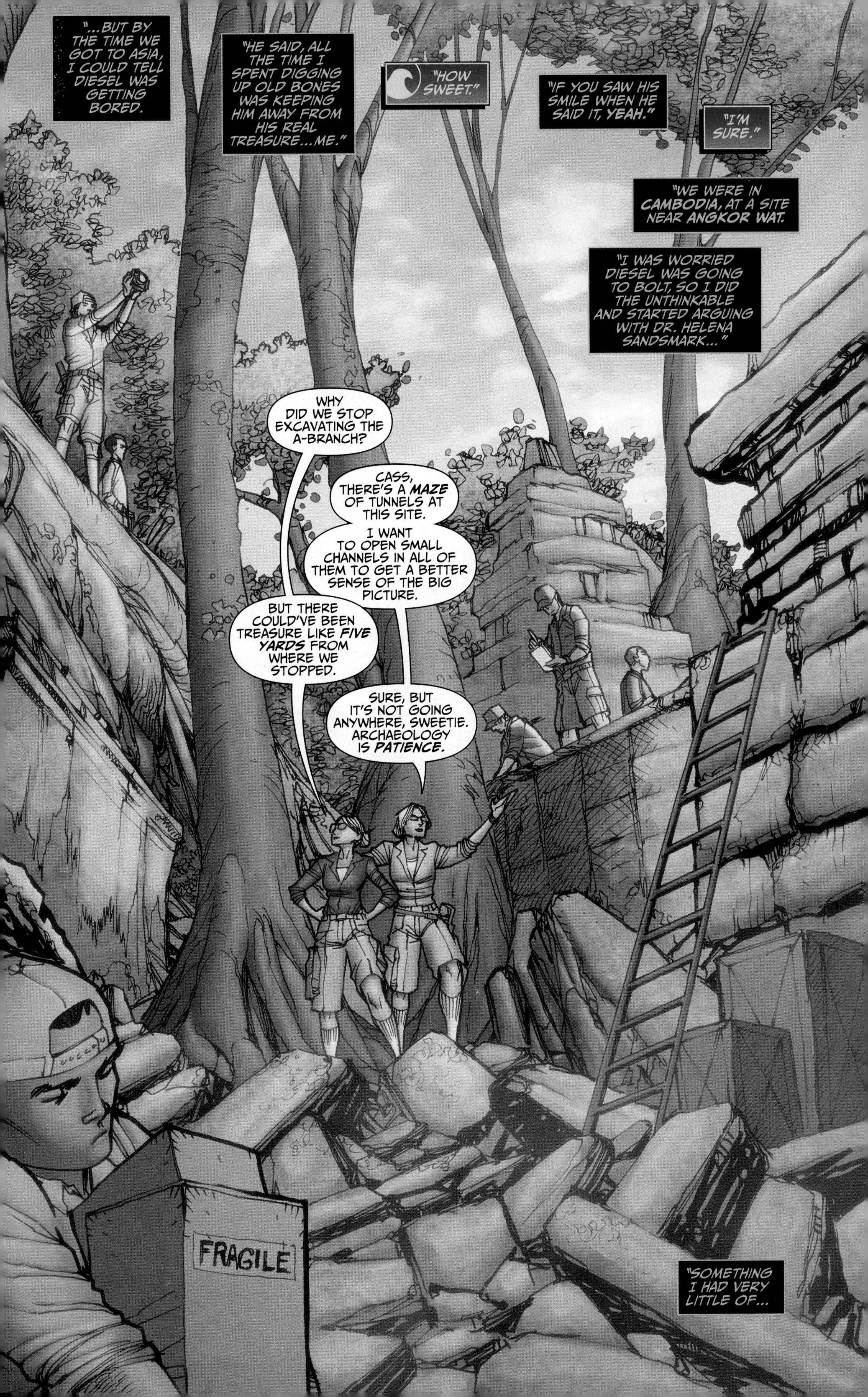
"...BUT BY THE TIME WE GOT TO ASIA, I COULD TELL DIESEL WAS GETTING BORED.
"HE SAID, ALL THE TIME I SPENT DIGGING UP OLD BONES WAS KEEPING HIM AWAY FROM HIS REAL TREASURE...ME."
"HOW SWEET."
"IF YOU SAW HIS SMILE WHEN HE SAID IT, YEAH."
"I'M SURE."
"WE WERE IN CAMBODIA, AT A SITE NEAR ANGKOR WAT.
"I WAS WORRIED DIESEL WAS GOING TO BOLT, SO I DID THE UNTHINKABLE AND STARTED ARGUING WITH DR. HELENA SANDSMARK..."
WHY DID WE STOP EXCAVATING THE A-BRANCH?
CASS, THERE'S A MAZE OF TUNNELS AT THIS SITE.
I WANT TO OPEN SMALL CHANNELS IN ALL OF THEM TO GET A BETTER SENSE OF THE BIG PICTURE.
BUT THERE COULD'VE BEEN TREASURE LIKE FIVE YARDS FROM WHERE WE STOPPED.
SURE, BUT IT'S NOT GOING ANYWHERE, SWEETIE. ARCHAEOLOGY IS PATIENCE.
FRAGILE
"SOMETHING I HAD VERY LITTLE OF...

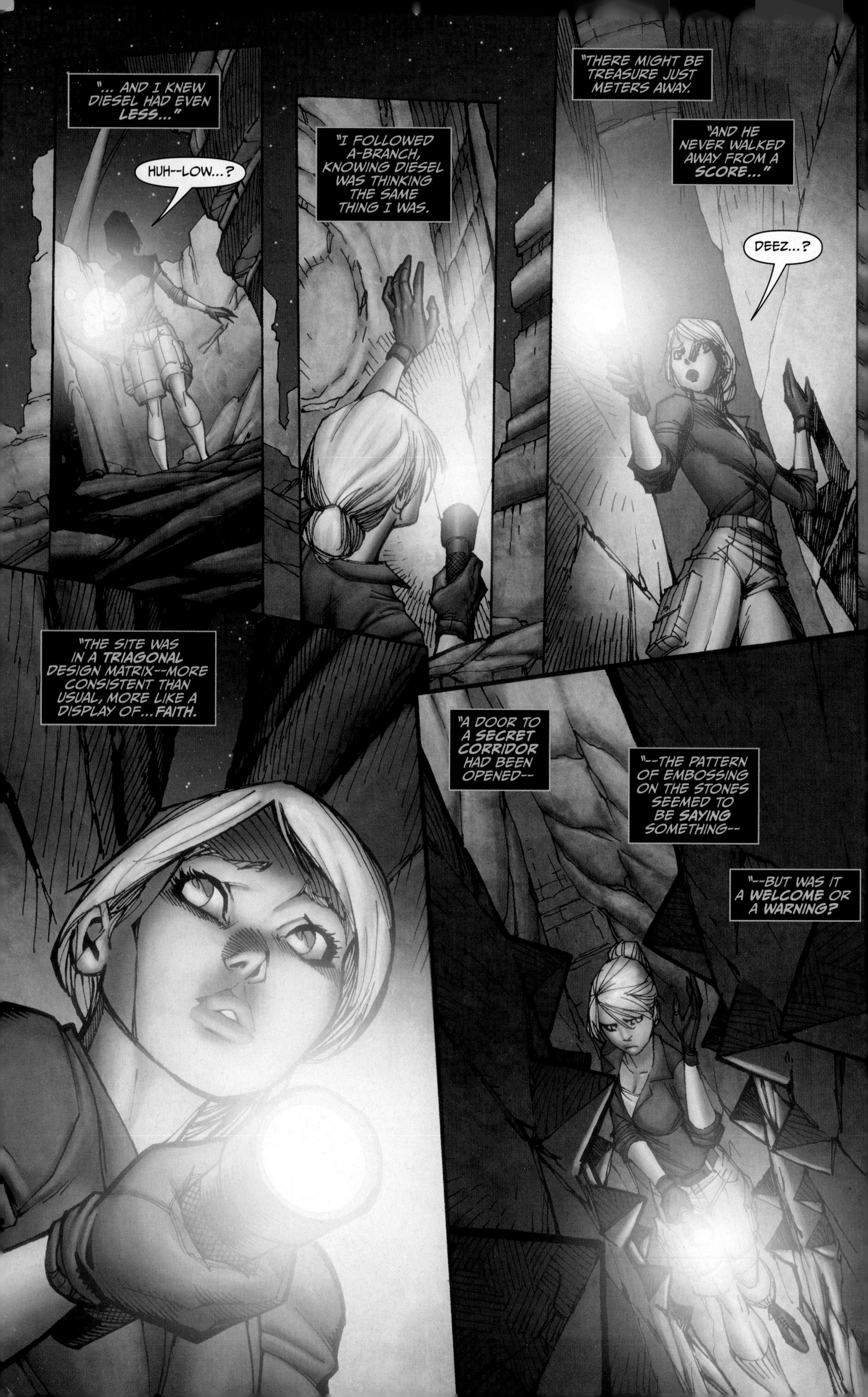
"... AND I KNEW DIESEL HAD EVEN LESS..."
HUH--LOW...?
"I FOLLOWED A-BRANCH, KNOWING DIESEL WAS THINKING THE SAME THING I WAS.
"THERE MIGHT BE TREASURE JUST METERS AWAY.
"AND HE NEVER WALKED AWAY FROM A SCORE..."
DEEZ...?
"THE SITE WAS IN A TRIAGONAL DESIGN MATRIX--MORE CONSISTENT THAN USUAL, MORE LIKE A DISPLAY OF...FAITH.
"A DOOR TO A SECRET CORRIDOR HAD BEEN OPENED--
"--THE PATTERN OF EMBOSSING ON THE STONES SEEMED TO BE SAYING SOMETHING--
"--BUT WAS IT A WELCOME OR A WARNING?

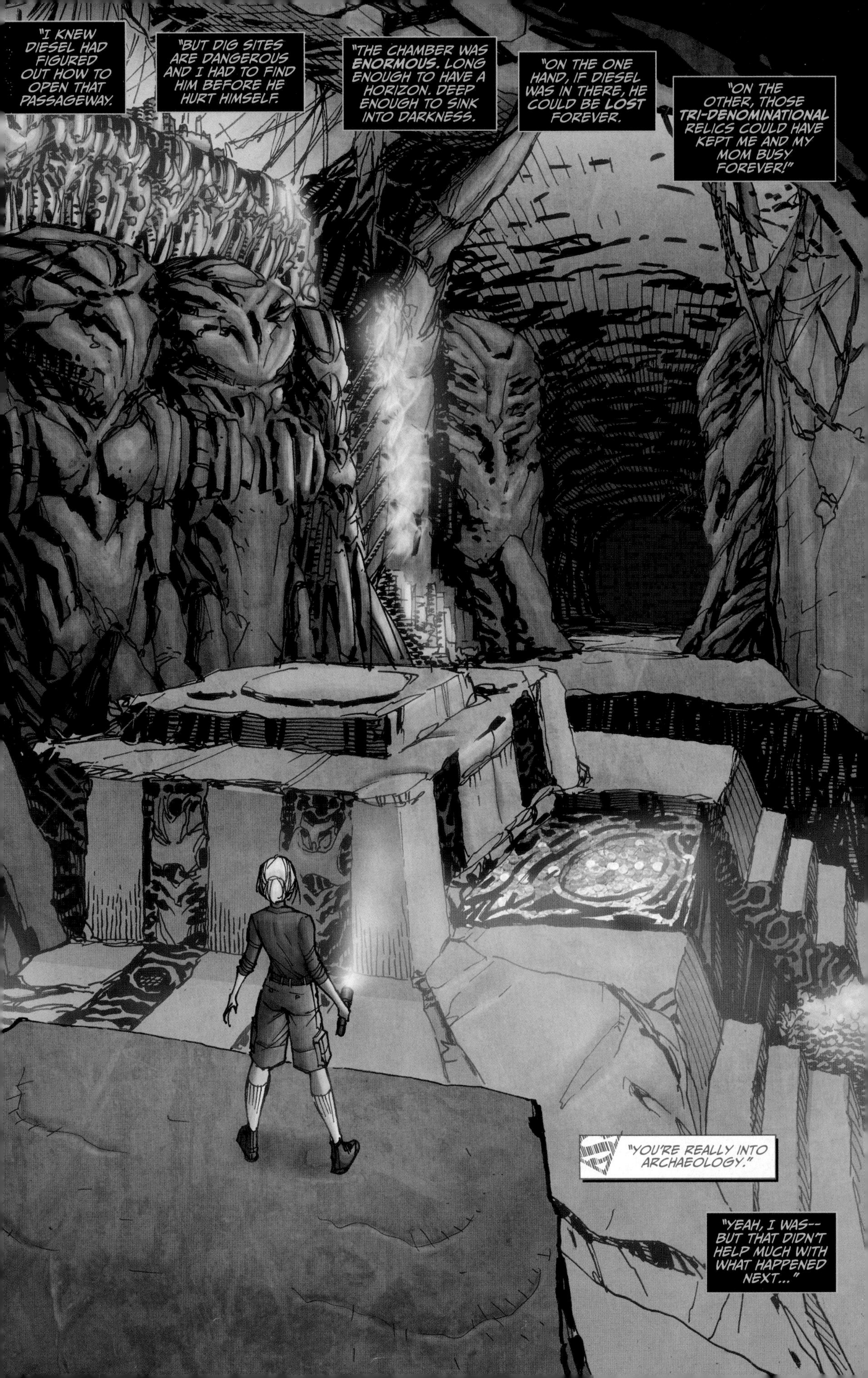
"I KNEW DIESEL HAD FIGURED OUT HOW TO OPEN THAT PASSAGEWAY.
"BUT DIG SITES ARE DANGEROUS AND I HAD TO FIND HIM BEFORE HE HURT HIMSELF.
"THE CHAMBER WAS ENORMOUS. LONG ENOUGH TO HAVE A HORIZON. DEEP ENOUGH TO SINK INTO DARKNESS.
"ON THE ONE HAND, IF DIESEL WAS IN THERE, HE COULD BE LOST FOREVER.
"ON THE OTHER, THOSE TRI-DENOMINATIONAL RELICS COULD HAVE KEPT ME AND MY MOM BUSY FOREVER!"
"YOU'RE REALLY INTO ARCHAEOLOGY."
"YEAH, I WAS-- BUT THAT DIDN'T HELP MUCH WITH WHAT HAPPENED NEXT..."

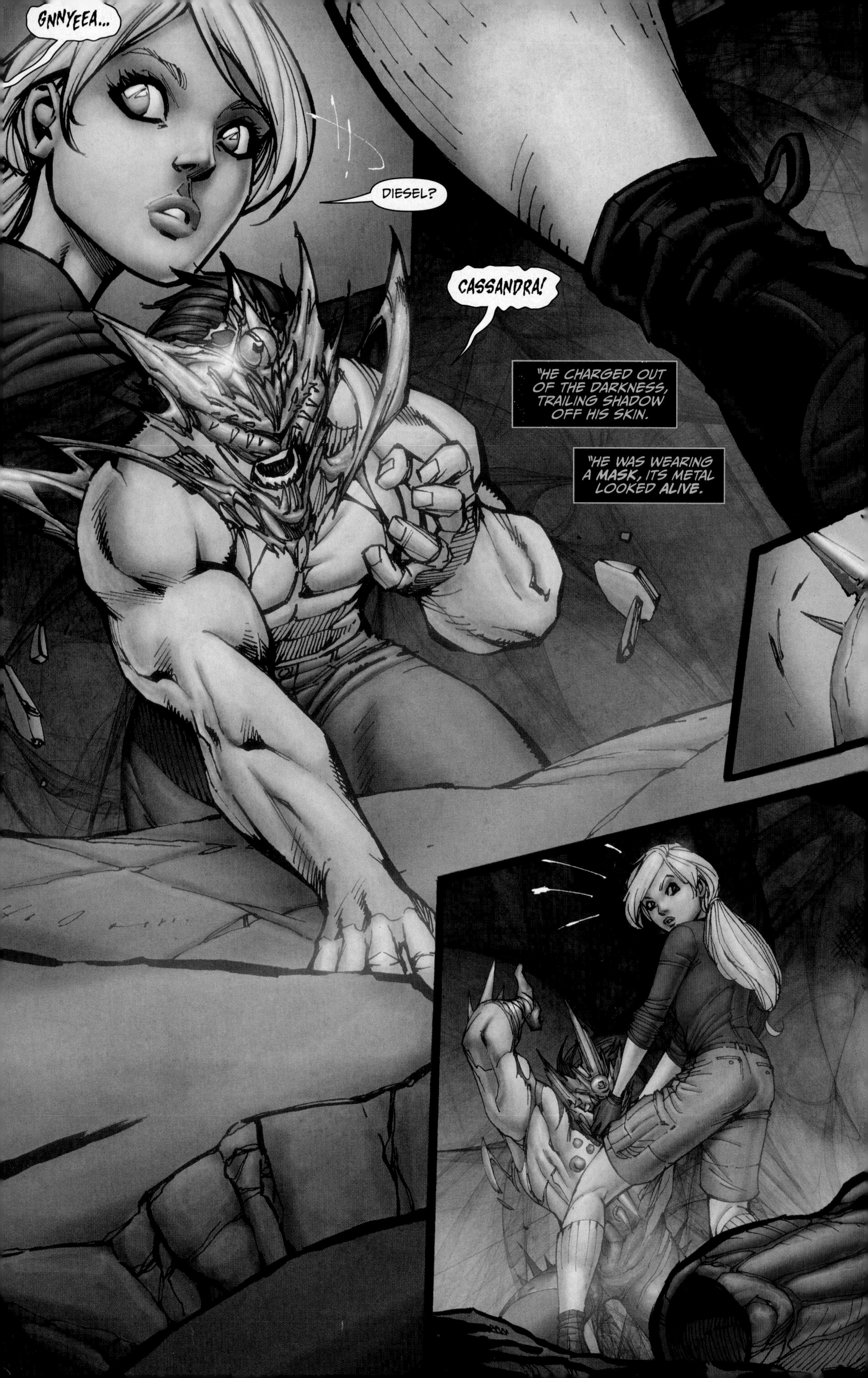
GNNYEEA...
DIESEL?
CASSANDRA!
"HE CHARGED OUT OF THE DARKNESS, TRAILING SHADOW OFF HIS SKIN.
"HE WAS WEARING A MASK, ITS METAL LOOKED ALIVE.

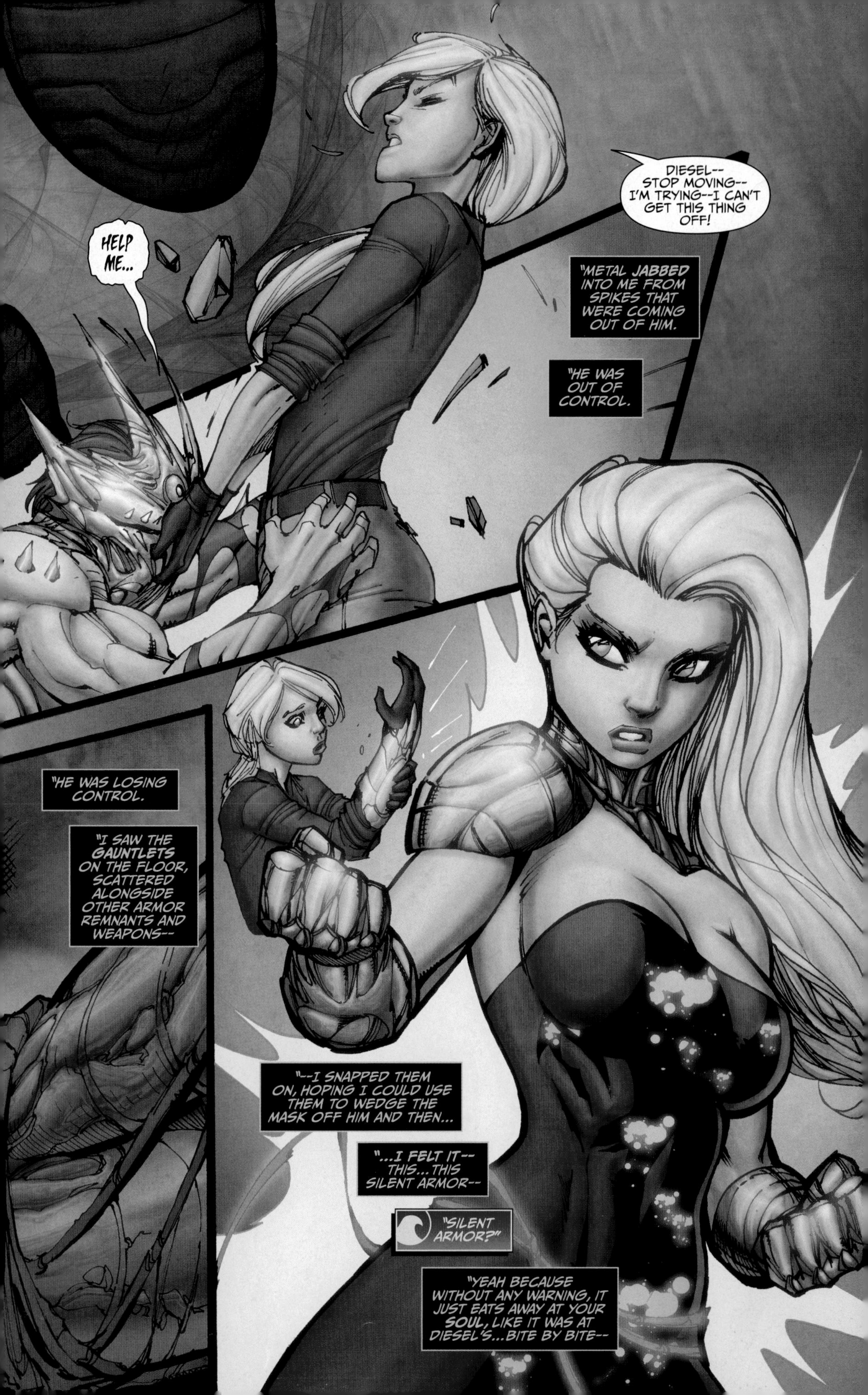

DIESEL-- STOP MOVING-- I'M TRYING--I CAN'T GET THIS THING OFF!
HELP ME...
"METAL JABBED INTO ME FROM SPIKES THAT WERE COMING OUT OF HIM.
"HE WAS OUT OF CONTROL.
"HE WAS LOSING CONTROL.
"I SAW THE GAUNTLETS ON THE FLOOR, SCATTERED ALONGSIDE OTHER ARMOR REMNANTS AND WEAPONS--
"--I SNAPPED THEM ON, HOPING I COULD USE THEM TO WEDGE THE MASK OFF HIM AND THEN...
"...I FELT IT-- THIS...THIS SILENT ARMOR--
"SILENT ARMOR?"
"YEAH BECAUSE WITHOUT ANY WARNING, IT JUST EATS AWAY AT YOUR SOUL, LIKE IT WAS AT DIESEL'S...BITE BY BITE--

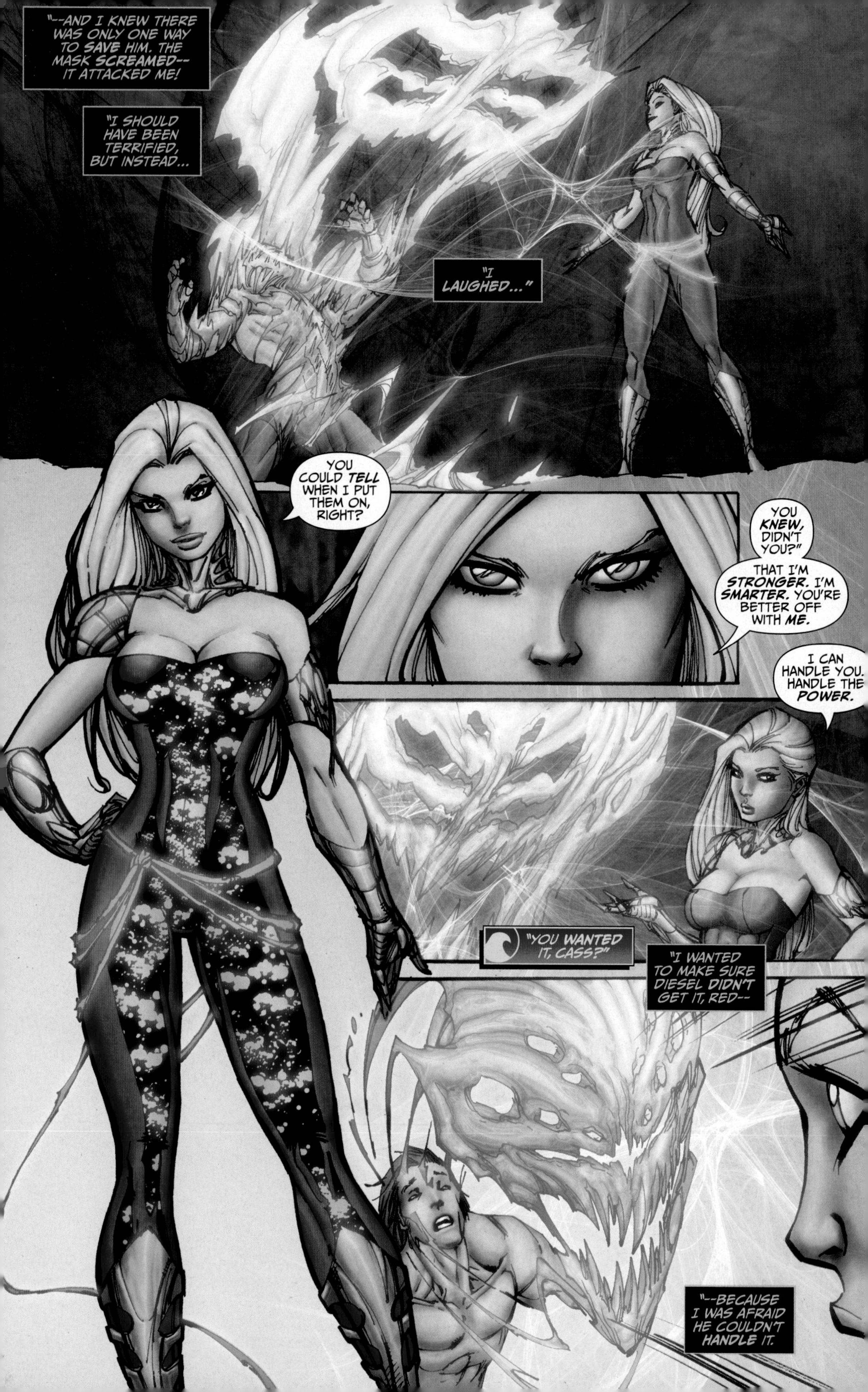
"--AND I KNEW THERE WAS ONLY ONE WAY TO SAVE HIM. THE MASK SCREAMED-- IT ATTACKED ME!
"I SHOULD HAVE BEEN TERRIFIED, BUT INSTEAD...
"I LAUGHED..."
YOU COULD TELL WHEN I PUT THEM ON, RIGHT?
YOU KNEW, DIDN'T YOU?"
THAT I'M STRONGER. I'M SMARTER. YOU'RE BETTER OFF WITH ME.
I CAN HANDLE YOU. HANDLE THE POWER.
"YOU WANTED IT, CASS?"
"I WANTED TO MAKE SURE DIESEL DIDN'T GET IT, RED--
"--BECAUSE I WAS AFRAID HE COULDN'T HANDLE IT.

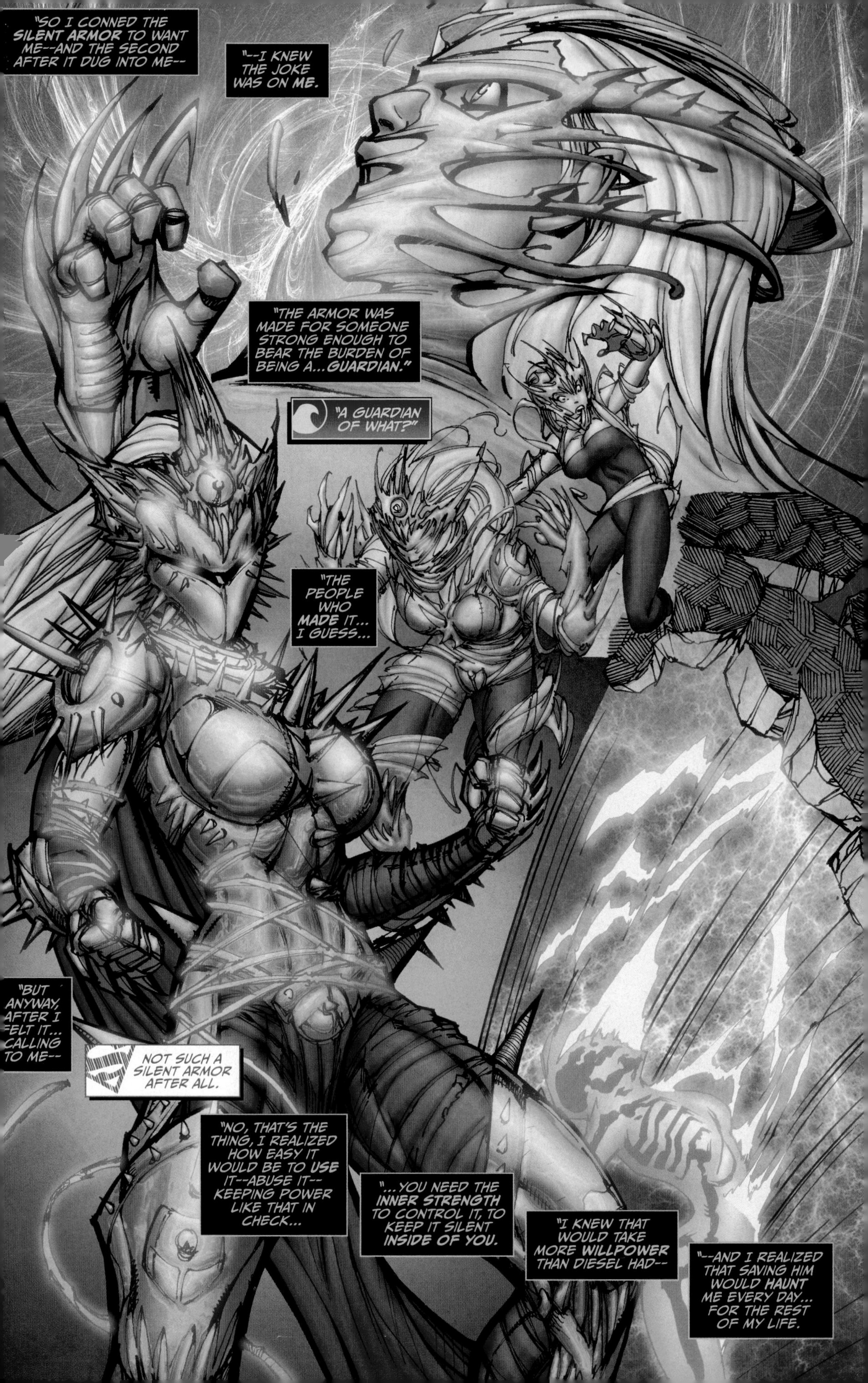
"SO I CONNED THE SILENT ARMOR TO WANT ME--AND THE SECOND AFTER IT DUG INTO ME--
"--I KNEW THE JOKE WAS ON ME.
"THE ARMOR WAS MADE FOR SOMEONE STRONG ENOUGH TO BEAR THE BURDEN OF BEING A...GUARDIAN."
"A GUARDIAN OF WHAT?"
"THE PEOPLE WHO MADE IT... I GUESS...
"BUT ANYWAY, AFTER I FELT IT... CALLING TO ME--
NOT SUCH A SILENT ARMOR AFTER ALL.
"NO, THAT'S THE THING, I REALIZED HOW EASY IT WOULD BE TO USE IT--ABUSE IT--KEEPING POWER LIKE THAT IN CHECK...
"...YOU NEED THE INNER STRENGTH TO CONTROL IT, TO KEEP IT SILENT INSIDE OF YOU.
"I KNEW THAT WOULD TAKE MORE WILLPOWER THAN DIESEL HAD--
"--AND I REALIZED THAT SAVING HIM WOULD HAUNT ME EVERY DAY... FOR THE REST OF MY LIFE.

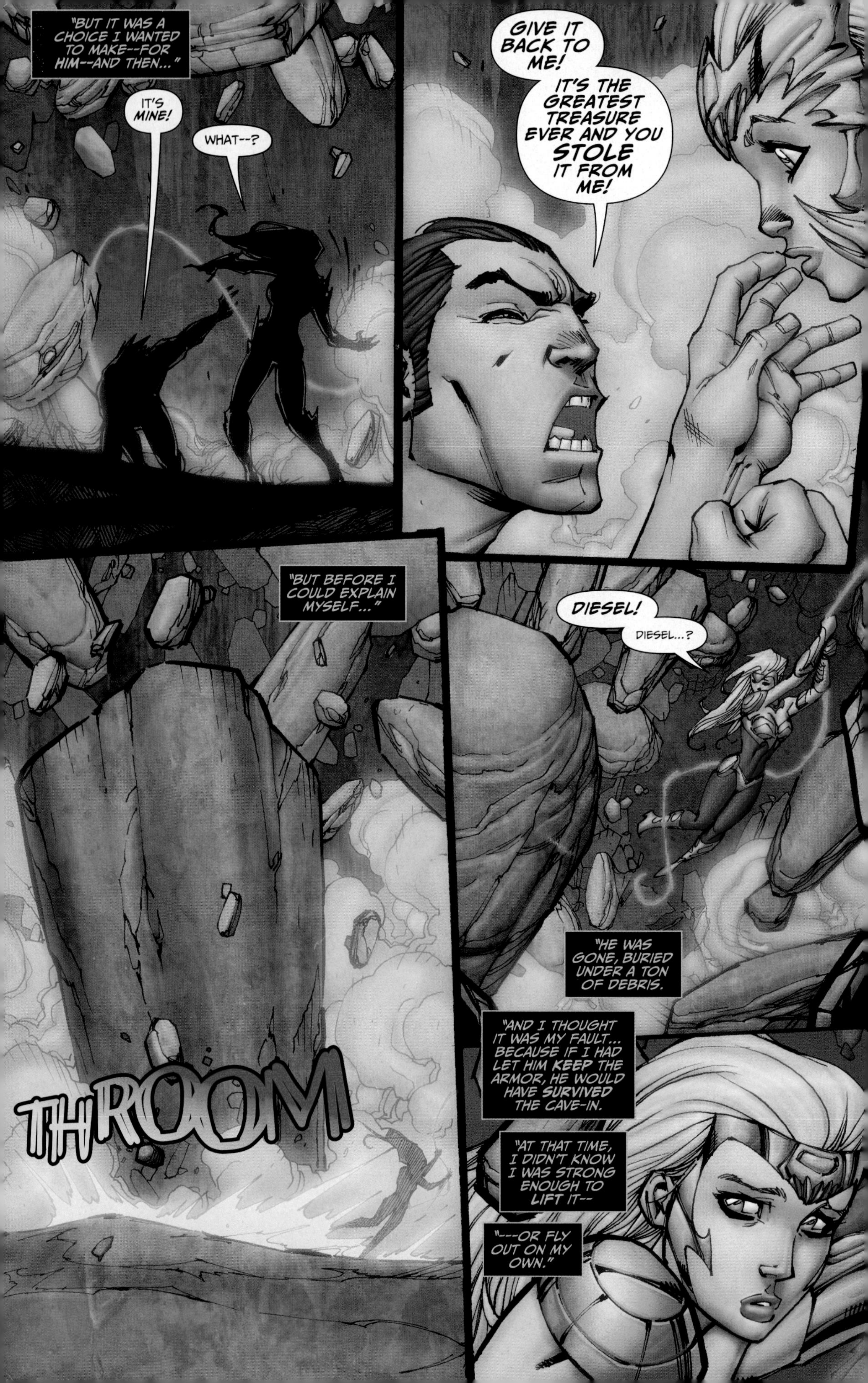
"BUT IT WAS A CHOICE I WANTED TO MAKE--FOR HIM--AND THEN..."
IT'S MINE!
WHAT--?
GIVE IT BACK TO ME!
IT'S THE GREATEST TREASURE EVER AND YOU STOLE IT FROM ME!
"BUT BEFORE I COULD EXPLAIN MYSELF..."
THROOM
DIESEL!
DIESEL...?
"HE WAS GONE, BURIED UNDER A TON OF DEBRIS.
"AND I THOUGHT IT WAS MY FAULT... BECAUSE IF I HAD LET HIM KEEP THE ARMOR, HE WOULD HAVE SURVIVED THE CAVE-IN.
"AT THAT TIME, I DIDN'T KNOW I WAS STRONG ENOUGH TO LIFT IT--
"---OR FLY OUT ON MY OWN."

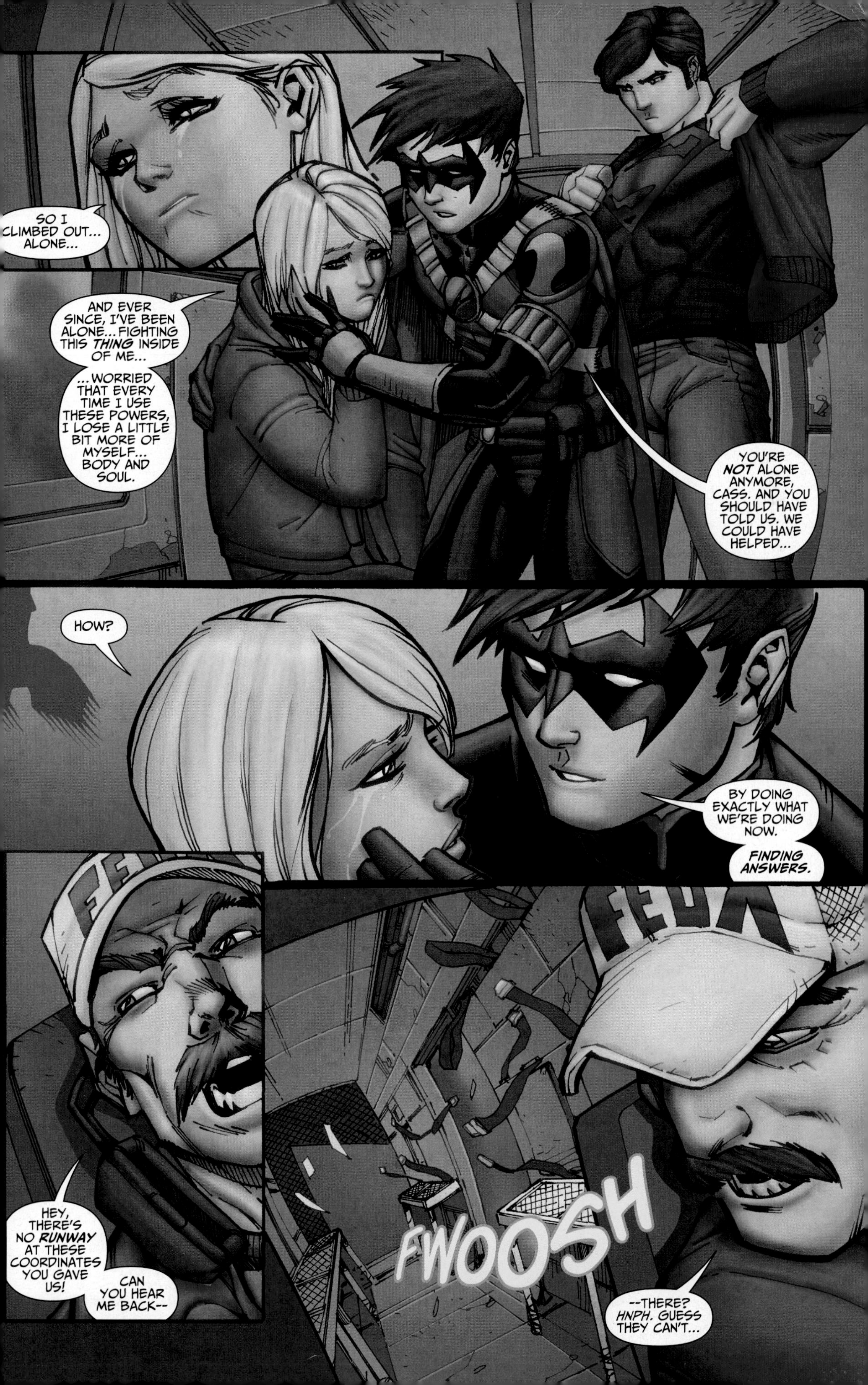
SO I CLIMBED OUT... ALONE...
AND EVER SINCE, I'VE BEEN ALONE... FIGHTING THIS *THING* INSIDE OF ME...
...WORRIED THAT EVERY TIME I USE THESE POWERS, I LOSE A LITTLE BIT MORE OF MYSELF... BODY AND SOUL.
YOU'RE *NOT* ALONE ANYMORE, CASS. AND YOU SHOULD HAVE TOLD US. WE COULD HAVE HELPED...
HOW?
BY DOING EXACTLY WHAT WE'RE DOING NOW.
FINDING ANSWERS.
HEY, THERE'S NO *RUNWAY* AT THESE COORDINATES YOU GAVE US!
CAN YOU HEAR ME BACK--
FWOOSH
--THERE? *HNPH.* GUESS THEY CAN'T...

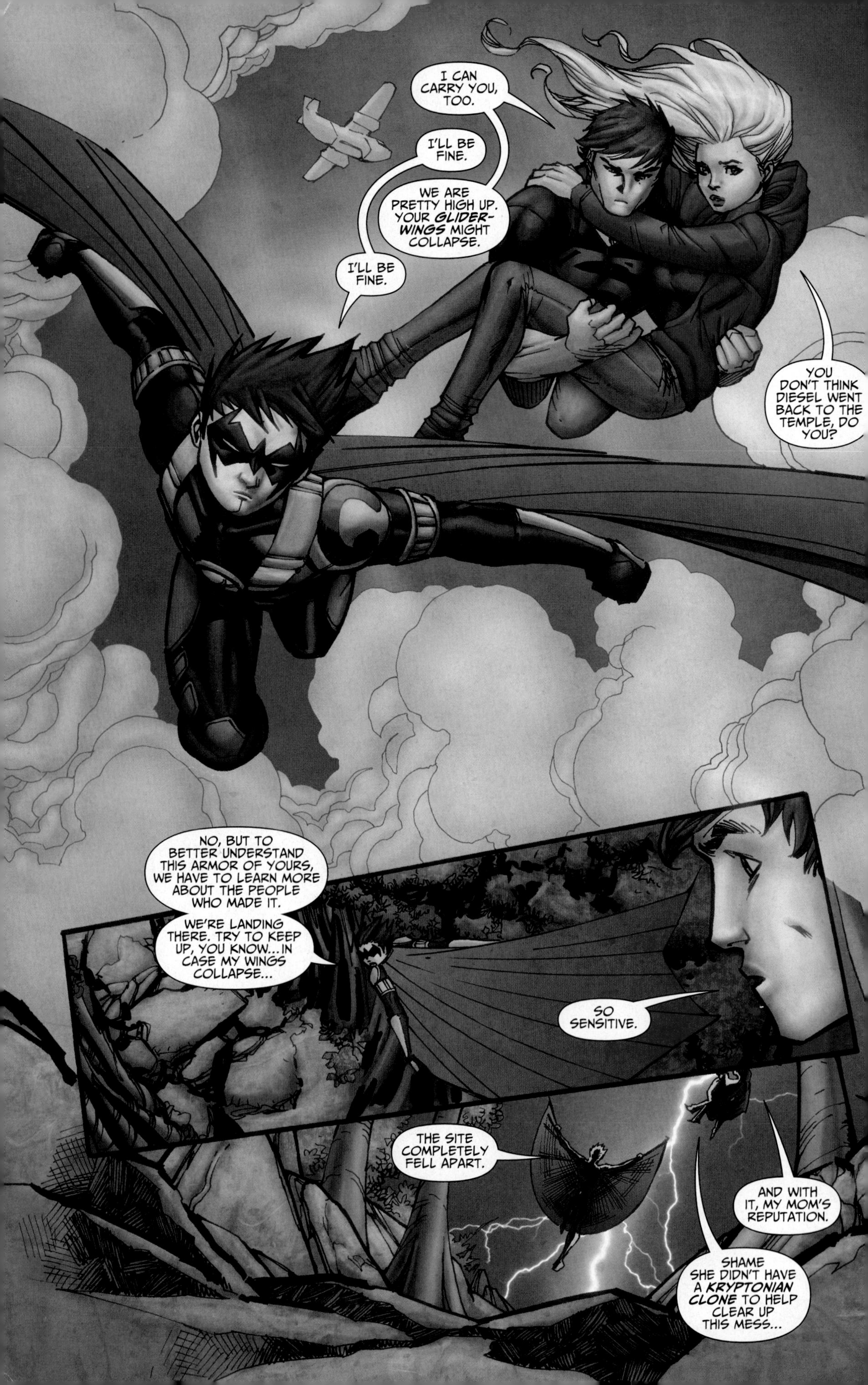
I CAN CARRY YOU, TOO.
I'LL BE FINE.
WE ARE PRETTY HIGH UP. YOUR GLIDER-WINGS MIGHT COLLAPSE.
I'LL BE FINE.
YOU DON'T THINK DIESEL WENT BACK TO THE TEMPLE, DO YOU?
NO, BUT TO BETTER UNDERSTAND THIS ARMOR OF YOURS, WE HAVE TO LEARN MORE ABOUT THE PEOPLE WHO MADE IT.
WE'RE LANDING THERE. TRY TO KEEP UP, YOU KNOW...IN CASE MY WINGS COLLAPSE...
SO SENSITIVE.
THE SITE COMPLETELY FELL APART.
AND WITH IT, MY MOM'S REPUTATION.
SHAME SHE DIDN'T HAVE A KRYPTONIAN CLONE TO HELP CLEAR UP THIS MESS...

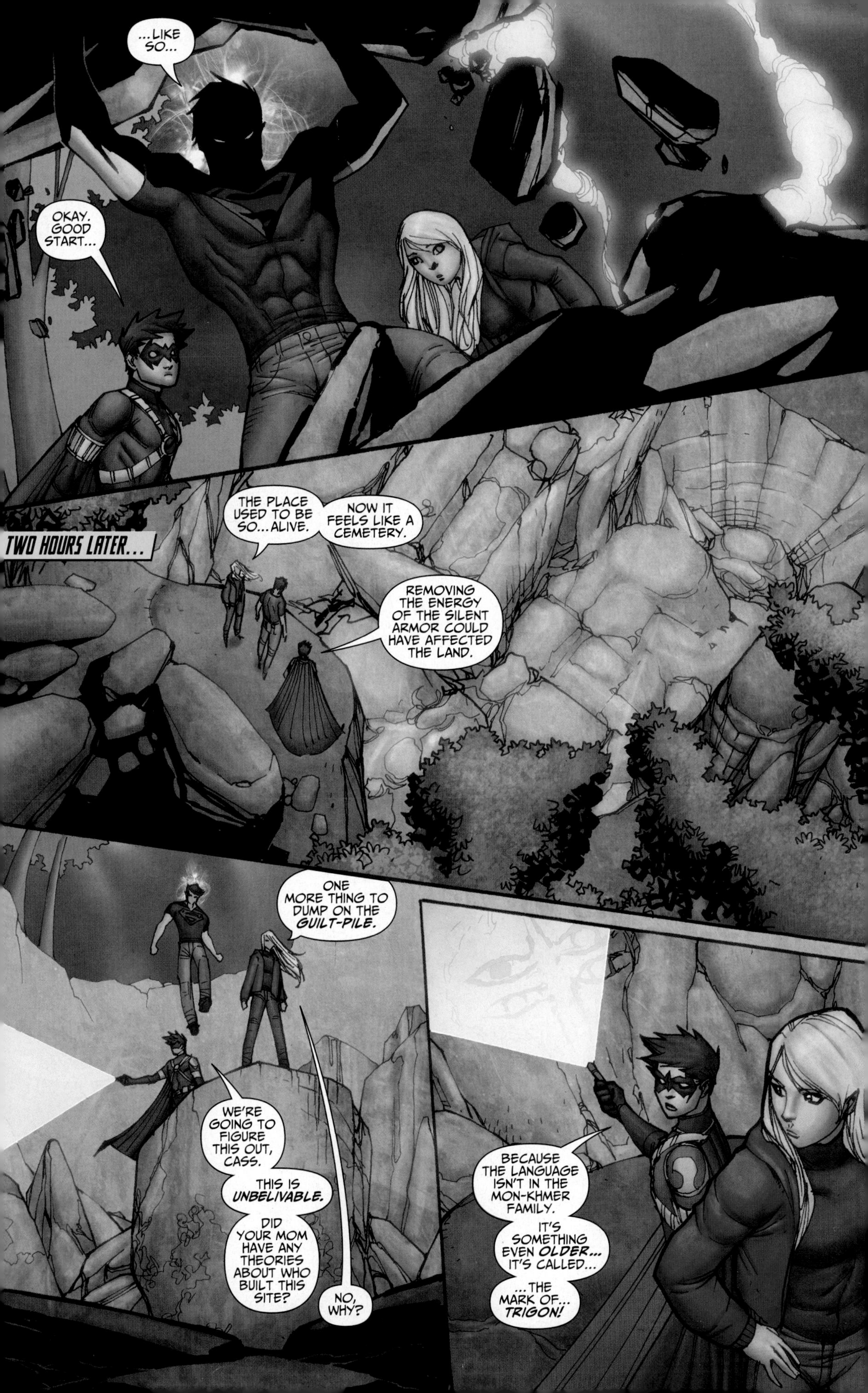
...LIKE SO...
OKAY. GOOD START...
TWO HOURS LATER...
THE PLACE USED TO BE SO...ALIVE.
NOW IT FEELS LIKE A CEMETERY.
REMOVING THE ENERGY OF THE SILENT ARMOR COULD HAVE AFFECTED THE LAND.
ONE MORE THING TO DUMP ON THE GUILT-PILE.
WE'RE GOING TO FIGURE THIS OUT, CASS.
THIS IS UNBELIVABLE.
DID YOUR MOM HAVE ANY THEORIES ABOUT WHO BUILT THIS SITE?
NO, WHY?
BECAUSE THE LANGUAGE ISN'T IN THE MON-KHMER FAMILY.
IT'S SOMETHING EVEN OLDER... IT'S CALLED...
...THE MARK OF... TRIGON!

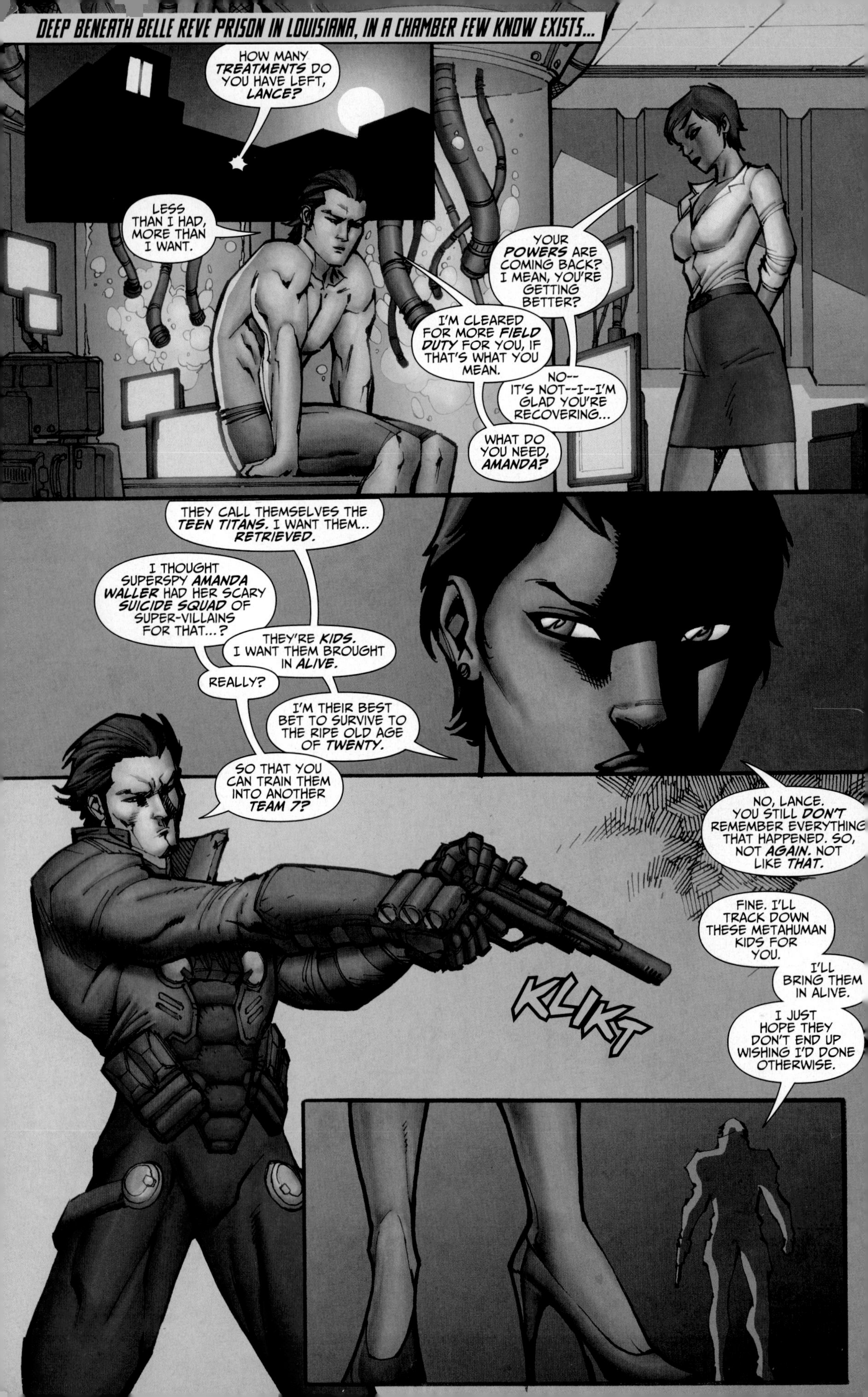

DEEP BENEATH BELLE REVE PRISON IN LOUISIANA, IN A CHAMBER FEW KNOW EXISTS...
HOW MANY TREATMENTS DO YOU HAVE LEFT, LANCE?
LESS THAN I HAD, MORE THAN I WANT.
YOUR POWERS ARE COMING BACK? I MEAN, YOU'RE GETTING BETTER?
I'M CLEARED FOR MORE FIELD DUTY FOR YOU, IF THAT'S WHAT YOU MEAN.
NO-- IT'S NOT--I--I'M GLAD YOU'RE RECOVERING...
WHAT DO YOU NEED, AMANDA?
THEY CALL THEMSELVES THE TEEN TITANS. I WANT THEM... RETRIEVED.
I THOUGHT SUPERSPY AMANDA WALLER HAD HER SCARY SUICIDE SQUAD OF SUPER-VILLAINS FOR THAT...?
THEY'RE KIDS. I WANT THEM BROUGHT IN ALIVE.
REALLY?
I'M THEIR BEST BET TO SURVIVE TO THE RIPE OLD AGE OF TWENTY.
SO THAT YOU CAN TRAIN THEM INTO ANOTHER TEAM 7?
NO, LANCE. YOU STILL DON'T REMEMBER EVERYTHING THAT HAPPENED. SO, NOT AGAIN. NOT LIKE THAT.
FINE. I'LL TRACK DOWN THESE METAHUMAN KIDS FOR YOU.
I'LL BRING THEM IN ALIVE.
I JUST HOPE THEY DON'T END UP WISHING I'D DONE OTHERWISE.
KLIKT

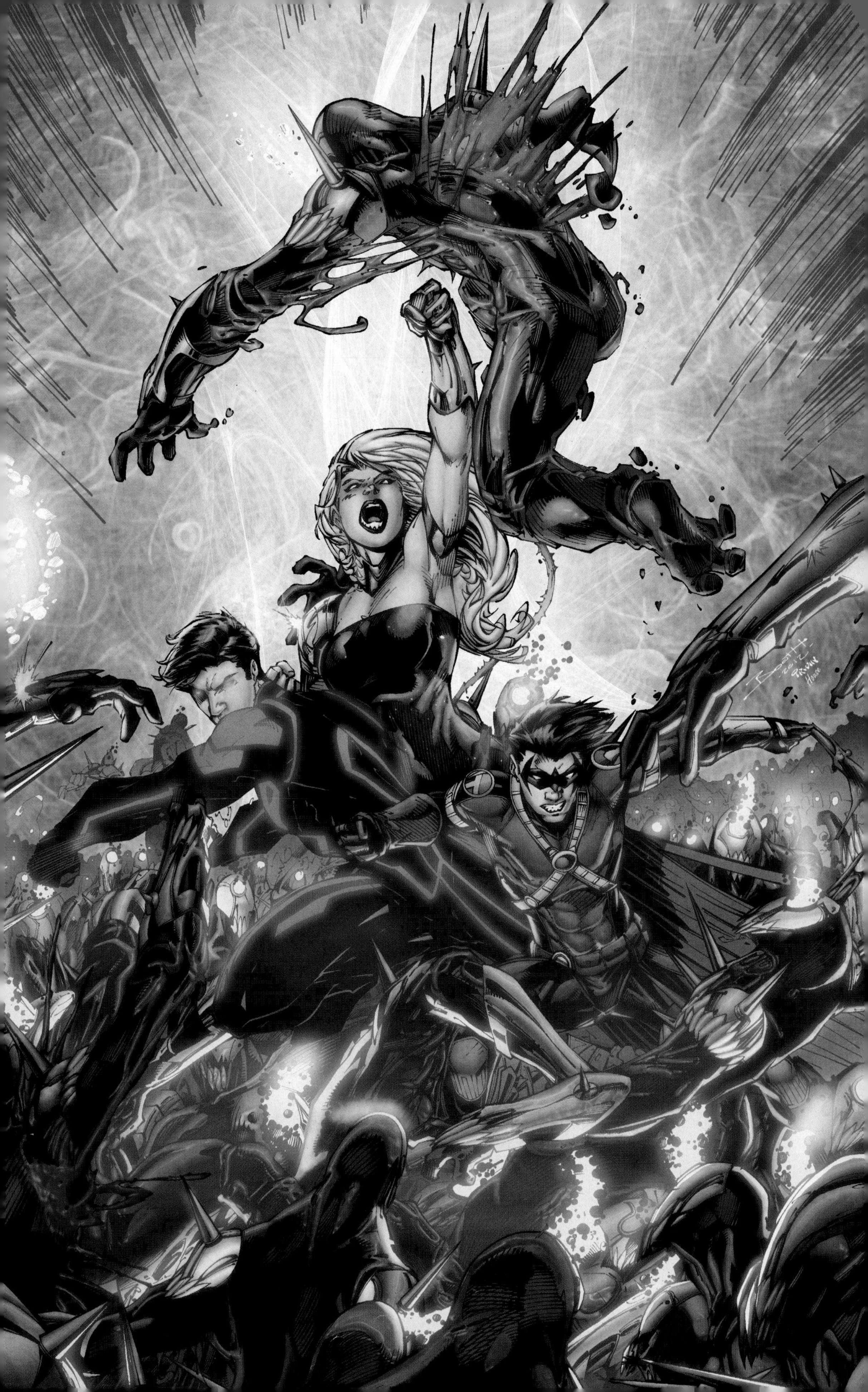

THE ORIGIN OF WONDER GIRL part two

SCOTT LOBDELL
writer

FABIAN NICIEZA
scripter

ALÉ GARZA
artist

cover art by
BRETT BOOTH, MARK IRWIN & ANDREW DALHOUSE

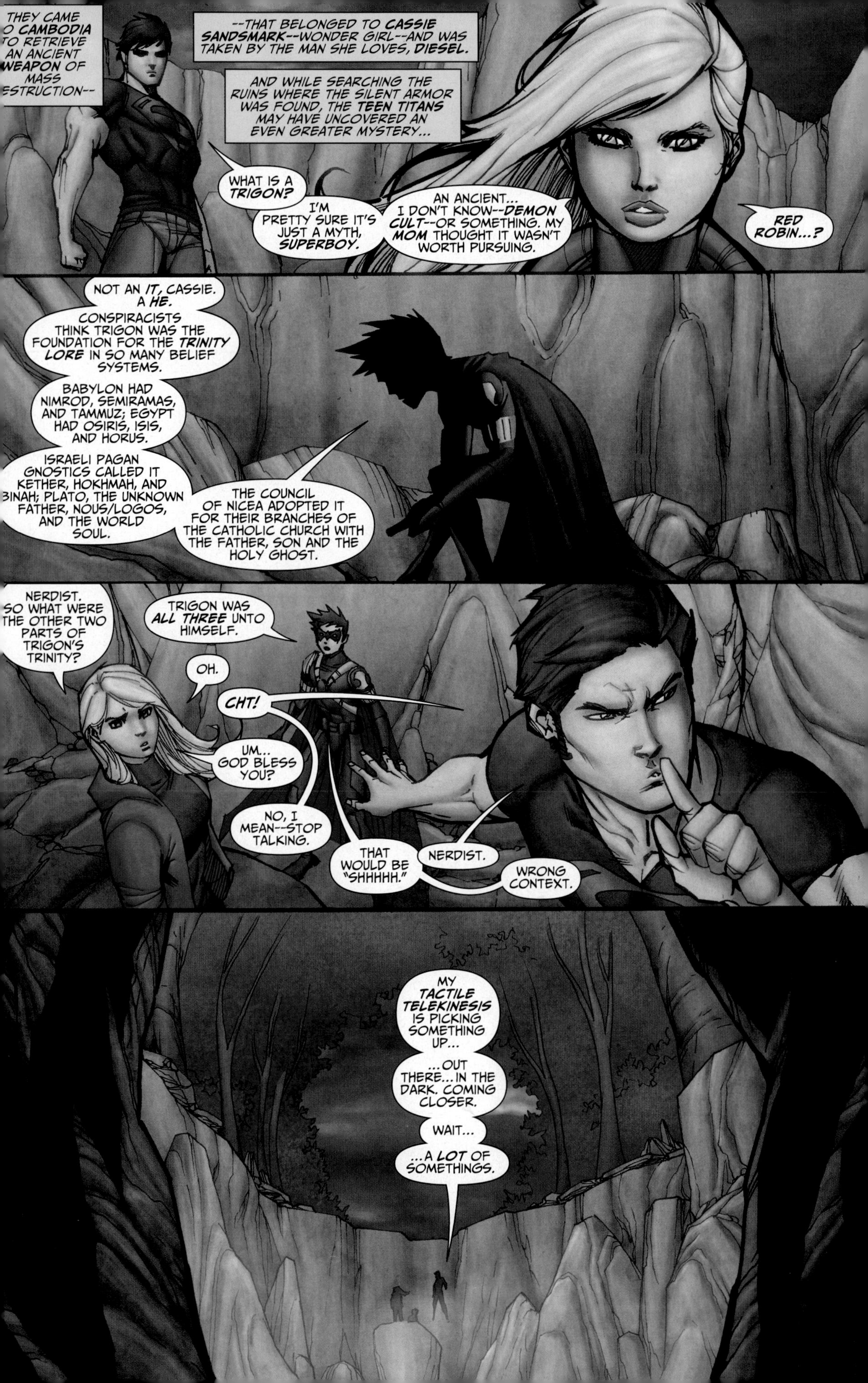
THEY CAME TO CAMBODIA TO RETRIEVE AN ANCIENT WEAPON OF MASS DESTRUCTION--
--THAT BELONGED TO CASSIE SANDSMARK--WONDER GIRL--AND WAS TAKEN BY THE MAN SHE LOVES, DIESEL.
AND WHILE SEARCHING THE RUINS WHERE THE SILENT ARMOR WAS FOUND, THE TEEN TITANS MAY HAVE UNCOVERED AN EVEN GREATER MYSTERY...
WHAT IS A TRIGON?
I'M PRETTY SURE IT'S JUST A MYTH, SUPERBOY.
AN ANCIENT... I DON'T KNOW--DEMON CULT--OR SOMETHING. MY MOM THOUGHT IT WASN'T WORTH PURSUING.
RED ROBIN...?
NOT AN IT, CASSIE. A HE.
CONSPIRACISTS THINK TRIGON WAS THE FOUNDATION FOR THE TRINITY LORE IN SO MANY BELIEF SYSTEMS.
BABYLON HAD NIMROD, SEMIRAMAS, AND TAMMUZ; EGYPT HAD OSIRIS, ISIS, AND HORUS.
ISRAELI PAGAN GNOSTICS CALLED IT KETHER, HOKHMAH, AND BINAH; PLATO, THE UNKNOWN FATHER, NOUS/LOGOS, AND THE WORLD SOUL.
THE COUNCIL OF NICEA ADOPTED IT FOR THEIR BRANCHES OF THE CATHOLIC CHURCH WITH THE FATHER, SON AND THE HOLY GHOST.
NERDIST. SO WHAT WERE THE OTHER TWO PARTS OF TRIGON'S TRINITY?
TRIGON WAS ALL THREE UNTO HIMSELF.
OH.
CHT!
UM... GOD BLESS YOU?
NO, I MEAN--STOP TALKING.
THAT WOULD BE "SHHHHH."
NERDIST.
WRONG CONTEXT.
MY TACTILE TELEKINESIS IS PICKING SOMETHING UP...
...OUT THERE... IN THE DARK. COMING CLOSER.
WAIT...
...A LOT OF SOMETHINGS.

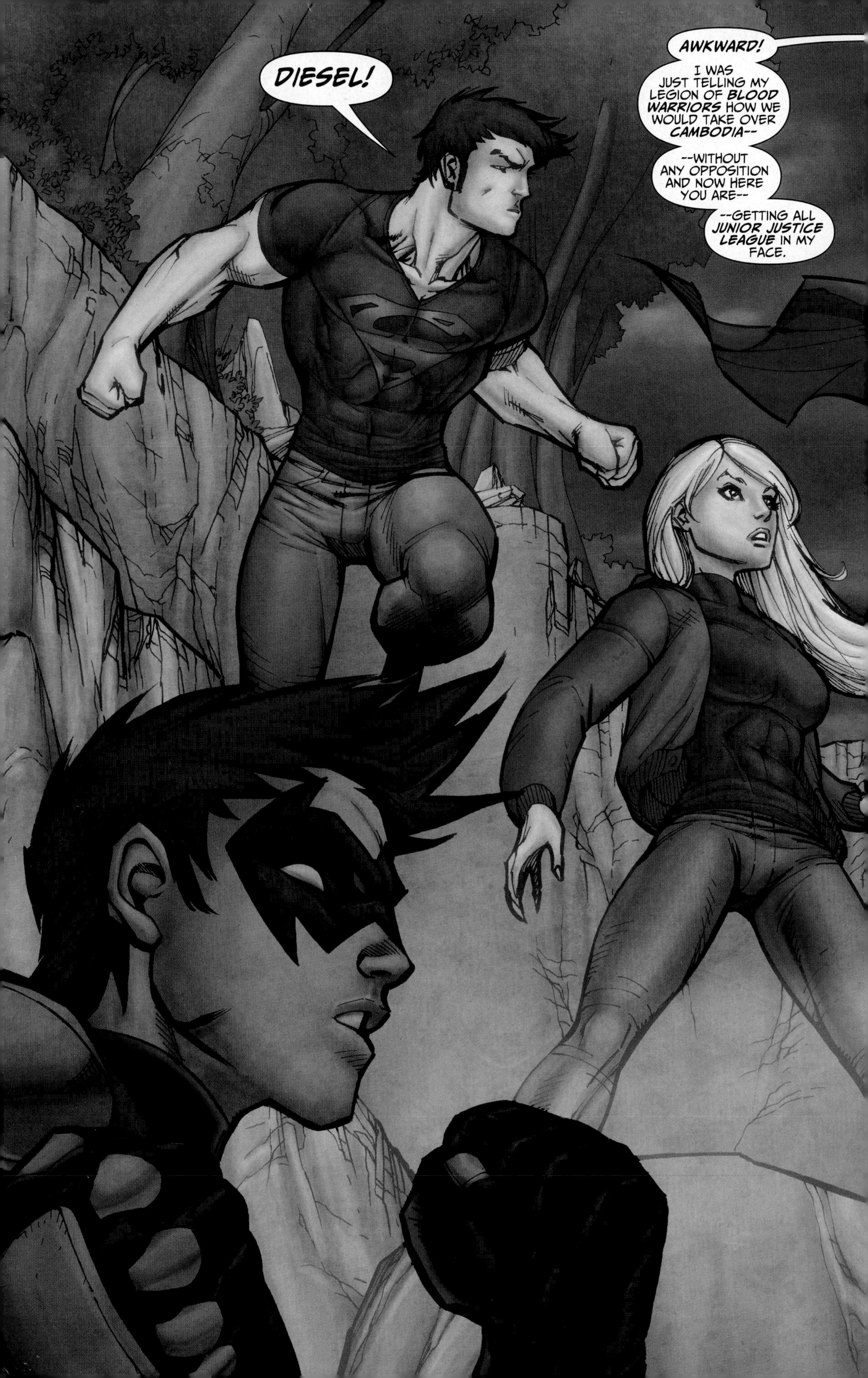
DIESEL!
AWKWARD!
I WAS JUST TELLING MY LEGION OF BLOOD WARRIORS HOW WE WOULD TAKE OVER CAMBODIA--
--WITHOUT ANY OPPOSITION AND NOW HERE YOU ARE--
--GETTING ALL JUNIOR JUSTICE LEAGUE IN MY FACE.

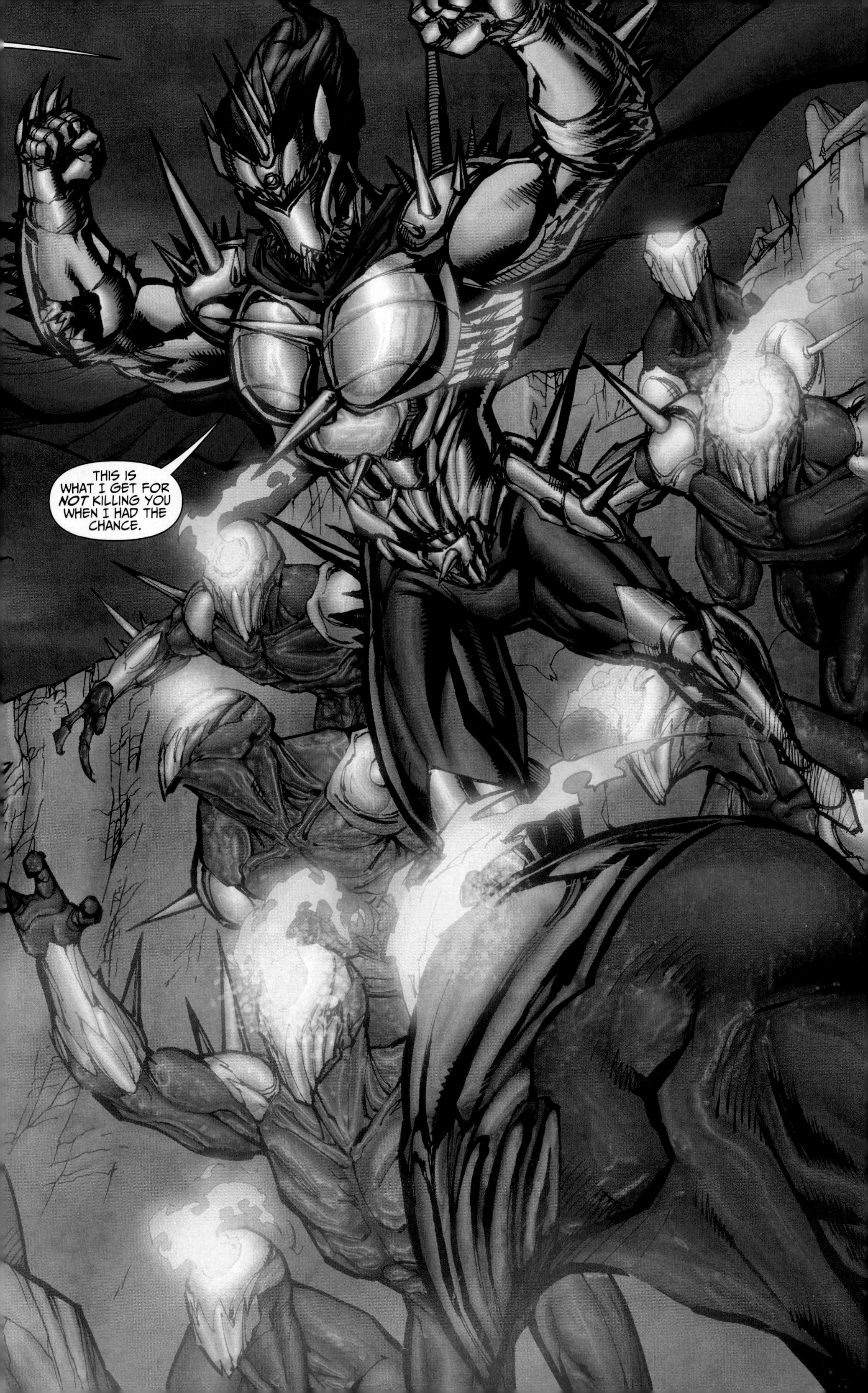
THIS IS WHAT I GET FOR *NOT* KILLING YOU WHEN I HAD THE CHANCE.

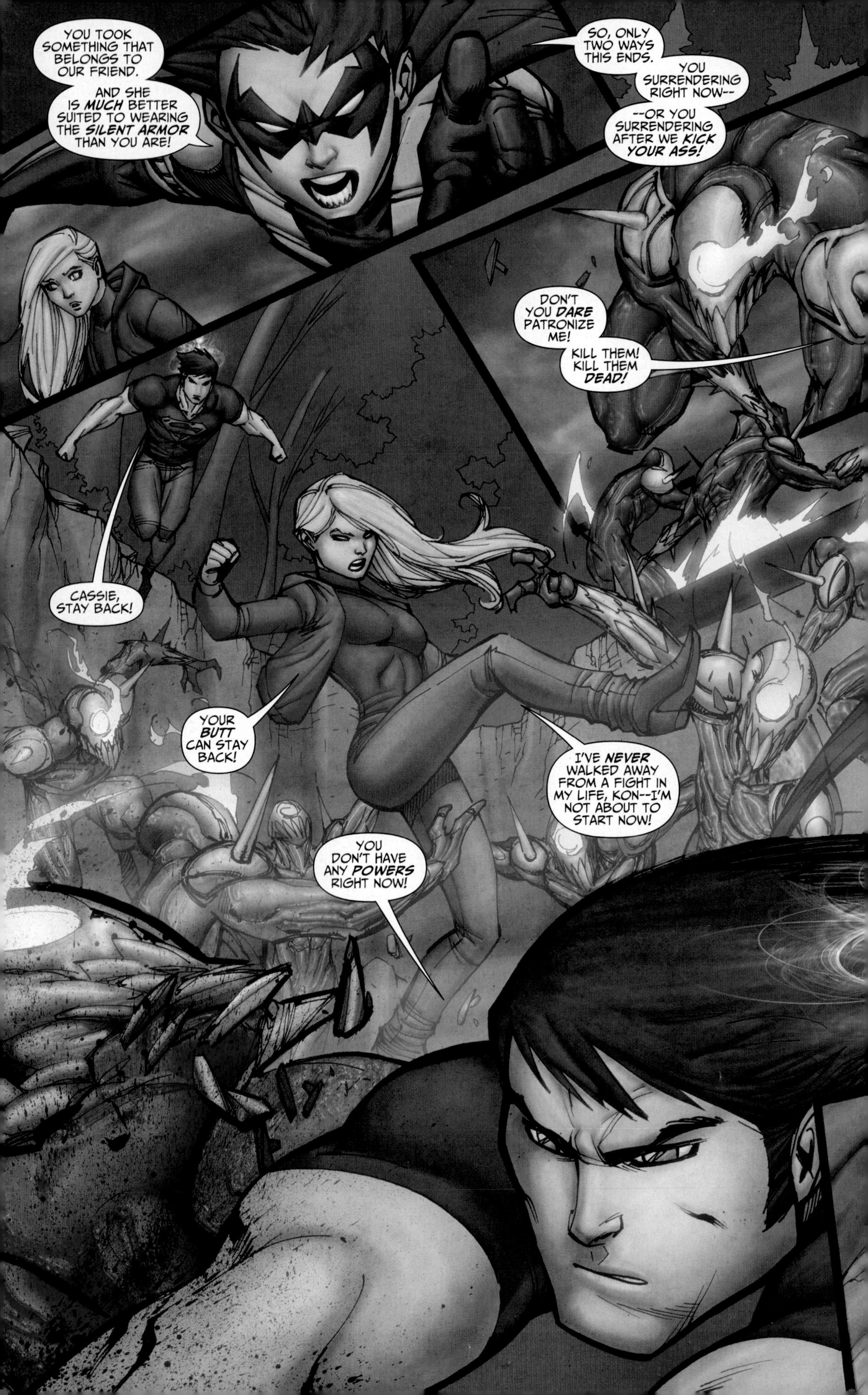
YOU TOOK SOMETHING THAT BELONGS TO OUR FRIEND.
AND SHE IS MUCH BETTER SUITED TO WEARING THE SILENT ARMOR THAN YOU ARE!
SO, ONLY TWO WAYS THIS ENDS.
YOU SURRENDERING RIGHT NOW--
--OR YOU SURRENDERING AFTER WE KICK YOUR ASS!
DON'T YOU DARE PATRONIZE ME!
KILL THEM! KILL THEM DEAD!
CASSIE, STAY BACK!
YOUR BUTT CAN STAY BACK!
I'VE NEVER WALKED AWAY FROM A FIGHT IN MY LIFE, KON--I'M NOT ABOUT TO START NOW!
YOU DON'T HAVE ANY POWERS RIGHT NOW!

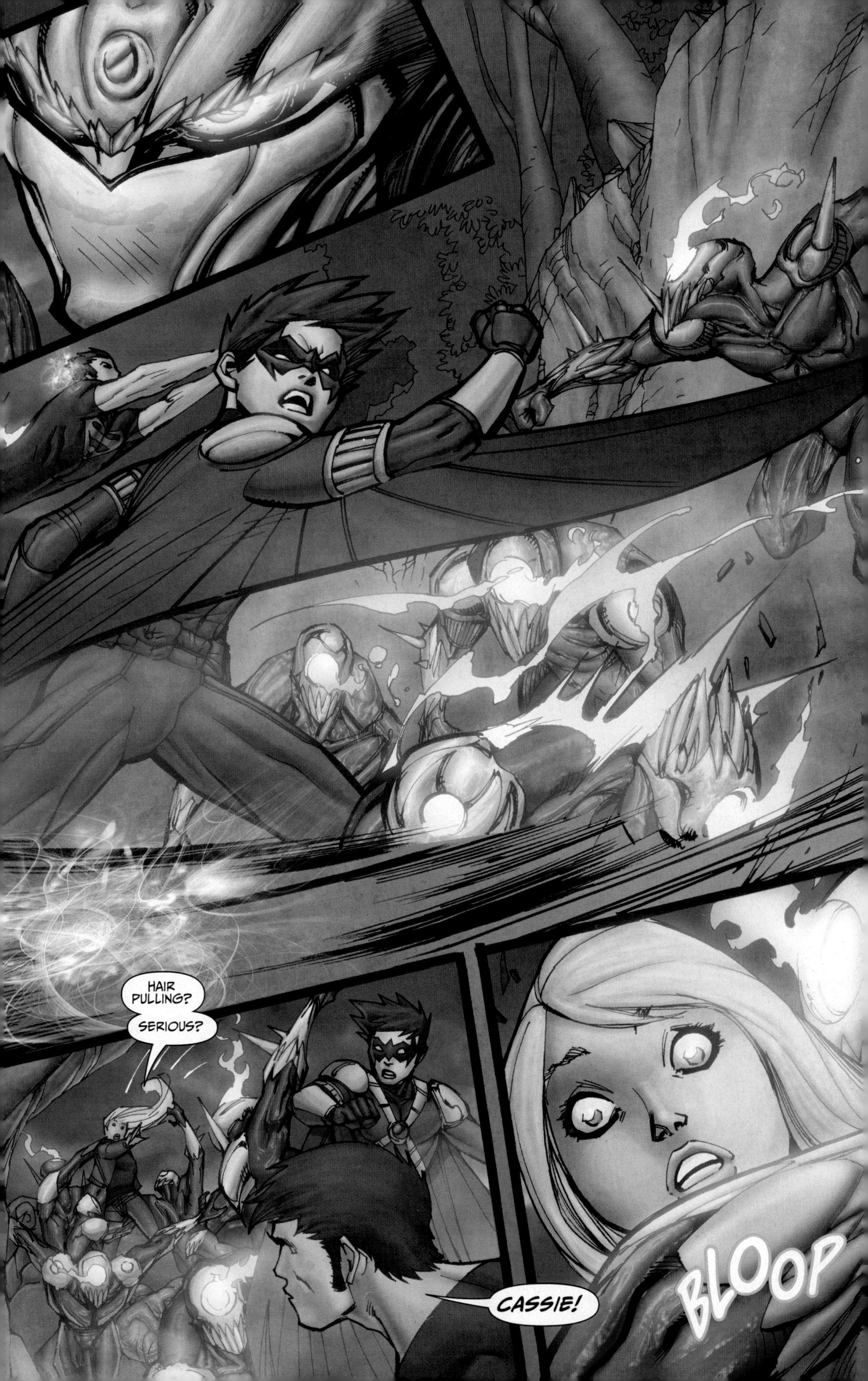
HAIR PULLING?
SERIOUS?
CASSIE!
BLOOP

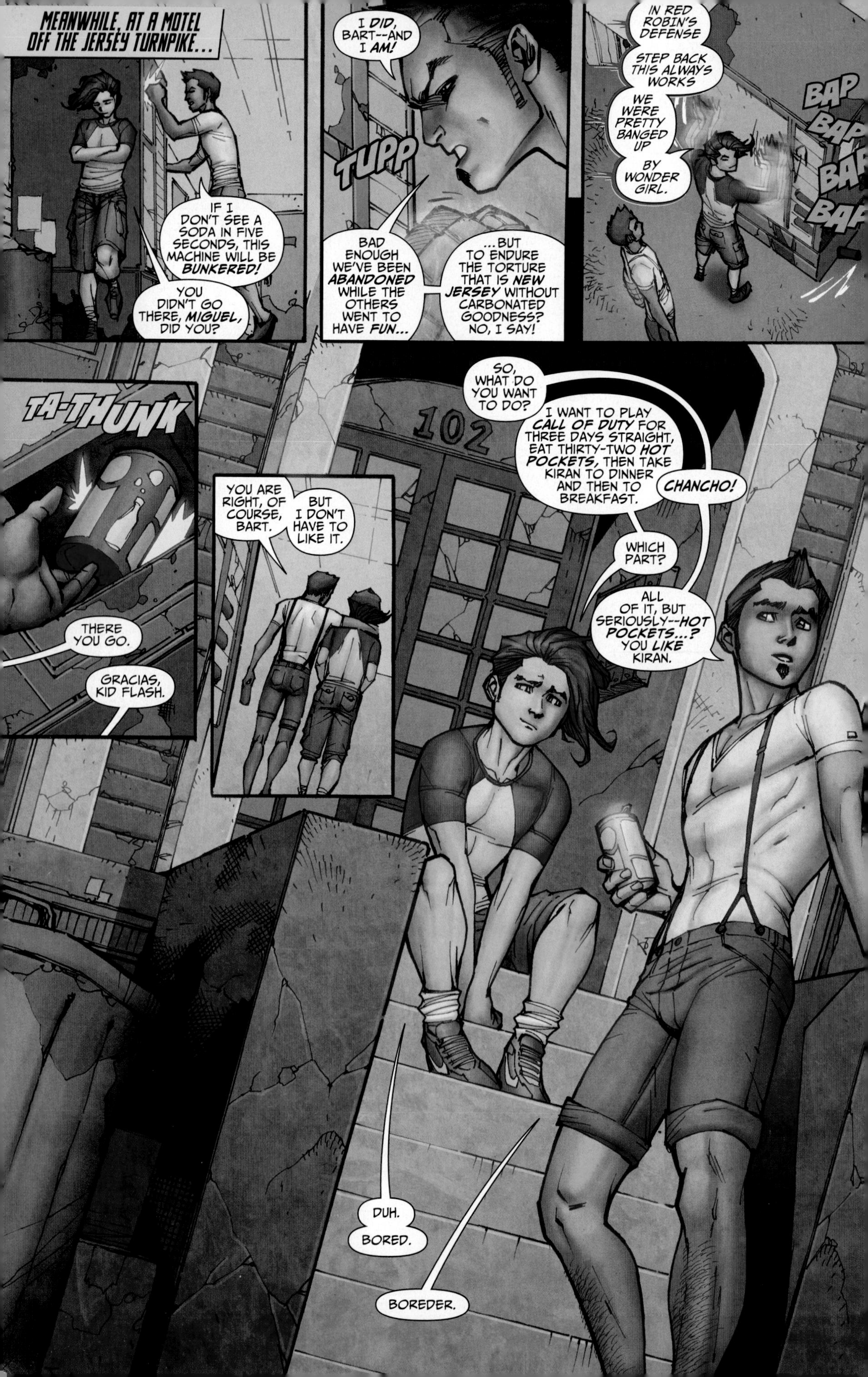
MEANWHILE, AT A MOTEL OFF THE JERSEY TURNPIKE...
IF I DON'T SEE A SODA IN FIVE SECONDS, THIS MACHINE WILL BE BUNKERED!
YOU DIDN'T GO THERE, MIGUEL, DID YOU?
I DID, BART--AND I AM!
TUPP
BAD ENOUGH WE'VE BEEN ABANDONED WHILE THE OTHERS WENT TO HAVE FUN...
...BUT TO ENDURE THE TORTURE THAT IS NEW JERSEY WITHOUT CARBONATED GOODNESS? NO, I SAY!
IN RED ROBIN'S DEFENSE
STEP BACK THIS ALWAYS WORKS
WE WERE PRETTY BANGED UP
BY WONDER GIRL.
BAP BAP BAP BAP
TA-THUNK
THERE YOU GO.
GRACIAS, KID FLASH.
YOU ARE RIGHT, OF COURSE, BART.
BUT I DON'T HAVE TO LIKE IT.
102
SO, WHAT DO YOU WANT TO DO?
I WANT TO PLAY CALL OF DUTY FOR THREE DAYS STRAIGHT, EAT THIRTY-TWO HOT POCKETS, THEN TAKE KIRAN TO DINNER AND THEN TO BREAKFAST.
CHANCHO!
WHICH PART?
ALL OF IT, BUT SERIOUSLY--HOT POCKETS...? YOU LIKE KIRAN.
DUH.
BORED.
BOREDER.

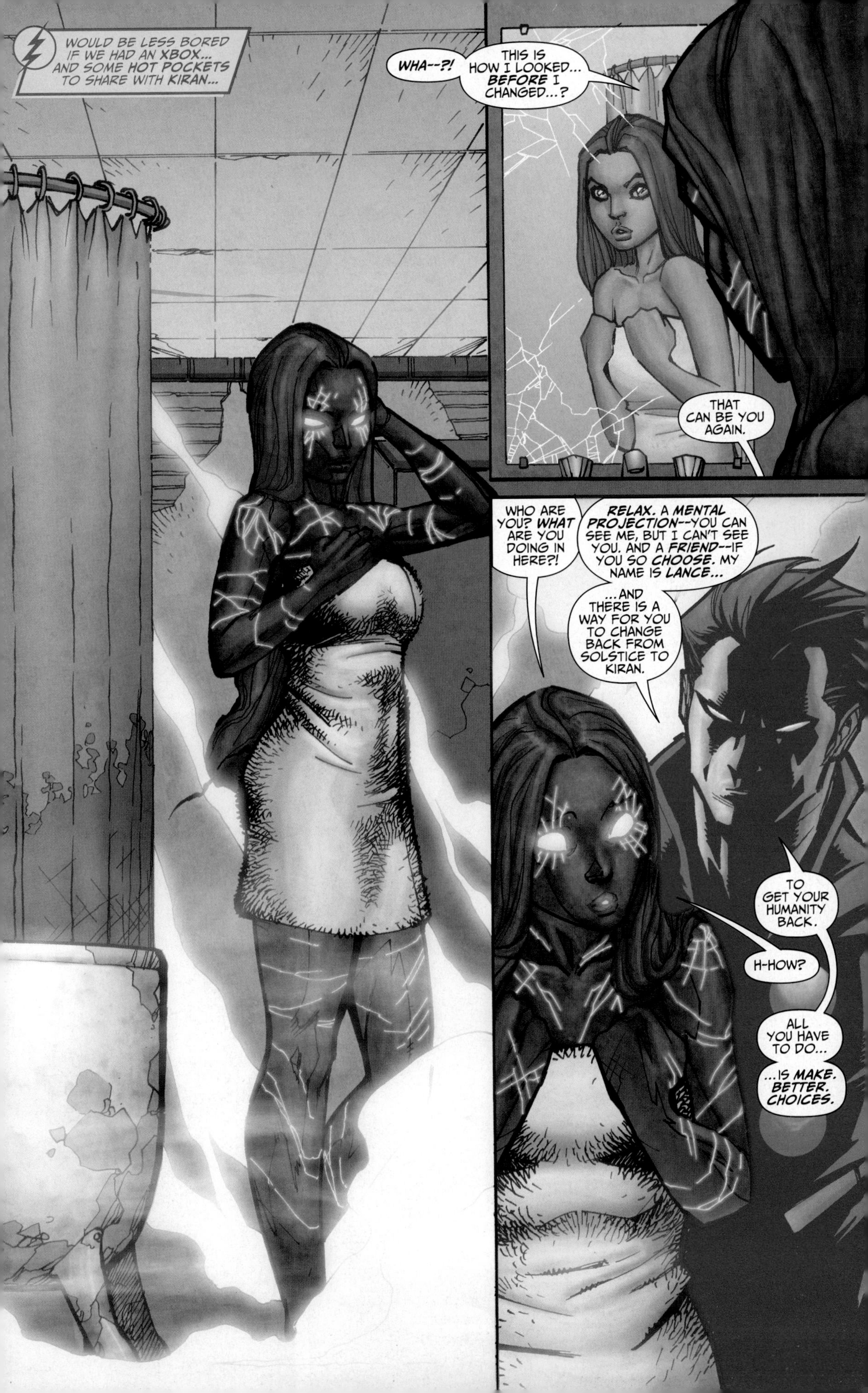

WOULD BE LESS BORED IF WE HAD AN XBOX... AND SOME HOT POCKETS TO SHARE WITH KIRAN...
WHA--?!
THIS IS HOW I LOOKED... BEFORE I CHANGED...?
THAT CAN BE YOU AGAIN.
WHO ARE YOU? WHAT ARE YOU DOING IN HERE?!
RELAX. A MENTAL PROJECTION--YOU CAN SEE ME, BUT I CAN'T SEE YOU. AND A FRIEND--IF YOU SO CHOOSE. MY NAME IS LANCE...
...AND THERE IS A WAY FOR YOU TO CHANGE BACK FROM SOLSTICE TO KIRAN.
TO GET YOUR HUMANITY BACK.
H-HOW?
ALL YOU HAVE TO DO...
...IS MAKE. BETTER. CHOICES.

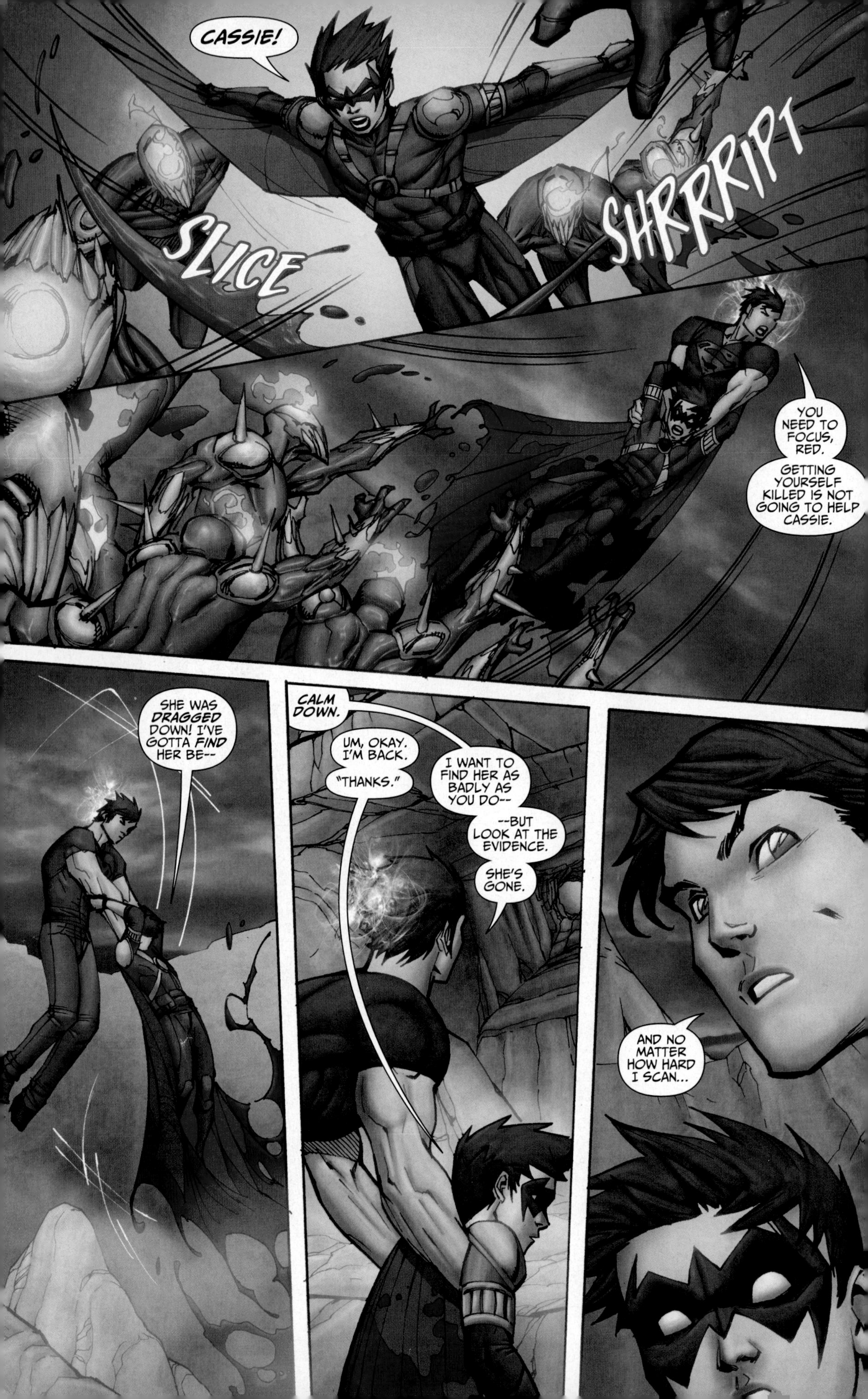
CASSIE!
SLICE
SHRRIPT
YOU NEED TO FOCUS, RED.
GETTING YOURSELF KILLED IS NOT GOING TO HELP CASSIE.
SHE WAS DRAGGED DOWN! I'VE GOTTA FIND HER BE--
CALM DOWN.
UM, OKAY. I'M BACK.
"THANKS."
I WANT TO FIND HER AS BADLY AS YOU DO--
--BUT LOOK AT THE EVIDENCE.
SHE'S GONE.
AND NO MATTER HOW HARD I SCAN...

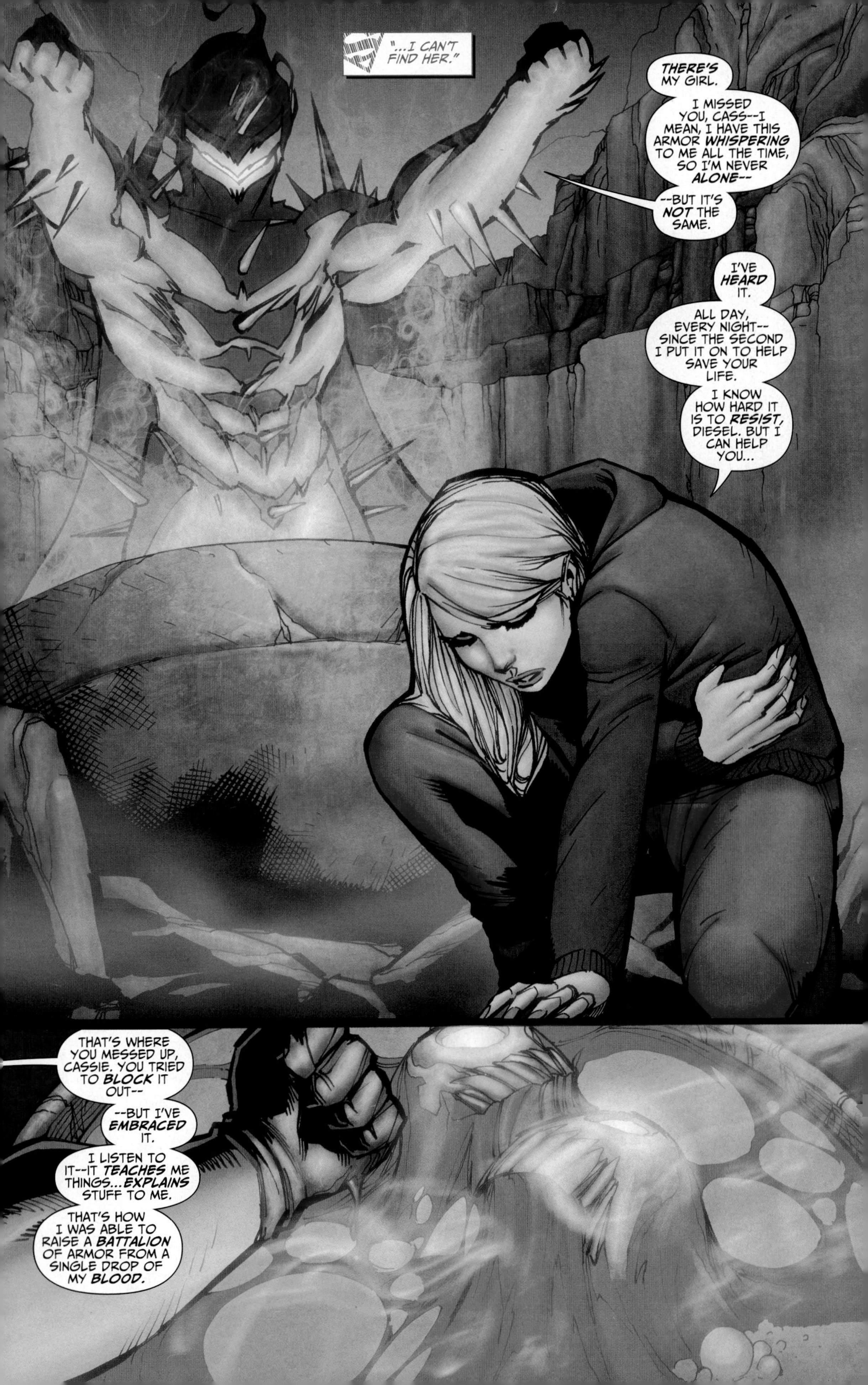
"...I CAN'T FIND HER."
THERE'S MY GIRL.
I MISSED YOU, CASS--I MEAN, I HAVE THIS ARMOR WHISPERING TO ME ALL THE TIME, SO I'M NEVER ALONE--
--BUT IT'S NOT THE SAME.
I'VE HEARD IT.
ALL DAY, EVERY NIGHT--SINCE THE SECOND I PUT IT ON TO HELP SAVE YOUR LIFE.
I KNOW HOW HARD IT IS TO RESIST, DIESEL. BUT I CAN HELP YOU...
THAT'S WHERE YOU MESSED UP, CASSIE. YOU TRIED TO BLOCK IT OUT--
--BUT I'VE EMBRACED IT.
I LISTEN TO IT--IT TEACHES ME THINGS...EXPLAINS STUFF TO ME.
THAT'S HOW I WAS ABLE TO RAISE A BATTALION OF ARMOR FROM A SINGLE DROP OF MY BLOOD.

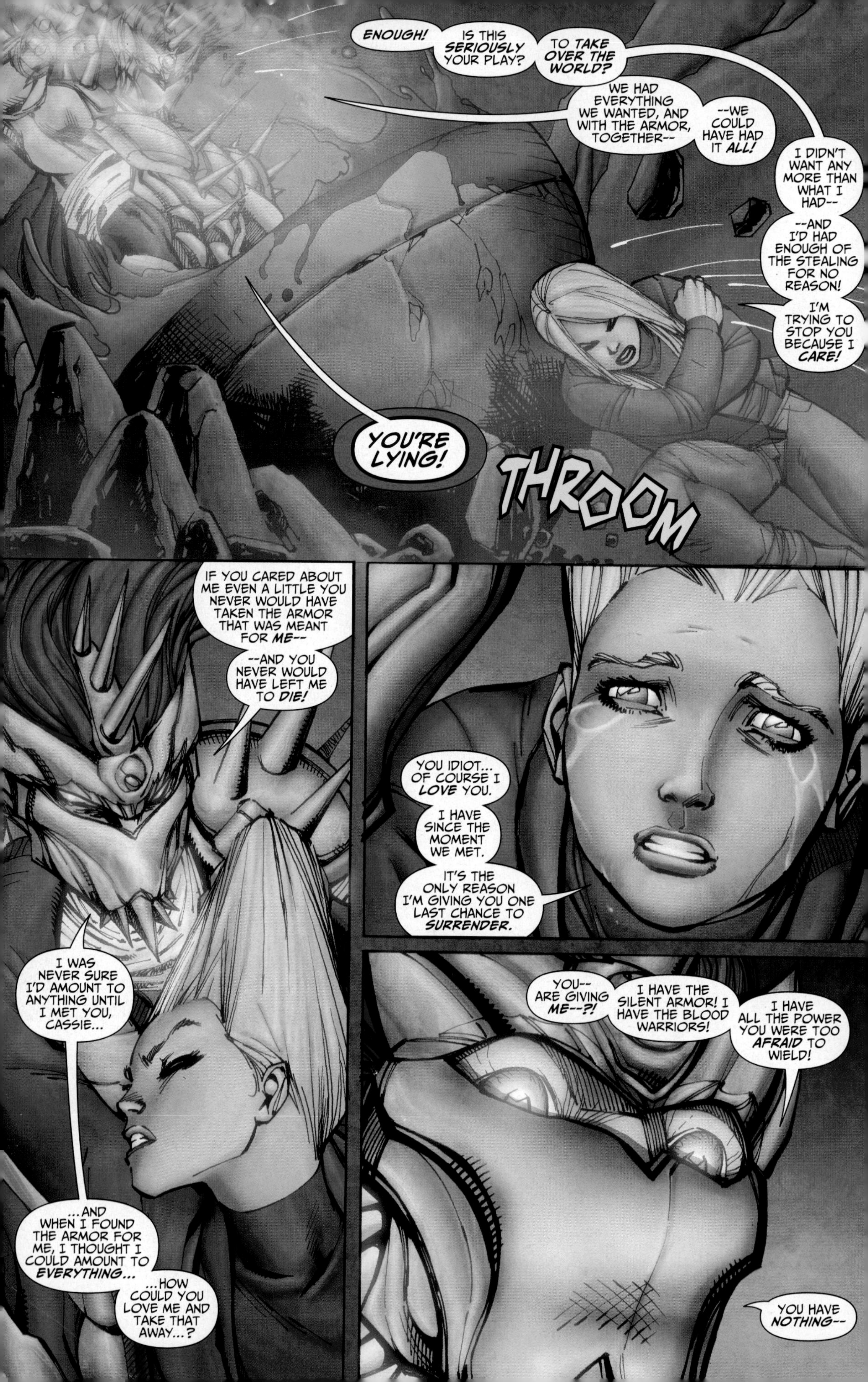
ENOUGH!
IS THIS SERIOUSLY YOUR PLAY?
TO TAKE OVER THE WORLD?
WE HAD EVERYTHING WE WANTED, AND WITH THE ARMOR, TOGETHER--
--WE COULD HAVE HAD IT ALL!
I DIDN'T WANT ANY MORE THAN WHAT I HAD--
--AND I'D HAD ENOUGH OF THE STEALING FOR NO REASON!
I'M TRYING TO STOP YOU BECAUSE I CARE!
YOU'RE LYING!
THROOM
IF YOU CARED ABOUT ME EVEN A LITTLE YOU NEVER WOULD HAVE TAKEN THE ARMOR THAT WAS MEANT FOR ME--
--AND YOU NEVER WOULD HAVE LEFT ME TO DIE!
I WAS NEVER SURE I'D AMOUNT TO ANYTHING UNTIL I MET YOU, CASSIE...
...AND WHEN I FOUND THE ARMOR FOR ME, I THOUGHT I COULD AMOUNT TO EVERYTHING...
...HOW COULD YOU LOVE ME AND TAKE THAT AWAY...?
YOU IDIOT... OF COURSE I LOVE YOU.
I HAVE SINCE THE MOMENT WE MET.
IT'S THE ONLY REASON I'M GIVING YOU ONE LAST CHANCE TO SURRENDER.
YOU-- ARE GIVING ME--?!
I HAVE THE SILENT ARMOR! I HAVE THE BLOOD WARRIORS!
I HAVE ALL THE POWER YOU WERE TOO AFRAID TO WIELD!
YOU HAVE NOTHING--

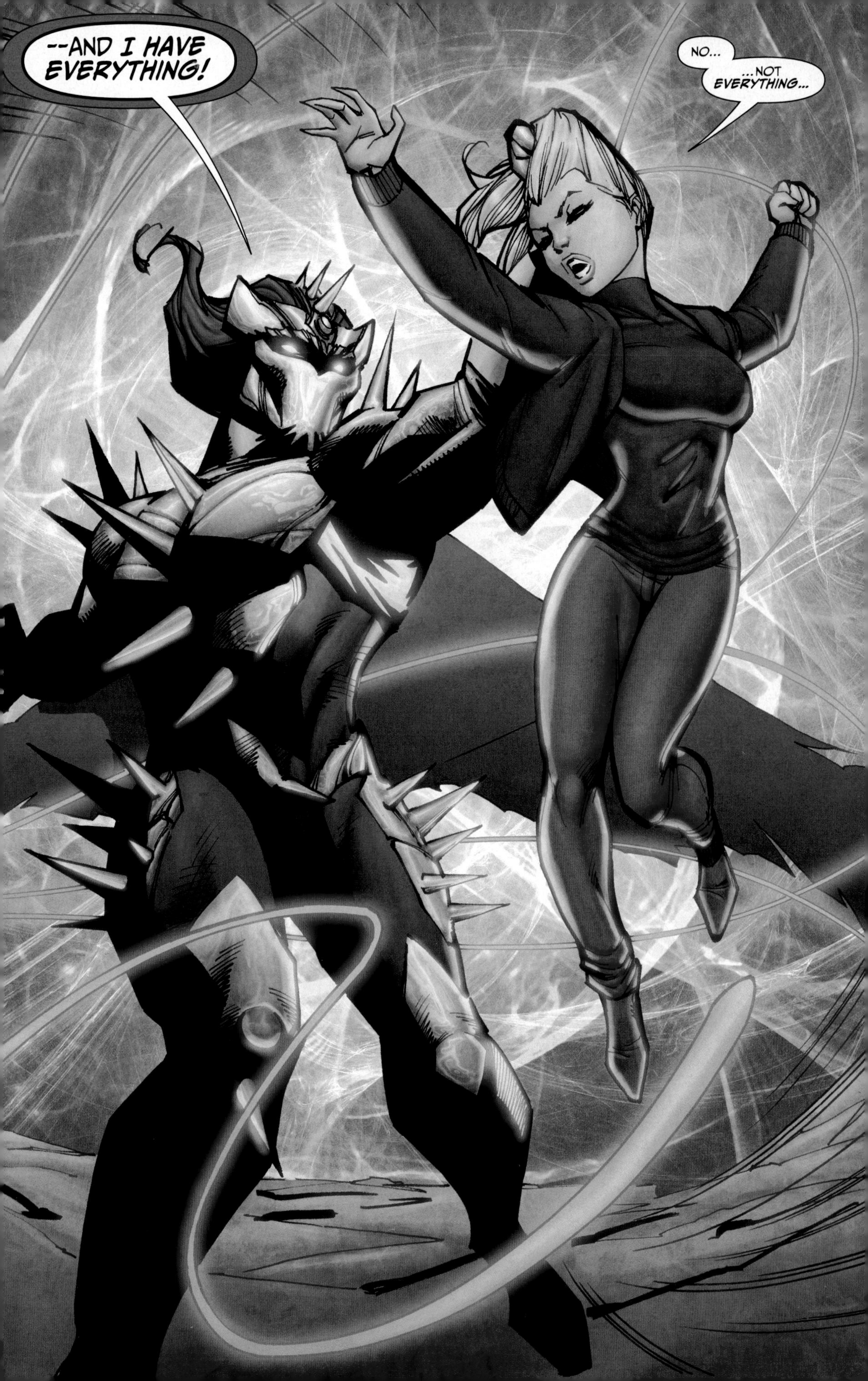
--AND I HAVE EVERYTHING!
NO...
...NOT EVERYTHING...

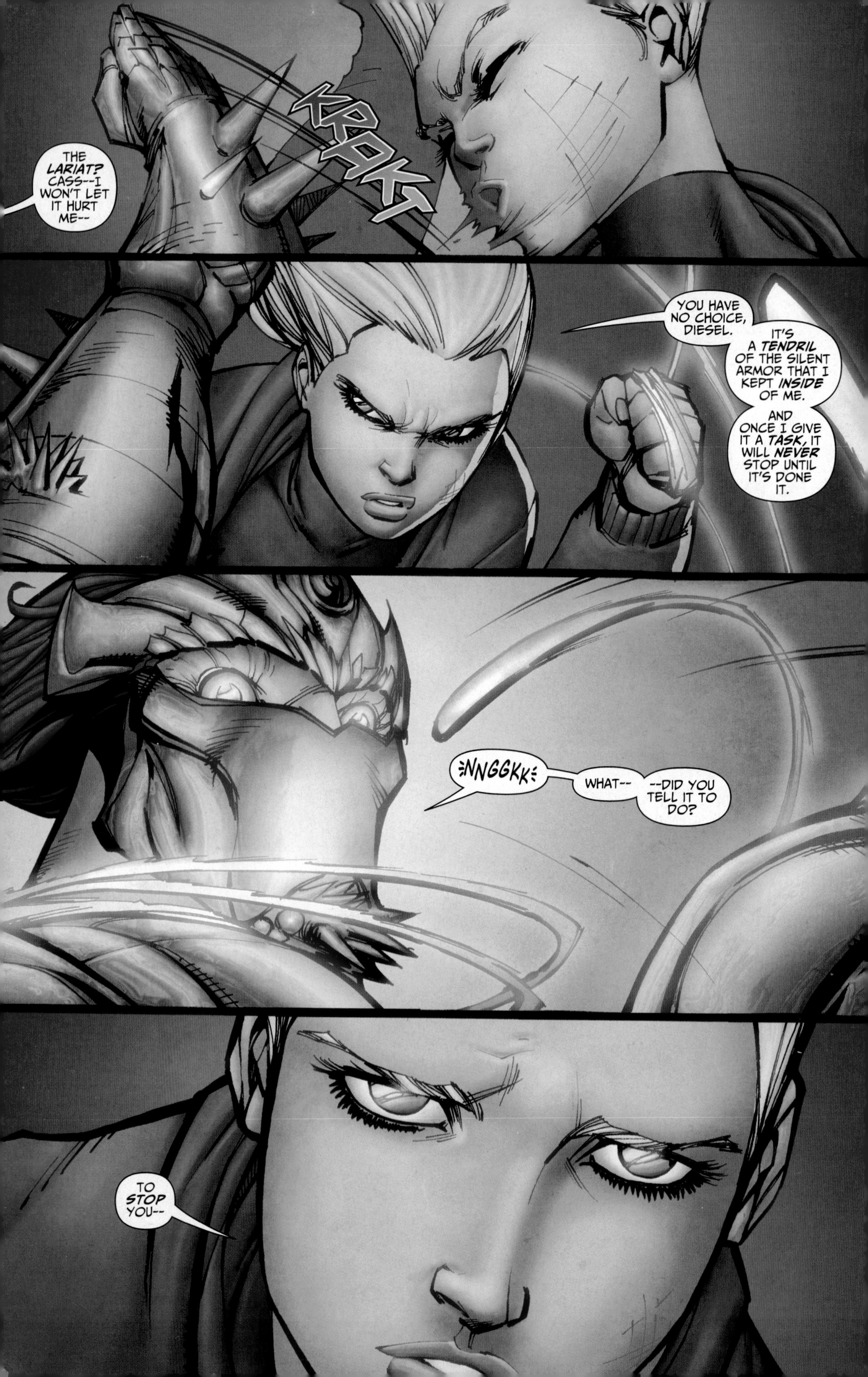
THE *LARIAT?* CASS--I WON'T LET IT HURT ME--
KRAKT
YOU HAVE NO CHOICE, DIESEL.
IT'S A *TENDRIL* OF THE SILENT ARMOR THAT I KEPT *INSIDE* OF ME.
AND ONCE I GIVE IT A *TASK,* IT WILL *NEVER* STOP UNTIL IT'S DONE IT.
NNGGKK
WHAT--
--DID YOU TELL IT TO DO?
TO *STOP* YOU--

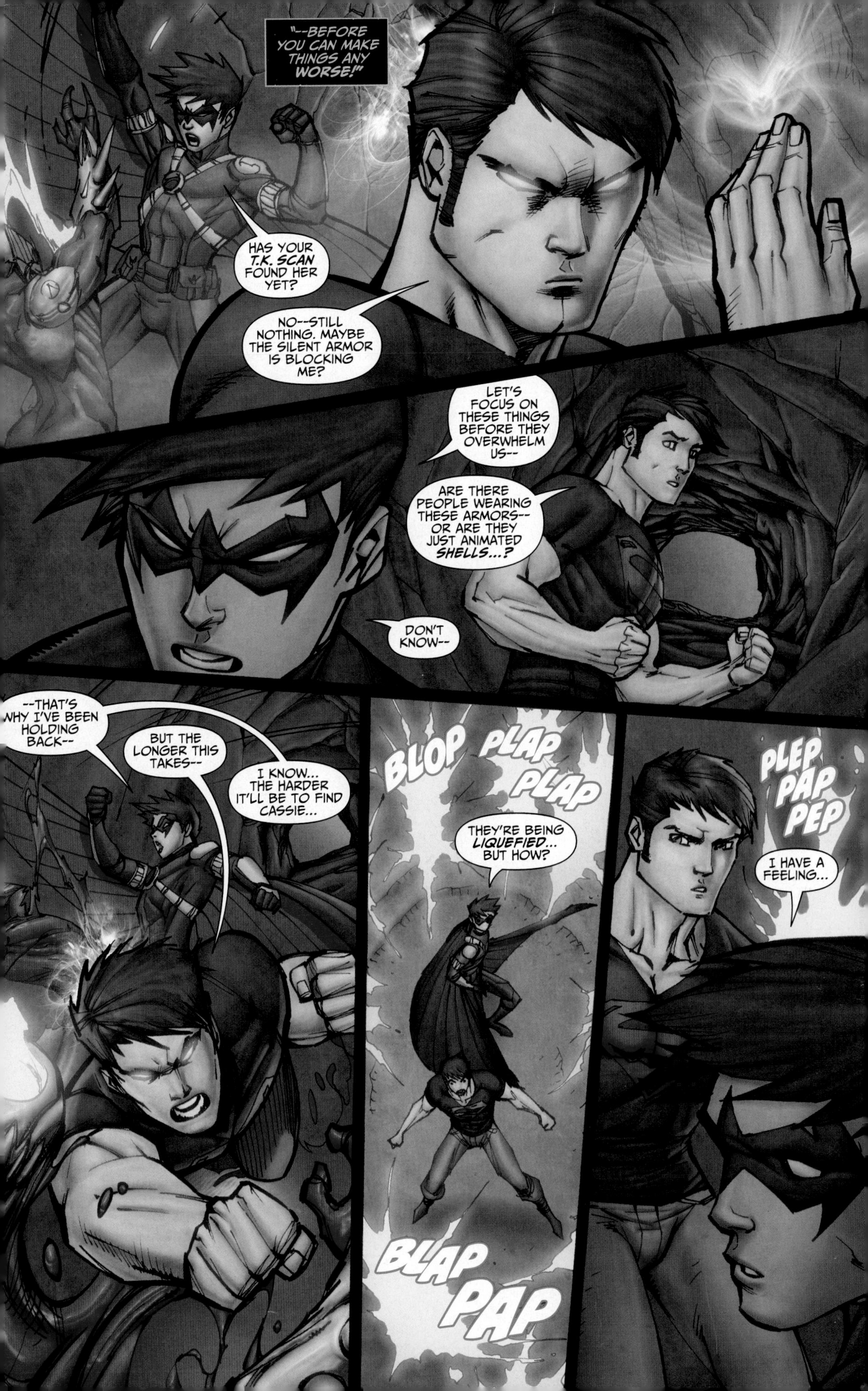
"--BEFORE YOU CAN MAKE THINGS ANY WORSE!"
HAS YOUR T.K. SCAN FOUND HER YET?
NO--STILL NOTHING. MAYBE THE SILENT ARMOR IS BLOCKING ME?
LET'S FOCUS ON THESE THINGS BEFORE THEY OVERWHELM US--
ARE THERE PEOPLE WEARING THESE ARMORS-- OR ARE THEY JUST ANIMATED SHELLS...?
DON'T KNOW--
--THAT'S WHY I'VE BEEN HOLDING BACK--
BUT THE LONGER THIS TAKES--
I KNOW... THE HARDER IT'LL BE TO FIND CASSIE...
BLOP PLAP PLAP
THEY'RE BEING LIQUEFIED... BUT HOW?
BLAP PAP
PLEP PAP PEP
I HAVE A FEELING...

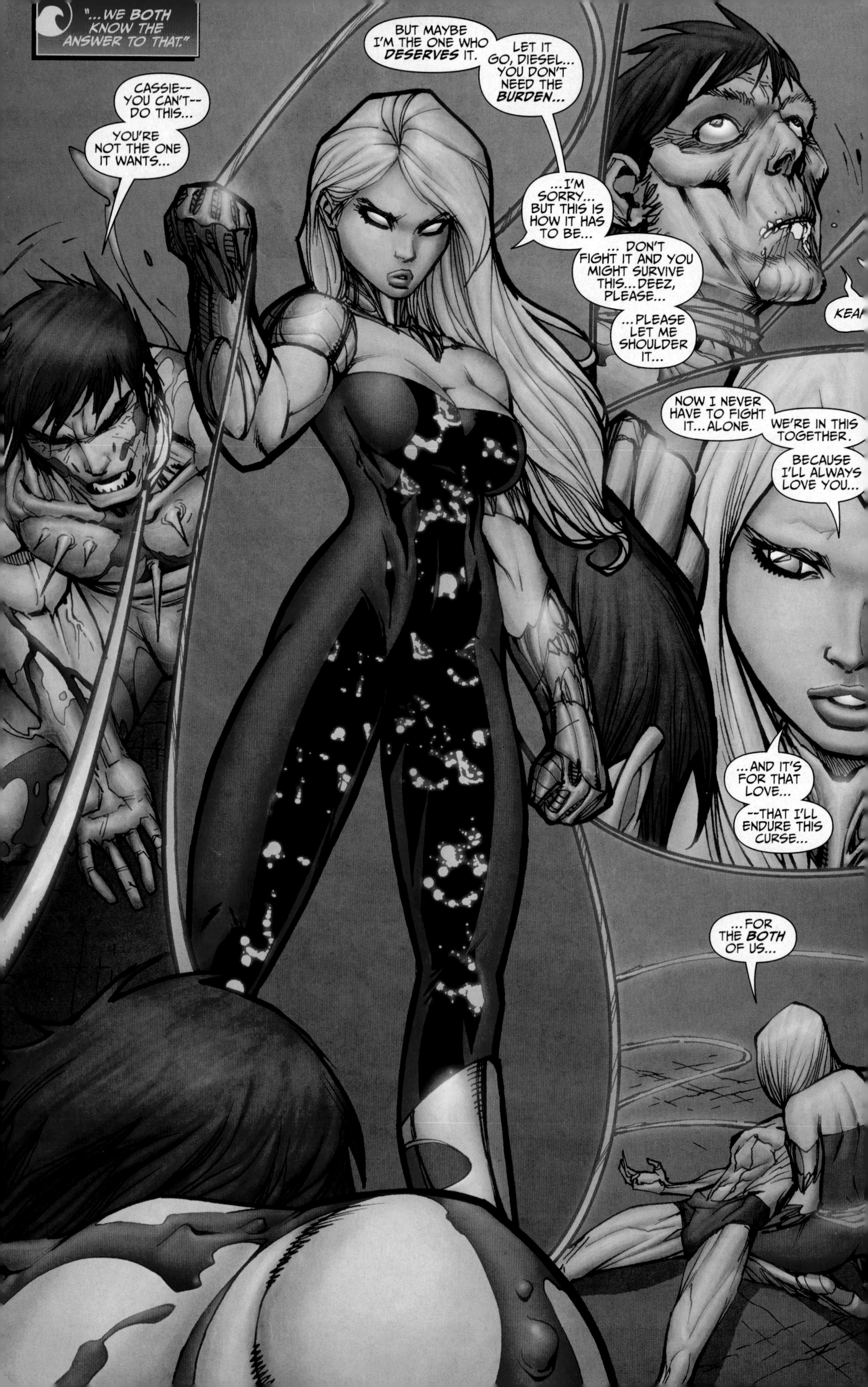
"...WE BOTH KNOW THE ANSWER TO THAT."
CASSIE-- YOU CAN'T-- DO THIS...
YOU'RE NOT THE ONE IT WANTS...
BUT MAYBE I'M THE ONE WHO DESERVES IT.
LET IT GO, DIESEL... YOU DON'T NEED THE BURDEN...
...I'M SORRY... BUT THIS IS HOW IT HAS TO BE...
... DON'T FIGHT IT AND YOU MIGHT SURVIVE THIS...DEEZ, PLEASE...
...PLEASE LET ME SHOULDER IT...
NOW I NEVER HAVE TO FIGHT IT... ALONE.
WE'RE IN THIS TOGETHER.
BECAUSE I'LL ALWAYS LOVE YOU...
...AND IT'S FOR THAT LOVE...
--THAT I'LL ENDURE THIS CURSE...
...FOR THE BOTH OF US...

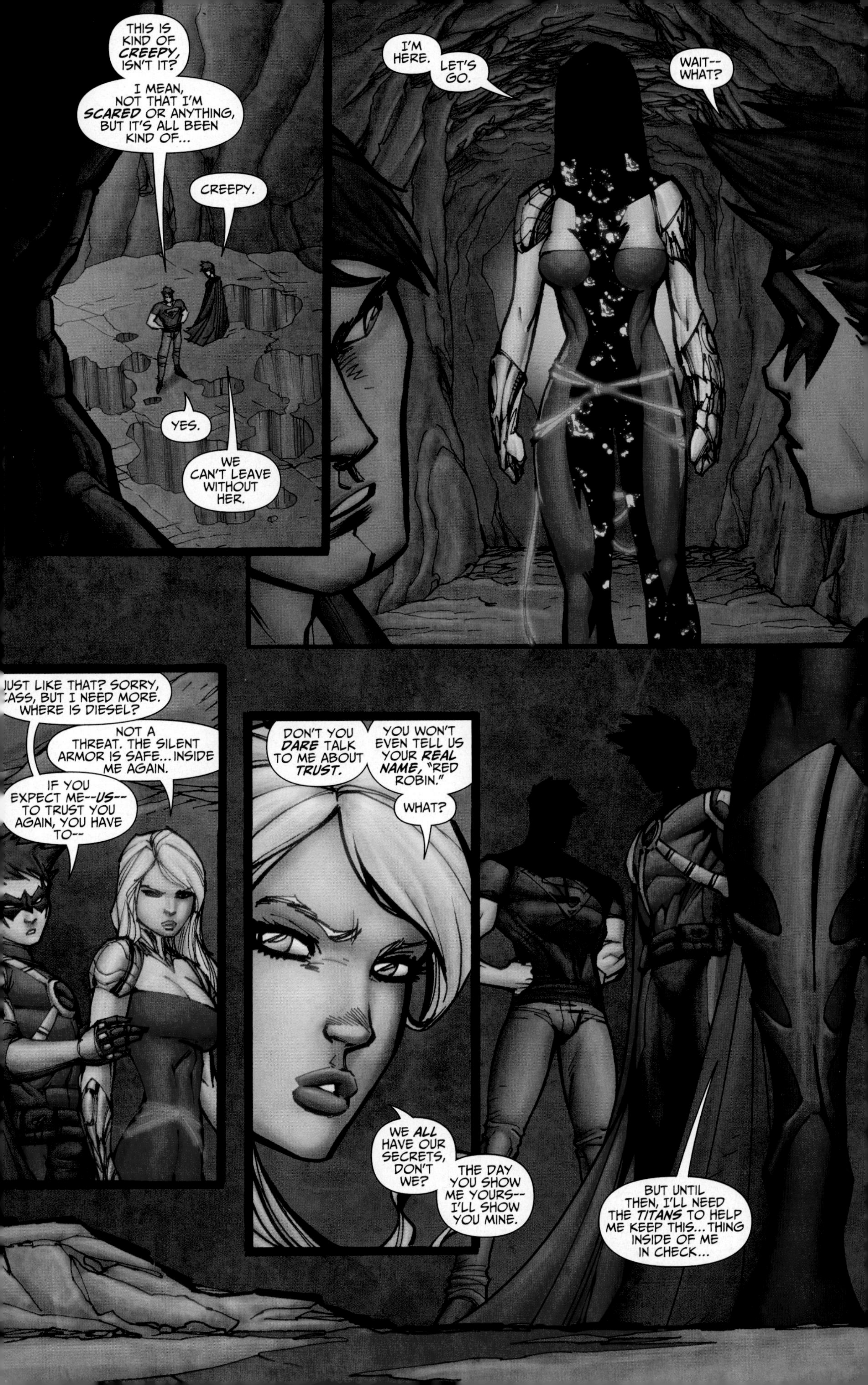

THIS IS KIND OF CREEPY, ISN'T IT?
I MEAN, NOT THAT I'M SCARED OR ANYTHING, BUT IT'S ALL BEEN KIND OF...
CREEPY.
YES.
WE CAN'T LEAVE WITHOUT HER.
I'M HERE.
LET'S GO.
WAIT-- WHAT?
JUST LIKE THAT? SORRY, CASS, BUT I NEED MORE. WHERE IS DIESEL?
NOT A THREAT. THE SILENT ARMOR IS SAFE... INSIDE ME AGAIN.
IF YOU EXPECT ME--US-- TO TRUST YOU AGAIN, YOU HAVE TO--
DON'T YOU DARE TALK TO ME ABOUT TRUST.
YOU WON'T EVEN TELL US YOUR REAL NAME, "RED ROBIN."
WHAT?
WE ALL HAVE OUR SECRETS, DON'T WE?
THE DAY YOU SHOW ME YOURS-- I'LL SHOW YOU MINE.
BUT UNTIL THEN, I'LL NEED THE TITANS TO HELP ME KEEP THIS... THING INSIDE OF ME IN CHECK...

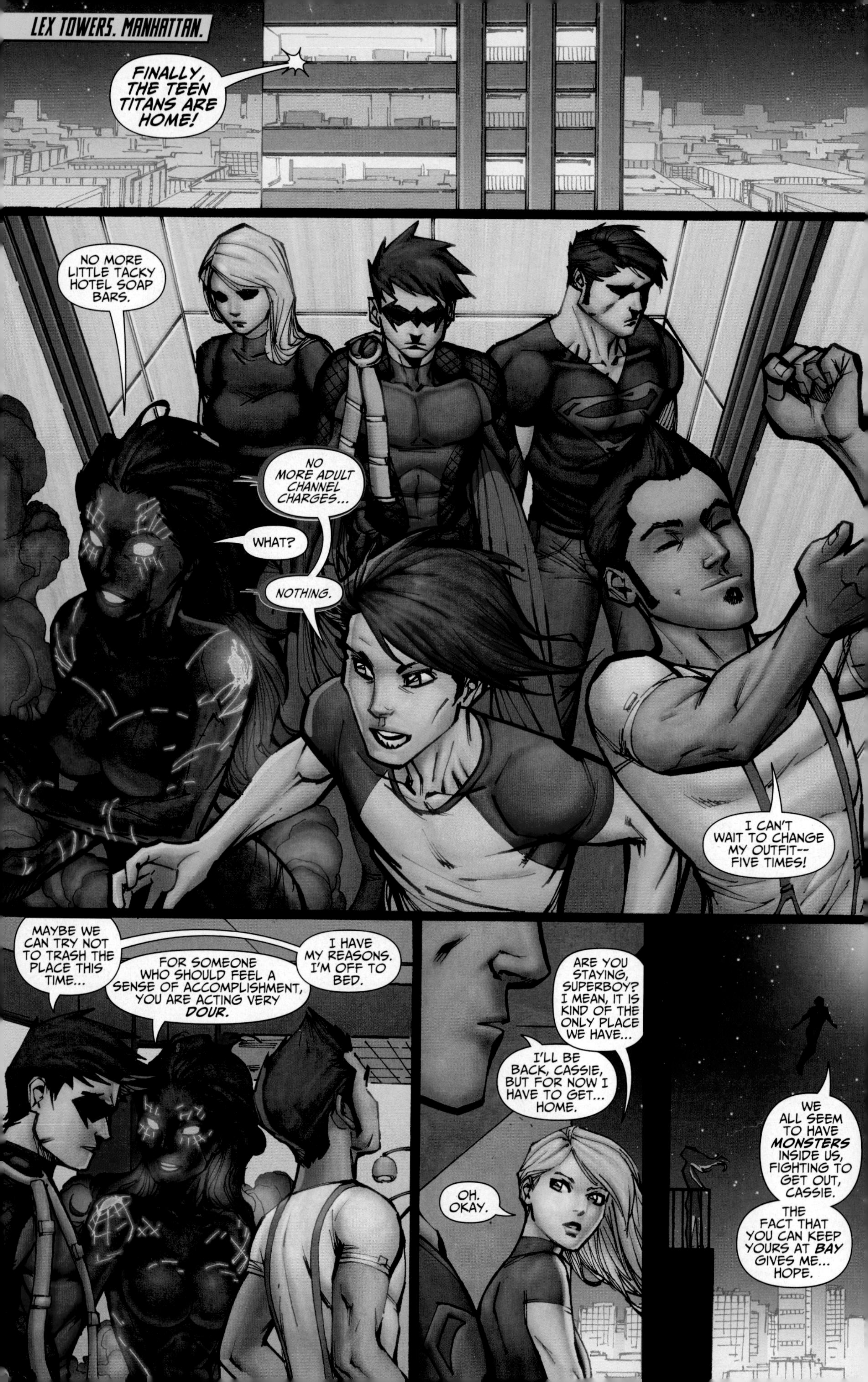
LEX TOWERS. MANHATTAN.
FINALLY, THE TEEN TITANS ARE HOME!
NO MORE LITTLE TACKY HOTEL SOAP BARS.
NO MORE ADULT CHANNEL CHARGES...
WHAT?
NOTHING.
I CAN'T WAIT TO CHANGE MY OUTFIT-- FIVE TIMES!
MAYBE WE CAN TRY NOT TO TRASH THE PLACE THIS TIME...
FOR SOMEONE WHO SHOULD FEEL A SENSE OF ACCOMPLISHMENT, YOU ARE ACTING VERY DOUR.
I HAVE MY REASONS. I'M OFF TO BED.
ARE YOU STAYING, SUPERBOY? I MEAN, IT IS KIND OF THE ONLY PLACE WE HAVE...
I'LL BE BACK, CASSIE, BUT FOR NOW I HAVE TO GET... HOME.
OH. OKAY.
WE ALL SEEM TO HAVE MONSTERS INSIDE US, FIGHTING TO GET OUT, CASSIE.
THE FACT THAT YOU CAN KEEP YOURS AT BAY GIVES ME... HOPE.

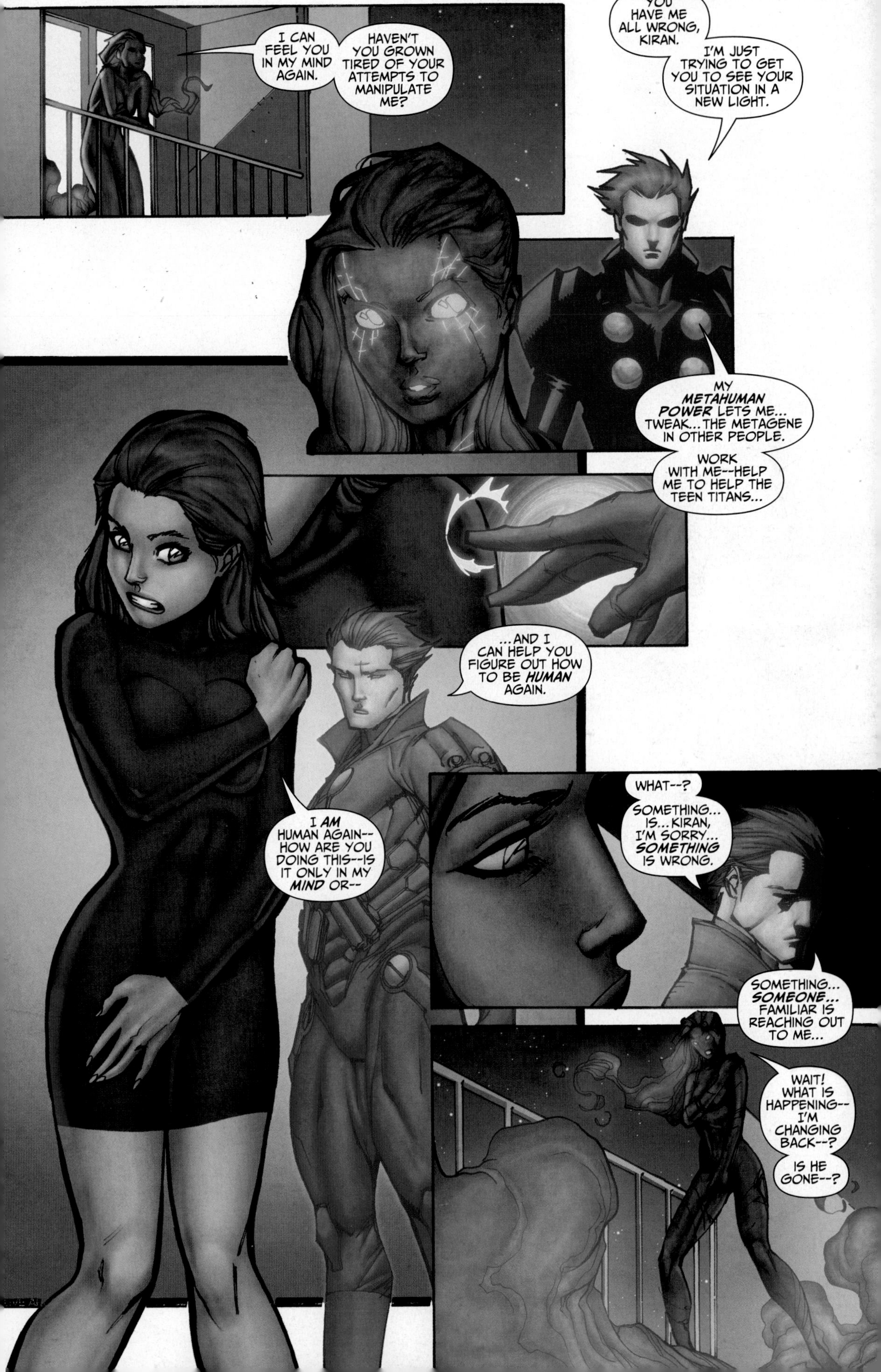

I CAN FEEL YOU IN MY MIND AGAIN.
HAVEN'T YOU GROWN TIRED OF YOUR ATTEMPTS TO MANIPULATE ME?
YOU HAVE ME ALL WRONG, KIRAN.
I'M JUST TRYING TO GET YOU TO SEE YOUR SITUATION IN A NEW LIGHT.
MY ***METAHUMAN POWER*** LETS ME... TWEAK... THE METAGENE IN OTHER PEOPLE.
WORK WITH ME--HELP ME TO HELP THE TEEN TITANS...
...AND I CAN HELP YOU FIGURE OUT HOW TO BE ***HUMAN*** AGAIN.
I ***AM*** HUMAN AGAIN--HOW ARE YOU DOING THIS--IS IT ONLY IN MY ***MIND*** OR--
WHAT--?
SOMETHING... IS... KIRAN, I'M SORRY... ***SOMETHING*** IS WRONG.
SOMETHING... ***SOMEONE...*** FAMILIAR IS REACHING OUT TO ME...
WAIT! WHAT IS HAPPENING--I'M CHANGING BACK--?
IS HE GONE--?

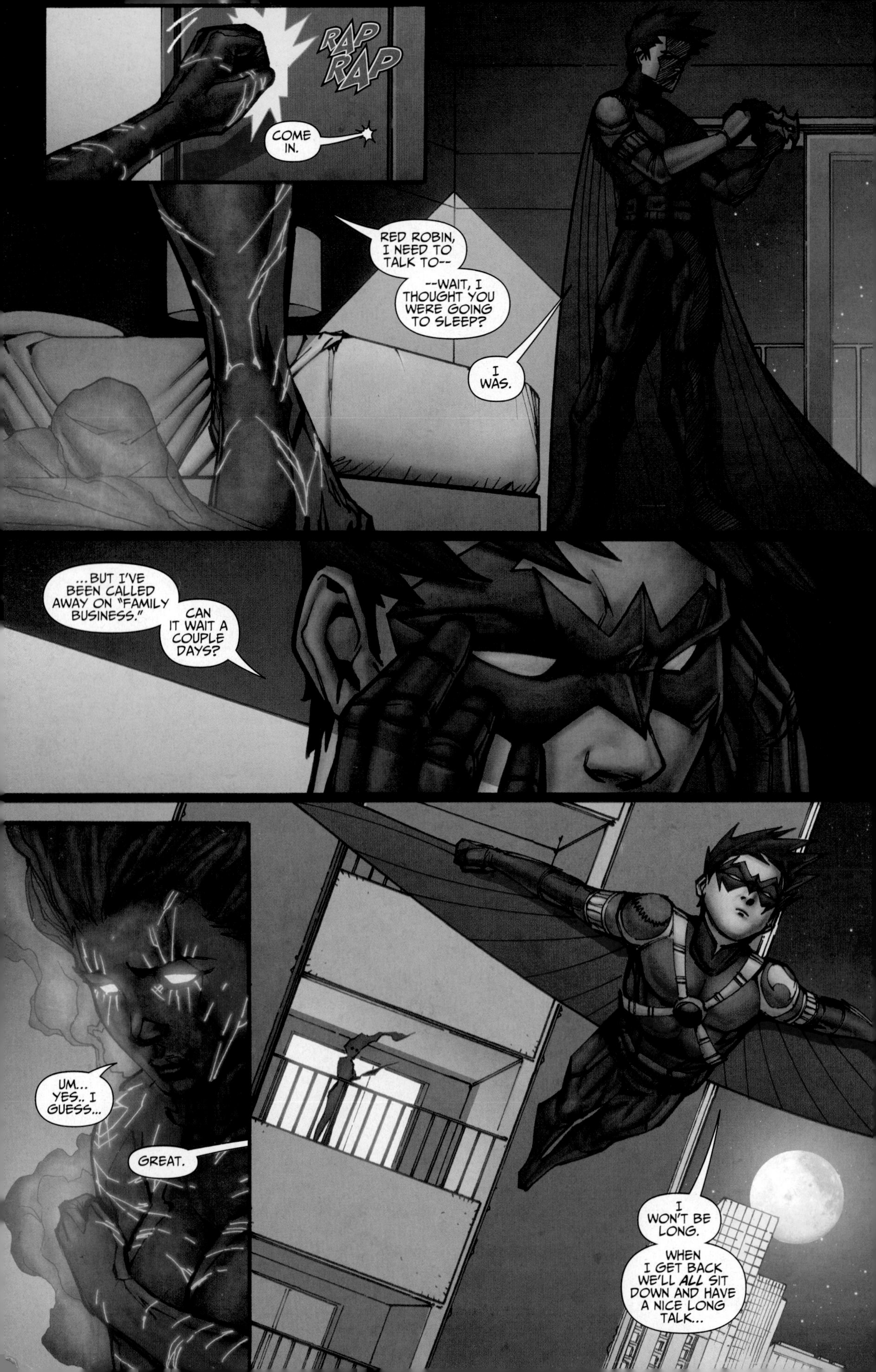
RAP
RAP
COME IN.
RED ROBIN, I NEED TO TALK TO--
--WAIT, I THOUGHT YOU WERE GOING TO SLEEP?
I WAS.
...BUT I'VE BEEN CALLED AWAY ON "FAMILY BUSINESS."
CAN IT WAIT A COUPLE DAYS?
UM... YES.. I GUESS...
GREAT.
I WON'T BE LONG.
WHEN I GET BACK WE'LL *ALL* SIT DOWN AND HAVE A NICE LONG TALK...

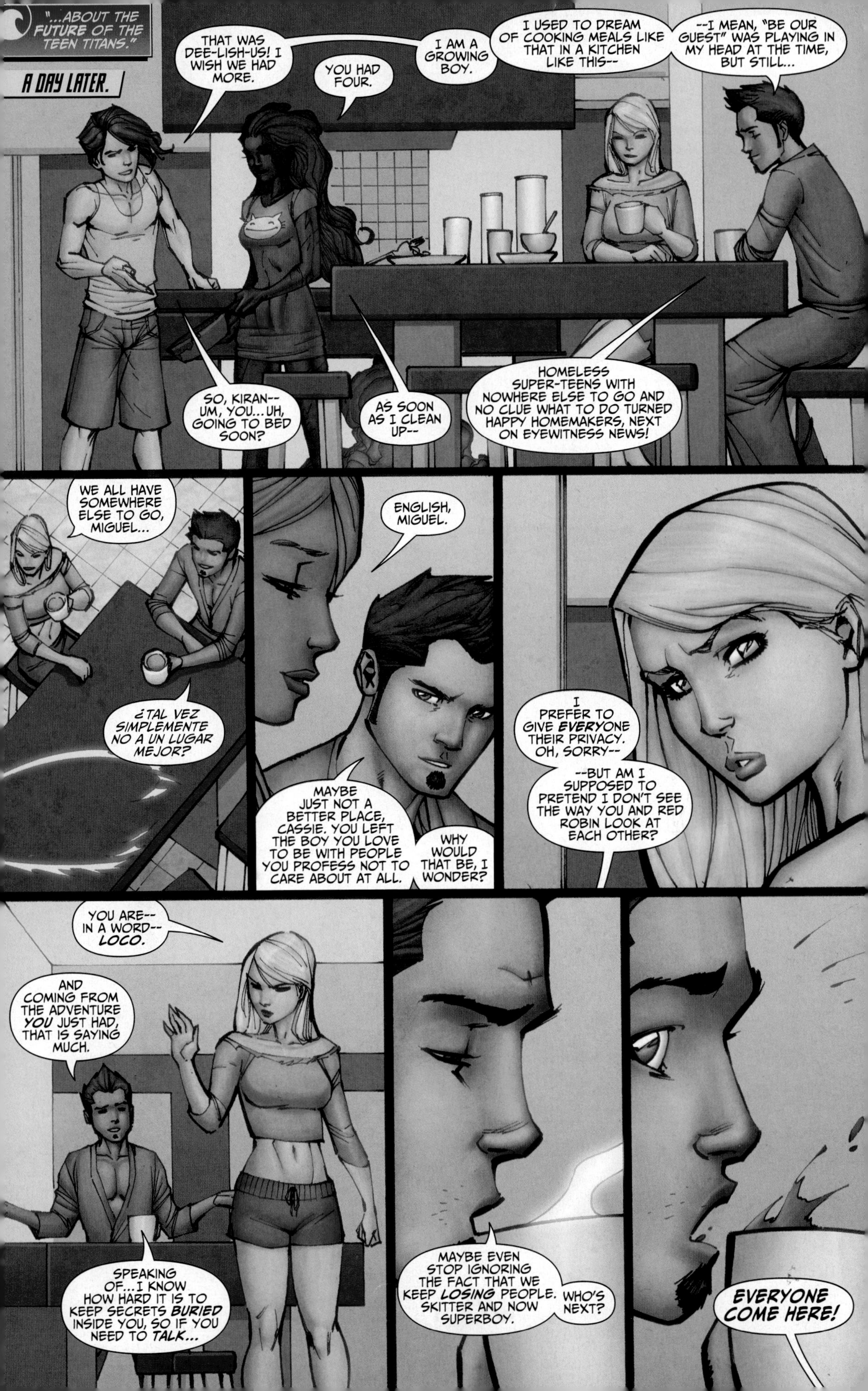
"...ABOUT THE FUTURE OF THE TEEN TITANS."
A DAY LATER.
THAT WAS DEE-LISH-US! I WISH WE HAD MORE.
YOU HAD FOUR.
I AM A GROWING BOY.
I USED TO DREAM OF COOKING MEALS LIKE THAT IN A KITCHEN LIKE THIS--
--I MEAN, "BE OUR GUEST" WAS PLAYING IN MY HEAD AT THE TIME, BUT STILL...
SO, KIRAN--UM, YOU...UH, GOING TO BED SOON?
AS SOON AS I CLEAN UP--
HOMELESS SUPER-TEENS WITH NOWHERE ELSE TO GO AND NO CLUE WHAT TO DO TURNED HAPPY HOMEMAKERS, NEXT ON EYEWITNESS NEWS!
WE ALL HAVE SOMEWHERE ELSE TO GO, MIGUEL...
¿TAL VEZ SIMPLEMENTE NO A UN LUGAR MEJOR?
ENGLISH, MIGUEL.
MAYBE JUST NOT A BETTER PLACE, CASSIE. YOU LEFT THE BOY YOU LOVE TO BE WITH PEOPLE YOU PROFESS NOT TO CARE ABOUT AT ALL.
WHY WOULD THAT BE, I WONDER?
I PREFER TO GIVE EVERYONE THEIR PRIVACY. OH, SORRY--
--BUT AM I SUPPOSED TO PRETEND I DON'T SEE THE WAY YOU AND RED ROBIN LOOK AT EACH OTHER?
YOU ARE--IN A WORD--LOCO.
AND COMING FROM THE ADVENTURE YOU JUST HAD, THAT IS SAYING MUCH.
SPEAKING OF...I KNOW HOW HARD IT IS TO KEEP SECRETS BURIED INSIDE YOU, SO IF YOU NEED TO TALK...
MAYBE EVEN STOP IGNORING THE FACT THAT WE KEEP LOSING PEOPLE. SKITTER AND NOW SUPERBOY.
WHO'S NEXT?
EVERYONE COME HERE!

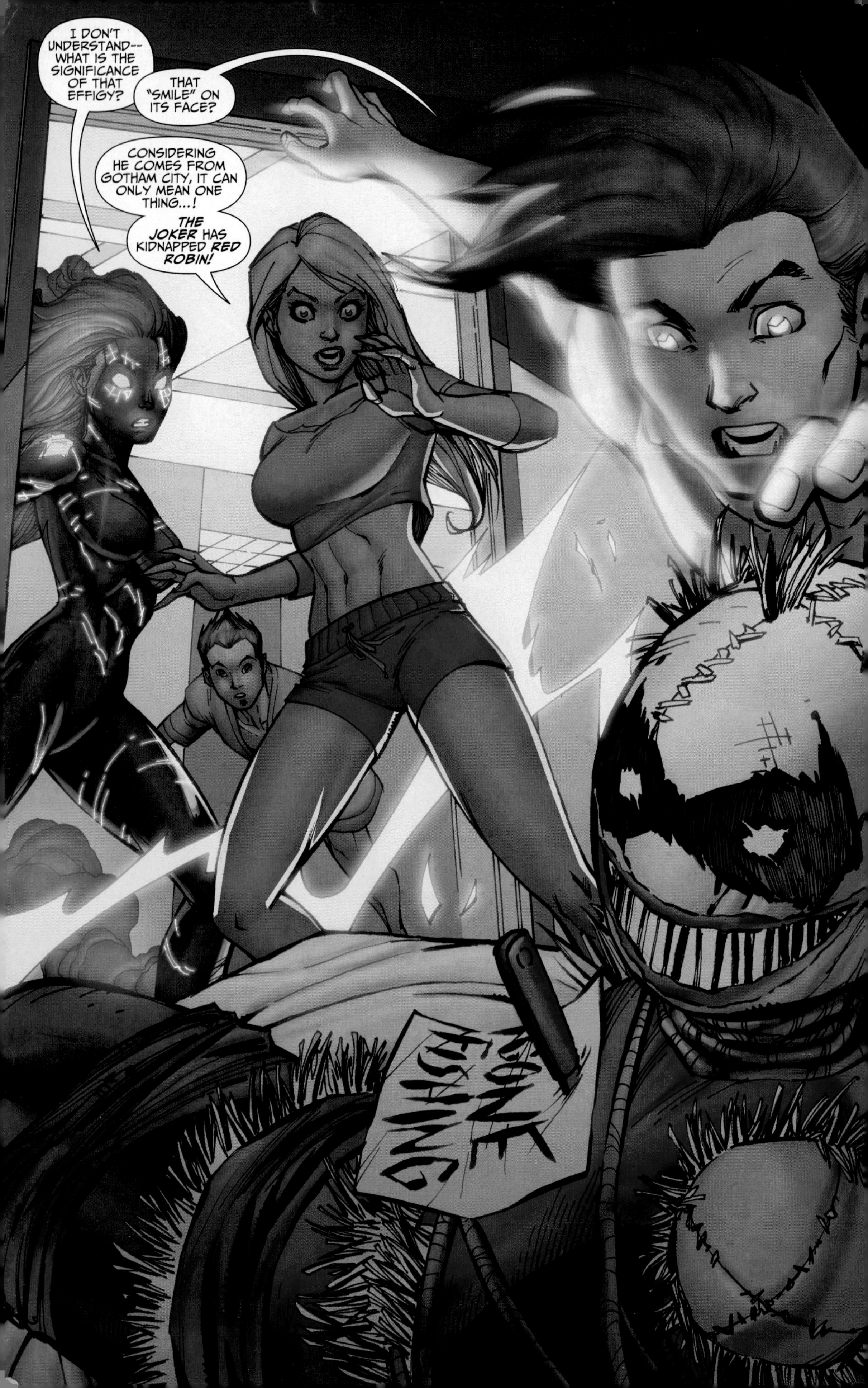

I DON'T UNDERSTAND-- WHAT IS THE SIGNIFICANCE OF THAT EFFIGY?
THAT "SMILE" ON ITS FACE?
CONSIDERING HE COMES FROM GOTHAM CITY, IT CAN ONLY MEAN ONE THING...!
THE JOKER HAS KIDNAPPED RED ROBIN!
GONE FISHING

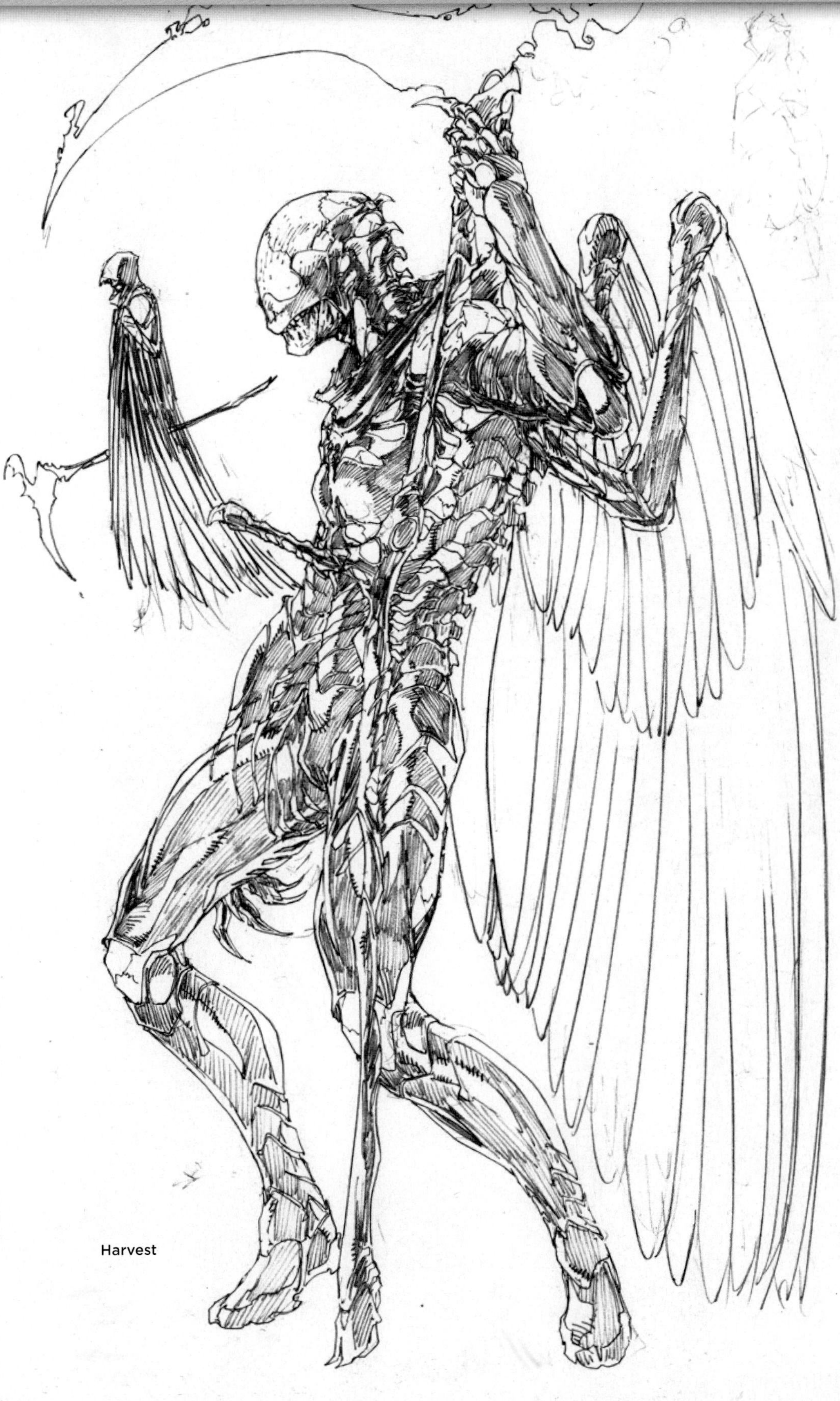

Harvest

The Colony

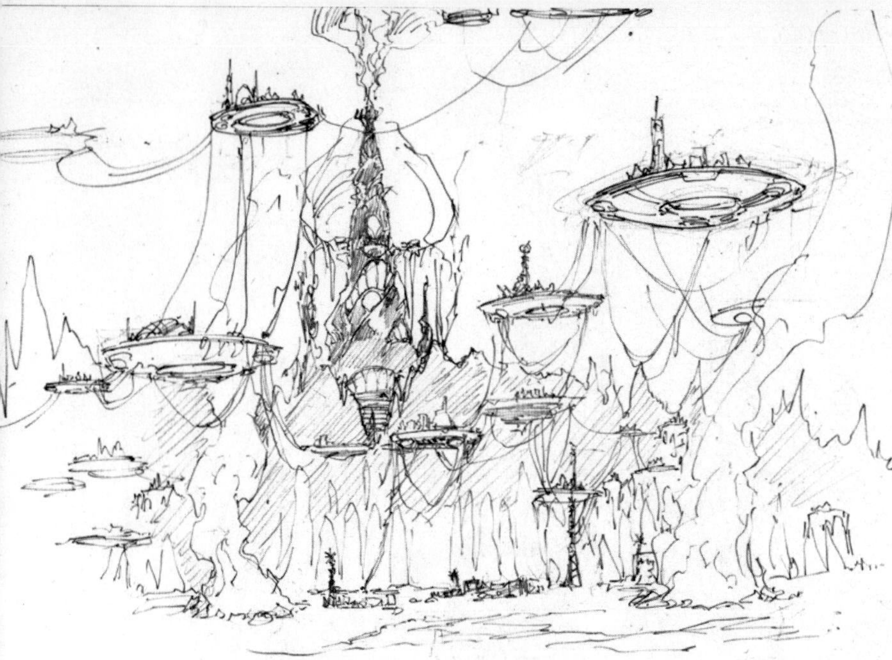

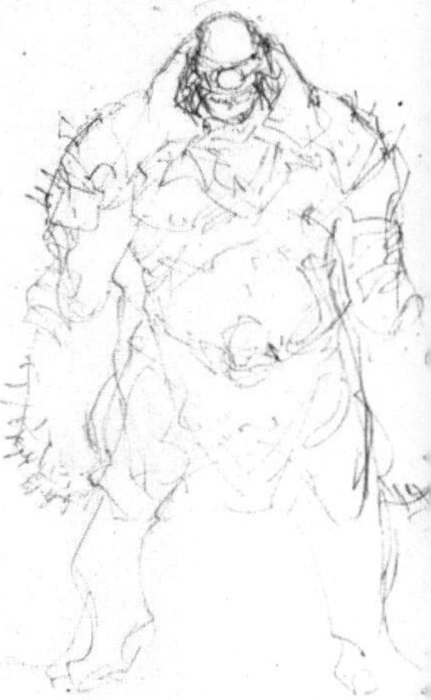

Leash

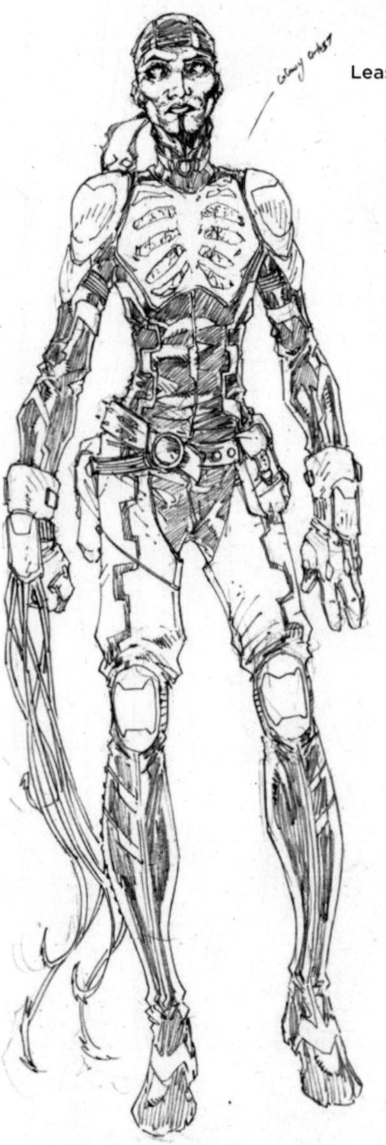

Omen

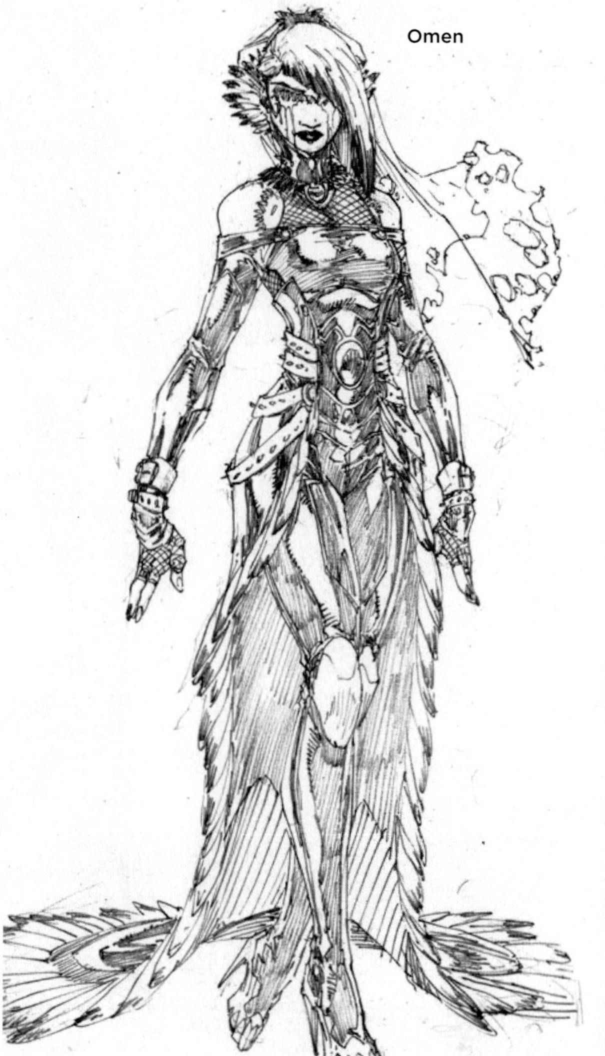

Unused version of TEEN TITANS #11 page 1

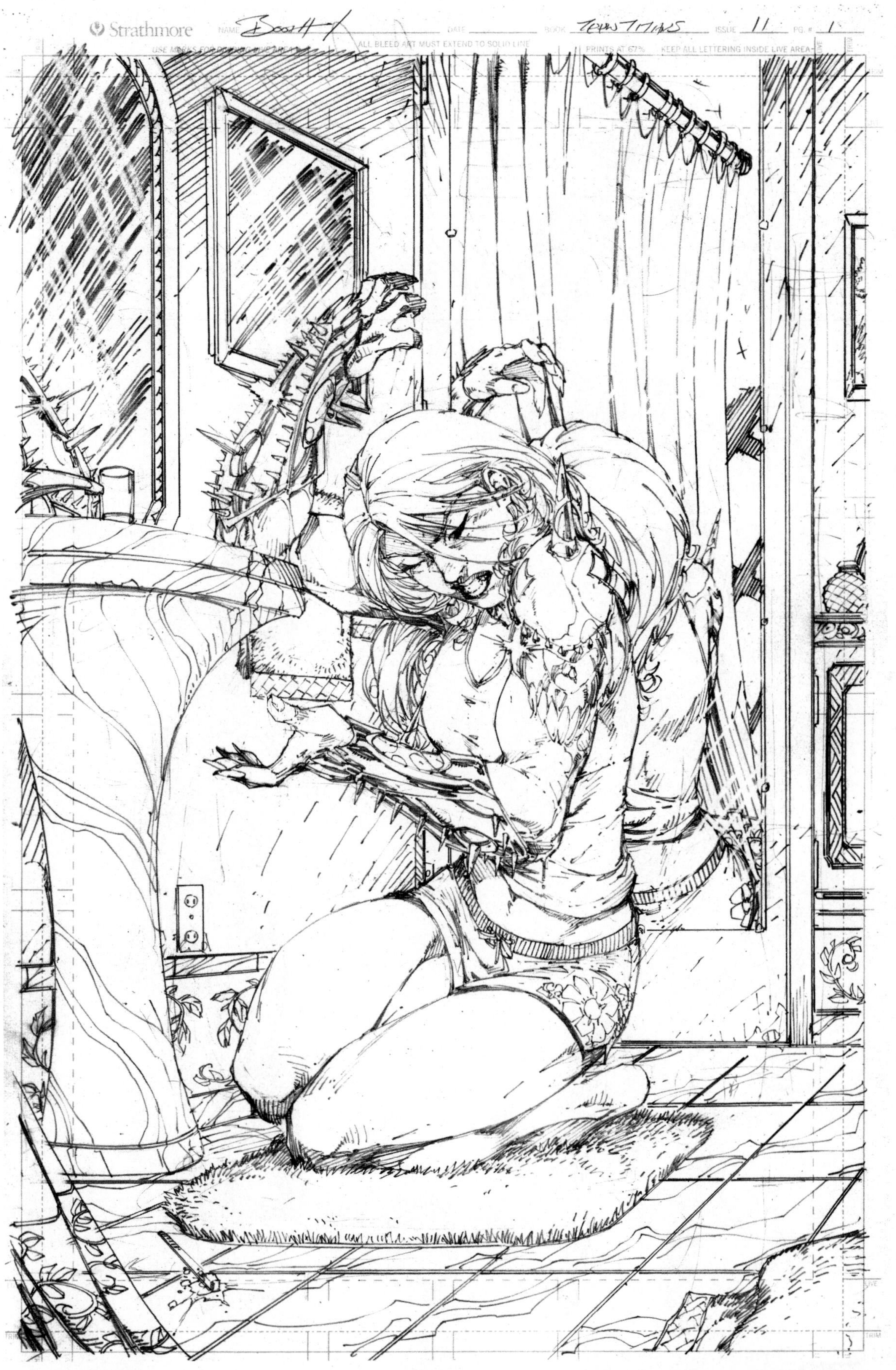
Strathmore
TEEN TITANS
11
1
ALL BLEED ART MUST EXTEND TO SOLID LINE
PRINTS AT 67%
KEEP ALL LETTERING INSIDE LIVE AREA

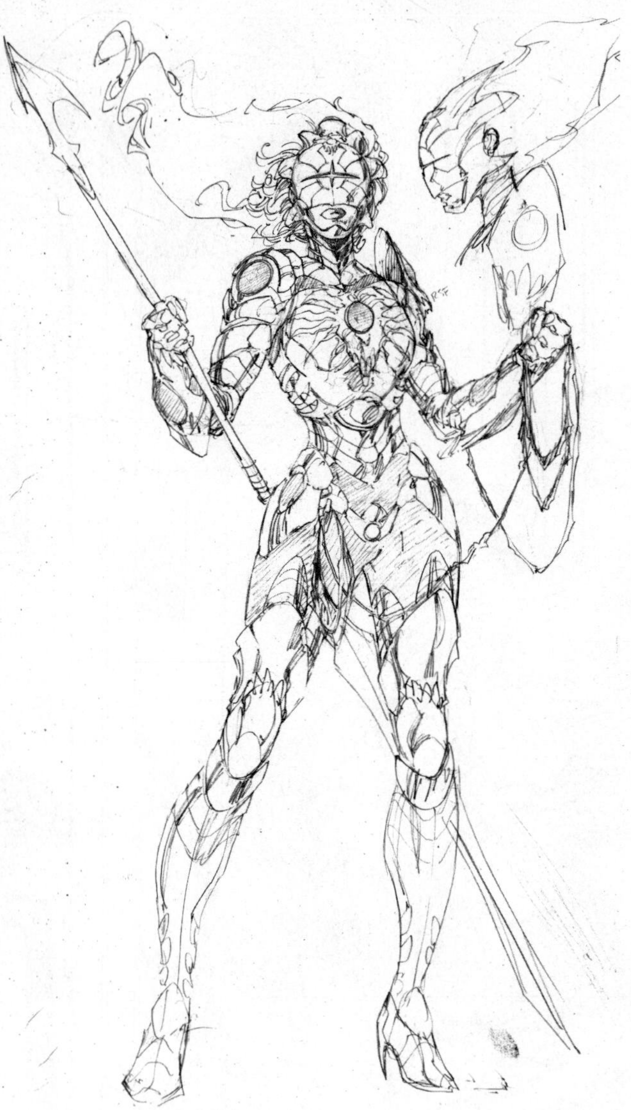

Cassie in the Silent Armor

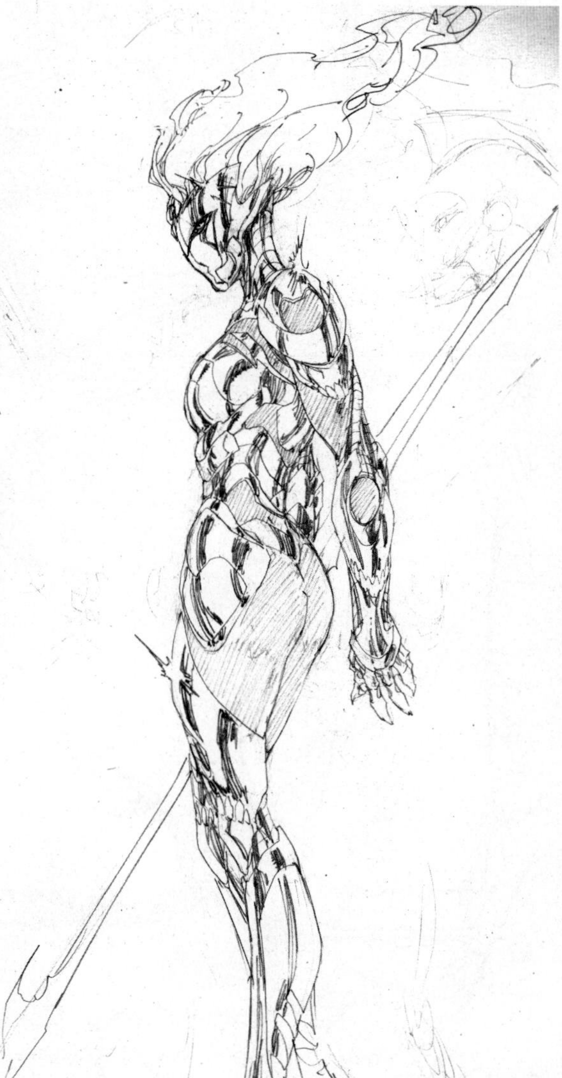

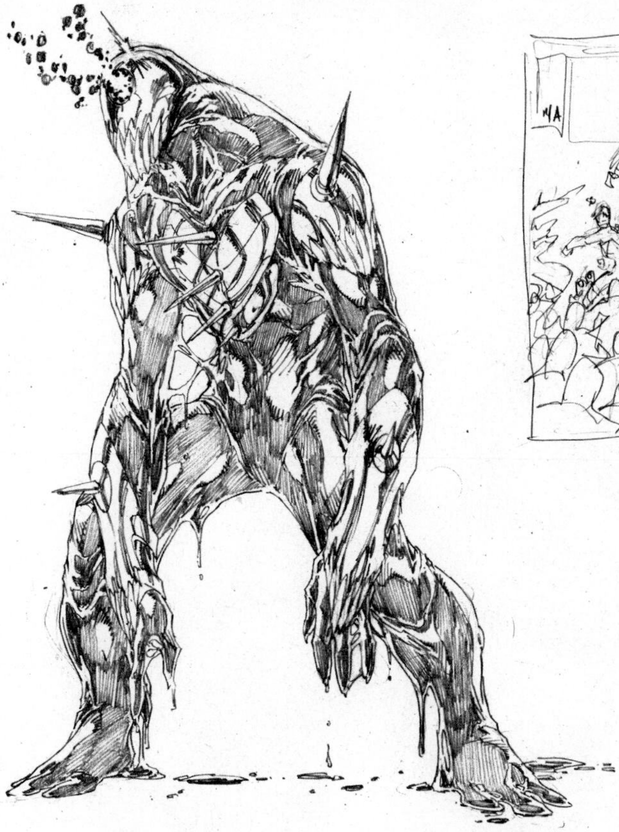

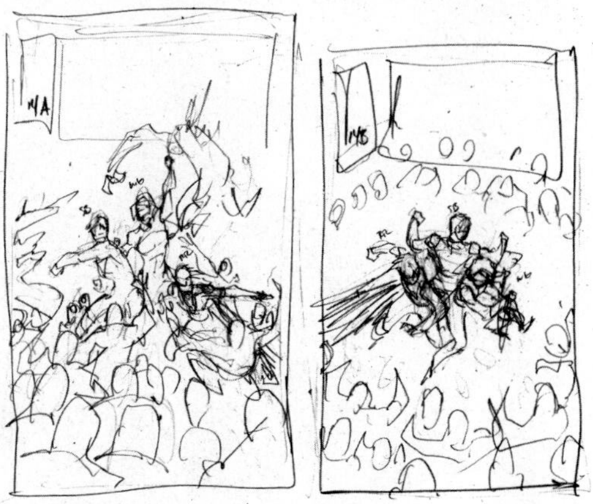

TEEN TITANS #14 cover sketches

Blood Warrior

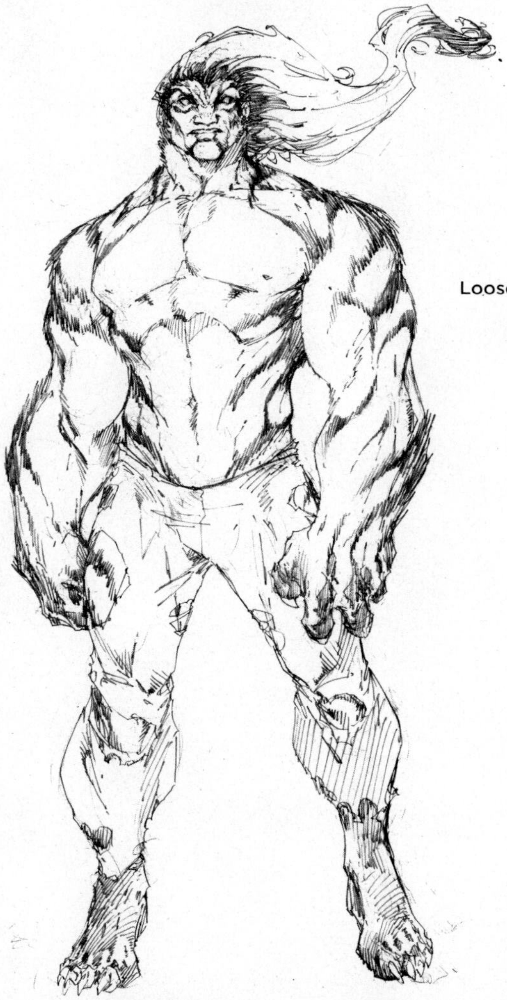

Loose Cannon

Dac

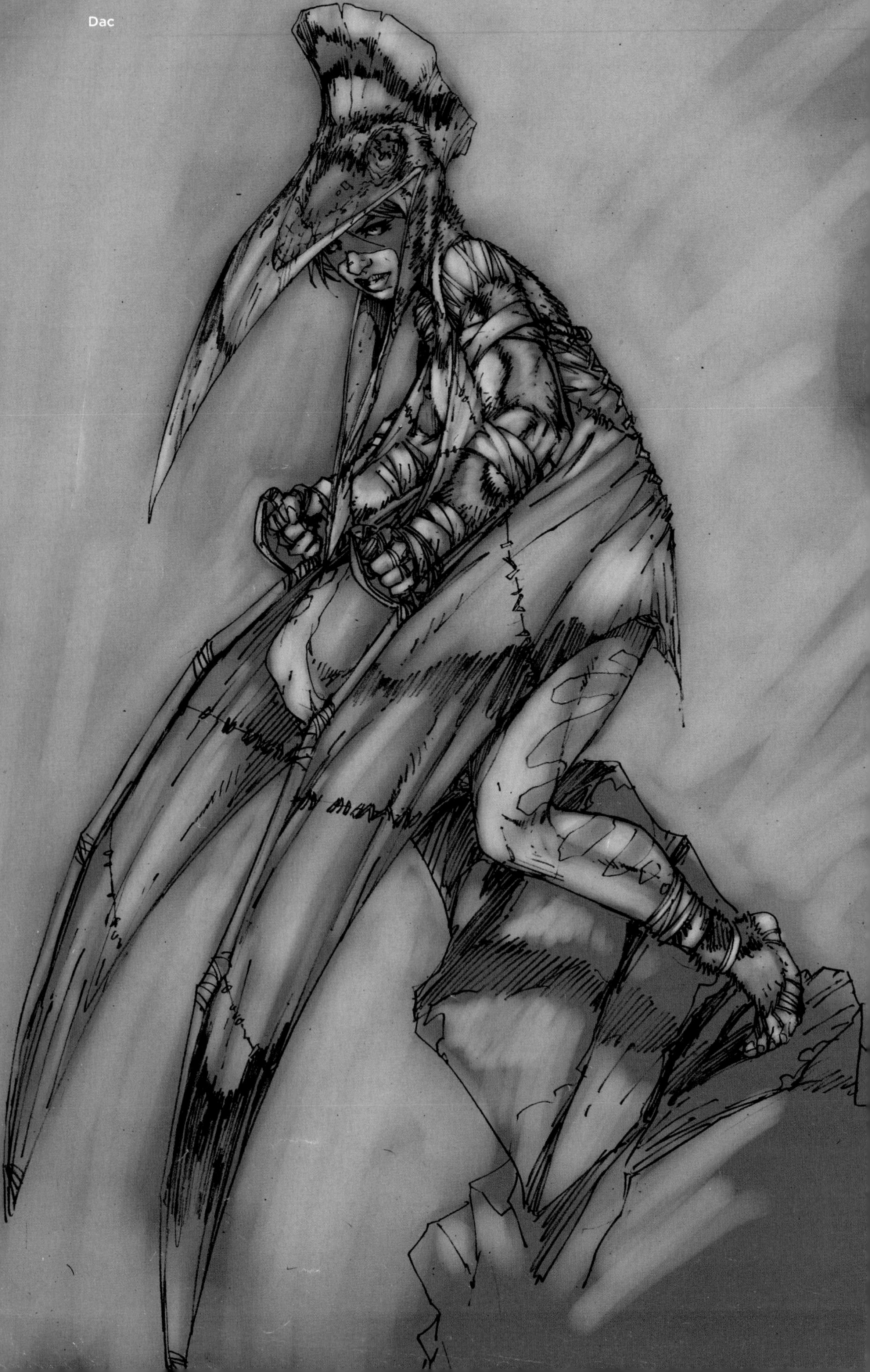

START AT THE BEGINNING!

JUSTICE LEAGUE VOLUME 1:ORIGIN

AQUAMAN
VOLUME 1:
THE TRENCH

THE SAVAGE
HAWKMAN VOLUME 1:
DARKNESS RISING

GREEN ARROW
VOLUME 1:
THE MIDAS TOUCH

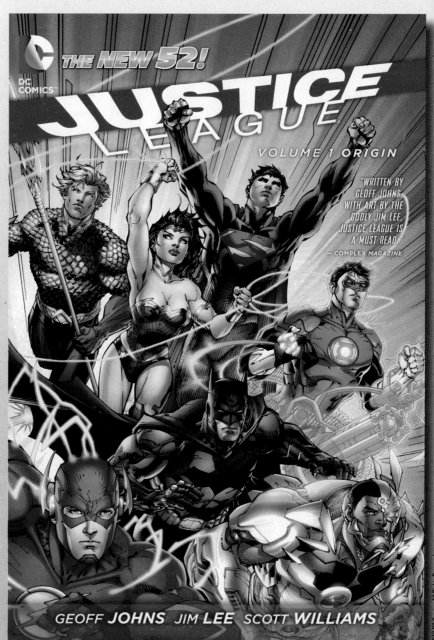

GEOFF **JOHNS** JIM **LEE** Scott **WILLIAMS**

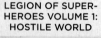